A-Level Physical Education

The Reflective Performer

A-Level Physical Education
The Reflective Performer

David Kirk, PhD

Loughborough University

Dawn Penney, PhD

Loughborough University

Robin Burgess-Limerick, PhD

The University of Queensland

Trish Gorely, PhD

Loughborough University

Colette Maynard, BEd

Worcestershire Local Education Authority

Human Kinetics

Library of Congress Cataloging-in-Publication Data

A-level physical education : the reflective performer / David Kirk . . . [et al.].
     p. cm.
   Includes bibliographical references and index.
   ISBN 0-7360-3392-0
     1. Physical education and training--Great Britain. 2. Performance. I. Kirk, David.
   1958-

GV245.A62 2002
613.7'1'071241--dc21   2001039457

ISBN: 0-7360-3392-0

Acquisitions Editor: Scott Wikgren
Developmental Editor: Rebecca Crist
Assistant Editor: Mark E. Zulauf
Copyeditor: Peter Kirkham
Proofreader: Erin Cler
Indexer: Joan Griffitts
Permission Manager: Dalene Reeder
Production Manager: Heather Munson
Graphic Designer: Robert Reuther
Graphic Artists: Angela K. Snyder and Denise Lowry
Photo Managers: Les Woodrum and Kelly Hendren
Cover Designer: Kristin Darling
Photographer (cover): Richard Hamilton Smith
Art Managers: Craig Newsom and Carl Johnson
Printer: United Graphics

Printed in the United States of America   10 9 8 7 6 5 4 3 2 1

Human Kinetics

Web site: www.humankinetics.com

United States: Human Kinetics
P.O. Box 5076
Champaign, IL 61825-5076
800-747-4457
e-mail: humank@hkusa.com

Canada: Human Kinetics
475 Devonshire Road Unit 100
Windsor, ON N8Y 2L5
800-465-7301 (in Canada only)
e-mail: orders@hkcanada.com

Europe: Human Kinetics
Units C2/C3 Wira Business Park
West Park Ring Road
Leeds LS16 6EB, United Kingdom
+44 (0) 113 278 1708
e-mail: hk@hkeurope.com

Australia: Human Kinetics
57A Price Avenue
Lower Mitcham, South Australia 5062
08 8277 1555
e-mail: liahka@senet.com.au

New Zealand: Human Kinetics
P.O. Box 105-231, Auckland Central
09-523-3462
e-mail: hkp@ihug.co.nz

Contents

Preface

The purpose of this book is to support students studying A-level physical education. You will find in this text a comprehensive range of information that covers the requirements of the four major accredited examination board courses. The common reference point for each of these specifications from September 2000 onwards is the Qualification Curriculum Authority's (QCA) criteria for A-level physical education. A key feature of this book is that it is addresses these criteria specifically, particularly the requirements for integrating knowledge, making knowledge personal, equity and inclusion, and synopsis. How the book does this is explained in chapter 1.1. The book is also written to address the key learning processes specified by the QCA, including the acquisition, application, evaluation and appreciation of knowledge in physical education.

We have described the book as a complete guide to A-level study partly because it provides you with a comprehensive range of information. However, the book is a complete guide because it also provides you with opportunities to develop the key skills of communication, working with others, problem solving and improving your own learning and performance. You will find in each chapter short sections with the heading Over To You (see Key to Icons). You can use these sections by yourself as a way of testing and improving your own comprehension; or they can be used by your teacher as a basis for organising learning experiences for your class. You will also find at the end of each chapter Test Yourself Questions written in the style of exam questions. Answers are provided at the back of the book.

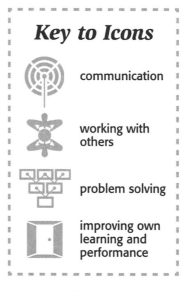

Key to Icons

communication

working with others

problem solving

improving own learning and performance

The book is also a complete guide to A-level study because it is linked to a web page and supported by an electronic Instructor's Guide. The Instructor's Guide provides your teacher with ideas and information for using this book in relation to the particular exam board course you are studying. The web page is updated regularly and provides you with a one-stop shop for addresses to other useful websites to support your studies, and extension activities to extend your learning and achievement.

You will find up-to-date, accurate and highly relevant information in this book. This is because it is written by people who are actively involved as researchers and teachers in their specialist fields. This means that the book is useful not only for A-level study, but will also assist you if you decide to study physical education, sport science or a related field at university.

Credits

Page 2 Photo copyright Sport, The Library/Michael Rayner.

Pages 14, 26, 38, 56, 74, 84 and 98 Photos copyright Claus Andersen.

Page 106 Photo copyright Nigel Farrow.

Page 116 Photo copyright Sport, The Library.

Page 134 Photo copyright iPhotoNews.com/Brooks.

Pages 144, 154 and 264 Photos copyright Human Kinetics.

Page 166 Photo copyright Empics.

Pages 176 and 240 Photos copyright Alvey & Towers Picture Library.

Page 188 Photo copyright The Sporting Image.

Page 200 Photo copyright Paul Souders/WorldFoto.

Page 210 Photo copyright Richard Hamilton Smith Photography.

Page 224 Photo copyright Photo Network.

Page 252 Photo copyright 99 Tom Roberts.

Page 278 Photo copyright Empics.

Page 290 Photo copyright International Stock/Michael Manheim.

Page 304 Photo copyright International Stock/Sunstar.

Page 316 Photo copyright International Stock/Tony Demin.

Figure 1 Reprinted, by permission, from L.T. Mackinnon, R.J. Neal, V. Kippers, and S.J. Hanrahan, 1996, *The biophysical foundations of human movement* (Champaign: Human Kinetics), 300.

Figure 2 Reprinted, by permission, from M. Mosston and S. Ashworth, 1994, *Teaching physical education,* 4th ed. (Boston: Allyn and Bacon).

Figures 3, 4, 28, 29, 30, 31, 32, 33, 34, 35, 36, 37, 38, 39, 40, 41, 42, 44, 45, 46, 47, 48, 49, 50, 51, 52, 53, 54, 55a, 55b and 61 Reprinted, by permission, from D. Kirk, R. Burgess-Limerick, M. Kiss, J. Lahey, and D. Penney, 1999, *Senior physical education: An integrated approach* (Champaign: Human Kinetics), 22, 25, 78, 79, 80, 80, 81, 82, 83, 85, 92, 92, 93, 95, 95, 97, 98, 44, 45, 49, 49, 50, 50, 57, 57, 58, 61, 63, 66, 61, 64, 65, 183.

Figure 5 Reprinted, by permission, from Weinberg and Gould, 1999, *Foundations of sport and exercise psychology,* 2nd ed. (Champaign: Human Kinetics), 84.

Figures 7, 9, 13, 15, 19, and 22 Reprinted, by permission, from R.S. Behnke, *Kinetic anatomy,* 2001 (Champaign, IL: Human Kinetics), 5, 10, 207, 137, 13.

Figure 8 © K. GalasynWright 1994.

Figures 10, 17a, 17b, 24 and 26 Reprinted, by permission, from P.M. McGinnis, 1999, *Biomechanics of sport and exercise* (Champaign: Human Kinetics), 232, 233, 271, 273.

Figure 16 Reprinted, by permission, from D.L. Butler, E.S. Grood, F.R. Nages, and R.F. Zernicke, 1978, Biomechanics of ligaments and tendons. In *Exercise and Sport Sciences Reviews,* 145.

Figure 18 Reprinted, by permission, from J.E. Donnelly, 1990, *Living anatomy,* 2nd ed. (Champaign, IL: Human Kinetics), 132.

PART 1

Educational, Ethical and Psychological Dimensions of Reflective Performance in Physical Education

*I*n this section you will find four chapters that are concerned with the educational, ethical and psychological dimensions of reflective performance in physical education. Chapter 1.1 introduces you to physical education as a field of study and to some of the important principles and processes that underpin study in this field. In chapter 1.2, you can read about equity and inclusion and how these impact on your performance, and others', in physical education. Chapter 1.3 focuses on how people learn in physical education and provides you with some useful tools for analysing and improving your own learning and performance. Chapter 1.4 provides you with further help in improving your own performance by examining psychological concepts such as motivation, goal setting and team cohesion.

CHAPTER 1.1

The Reflective Performer in Physical Education: The Field of Study

Learning Outcomes

When you have studied this chapter, you should be able to

- ☑ list the categories of physical activities and subject matter knowledge that make up the field of study,
- ☑ identify and describe the four key learning processes in physical education,
- ☑ identify and describe the four educational principles informing physical education,
- ☑ define the 'reflective performer' in physical education, and
- ☑ explain the idea that physical education is socially constructed.

INTRODUCTION

Physical education is a challenging and demanding subject to study. This is because the subject covers a broad range of physical activities and subject matter. The combination of physical activities and subject matter is what makes the subject challenging and demanding for you as a learner. Few individuals can become experts in each individual component of physical education. In any case, this is not what *physical education* aims to do. You may be a good netball or basketball player; or you may be interested in the physiology of sport. But expertise in isolated aspects of physical education is not the same thing as developing expertise in physical education.

So what is physical education if it is not merely a collection of isolated physical activities and subject matter? Becoming a **reflective performer** in physical education is a process of learning *in* the physical domain, learning *about* physical activity and learning *through* physical activity.

The range of physical activities offered in physical education programmes is the medium for learning *in* the physical domain. The **subject matter** of the subdisciplines such as biomechanics and sociology of sport facilitates your learning *about* physical activity. In the process of engaging in the physical activities and subject matter of physical education, you learn *through* physical activity other social values such as teamwork and fair play.

What makes physical education unique is that it is a field that integrates physical activity, subject matter knowledge and social values. It is this integration that makes the field challenging and demanding, and also educationally worthwhile.

In this chapter, you will find a brief overview of the field of study in relation to physical activities and subject matter knowledge. You will also find information on the learning processes and educational principles underpinning physical education as a field of study. And finally, you will discover that the subject, like all other fields of study in schools, is socially constructed and contested.

PHYSICAL EDUCATION: THE FIELD OF STUDY

There is a wide range of physical activities that can be, and often are, studied as part of school physical education programmes. There is also a wide range of subject matter that has developed in higher education institutions such as universities and is increasingly recognised as a legitimate part of the study of physical education in schools.

Categories of Physical Activities

The National Curriculum for Physical Education (NCPE) identifies six categories of physical activities that form a central component of the study of physical education. You can read more about the National Curriculum for Physical Education in part 4 of this text. The categories are games, gymnastics, athletics, dance, outdoor and adventurous activities, and swimming and water safety. Within each of these categories there are further subdivisions. For instance, within the category of games there are team games such as cricket and hockey, and individual games such as golf and squash.

Because of the range of activities that exists in each of these categories, most school physical education programmes include only a selection from each category. The selection of activities is most often made by teachers and involves consideration of their interests and expertise, your interests as students, the facilities available to the school, equipment and local traditions.

Even though there is a wide range of potential activities available for inclusion in physical education programmes, research since the 1960s has shown that traditional

Reflective performers in physical education are people who think and do at the same time.

Subject matter knowledge draws on the subdisciplines of the physical activity field as it is studied in higher education.

team games tend to be allocated more time and resources in schools than other games or activities from other categories. Some physical educators have questioned whether other games and sports such as snooker, darts, skateboarding and in-line skating are suitable for inclusion in physical education.

Questions about what activities should properly be included in physical education reveal that the six categories of activities identified in the NCPE as appropriate represent only one way of thinking about physical activities. There are alternative approaches. For example, in Queensland, Australia, in the academic discipline senior physical education, which is the equivalent of an A level, physical activities are categorised as

- direct interceptive activities — such as football, netball and water polo, but also fencing, karate and judo;
- indirect interceptive activities — such as badminton, croquet and volleyball, but also softball, billiards and bocce;
- performance activities — such as athletics, swimming and cycling, but also archery, waterskiing and weightlifting; and
- **aesthetic** activities — such as jazz, ballet, ballroom dance and figure skating, but also equestrian dressage, surfboard riding and artistic gymnastics.

Aesthetics is the field of study concerned with the art of movement.

Another approach to categorising games has been widely used in Britain. Based on Teaching Games for Understanding (TGfU), games have been categorised as invasion games, net–wall games and striking–fielding games.

Invasion games include football, rugby union and rugby league, basketball, netball and hockey. These games have the following things in common:

- The common tactical features of invading territory to make space in attack
- The containment of space in defence
- The use of a goal or similar target for scoring

Net–wall games such as tennis, table tennis and volleyball have these things in common:

- A target area on the floor
- The need for all players to serve and receive the ball
- The need for playing areas to be divided by a net (except for squash, although the same tactical concepts apply)

Striking–fielding games such as cricket, baseball and rounders have these things in common:

© Human Kinetics

Invading territory to attack is one feature of invasion games.

- Players strike objects into open spaces in order to score runs.
- Fielders are placed strategically to prevent runs from being scored.

The TGfU categories are important because they identify common tactical features of games. This is not a merely arbitrary way of grouping physical activities. It is instead based on a sound educational argument and has important implications for how teachers organise learning experiences for students of physical education. This is because it is possible to modify the form of the adult game and to learn the key tactics and strategies for a number of similar games at the same time.

The existence of alternative ways of categorising physical activities suggests that the NCPE approach is just one way of organising physical activities for programmes of study. As you will read later when we discuss the social construction of physical education, the current NCPE approach is an outcome of historical and social forces.

Over to You

With a partner, list the activities that should/should not be considered part of physical education. Now write a one-page defence of your choices. Share these with other members of the class. Use these short papers as the basis for a class discussion on these issues. Write a brief summary of the discussion, noting the key points of agreement and disagreement.

Subdisciplines and Subject Matter

A-level physical education includes a wide range of subject matter in addition to physical activities. This subject matter draws on the subdisciplines of the physical activity field developed in universities since the middle of the 20th century. Although the categories of subdisciplines continue to develop and expand, the subdisciplines most often represented in school physical education include

Biomechanics is the field of study concerned with the physics of movement.

- **biomechanics** — the application of physics to physical activity;
- exercise and sport physiology — the study of the biology and biochemistry of physical activity;
- exercise and sport psychology — individual psychological factors that influence physical activity;
- functional anatomy — the study of the structure and function of the body in relation to physical activity;
- history of sport and physical education — the study of the past in order to better understand the present and possible futures;

Pedagogy is the field of study concerned with the learning and teaching of physical activities.

- **pedagogy** of physical activity — the study of teaching and coaching, learning and curriculum in physical activity settings;
- motor learning and control — a subdiscipline concerned with the neural basis of physical activity and the acquisition of skill; and
- sociology of sport and leisure — the study of social processes in and around physical activity settings.

Other subdisciplines exist in the physical activity field in higher education, such as the politics of sport, the economics of sport and the philosophy of sport—but these subdisciplines appear less frequently in school programmes of study than do the subdisciplines just listed.

The relevance of this subject matter for the study of physical education in schools is sometimes questioned. One danger of including this subject matter in physical education is that it crosses the biological, physical and social sciences. This makes the subject very challenging for students. Another danger is treating subdisciplines in isolation from physical activities and from other subdisciplines. Together, these factors could result in this subject matter's appearing too theoretical and irrelevant to the study of physical education.

In order to minimise these dangers and to distinguish physical education from a collection of disconnected and isolated physical activities and subject matter knowledge, key learning processes and educational principles have been identified. In A-level programmes, these processes and principles have been focused on the idea of the 'reflective performer' in physical education. This idea and the processes and principles that support it are essential ingredients in making physical education a coherent and educationally valuable field of study in its own right.

Over to You

Consider your A-level course of study. In a small group of up to four people, consult your teacher and make a list of the factors that you and your teacher think have influenced the selection of activities and subject matter. Discuss and note any alternatives that exist for your programme of study.

THE REFLECTIVE PERFORMER IN PHYSICAL EDUCATION

Too often in the past, participation in physical education has been stereotyped as a purely physical activity that requires little or no thought. Today we understand that this idea is inaccurate and misleading. To study physical activity, you must work cognitively as well as physically. Acknowledging the nature of learning in physical education as both physical and cognitive is very challenging and demanding. This is because thinking and acting must be integrated in order to be effective in the **performance** of sport and other physical activities.

Another stereotypical idea is that the word 'performance' applies only to individuals at the elite end of the sport spectrum. Throughout this book the term 'performance' refers to participation in physical activity and sport at many levels, including elite, recreational, school, club, national and international levels. There are limitations in making a distinction between performance and participation. This distinction invariably has particular forms and levels of participation and performance in mind. Typically, performance is used to refer to participation at elite levels, whereas participation is associated with recreational sport. Challenging these common-sense ideas is important if we are to achieve the goal of making physical education inclusive so that all young people can learn to lead active and healthy lives.

So the way in which performance is used in the context of your A-level course is different from the elite idea of performance. Performance refers to actual engagement *in* physical activity. Physical activity is the essential ingredient of any course that is labelled physical education. This is because physical activity is both a medium for learning and a source of information. There are some things, such as kinaesthetic awareness, that cannot be learned in any way other than participation in physical activity. The essential dimension of participation in physical activity is expressed in this notion of performance.

Reflective performers are able to learn effectively from their experiences of engaging in physical activities. A popular misconception of reflection is the idea that you sit in an armchair and contemplate, rather than actively engage in, physical activity. In contrast, the process of reflection in the context of your A-level course refers to the ability to use available information in an orderly and systematic way to improve performance. You have to be willing to subject yourself to some degree of self-criticism to be a reflective performer.

Reflective performers in physical education are people who think and do at the same time. Typically, as you work harder and learn more in, about and through physical activities, you become better educated physically. As a physically educated person, you learn these things:

Performance refers to participation in physical activity and sport in many sites, including elite, recreational, school, club, national and international arenas.

Becoming a reflective performer in physical education is a process of learning *in* the physical domain, learning *about* physical activity and learning *through* physical activity.

Physical competencies are the skills and techniques you can perform.

Physical literacy is your vocabulary of physical competencies.

- Make appropriate use of a range of **physical competencies,** particularly fine and gross motor skills, required to accomplish the many and varied tasks you encounter in your everyday life. In short, you develop a sophisticated level of **physical literacy.**

- Lead an active and healthy life in a manner appropriate to your circumstances, adapting physical activities to suit your needs at any given time, while practising activities that minimise the risk of injury and that are sustainable over prolonged periods of time.

- Play several games or sports in a recreational or competitive context at a level of competence that produces for you feelings of achievement and enjoyment, particularly activities, games or sports that are commonly pursued well into mature adulthood.

- Make informed judgements about the quality of products of the sport, leisure and exercise industries, and become a critical consumer of these products.

- Practise the skills of leadership and citizenship, including cooperation, self-control and conflict resolution.

Over to You

In a small group, consider the points just listed. Decide as a group whether you wish to make any changes to the list. Make the changes and write down the reasons for making them. If the group does not wish to make changes, write down your reasons why.

There are a number of key learning processes that reflective performers engage in, including acquiring and developing physical skills, applying and evaluating knowledge to improve performance, and developing an appreciation of the value of physical activity and health. These learning processes are underpinned and informed by a series of principles, including equity and inclusion, personalisation, integration and synopsis. Together, these processes and principles are essential to reflective performance and contribute to your physical education.

LEARNING PROCESSES IN PHYSICAL EDUCATION

There are four key learning processes that are important in studying physical education: acquiring knowledge and skills, applying knowledge, evaluating this knowledge, and appreciating the value of physical activity. The actual performance of physical activity is a key part of each of these processes in physical education.

Acquiring Knowledge and Skills

Acquiring knowledge in physical education involves collecting and remembering information, and repetitious practising.

You **acquire knowledge** and skills in physical education through processes such as collecting, remembering and repetitious practising. Knowledge and skills are acquired from sources such as books, journals, videos and websites, through participation in physical activities and by observing the performances of others. Here are tests that show whether you have acquired knowledge and skills relevant to your programme of study:

- Recall facts, definitions and terminology.
- Organise and classify information.
- Record relevant information.

- Recognise appropriate and important information.
- Demonstrate and replicate techniques and skills consistently.

Applying Knowledge and Skills

You **apply knowledge** and skills in physical education by analysing, manipulating and interpreting information from books, journals, videos and websites, through participation in physical activities and by observing the performances of others. Here are tests of whether you are able to apply knowledge and skills relevant to your programme of study:

- Integrate new information into your performance of physical activity.
- Explain the outcomes of your own and others' performances.
- Adapt activities to suit particular conditions.
- Develop plans and strategies for improving performance.

Applying knowledge and skills in physical education involves analysing, manipulating and interpreting information.

Evaluating Knowledge and Skills

You **evaluate knowledge** and skills in physical education by synthesising, justifying, assessing and hypothesising. Here are tests of whether you are able to evaluate knowledge and skills relevant to your programme of study:

- Predict probable outcomes of a performance.
- Defend and justify predictions of outcomes.
- Make informed decisions during, and about, performances of physical activities.
- Reflect on your performances and plan strategies for improvement.

Evaluating knowledge and skills in physical education involves synthesising, justifying, assessing and hypothesising.

Appreciating and Valuing Physical Activity

Appreciating the value of physical activities from social, aesthetic, moral and cultural perspectives happens in conjunction with acquiring, applying and evaluating knowledge and skills in physical education. Typically, it is difficult to test your appreciation of these values in the same ways as the other three processes. Nevertheless, appreciation is a key educational process in physical education. Unless you learn to appreciate the values associated with physical activities, it is unlikely that you will develop the depth of understanding required of a reflective performer. People tend to learn to value physical activity when their learning experiences are positive, supported and enjoyable, and when they have improved their performances.

Appreciating the value of physical activities happens in conjunction with acquiring, applying and evaluating knowledge and skills in physical education.

Over to You

With a partner, consider the four learning processes just outlined. Write down a specific example of each process as it applies to an area of practical activity you are studying.

PRINCIPLES OF A-LEVEL PHYSICAL EDUCATION

There are four key educational principles that underpin the study of physical education at A level: the integration of knowledge from different sources, making knowledge personal, equity and inclusion, and synopsis. In conjunction with the four learning processes just described, these principles inform the development of your programme of study and help you to become a reflective performer.

Integration of Knowledge

Integration refers to linking the learning of subject matter such as physiology or history with learning physical activities such as badminton or swimming. This principle is informed by the work of several educational philosophers who have described physical education as a process of learning in, about and through physical activity. You have already met these ideas earlier in the chapter. Here you have the chance to consider them in more detail in relation to the notion of integration.

- Learning *in* the physical domain refers to the acquisition and development of the techniques that enable you to execute a movement efficiently and to apply techniques appropriately as part of your overall performance.

- Learning *about* physical activity refers to improving performance by acquiring, applying and evaluating physiological, psychological, biomechanical and sociological knowledge, and integrating this understanding with knowledge and practical experience of the physical activity.

- Learning *through* physical activity refers to learning to appreciate a whole range of social values such as responsibility for your actions and caring for and supporting others.

Recently, physical educators have been attempting to find ways of applying this principle of integration to school programmes. They have done this by developing learning experiences that provide learners with opportunities to make connections and links between the content of sociology or biomechanics, for example, and physical activities such as basketball or aquatics. Examples of these learning experiences can be found in some of the tasks in this chapter of the book.

Making Knowledge Personal

The notion of making knowledge personal has been informed by recent advances in the fields of educational learning theory, motor control and the psychology of sport and exercise. **Personalisation** refers to the ways in which new information can be made meaningful to you as an individual. Improving performance in physical education largely depends on the extent to which knowledge and skills can be personalised.

Making knowledge personal is not simply a matter of finding some aspect of new information that is recognisable, familiar or comfortable. The application of this principle also involves

- discovering the links between what you already know or can do and the new information and physical challenges you encounter;

- working out which pieces of information within a whole range of new knowledge you should attend to;

- becoming more aware of how you learn and being better able to learn from experience;

- seeing the relationships between local, national and global environments and adapting this information to suit the local, national and global contexts in which you live; and

- learning through critical reflection on your own experience and the experiences of others.

As you read through this textbook, you will come across a series of exercises in each chapter that are headed 'Over to You'. These exercises implement the notion

Integration refers to linking learning in, about and through physical activities.

Making knowledge personal refers to the ways in which new information can be made meaningful to you as an individual.

of personalisation by providing you with opportunities to relate new information encountered in the text to your own personal experience and to the experience of others in your class, school, family or community. The exercises are intended to assist you to make sense of new information by encouraging you to apply the information to situations with which you are familiar and to real-life examples other than those provided in the book.

Equity and Inclusion

In physical education and sport most people would agree that it is important to help more people to lead an active and healthy life. Making physical education and sport more inclusive involves our accepting and promoting a commitment to equity. What does such a commitment entail? You need to approach equity in positive rather than negative ways. Having a commitment to **equity** and **inclusion** in physical education and sport means valuing and celebrating, rather than 'accommodating', difference and diversity in performances, in ambitions and interests relating to sport, and in body shapes and sizes.

Developing equity requires that we not only recognise but also value individual and collective differences between societies and cultures in relation to sporting interests, traditions and behaviours. By valuing difference and diversity we can ensure that physical education and sport are, in a meaningful sense, inclusive. We can also emphasise the need to move beyond thinking of equity as concerned only with gender, race, age, class or ability. Promoting equity involves thinking about real people, not labels.

In chapter 1.2, you will find more detail on the implications of equity and inclusion in physical education and sport for you and your classmates, teachers, coaches, administrators and spectators. You will also find information on the active role we all play in reinforcing long-standing inequities in physical education and sport, and what you can do to change this situation.

A commitment to equity and inclusion in physical education and sport means valuing and celebrating difference and diversity in performances.

Synopsis

This book contains chapters that address specific subdiscipline knowledge associated with the study of physical education and sport. However, it is important that you also explore links between subdisciplines through **synoptic** study. In particular, you will find through your A-level course ways to draw on knowledge and understanding from a combination of subdisciplines to help you develop a better understanding of physical education. You will also be able to consider ways in which you may improve your own and others' performances and experiences in sport through synoptic inquiry.

To understand why particular performances are achieved and achievable, you need to acknowledge the many factors influencing abilities and opportunities at any given time and in a range of contexts. If you rely on subject matter from only one subdiscipline, say sociology or physiology, you risk developing only a partial understanding of physical education. You could miss key factors for possible improvements in performance.

A synopsis involves drawing on knowledge and understanding from a combination of subdisciplines to help you develop more comprehensive understandings of the field of physical education.

Over to You

In conversation with your teacher, consider the implications of each principle for teaching or coaching in physical education or sport. Make a list of the things a teacher or coach would do to implement each principle.

THE SOCIAL CONSTRUCTION
OF PHYSICAL EDUCATION

The social construction of physical education refers to the organisation of knowledge according to the preferences, interests and cultures of individuals and groups of people.

This chapter's description of physical education as a field of study represents only one version of the subject. Using historical and sociological methods, you will discover other versions of physical education advocated at different times in history and in various parts of the world. Later in this book, you will find out how physical education as a subject has been constructed according to the social class interests and gender interests of particular groups of people. For example, you will discover that physical education has been strongly influenced by gender considerations. That is why it is still common today for schools in Britain to offer single-sex classes for girls and boys.

So the version of physical education described here is a **social construction**. This means that it stresses the need for integrating subject matter knowledge and practical knowledge, and making a commitment to equity and inclusion.

Acknowledging physical education as a social construction does not mean that anything goes, however. Teachers, curriculum developers and researchers have developed the version of physical education you are studying for A level only after years of experience. In its present form, it is the latest and most appropriate version for programmes of study at A level. However, because physical education is a social construction, the form can be changed if it later proves to be inappropriate to the needs and interests of new generations of A-level students. You will learn more about the idea that physical education is socially constructed as you work through this book.

> The social construction of physical education refers to the organisation of knowledge according to the preferences, interests and cultures of individuals and groups of people.

Over to You

Discuss in class what it means to say that physical education is socially constructed. Write down as many implications as you can of the idea that physical education is socially constructed. Then identify any specific action points for you as a reflective performer that your analysis has produced.

SUMMARY

Physical education has two major components: practical physical activities and subject matter knowledge. Each of these components can be categorised in various ways. What makes physical education educationally worthwhile is the integration of learning in, about and through physical activity. You are assisted to become a reflective performer in physical education through the application of four learning processes and four educational principles. The version of the field of study outlined here is a social construction, and the chapter briefly explores the implication of this idea.

Test Yourself Questions

1. List the six categories of physical activities that make up the field of study.

2. Provide four examples of the subdisciplines that contribute to the subject matter of the field of study.

3. List the four key learning processes in physical education.

4. List and describe four educational principles that inform the study of physical education.

5. Define the 'reflective performer' in physical education.

6. Explain what we mean when we say that physical education is socially constructed. Give examples.

Equity in Physical Education: Principles in Practice

Chapter Overview

Learning Outcomes

When you have studied this chapter, you should be able to

☑ explain the differences between equality of access, equality of opportunity and equity in physical education and sport;

☑ appreciate a range of issues that need to be addressed if physical education and sport are to be inclusive;

☑ explain, using Figueroa's framework, the various ways in which inequity can be challenged; and

☑ identify how you can personally play a part in achieving equity in and through physical education and sport.

INTRODUCTION

Although you may not realise it, whenever you participate in physical education and sport, you either contribute to or challenge inequities in schools, sport and societies. You may be able to recall a situation in which you chose not to pass to another player who you felt would be clumsy or slow or who might let your team down. Or perhaps you are someone who has been marginalised or excluded from play in this way. This is just one example of inequity in sport. We all have a role to play in making sport a more equitable and enjoyable experience for more people. This chapter explores the complexities of equity and the various ways in which we may challenge inequities in physical education and sport.

SO WHAT IS EQUITY?

Uncertainty about the meaning of the term 'equity' is understandable. It is a term widely used in relation to policies and practices in physical education and sport. But a shared understanding of equity is still lacking. Often 'equity' is interchanged with 'equality' or 'equal opportunities'. Taking a closer look at these words is a useful starting point for our discussion of equity.

EQUALITY: ACCESS, OPPORTUNITY AND INCLUSION

Many of the developments that have claimed to promote 'equality' or 'equal opportunities' in physical education and sport have focused on the issue of access to activities and facilities. A school or club may be concerned to extend a provision to enable a group of people currently not participating to have access to the particular activity or sport. For example, your school may arrange for both boys and girls to play football, rather than this being a sport that is available for boys only.

If football is introduced into physical education for both boys and girls, all pupils have access to football. But does this mean that there is equality in physical education or that the school is ensuring 'equal opportunity'? If we consider the many and varied experiences that you and your classmates have in the football lessons, we can begin to appreciate that equal access and equal opportunity are not the same thing.

For both boys and girls there will be notable and unavoidable differences in experiences of lessons. Several differences in experiences are relevant in relation to equal opportunities. Does everyone have an equal chance to play an active role in the lesson? Or do some players dominate the lesson? Does everyone have an equal chance to improve their own skills? Or do the practices and standards expected suit some, but not all, players?

© Human Kinetics

Equal access to a physical education lesson does not mean that boys and girls will share the same experience of it.

Differences in skills and abilities are an important consideration if teachers, coaches and clubs are interested in offering everyone an equal opportunity to participate in physical education and sport and to improve their personal performance. Acknowledging these differences and developing practices that are 'personalised' are very important to inclusion in physical education and sport.

Over to You

For (a) physical education in curriculum time and (b) extracurricular physical education, ask yourself, Who has access to what opportunities? Whose needs and interests are being met by provision? Whose are being marginalised or overlooked? Discuss in a small group what you have found and summarise the discussion.

Policy makers and providers have considered issues of access and opportunity in relation to physical education and sport. Many initiatives have attempted to extend participation by removing barriers to physical activity and sport. Often the barriers have been associated with particular groups in society.

Women, young people, disabled people, people over 50 and members of ethnic groups have all, at various times, been defined as 'target groups' by sport policy makers. Initiatives have attempted to overcome barriers such as the location of facilities or clubs, the cost of participation, the timing of sessions and whether individuals are happy or willing to participate in mixed sex settings. The stated aim has been to offer more people the opportunity to participate in physical activity and sport.

However, such aims, policies and initiatives need to be explored in depth if we are interested in equity. Of particular interest here are questions such as

- What exactly is being presented as an opportunity for the individuals within the various groups?
- What assumptions are being made about the needs and interests of those individuals?
- Whose values and interests are expressed in, and furthered by, the initiatives?
- What is the basis of inclusion in physical activity and sport?

Questions such as these help us begin to address issues that are of central concern in any consideration of equity in physical education and sport. The key issues are the ways in which we view individual, social and cultural differences in attitudes, values and behaviours, and how differences are acknowledged in equality and equity policies and programmes.

Often policy makers and providers tend to deny the many individual differences that we can see present in any identified social group. Members of an identified group may have one characteristic in common such as their age. But policy makers and providers need to acknowledge that this is only one characteristic. Individuals within the group will vary in, for example, their abilities, their religious beliefs, their disposable income and family responsibilities. All of these differences will influence people's ability to access the opportunities provided for a target group that they may belong to.

In addition, difference is often viewed in terms of deficit. Many policies and initiatives privilege one set of **values for participation and achievement** in physical activity and sport and imply that these values are appropriate and desirable for everyone. Then, individuals and groups are identified who do not meet the expectations set out in the policies. Strategies are then developed in an attempt to reduce the perceived imbalances in participation and performance statistics.

In considering whose values and interests, think of which particular groups celebrate participation and achievement in particular sports.

In considering the basis for inclusion, try to identify the starting point for planning for inclusion.

The assumptions and value judgements inherent in such strategies are rarely questioned. Few people stop to consider that the initiatives reflect a particular and sometimes limited approach to inclusion in physical activity and sport. The assumption is made that the established forms of physical activity and sport are desirable for, and desired by, nonparticipants. **Interests in different forms of activity,** and participation for different reasons, are often overlooked.

Some of these assumptions are evident when we consider attempts to increase the number of young people who are active participants in sport. Many policies have focused on recruiting more young people to become members of sports clubs. Policy makers assume that this is the type of opportunity young people want. Obviously, some young people will welcome the opportunity to pursue their ability in a particular sport and will have ambitions to become involved in high-level competition in that sport. You may be one of those people.

However, you may also be able to think of friends who have no such desires or ambitions. They may want to be involved in physical activity and sport, but for very different reasons, perhaps for fun, friendship and general health. Can junior sports clubs provide for their needs and interests?

Many young people may not want to commit themselves to a particular sport. They may, instead, want to have a go at several activities. Similarly, some people may not want sessions to be dominated by coaching directed towards improvements in performance. They may just want to take part to enjoy it, unconcerned to reach higher levels of performance.

Regrettably, policy makers and providers often overlook the appeal of participation in sport as a social activity by focusing instead on performance agendas. So, we can begin to appreciate the limits to the inclusivity of policies and initiatives. Essentially, such inclusion is on terms that present particular forms of physical activity and sport (performance at elite levels) as of more value than others. Differences in interests and needs are denied or marginalised.

Over to You

The English Sports Council (subsequently known as Sport England) promoted many initiatives in the 1980s and 1990s aimed at encouraging different groups of people to participate in sport. Identify some of the groups targeted by such an initiative ('Ever thought of sport?', for example). Use the group names as headings and list under each header how their needs and interests were met by the initiative.

Find out about a campaign or initiative in your local area that has attempted to increase participation among a particular group of people (for example, women, over-50s, young people). Describe the key characteristics of the campaign or initiative, and reflect on the assumptions that underpin the attempt to establish inclusion in physical activity and sport locally. Write a brief report on what you have found.

The revised National Curriculum for Physical Education at Key Stage 4 has attempted to offer participation opportunities for young people through a variety of experiences such as officiating, coaching, choreographing, performing for general health and performing for competitive preparation. Speak to your physical education teachers. How do they feel the new orders have affected the provision and presentation of activities at Key Stage 4? Speak to year 10 and 11 students. What are their thoughts regarding the choice of activities and equality of opportunity to improve in physical education? Discuss your findings in a small group and produce a co-authored report.

A COMMITMENT TO EQUITY

So far, you have read about some shortcomings in the ways in which equality and equal opportunities have been approached in physical education and sport. How does a commitment to equity overcome these shortcomings?

The notion of difference is a key consideration, especially the way in which it is perceived and approached by policy makers and providers. Being committed to equity in physical education and sport means not just acknowledging difference. It means celebrating and valuing difference. It means that no one set of values or behaviours is regarded as superior to others. Nor is one set of values regarded as the norm against which others are measured or judged. Rather, there is recognition that behaviours and values always need to be located, temporally and culturally. At different times, in different places and cultures, different behaviours and values will be regarded as normal and desirable.

For physical education and sport to be equitable demands that we not only recognise social and cultural differences but value them as a richness of societies. Similarly, to be equitable, policies and practices need to regard individual differences in a positive manner. Individual differences in interests and abilities are not to be viewed as a problem. Individuals are not to be seen as deficient if they do not match with particular perceptions about desired participation or ability in sport.

Instead, differences should be respected, valued and provided for. Evans and Davies on page 19 of *Equality, Education and Physical Education* (1993) explain the following:

> The issue must not be whether differences can be dissolved … but how they can be celebrated in ways which negate prejudice and stereotyping and at the same time respect individual cultural identity.

From an equity perspective, 'inclusion' has quite different meanings and implications to those implied in our discussion of equality. It means questioning many long-standing assumptions about the form that physical education and sport should take, and being open to the introduction of new forms that reflect different interests and values. The next section explores the complex ways in which such assumptions are embedded in our own actions, and in the institutions, societies and cultural groups of which we are a part. It addresses the many dimensions to equity and the various arenas in which action is needed if we are to achieve equity in physical education and sport.

EQUITY: A FRAMEWORK FOR UNDERSTANDING AND ACTION

Equity is a complex and challenging concept, with many dimensions and wide-reaching implications for policies and practices in physical education and sport. A framework developed by Figueroa (1993) is useful in exploring the dimensions and their implications at various levels of provision of physical education and sport. The framework consists of five levels that link up. The relationship between the levels is two-way so that any level is to some extent shaped by that above it. At the same time, it also plays a part in shaping the level above. The interaction of levels shows that we all play an active part in either creating or reinforcing inequities or, in contrast, challenging them.

Stereotyping reflects the belief that every individual belonging to a particular group displays characteristics that are associated with that group. Effectively, stereotyping labels all individuals within a group as 'the same' in particular respects.

Prejudice refers to the practice of making judgements or holding beliefs about people on the basis of assumptions about characteristics of the groups to which they belong rather than on the basis of personal knowledge about an individual.

The Individual Level

One of Figueroa's levels is directly concerned with us as individuals. The individual level considers the attitudes and beliefs that we each hold, for example, about other people, about desirable and undesirable behaviours in sport, about body shape, about forms of participation and about achievement in sport. These attitudes and beliefs contribute to the creation of inequitable situations when they mean that we value some people more than others and judge people on the basis of **stereotypes.**

Over to You

What are your beliefs about other people, about desirable and undesirable behaviours in sport, about body shape, about forms of participation and about achievement in sport? Discuss and compare beliefs with others in your group. Note and summarise similarities and differences in beliefs.

Becoming more aware of our own attitudes and beliefs is an important first step if we are to achieve equity in physical education and sporting contexts. **Our attitudes and beliefs** are, of course, shaped by our experiences as members of particular families, clubs, schools, societies and cultural groups. However, as members of these various institutions and groups we actively contribute to the attitudes and beliefs that they continue to instil in others.

The Interpersonal Level

The dynamic between ourselves and others brings us to the next level in this framework for equity, the interpersonal level. This level is concerned with the ways in which we interact with one another. This includes all forms of communication, including oral communication and body language. In contexts of physical education and sport, what people say to one another is an important consideration. But there are also many nonverbal interactions. As a member of a team you may not say anything to anyone on either your own or the opposing team. However, in the way you play, interact with other players, whom you pass or do not pass to, how you react to an aggressive tackle or a decision that you do not agree with; all of these contribute to the creation of either an equitable or inequitable environment.

It is appropriate here to recall the emphasis on valuing difference and our concern to promote inclusiveness in physical education and sport. Particularly in school physical education, how pupils treat one another can influence how individuals feel about themselves. Unfortunately, because of the way they are treated by other pupils, many young people may leave school with no desire to participate further in physical activity and sport.

Teachers and coaches can influence an individual's feelings of competence. They can be key people in encouraging involvement. Developing personalised programmes and goals to suit individual abilities and interests is critical to ensuring that everyone gets the most benefit out of their participation in an activity. To promote equity, teachers and coaches need to develop practices and set goals for everyone in class.

Over to You

After reading about personal and interpersonal levels of equity, reflect on your own attitudes and beliefs relating to ability and involvement in sport. Whom do you feel sport is for? Whose participation and performances should we encourage and celebrate? In your physical education lessons, who do you want to be on your team and who would you not chose? Think of situations in which the actions of some pupils mean that other pupils may leave the lesson feeling that they are failures. Identify ways in which you and other pupils may act differently to ensure that everyone enjoys physical education and feels that they have achieved something. Make a list of things to do.

How can teachers, coaches and student leaders influence and encourage involvement by everyone? With a partner, develop and write down some strategies that would work at your school.

The Institutional Level

Third in our equity framework is the institutional level. At this level we are concerned with the way routine practices in society and its institutions, such as schools, sports clubs and organisations, place particular groups of people in positions of advantage and disadvantage. Rules, regulations and procedures are often firmly established in institutions and organisations.

Often, regular ways of operating are not questioned. Rather, they are uncritically accepted as common practice or regarded as the only or the best way for things to be. We rarely pause to consider the implications of regulations or procedures. Routine practices in physical education and sport have many implications for participation and, specifically, the degree to which different people may become active participants and improve their performance.

Extracurricular sport in schools provides a good example of inequity operating at the institutional level. Invariably, male teachers are given responsibility for organising activities for boys, and female teachers have responsibility for activities for girls. Many people regard these arrangements as normal. But research has shown that a shortage of female teachers for extracurricular activities means that boys have a greater range of activities offered to them than girls.

Few schools have considered alternatives, such as teachers' having responsibility for running extracurricular sports clubs for both boys and girls. Extracurricular sport may also be unfavourable to less able individuals. In many instances, it is only a few of the most able students who have opportunities to play in matches after school. It is the focus on competing with other schools that creates this situation. Once again, we can consider alternative arrangements that may be more equitable. With a focus on students' playing with and against students from the same school, more may have an opportunity to participate and improve their ability in various sports.

Barriers to Participation. We referred earlier to 'barriers to participation'. In some instances, institutional practices represent very real barriers to the involvement of individuals. For example, because of their religious beliefs, some girls and women may not be able to participate in swimming unless lessons are single sex. If clubs and facility managers are seriously committed to equity and inclusiveness in sport, they need to consider such issues when decisions are being made about timetabling of sessions and the design of facilities.

Scheduling Facilities. Think about who has priority use of sports facilities. Are they recreational groups or competitive teams? Are the arrangements fair to everyone who wants to use the facilities? Decisions on these matters are not neutral. Inevitably, some people's needs and interests are favoured over others. For example, masters swimming clubs often find that the only pool time available to them is late in an evening. Other users, with different interests, are given priority at peak times. In part this reflects commercial interests and pressures. But in some facility time-tabling we also see particular types of participation and standards of performance advanced at the expense of others.

Dress and Equipment. Most sports clubs and schools have rules and regulations about suitable clothing and equipment for participation in physical activities. In

Extracurricular sport refers to sport that is provided outside the normal curriculum hours. It therefore includes activities provided before the start of the school day, at lunchtimes, after school and at weekends.

some cases, rules clearly relate to safety and so have been developed in the best interests of everyone. In other cases, the dress and equipment regulations may reflect long-standing traditions of a sport or an institution.

Whatever the origins of such regulations, they can sometimes restrict participation. This is because owning or being able to borrow or hire clothing or equipment is a prerequisite to participating. The exclusion of young people from lower income groups from particular sports such as competitive showjumping is still evident in Britain. Some effort has been made to reduce obvious costs associated with some sports, such as club membership or green fees for golf. However, the hidden costs associated with regular participation in sport remain a barrier to involvement for many people.

The location and timing of many sports club sessions in the community mean that participation is only possible for people who have access to a car for transport. This is particularly true in the case of young people who wish to train hard to reach higher levels of performance. Without supportive parents, who own at least one car, pursuing such ambitions may be very difficult. So, routine arrangements associated with access to sports clubs and facilities both directly and indirectly have implications for equity.

In addition, achieving excellence in sports performance is not determined solely by physical factors. Possessing and developing a particular physique will help performance in particular sports. But physique alone does not determine who can reach elite levels. Technique and biomechanical factors are also important, as are psychological aspects, including motivation. However, there is always also an interaction of these factors with social, economic and cultural issues, such that two people with similar potential in sport may be very differently placed in terms of the chances that they have to fulfil that potential. Schools and sports clubs concerned to promote equity in sport need to consider ways in which their practices take account of social, economic and cultural factors.

Over to You

Visit a sports facility or club in your local area. Find out about policies and regulations relating to membership and when individuals and groups can use the facilities. Note and critically reflect on whose needs and interests are being privileged by the policies and regulations, and who is being excluded from participation.

Audit access to facilities and equipment in your school. Make notes on which individuals and groups use the facilities, when and how often. Interview boys and girls at each year level. What do they perceive to be the barriers to their and others' increased involvement in physical activity at school?

The Structural Level

The next level in our framework is the structural level. This level is directly concerned with some of the inequities that we can see within institutions. The structural level helps us to address matters such as the uneven distribution of **resources** and **rewards** within sport and society. It also helps us to address the different social position and status that are accorded to different people, different sports and different types and levels of participation.

Inequities at the structural level are reflected in many arenas and institutions. Media coverage of sport provides clear evidence of the different status accorded to sports and to men's and women's participation in sport. Men's sports, elite performances in sport and in Britain sports such as football dominate the sports pages of national newspapers.

Resources may refer to physical and human resources, and therefore includes, for example, funding for development, provision of facilities, equipment and coaching.

Rewards may be direct or indirect. Differences in rewards may relate to particular sports or particular groups of individuals.

⊟ ▦ ▦ ▦ ▦ ▦ ▦ ▦ *Over to You* ▦ ▦ ▦ ▦ ▦ ▦ ▦

What are the intrinsic and extrinsic rewards for the two sports that you are studying? What status do the sports and the performers have in Britain when the sports are played at an elite competitive level and at a recreational level? Make a record of either newspaper, television or radio coverage for your two sports during one week. Note how often the sport is covered. How much time or column space is allocated to reporting? Are all groups represented? Note which levels (recreational, competitive) of participation are represented. Are men and women represented equally?

▦ The Cultural Level

Selective coverage of sport by the media develops and sustains attitudes and values, and so requires analysis at the cultural level. Media coverage of sport reflects dominant beliefs, values and behavioural norms that feature in British society. Analysis at the cultural level is concerned with our shared assumptions, beliefs and values, particularly as they relate to matters such as gender and race. Sometimes these assumptions or beliefs are misguided or simplify complex issues.

For example, many sports are still regarded as men's or women's sports, with particular abilities or behaviours regarded as exclusive to either men or women. Assumptions and beliefs about the capabilities of men and women, and of the types of participation appropriate for men and women, deny the diversity of abilities and interests that exists in these two groups.

Not all men are the same, nor are all women. Among both men and women there will be a considerable range of abilities and interests relating to physical activity and sport. Inequity operating at a cultural level often means that this diversity is overlooked or denied and becomes explicit at other levels in the framework such that opportunities for participation by both men and women are limited in various ways. Within your school you can perhaps see evidence of inequity operating in this way, with certain sports provided for boys and others for girls.

Comparative studies are particularly useful in drawing attention to inequity at the cultural level. Differences between countries can draw attention to assumptions about cultural values and norms and the ways in which these differences are then reflected in, and actively reinforced by, society and its institutions.

Sport and physical education continue to be arenas in which the reinforcement of social and cultural norms, beliefs and values is at times very obvious and, at other times, subtle. Often we remain unaware of these processes of social and cultural reproduction and our own part in sustaining inequities in sport, in schools and in society. We can celebrate the good things sport has to offer to many people in society. But we must not forget to ask who is marginalised or excluded from the enjoyment and sense of achievement that sport participation can provide.

In addition, we must always look critically at the values that are being promoted by the events and achievements that we are celebrating. Major international events, such as the Olympic Games, provide a useful focus for such enquiry. We can question what and whose values and interests are reflected in the modern Olympics, which groups in society benefit from such events, and what social values are promoted by the Olympic Games.

Challenging long-standing practices, assumptions and attitudes is never easy. It needs to start with our own thinking and actions as individuals. Figueroa's framework demonstrates the capacity for this thinking and action to have wide-reaching effects, and also the way in which we need to question the practices that we routinely engage in as we participate in physical activity and sport. Can you see ways you can contribute to equity in physical education and sport?

Over to You

Conduct a case study that focuses on the reproduction of inequity in sport at each of the five levels. For your school sports day or a tournament that you participate in, observe and describe the ways in which inequity is evident in individual attitudes (your own or fellow players or competitors), interactions between players or competitors, between players or competitors and teachers or coaches, and institutional aspects of the event. In what ways does the event or tournament reflect and reinforce inequity at the structural and cultural levels?

When you have completed the case study, make a list of ways in which you could change the focus or arrangements for the event to create a more equitable sporting environment.

SUMMARY

This chapter addresses equity in physical education and sport. Differences in equality of access, equal opportunities and equity are discussed, and attention is drawn to the complex issues that need to be addressed if physical education and sport are to become more inclusive. A framework for understanding ways in which inequities may be either reinforced or challenged is presented, and the role that individuals and institutions play in reinforcing or challenging inequity in physical education and sport is outlined. Throughout the chapter you are challenged to identify practical ways in which you can personally contribute to the development of greater equity and inclusion in physical education and sport.

Test Yourself Questions ▧ ▧ ▧ ▧ ▧ ▧ ▧ ▧ ▧ ▧ ▧ ▧

1. Provide an example of a change in provision in physical education that can be regarded as a move to achieve equality of access. Explain why such a change may fail to address equality of opportunity in physical education.

2. Explain the way in which differences between individuals and in society are viewed (a) from an equality perspective and (b) from an equity perspective.

3. Identify differences between children that are important for teachers or sports coaches to consider if they are committed to equity and inclusion. Explain the changes that may need to be made to the content and organisation of physical education and junior sports clubs in order to achieve greater equity and inclusion.

4. Briefly outline the five levels of Figueroa's framework for equity. Explain the two-way links between the various levels.

Learning to Become a Reflective Performer

Learning Outcomes

When you have studied this chapter, you should be able to

☑ describe the traditional approach to learning physical activities and list some weaknesses,

☑ identify the main features of an information-processing approach to learning,

☑ identify the main features of a constructivist approach to learning,

☑ list possible advantages and disadvantages of the information-processing and constructivist approaches,

☑ describe the implications of a constructivist approach for teaching/coaching, and

☑ apply concepts from this chapter to analyse your own learning as a reflective performer and show how you can use these concepts to plan for improvement.

INTRODUCTION

The manner in which physical activity teachers and coaches have gone about their jobs in the past has had a profound influence on how we think about acquiring physical skills. Traditionally, teachers practised a command-style method of instruction where learners were thought to be passive recipients of information. Over time, researchers recognised that developmental and personal differences, as well as cognitive processes, greatly influence how we learn physical skills. Researchers also found that personal needs and interests are important. From this new knowledge about learning, teachers and coaches have begun to adopt a range of teaching styles that have been informed by information-processing and constructivist theories of learning. These theories support the teacher in the role of facilitating your learning to be a reflective performer.

THE TRADITIONAL APPROACH
TO LEARNING PHYSICAL SKILLS

Swedish gymnastics is a system of freestanding exercises developed by Per Henrik Ling in Sweden at the end of the nineteenth century, called callisthenics in the United States.

From the 1880s until the 1950s, militaristic forms of instruction dominated physical education in schools. Children who attended government schools participated in a system of drilling and exercising known as **Swedish gymnastics,** also known as callisthenics. In this form of physical education, the teacher shouted commands and learners were supposed to follow these directions and any demonstrations given by the teacher. The teacher stood out in front of the class, and the learners were supposed to move in unison. There was no room for individual differences in ability or interest among individual children. Needless to say, this proved to be an unpopular form of physical education.

Through the 1950s, games and sports began to replace drilling and exercising as the content of physical education programmes in schools. Whereas this innovation provided teachers with opportunities to change their methods of teaching, the old militaristic or command style of teaching remained influential in certain important respects. One of these was the way in which it encouraged people to think about the acquisition of physical skills. The command style of teaching assumes that learners are passive recipients of information. Information moves in one direction only, from the teacher to the learner. It is the learner's job to follow as closely as possible the teacher's instructions. Learning is thought to have occurred when the learner is able to reproduce the skills in a form that closely resembles the teacher's instructions and demonstrations.

An analogy that might describe the way learning is assumed to happen in traditional physical education is that students are like mirrors who passively reflect the actions of the teacher. This view, in which the teacher is assumed to be the most important person in the equation, is not restricted to physical education. In other school subjects, similar analogies have been used. The empty bucket model of learning describes a passive learner whose head is like an empty bucket ready to be filled with information. The sponge analogy imagines learning takes place by the learner absorbing information just like a sponge absorbs water.

Attractive though these analogies may seem, they fail to explain how learning actually takes place. They also fail to provide guidelines on how someone can learn to become a reflective performer.

Today we know that the traditional way of thinking about learning physical skills fails to acknowledge that cognitive processes are central to the acquisition of physical skills. Traditional thinking assumes that acquiring physical skills is simply a matter of getting the movements right, and demands little cognitive activity of the learner. Because this approach does not include cognitive processes in the acquisition of skill, it cannot explain how people learn to apply physical skills creatively or to perform well in novel situations. Nor is it able to account for the critical evaluation of game play that is a key part of using strategies and tactics.

MOTOR LEARNING APPROACHES TO LEARNING PHYSICAL SKILLS

The information-processing approach to learning responds to the problem of how people manage to produce controlled and coordinated movements in all aspects of their daily lives. To produce even the simplest of movements, we need to vary the forces produced by a large number of muscles of the body and do so with appropriate timing.

To get an idea of how difficult even simple movements are, watch a very young baby try to grasp a toy with her hand. Her arm jerks about and, initially at least, the baby's hand has little chance of getting to its destination. Why? Not because of a physical limitation preventing the baby grasping the toy, but because she has not yet mastered the complexity of her neuromuscular system.

So how do adults manage to produce controlled and coordinated movements, often without even appearing to think consciously about it? The information-processing approach offers a simple way to think about learning to become a reflective performer.

Motor learning uses a similar kind of **information-processing** model to a software program that controls the operations of a computer system. Think of a human being as a system that receives input through the senses, just as a computer receives input from a keyboard or other device. The person's central nervous system then processes the input, just as a computer's central processing unit processes information. Finally, the central nervous system sends a message to the muscles in the form of neural commands, just as a computer sends output to a printer. In this analogy, motor learning is parallel to a computer program; it translates neural impulses into a desired and specific muscle activity and movement pattern.

The information-processing approach is based on an analogy that learning in humans is similar to the way in which computers process information.

■ Phases of Performance

The information-processing approach to learning stresses the importance of perception and decision making. It focuses attention on how people learn to interpret information in their environment and use their interpretation to make effective decisions about movement execution. This approach assumes, as shown in figure 1, that there are three sequential phases in skilful performance: perceiving, deciding and acting.

During the *perceiving* phase you are trying to determine what is happening and to identify what information is relevant in a particular set of circumstances. For example, you are a basketball player who has just received the ball. You must interpret a range of information in the immediate environment. You perceive the position of team-mates and opponents, your own position on court, your distance from goal, the stage of the game, the score, levels of fatigue, and so on. The ability to sift the important information from other information quickly and accurately is a key characteristic of expert players.

Next is the *deciding* phase, which is when you decide the best course of action. As mentioned previously, you have just received the ball and perceived a range of information. Now you must decide whether to pass, dribble or shoot, and decide the most appropriate kind of pass, dribble or shot. Typically, expert players are much more efficient and faster at making decisions than novices are because they have learned through experience which actions to link to which circumstances in the game.

During the *acting* phase a series of neural impulses recruit muscles to execute your selected movements with appropriate timing, coordination and force. You now act

Figure 1 Central processing stages in a typical information-processing model of motor control.
Reprinted, by permission, from MacKinnon et al., 1996.

based on your perception of the situation and your decision on how to respond. Movement execution is a vital part of skilful physical performance, but it is not necessarily the most important part.

The three phases of perceiving, deciding and acting are interdependent and, in the case of expert performers, often happen very rapidly. Beginners take longer than experienced players to perceive the relevant information and have difficulty determining exactly *what* information is most relevant to their performance. It follows that expert players are also more rapid and effective decision makers than novices because they have the advantage of experience.

The information-processing approach to learning shows clearly that, in contrast to the traditional approach to learning, the execution of movement, or acting, is only one part of learning physical skills. It also demonstrates the significance of the cognitive processes of perceiving and deciding.

Over to You

Apply the information-processing approach to one of the physical activities you are currently studying. Set up a practice that will run for one minute, where you are involved in perceiving information, making decisions and executing techniques. As soon as you have completed the practice, sit down and write a list of everything you did during the one minute. Then make three headings, perceiving, deciding and acting. Under each heading, write down which aspect of your practice belongs in each category. For example, making a shot in netball might be categorised under 'acting'; the time between receiving the ball and shooting might go under 'deciding'; and the period immediately before receiving the ball might be located under 'perceiving'.

The emphasis on perceiving and deciding provides a basis for the development of the 'teaching games for understanding' approach. This approach aims to develop players' understanding of strategies and improve their decision making while simultaneously developing their techniques. The information-processing approach suggests there is no single best way to execute a movement because so much depends on the circumstances within which the movement is performed and on the player's perception and decision-making capabilities.

The Role of Feedback

As figure 1 suggests, an integral part of an information-processing model of movement control is a **feedback loop.** This loop indicates that successful movement execution involves using information about the movement obtained through your senses. Information is available from a variety of sources. One important source is vision. As a person moves, vision provides information about how you are moving in your environment. Vision also provides information about the location of your arms and legs if you can see them.

Whenever you move, neural impulses are also transmitted by receptors located in your muscles, tendons, ligaments and skin. These neural impulses provide information about the position and velocity of your body, and have been called **kinaesthetic information.** Kinaesthetic information might be thought of as how a movement feels. Information about the orientation and movement of your head is also provided by the vestibular receptors in the ears. Auditory information may also be useful in some situations.

> A feedback loop is the information you receive from a variety of senses on the outcomes of your movements.

> Kinaesthetic information concerns the ability of the body, through the use of proprioceptors, to know where body parts are positioned in relation to each other.

Over to You

Stand still, close your eyes and start with your arms by your sides. Then, with your eyes still closed, move your arm to touch your nose with your right forefinger. Put your arms by your side again. Do the same thing again with your left hand. Then, with eyes closed, lift one arm and hold it out to the side and straight so that it is parallel with the ground. Hold the position and open your eyes to check the result. How successful were you with each task? Discuss in a small group how such movements are possible without the use of visual feedback and write a note about your discussion.

All this feedback-type information is provided throughout every movement we make. Together, it constitutes the perceptual consequences of movement. Learning what the perceptual consequences of successful movement look, feel and sound like, is a critical part, and perhaps the most important part, of learning to execute a movement.

A coach or teacher can also provide information about how you performed a movement after the movement is completed. This could take the form of verbal information or by watching a video playback of the performance. Information about the outcome of the movement, such as Where did the ball go after it was hit? or How fast did I run?, is also a valuable source of feedback.

Over to You

Choose a skill (such as a spike in a volleyball game or a fake-and-drive to a lay-up shot in basketball). In a small group, teach this skill to some classmates. Experiment with different types of feedback. Try various sources such as visual (e.g., video playback), verbal and kinaesthetic (ask the learner how the movement feels). Write down the effects of each type of feedback in relation to learning the skill.

Acquiring a skill takes practice, but practice alone does not guarantee that your performance will improve. During practice you must make changes to the way you performed and decide whether the change was an improvement. One role of the teacher or coach is to facilitate learning by giving you opportunities to experience the perceptual consequences of successful movement. Another role is to provide you with additional information about the movement and its results, and to assist you to learn from this information. Knowing how to use good quality feedback is a key part of learning to become a reflective performer. A third role is to assist you to make changes to the movements that are likely to lead to the desired perceptual consequences. To be successful, these changes must be suggested in a way that you can understand and act on. This may involve demonstration or use of visual or other cues.

The information-processing approach to learning can be further developed when it is added to an educational learning theory known as constructivism.

CONSTRUCTIVIST APPROACHES TO LEARNING PHYSICAL SKILLS

Constructivist approaches to learning emphasise that learning is an active process. This involves your seeking out information in relation to the task at hand and the current environmental conditions. It also involves you trying out your techniques in relation to the task and environment.

Constructivism is consistent with the information-processing approach in its emphasis on perception and active interaction with the environment. It develops the information-processing approach further by adding that learning is developmental, both in the sense that there are identifiable phases to learning physical skills and that learning changes over time as you become more experienced. Constructivism also emphasises that learning is multidimensional, and that people typically learn more than one thing at a time.

These three features of learning as active, developmental and multidimensional are common features of a constructivist approach to learning.

■ Learning Is an Active Process

The idea that learning is an active process challenges the traditional approach to teaching and coaching physical activity where it is assumed that learners passively mirror the commands of the teacher. It also incorporates the information-processing approach's three phases of perceiving, deciding and acting.

Consistent with the information-processing approach, constructivist researchers claim that people actively attempt to make sense of specific tasks within a set of environmental conditions and in relation to what they know they can already do. An example of this would be your learning to use the lay-up shot in basketball. You bring to the task a range of prior experiences that influences your ability to learn to lay up. The task is the lay-up shot, which is typically a high percentage shot in basketball since it involves shooting from close range. The circumstances in which it is most appropriate to use the lay-up shot vary, but usually it is used when there is a reasonably clear path to the basket.

Performing a lay-up involves at least two things. First, you need to perform the combined and appropriately sequenced techniques of dribbling the ball, the pick-up, the step and jump, and the shot itself. Second, you need to decide when it's right to use the lay-up, based on your perceptions of the state of the game. Learning to perform this shot involves the three phases of perceiving, deciding and acting. It is not unusual for a player to be able to perform the actions of the lay-up shot in an unopposed practice, but then never to use the shot during a game, because they do not know how to recognise when the shot is the best option.

Constructivism is an approach to learning physical activities that proposes learning is active, developmental and multidimensional.

The interaction and interdependency of individual abilities, task demands and environmental conditions are evident in learning to lay up a basketball shot. These three factors feature in many other physical skills that are part and parcel of everyday life, as well as games and sports. People are continually required to make judgements about what they can already do in relation to what the task is asking them to do and in relation to particular sets of circumstances. In order to perform physical skills like the lay up shot successfully, learners need to make judgements about the relationships between these three factors.

The example of the lay-up shot in basketball shows that perception and cognition are central components of learning physical skills. The process of making judgements about what an individual can already do in relation to the task and environment is a cognitive process. A characteristic of improvement in performing a lay-up shot is that you become quicker and more accurate at picking out the environmental cues that tell you that the shot is 'on'. Technique also becomes smoother and capable of subtle variation. As a result, the reflective performer or experienced player is more likely than an unreflective player or novice to use the lay-up shot effectively and to score baskets in this way.

The idea that learning is an active process also takes into account your motivation and readiness to learn, which we discuss in chapter 1.4. A constructivist approach acknowledges that people have feelings and emotions that influence their willingness to work hard, to accept failure and not become discouraged, to experience discomfort and to feel elated when they succeed. People also display preferences for how they like to learn. Some prefer to watch, listen and experiment; others prefer to try an activity first and refine their learning through feedback. Your preferences may change, depending on the nature of the task and your prior experiences.

Over to You

For this task you need a video recording of a sport performance that you haven't seen before. A game such as tennis, badminton or volleyball is ideal for this task. Play the tape and pause the action as it becomes obvious that the player is about to perform a skill (for example, in tennis it might be the return of the ball over the net). Predict what will happen next by analysing the task (what the person is required to do, such as return the ball down the line); the abilities the player must have to accomplish the task (e.g., must be able to play a volley); and the environmental conditions (e.g., where the opponent is positioned, stage of the game, and so on). Try this a few times and write down your predictions and the actual results. Discuss your predictions and results in a small group. Decide which of these three factors has the biggest effect on the rate and quality of learning a physical skill. You may want to reread the preceding section of the text on learning as an active process. Write a brief summary of your discussion.

Learning Is Developmental

How you learn changes as you move from the status of beginner or novice to expert. You would expect an experienced basketball player to adapt to novel circumstances more easily than a beginner. Indeed, as we learned in the previous section, one way of distinguishing an expert from a novice is the speed and ease with which the expert adapts to changing circumstances.

Before you reach physical maturity, changes to your size and strength will have a pronounced effect on learning. Coping with these changes may be a source of clumsiness as some young people struggle to match their existing skills and expectations with changes to their bodies. Similarly, as people grow older and begin to experience physical deterioration, learning is also affected. This ongoing process of growth, development and maturation across the lifespan means that how people learn is never constant.

Within this broad lifespan perspective, we can also note that learning is developmental in relation to the phases people typically pass through as they are learning physical skills. Some researchers have suggested that there are three distinct phases in skill learning: the cognitive phase, the practice or associative phase and the autonomous phase. These phases describe a learner's journey from beginner to experienced performer.

The **cognitive phase** involves the person grasping the demands of the task to be learned and becoming aware of the circumstances or conditions under which it would typically be performed. Some researchers claim that the cognitive phase can last from a few minutes to several hours. However, it would seem that the duration of this phase depends on the nature of the task, the complexity of the environmental factors and the prior experiences of the learner. In most cases, it also seems unlikely that the cognitive phase ever ends, since even expert performers show that they are capable of learning to adapt skills in the face of changing circumstances. It is also clear that a person's understanding will deepen with greater experience and that the novice's understanding is likely to be immature, simplistic and unsophisticated.

The **associative, or practice, phase** involves the person in gradually improving his or her ability to cope with more and more information about the task and environment through practice and experience. In this phase, judging which shot to perform typically begins to require less conscious effort. The techniques of the lay-up and tennis shot, for example, become smoother, and you gradually attend to these less and less and take in other information from the environment while executing the techniques appropriately.

The **autonomous phase** is an extension of the associative phase. Typically, the autonomous phase is intended to be an end point in learning a physical skill. This is when the performance of the skill becomes so automatic that you don't need to attend consciously to the individual actions that make up the skill.

Some doubt whether this is a useful way to describe expert performance. In contrast with a novice, an expert's execution of a skill seems to be automatic. But this need not imply that the expert player is no longer capable of thinking, learning and improving.

Researchers who support the idea of an autonomous phase assume that it applies mainly at the level of **manual dexterity** in performing a technique. Once these techniques become automatic, you are freed up to attend to information in the environment.

However, this assumption is inconsistent with the notion of an active learner described previously, as learning skills is primarily concerned with learning the relationships between individual abilities, task demands and environmental circumstances. Skilful performance depends on the interlinking of perceiving, deciding and acting. The active learner and reflective performer is learning to deal with these relationships all of the time, not sometime after the physical demands of the task have been met.

If the autonomous phase is to remain a useful descriptor within the developmental process of learning, it perhaps needs to be reconsidered. It might usefully refer to those learners who have achieved a high level of proficiency in most aspects of an activity to the point where their performance is automatic, efficient and successful. This understanding of the autonomous phase need not imply that this highly proficient performer cannot go on learning, although it may be difficult to detect changes or improvements as these become increasingly finer and finer.

Learning Is Multidimensional

A third characteristic of constructivist approaches to learning is that learning is multidimensional. People typically learn more than one thing at a time. For instance,

The cognitive phase in skill learning involves grasping the demands of a task.

In the associative phase less attention is paid to the task, more attention to the environment.

During the autonomous phase, the execution of the task and decision making become automatic.

Manual dexterity relates to the technical competence and efficiency of movement.

your task may be to learn the lay-up shot in basketball. You may be trying very hard to learn how to perform this shot successfully. While working on the lay-up, you may also be learning that you enjoy or dislike basketball, that some of your team-mates are good to work with in the basketball class, whereas some others are too selfish with the ball and don't give others a fair go.

You may also be learning about your teachers or coaches. For example, you might be learning what they mean when they give advice in a certain way, when they are serious and when they are only joking. The whole time, everyone in your basketball class will be continuing to learn about appropriate behaviour in this setting and appropriate ways of being feminine or masculine.

Even though someone may be concentrating on only one task — for example, learning to lay up in basketball — other things are being learned at the same time. But clearly not all of this information is being acquired through a conscious effort. There are limits to the amount of information anyone can attend to fully at any one time. This means that much of the learning that goes on while you are acquiring, applying and evaluating your physical skills is reflexive. When learning is reflexive, it means that something is learned in conjunction with something else, as part of learning something else. An example of reflexive learning is learning to enjoy playing basketball while concentrating on the lay-up shot.

Recognising that learning is multidimensional is important because it highlights the complexity of acquiring even the most basic physical skills. It also allows you to begin to see how broader aspects of life such as the social construction of gender are taking place as you are learning physical skills. While learning a whole range of physical skills in physical education classes, for example, people are also learning reflexively such things as what is expected of them as a female or male student in this particular teacher's class, in this school, working with these friends and classmates, whether they are any good at these activities and so on.

It is only when some of the unspoken rules are broken that the things individuals learn in the process of learning physical skills are made explicit, such as not trying hard enough or talking when you should be listening. Researchers refer to the multidimensional character of learning as the hidden curriculum because this learning is often not visible or clearly stated as a part of the formal or explicit curriculum.

THE TEACHER OR COACH AS A FACILITATOR OF LEARNING

Learning as active, developmental and multidimensional processes has important implications for the role of the teacher or coach. Within the traditional approach to learning physical skills, the teacher or coach occupied centre stage in the learning process, often adopting a command or directive style of instruction, and provided a verbal feedback to learners about their performance. Learning to become a reflective performer requires a different style of teaching and coaching. Teachers and coaches need to be viewed as facilitators of learning.

As a facilitator of learning, the teacher or coach does not merely give learners information. The teacher's or coach's role now involves creating opportunities for people, who may have different prior experiences of a task and who may learn at different rates and through different styles, to learn physical skills using diverse kinds of feedback including visual, auditory and kinaesthetic information.

The idea that learning is an active process does not mean that the teacher or coach becomes passive. It does mean that the teacher or coach must use a wider range of instructional strategies than under the traditional approach. It also means that the teacher or coach must make effective and appropriate use of various forms of feedback.

One educational researcher named Muska Mosston has developed a spectrum of instructional styles consistent with the idea of learning to be a reflective performer. As figure 2 shows, active and independent learning features more obviously as the teacher or coach moves from a directing role to a facilitating role.

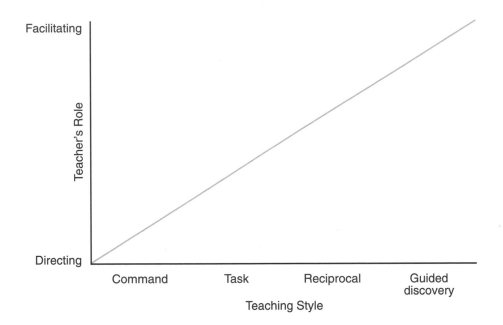

Figure 2   Mosston's spectrum of teaching styles.
Reprinted, with permission, from Mosston and Ashworth, 1994.

Task-based learning is one approach that provides you with slightly more independence and responsibility for your own learning than is typical within the traditional approach. Circuit training, where you use task cards and move from station to station, is a good example of task-based learning.

Reciprocal learning is another example of treating people as active and relatively independent learners. This approach usually involves working with a partner and providing feedback as you both work at a task.

Guided discovery is a third approach that, as the name suggests, involves your teacher guiding rather than directing you through a series of tasks. The goal with the guided discovery approach is for you to discover information or develop a skill through your own abilities to explore and search the environment for information.

Over to You

Experiment with the range of teaching styles in Mosston's spectrum. In a small group, design a series of short (five-minute) lessons in one of your areas of physical activity. The lessons should have an aim. Each member of the group should use a different teaching style. Teach the lessons. After each lesson, write some notes on what you liked or disliked about the teaching style and whether it was an effective means of achieving the lesson's aim.

These approaches — command, task-based, reciprocal, guided discovery and others — may be used by themselves or in combination. Choice of approach or approaches will depend on the physical skills to be learned; the ages and stages of the learners; the knowledge, interests and goals of the teacher or coach; and a range of other factors and circumstances such as available time, facilities and equipment.

As you read earlier in this chapter, constructivist approaches to learning physical skills emphasise the interdependence of individual abilities, the task and the environment. When teachers and coaches adopt the role of facilitator of learning, their main task is to organise learning experiences so that you are able to explore the relationships between your own abilities, the task and the environment. The main focus of the work of the teacher or coach in maximising skill learning is on tasks and environments. The instructor has a responsibility to design learning tasks and structure the environment in ways that are appropriate to the range of individual abilities in a group or class.

SUMMARY

This chapter is concerned with learning to become a reflective performer. The traditional approach to learning was considered inadequate for this purpose since it forced people to be passive learners and concentrated on the execution of technique at the expense of perceptual and cognitive dimensions of learning. The information-processing approach provided a model of learning that involves perceiving, deciding and acting. This approach is also consistent with constructivist theories of learning that involve active, developmental and multidimensional learning. Within both approaches, the teacher's and coach's role becomes the facilitator, rather than director of learning. It was concluded that information-processing and constructivist approaches are better suited to developing reflective performers.

Test Yourself Questions

1. List four key features of the traditional approach to learning physical activities.

2. In a sentence for each, identify three weaknesses with traditional approaches to learning physical activities.

3. The information-processing approach to learning rests on an analogy. Explain the analogy.

4. List and describe the three main phases of an information-processing approach to learning. Use an example from sport in your description.

5. List the three components of a constructivist approach to learning. Use an example from sport to describe one of the components.

6. How does a reflective, experienced performer differ from an unreflective player or novice? Relate your answers to a physical activity that you participate in.

7. Describe what the teacher or coach would do as a facilitator rather than a director of learning.

Psychological Factors Influencing Reflective Performance

Learning Outcomes

When you have studied this chapter, you should be able to

- ☑ identify your own optimal mental climate associated with your best performances;
- ☑ evaluate how participation motives, definitions of success and attributions influence motivation;
- ☑ explain, using theories and models, how arousal and anxiety affect performance;
- ☑ explain the link between confidence and performance;
- ☑ identify the components of effective concentration;
- ☑ explain the role and influence of cohesion in performance; and
- ☑ identify and explain strategies to manipulate or manage the psychological components of performance.

INTRODUCTION

It is now widely accepted that performance is influenced by psychological factors. Some sports people credit up to 95 per cent of their performance on any given day to their mental state. Motivation, anxiety, confidence and concentration can all affect the quality of our performance as individuals. How we relate to each other in team games can affect team performance. This chapter introduces some of the psychological influences on performance and highlights some strategies that reflective performers can use to maximise their psychological readiness before and during performance.

WHAT IS A GOOD PERFORMANCE?

For a long time it was thought that personality was a key psychological factor in sports performance. During the 1960s and 1970s a large part of the sport psychology research effort examined the role of personality in sport and physical activity participation and performance. From this work it became obvious that there are few personality differences between athletes and nonathletes.

What is interesting, however, is that some differences were found between successful and less successful athletes. The more successful athletes tended to possess a variety of psychological skills that assist good performance. These skills included well-developed mental preparation plans and skills to maintain confidence and focus and to cope with anxiety.

The most important lesson to learn from the personality research is that everyone is different and is going to respond differently in the same situation. For example, Mary may approach a competition with confidence and excitement, whereas John approaches the same competition with extreme nervousness. It is not these personality differences that determine performance but the skills people have to control their motivation, confidence, concentration and anxiety effectively, regardless of the situation.

Knowing this, to maximise our performance we have to develop better self-awareness. We also need to know how we react in different situations. With this understanding we can develop strategies and skills to perform at our best more often.

The idea that both the person and situation are important when looking at a person's behaviour is called the **interactionist perspective.** This perspective is common throughout psychology. You should keep the interactionist perspective in mind as you complete all the tasks in this chapter.

In performance psychology it is now understood that an individual's ability to consistently create the mental climate associated with his or her good performances helps to iron out the differences between good days and bad days. Although this doesn't guarantee winning, a positive mental climate raises the standard of performance overall. You can provide a platform on which your physical training and skills are more consistently displayed by becoming aware of your own **optimal mental climate** and working to recreate it before each performance.

The optimal mental climate for good performances is different for every person. For Abdul, a good performance happens when he feels calm and confident in his preparation, when he knows the opposition's game plan and when he feels he really wants to be there. Abdul feels successful when he plays to his potential and manages to include some new skills he has been learning in practice.

For Grace, a good performance happens when she feels excited and a little bit apprehensive about the event. The nerves seem to wake her up and get her focused on the task. Grace feels successful when she beats others, although she takes some pride from playing well even if she loses.

Interactionist perspective concerns behaviour influenced by both the person and the situation he or she is in.

Optimal mental climate is the combination of psychological factors associated with an individual's best performances.

Throughout this chapter you will be asked to reflect on your own performances, good and bad, and try to work out how different levels of motivation, arousal, anxiety, confidence, concentration and teamwork influence your optimal mental climate and performance.

Over to You

Based on what you've learned so far, design a brief questionnaire to find out someone's optimal mental climate. Think of a best-ever performance and try it on yourself first, then on the rest of your group.

Write down five situations in sport when your optimal mental climate might be challenged (e.g., performing in front of a large audience).

MOTIVATION AND PERFORMANCE

Motivation is central to all that we do. When we talk about motivation, we are talking about why people do what they do. We look at factors such as what they choose to participate in, how much effort they put in and how long they persist with an activity, especially when things aren't going well. Sometimes you will hear people say, 'Oh, Jo just has no motivation'. Strictly speaking, this is rarely true. People always have some level of motivation, although it just may be for some other activity.

Think about an activity that you do that you really like. Now ask yourself, 'What are my reasons for taking part in this activity'? You will probably come up with several different reasons. For example, you play tennis because you enjoy it, you meet new people, it helps keep you fit and you like the competition. As long as these different reasons are being met, your motivation is likely to remain high. So if we are looking to change someone's motivation, one thing we need to know is what are his or her reasons for participating.

Consider also that motivation levels are influenced by the person and the situation he or she is put in. For example, Sam likes running and is pretty good at it. At the school cross-country event he is keen and enthusiastic and puts in a lot of effort. However, at the school sports day on the track, he has to be convinced to participate and puts in very little effort, saying: 'I hate the track. It's so boring going round and round'. The basic activity, running, hasn't changed, but the situation has resulted in a decrease in motivation. So to influence motivation levels we have to consider the characteristics of the person and the situation. This is an example of the interactionist perspective.

> Motivation is about the effort and persistence we put into the activities we choose to do.

Over to You

Identify the two sports you have chosen to study in A-level physical education. What are your reasons (motives) for choosing these sports? Write them down. Compare your reasons with others in your class. Note similarities and differences.

Think of an activity that you have been involved in for several years. Have your motives for participating changed? Make a note.

In your own words define motivation. Write down the definition.

Goal Orientations: Task and Ego

Another important factor in understanding motivation is to understand how individuals define success. This way of looking at motivation is referred to as goal orientation. When someone defines success in terms of mastering a new skill or demonstrating skill, this is called a **'task orientation'**. People with a task orientation are interested in how well they perform a particular task and compare their performance with their own previous performances.

When someone defines success in terms of winning, this is called an **'ego orientation'**. People with an ego orientation focus on social comparison and how they compare to others.

Usually a person will have a mix of these two orientations. Sport psychologists believe that a high task orientation in combination with either high or low ego orientation is good for motivation. A strong focus on an ego orientation with a low task orientation is viewed as unsuitable — 'motivationally maladaptive'.

High task orientation is good because it provides greater personal control. You are focusing on what you do and how well you do it and not on how well someone else does. For example, a basketball team may have been working on a new attacking move. In the first game where the team tries the new move it works superbly. However, the opposition play better than all expectations and win by three points. Regardless of orientation, you are likely to be disappointed by this result. But with a task orientation you are more likely to look back at the game and feel satisfied that you played well and were successful with the new move.

With an ego orientation, you are more likely to continue to feel like a loser and think that the new move, and maybe the team, is no good. Individuals with high task orientation are likely to work harder and persist longer in difficult situations. Individuals with high ego orientation are likely to give up or make excuses when things aren't going their way.

Task orientation is about focusing on learning new skills and comparing performance with personal standards.

Ego orientation is about focusing on beating others and comparing performance against other people.

Over to You

Set up a practice match in one of your chosen activities where one team is focusing on winning as the only important outcome and the other team is focusing on mastering a set move or a newly learned skill. Afterwards discuss how the members of the two teams felt during the match. How would they feel if the outcome had been reversed? Make notes and write down a summary of the discussion.

Attributions

Motivation is also influenced by the **attributions** (reasons) people give for their performances. For example, a tenpin bowler, Chris, who is not playing well, might attribute her poor performance to lack of practice, poor technique or not being any good. The sorts of attributions people make affect their motivation. If Chris attributes her poor performances to lack of practice, she might get motivated to do something about it and practice. Likewise, if the attribution is to poor technique, she might ask a coach for help. However, if the attribution is 'I'm just no good', she may just give up.

Think of a successful performance you've had in a sport. Why were you successful? What was the main reason for your success? Now think of a poor or unsuccessful performance in that sport. Why were you unsuccessful? What was the main reason for your lack of success? Probably the reasons you will give fall under one of the following four headings:

Attributions are the reasons people give for success or failure.

1. Luck (e.g., chance events such as weather, the ref was on their side, and getting lucky)
2. Ability (e.g., you were the better player; your team was no good)
3. Effort (e.g., you worked really hard all of the game)
4. Task difficulty (e.g., the opponents were more experienced; you had the best grasp of tactics)

Although most attributions fall under these four headings, sport psychologist Bob Weiner suggests that what is more important is where these attributions fit along two dimensions. These dimensions are locus of causality and stability. Locus of causality relates to whether the cause is due to something inside or internal to the person, or something outside the person or external. Stability relates to whether the cause is likely to occur again in the future, in which case it is stable, or not, in which case it is unstable. The four common attributions can be placed in Weiner's dimensions as shown in table 1.

Internal and external attributions influence how a person feels about a performance. If you attribute success to internal factors, you experience greater pride and satisfaction than if you attribute success to external factors. If you attribute failure to internal factors, you experience greater shame than if you attribute failure to external factors. So it is best if you attribute success to internal factors and failure to external factors because this maximises feelings of pride and satisfaction and minimises feelings of shame.

Table 1 Four Common Attributions for Success or Failure

	Stable	Unstable
Internal	Ability	Effort
External	Task difficulty	Luck

The stability dimension influences our perceptions of whether success or failure is likely to occur again. If Jamie attributes success to a stable dimension, he will expect success to occur again. If he attributes failure to stable causes, he will expect to fail again in the future. These expectations of future success and failure influence a person's confidence and enthusiasm for future participation. When considering motivation it is important that we examine the attributions that we typically give and try to maximise their motivating power.

GOAL SETTING: A STRATEGY FOR INCREASING MOTIVATION

We can use goal setting to increase motivation, task orientation and appropriate attributions. This is a process where someone decides what they want to achieve and plans how they are going to get there. People tend to set goals spontaneously — 'I want to get on the school netball team', 'My aim is to be a doctor', 'My goal is to get fitter'. You can set goals in many different areas:

- Physical (e.g., to get fitter)
- Mental (e.g., to improve concentration)
- Skill (e.g., to learn to do breaststroke)
- Tactical (e.g., to learn a new defensive pattern)

However, not all goals are equally effective in helping you to do your best. But by following seven guidelines we can increase their effectiveness.

Guideline 1: Set Specific Goals

Clearly worded specific goals enhance motivation more than general goals. The idea of 'do your best' doesn't highlight what to work on. Likewise, a goal of 'I want to be a fast football player' is broad and imprecise compared with 'Because I am a striker, I need speed and power. I want to reduce my time for a 50-metre sprint by 1 second'. This last goal sets out exactly what you want to do and why.

Guideline 2: Set Challenging Goals

Goals are most motivating when they extend you from where you are. If goals are too easy, you are not likely to take them seriously. On the other hand, if they are too difficult you may feel that they are impossible to reach and won't try. The trick with goal setting is to set goals that are challenging but at the same time make the goals realistic enough that, with some effort on your part, you will achieve them.

Guideline 3: Set Long-term and Short-term Goals

Often our ultimate goal is a long way away. For example, at the start of the season the finals are a long way off. At the beginning of a new school year, final exams seem to be a long way off. Although these ultimate goals are very important, motivation is best served if you break the big goal down into a series of smaller, short-term goals. As you reach each of these smaller goals you feel you are moving closer to your ultimate goal (see figure 3). You can then re-evaluate what you need to do next to keep you moving in the right direction.

Figure 3 Long-term goals are essential to establish an athlete's direction. Multiple intermediate goals are stepping stones to the final target.
Reprinted, by permission, from Kirk et al., 1999.

Guideline 4: Set Performance Goals

Performance goals focus on what action you have to take to do your best. They contrast with outcome goals that focus on winning or doing better than others. You should be able to see the similarity between performance and outcome goals and task and ego orientation. For the same reasons that a task orientation is thought to be better than an ego orientation, performance goals are thought to be better for motivation than outcome goals. Performance goals increase your control of your performance so that you only need to concentrate to perform well. In addition, performance goals can help reduce anxiety and improve concentration because they assist you to focus on the task at hand rather than on the outcome.

Guideline 5: Identify Strategies That Will Help You Achieve Your Goal

One of the biggest mistakes people make when they set goals is forgetting to work out what they need to do to achieve the goal. Many people set goals that meet guidelines 1 to 4. But, unless you also work out what you need to do to reach the goal, the goal-setting process will not be effective. As an example, I have set a goal of increasing my percentage of successful shots from the free throw line in basketball from 60 per cent to 75 per cent. My next step would be to choose some exercises or drills to help me do this. I might decide that I am going to do 3 sets of 10 free throws each lunchtime for the next two weeks and record the number I score. I am also going to keep a record of the percentage I score in games. I might also decide to talk to my coach about my technique and check that it is correct and work on any exercises the coach suggests. By setting these strategies it is more motivating because I now know exactly what I am going to do to achieve my goal.

Guideline 6: Write Down Your Goals

Writing down goals prevents you from changing your mind when the going gets tough. If it's written down, you've got no option but to say, 'Yeah that's what I was aiming for'. Also writing down goals is effective because it means you can then display the goal somewhere prominent and constantly remind yourself of what you are trying to achieve.

Guideline 7: Evaluate Your Goals Regularly

Are you reaching your goals? Are they motivating you? You may need to readjust or reset your goals so that they remain challenging. If you are reaching your goals, regular evaluation allows you take pride in your improvements.

Over to You

Create an acronym to remind you of the seven goal-setting guidelines.

Give an example of a long-term goal for a sporting situation you are involved in. Identify five relevant short-term goals that help move you towards your long-term goal—remember all the different areas you can set goals in. Taking one of these short-term goals, complete the goal-setting process by addressing the following issues: My goal is . . . Date set . . . Date to be achieved by . . . What do I need to do to achieve my goal? Who can help me and how? How will I know I have achieved my goal? Check that you have followed guidelines 1 to 7. Switch with a friend and check that each of you has met the guidelines. Can you tell exactly what the person is going to do to achieve his or her goal?

Why Does Goal Setting Work?

There are many reasons why goal setting is effective in enhancing or maintaining motivation. By progressively achieving small goals on the way to a larger goal you can see where you have come from; you can see the improvements you are making towards your ultimate goal. This helps motivation remain high. By setting goals, you can also identify your strengths and weaknesses. You can then target key areas where improvements will lead to improved performance. Goals also help provide you with a sense of purpose and direction because they help you to determine what is important to work on now and why. Finally, goals help you look for new strategies to learn a skill.

Over to You

How could you use goal setting to help you study for your A- or AS-level physical education course?

ANXIETY, AROUSAL AND PERFORMANCE

Imagine yourself before an important event such as a race, an exam or a job interview. How are you feeling? The chances are you might have a few butterflies in the stomach, perhaps your heart is racing and your palms are sweaty, maybe you feel excited or worried, or your mind is full of thoughts about how you are going to perform.

Most of us have experienced some of these changes in arousal and anxiety before a performance. **Arousal** refers to changes in activation from deep sleep to high excitement. Arousal is associated with good events, such as doing well in your exams, and not-so-good events, such as falling off your bike. **Anxiety** is a negative response to these changes in arousal. Negative responses may be cognitively related, for example, to feelings of worry, or physiologically related, such as feelings of muscle tension.

How Do Arousal and Anxiety Affect Performance?

Many people assume that increases in arousal and anxiety lead to decreases in performance. This is not necessarily so. Most of us need an increase in arousal to perform at our best. In exams, for example, it helps to be awake, alert and interested. Even anxiety may not decrease performance. It is generally thought that **cognitive anxiety** is detrimental to performance. However, **physiological anxiety** can be a positive sign as long as we interpret it as meaning we are ready to perform at our best.

The Inverted-U Hypothesis

Several models and theories have been proposed to explain the relationship between arousal states and performance. One of the most widely cited is the inverted-U hypothesis (see figure 4). This hypothesis suggests that as arousal increases there will be an increase in performance up to a point where further increases in arousal lead to decreases in performance. This approach suggests that there is an optimal level of arousal that is associated with best performances. Any deviation from this optimal level will result in poorer performance.

Arousal is the level of psychological and physiological activation, ranging from deep sleep to high excitement.

Anxiety stems from a negative interpretation of changes in arousal.

Cognitive anxiety arises from feelings of nervousness and worry associated with changes in arousal.

Physiological anxiety is revealed in physiological responses such as increased heart rate and sweaty palms associated with increased arousal.

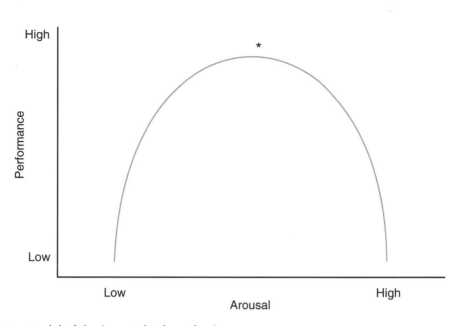

Figure 4   Model of the inverted-U hypothesis.
Reprinted, by permission, from Kirk et al., 1999.

It is likely that the optimal level of arousal will be different for different people. You can probably think of someone who seems to perform their best when they appear to be very calm and relaxed and of others who need to be really jumping out of their skin to perform their best. Also it is likely that the optimal level of arousal will be different for the same person, depending on the activity they are doing. For example, if you were going out to play hockey, your optimal arousal level is likely to be different from that associated with going out to play golf. It is likely to be different again, if you were going to play snooker.

Over to You

Other than the activity itself, make a list of factors that might influence arousal levels.

Make three copies of the X and Y axes from figure 4. On the graph, plot a curve that matches your arousal–performance relationship for three different activities. Discuss the differences with members of your group. What would you do to control your arousal to an optimum level for each activity?

Recently, researchers have suggested that the inverted-U hypothesis is too simplistic, and more complex models have been proposed. These new models try to separate the effects of cognitive anxiety and physiological arousal. For example, in catastrophe theory (figure 5) it is predicted that, if cognitive anxiety is low, increases in physiological anxiety will follow the inverted-U, with gradual decreases in performance beyond optimal levels. However, if cognitive anxiety is high, once physiological arousal passes an optimal level, there will be a sudden decline in performance, or a catastrophe. In this theory, the effects of physiological arousal are markedly different depending on the level of cognitive anxiety. This means that when trying to manage anxiety we need to be able to manage our thoughts and worries as well as our physical responses.

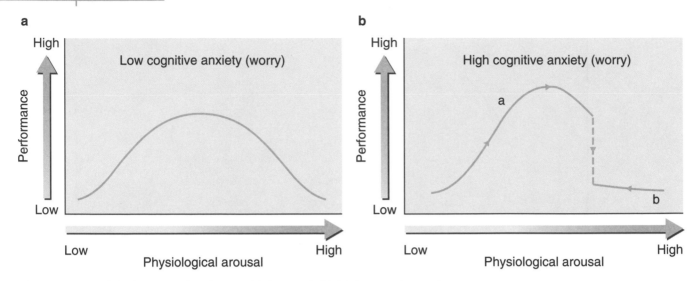

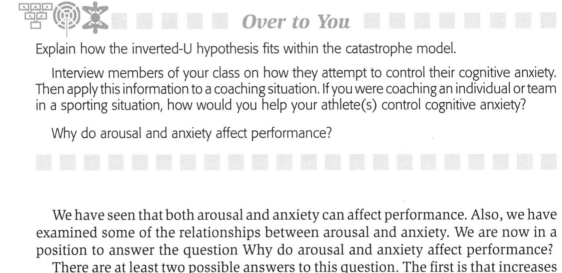

Figure 5 Model of catastrophe theory; (a) low and (b) high cognitive anxiety.
Reprinted, by permission, from Weinberg and Gould, 1999.

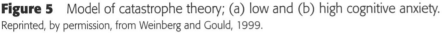

Over to You

Explain how the inverted-U hypothesis fits within the catastrophe model.

Interview members of your class on how they attempt to control their cognitive anxiety. Then apply this information to a coaching situation. If you were coaching an individual or team in a sporting situation, how would you help your athlete(s) control cognitive anxiety?

Why do arousal and anxiety affect performance?

We have seen that both arousal and anxiety can affect performance. Also, we have examined some of the relationships between arousal and anxiety. We are now in a position to answer the question Why do arousal and anxiety affect performance?

There are at least two possible answers to this question. The first is that increases in physiological anxiety may lead to increases in muscle tension that in turn lead to decreases in coordination. It is hard to move easily and competently if you are feeling tight and stiff.

The second explanation is that changes in psychological arousal result in changes to our concentration. When you are optimally aroused, you focus on the relevant details to perform the task. When you are underaroused your mind tends to wander and you take in irrelevant details such as what you had for tea last night or what colour shirt the opposition is wearing. In contrast, if you are overaroused and worrying about what is going to happen, you are likely to find your concentration becomes too narrow and you miss some vital cues. With a focus that is too broad or too narrow, you are unlikely to perform at your best.

CONFIDENCE

One of the most consistent findings in the research literature is the relationship between **confidence** and success. When we feel confident, we tend to perform well. When we lack confidence, we tend to perform poorly. Confidence is important because what you think or say to yourself before performing is critical. If you don't

Confidence is the realistic belief that you have the ability to achieve your goals.

Over to You

Techniques for managing your arousal and anxiety:

Step 1

What words would you use to describe yourself when you have (a) high cognitive anxiety, (b) low cognitive anxiety, (c) high physiological arousal and (d) low physiological arousal. Construct your own personal scale for cognitive anxiety and physiological arousal. For example, your cognitive anxiety scale might be 1 = whatever you wrote for (a) and 5 = whatever you wrote for (b).

Step 2

To be able to effectively manage your arousal and anxiety levels you have to know how you feel when you perform at your best. After every performance for a period of two to three months, complete a form containing the following information:

- Date:
- Opponent:
- Performance rank: (1 = the worst I can play, 10 = as good as I can play)
- Rate your cognitive anxiety and physiological arousal using the scale you constructed in step 1.
- Make note of any factors that might have influenced how you felt (e.g., weather, opponent, who was watching, importance of the game).

Step 3

When you have several of these ratings you should start to see a pattern between how you feel and how you perform. Use this information as a guide for managing your arousal and anxiety before performing.

Step 4

In a group, discuss ways to manage arousal and anxiety before performance. Remember to discuss ways to both increase and decrease these levels. Make a list of at least three ways up and three ways down for both cognitive anxiety and physiological arousal. Your list should be personal to you and include ways that you know or feel would work for you.

---

think you can achieve your goals, then you probably won't. For example, if you think your gymnastics routine is too difficult, then it will likely prove so.

Being confident does not guarantee you will perform well. But it certainly helps the process and enables you to ride out the rough patches more easily. For example, compared with someone who lacks confidence, a confident person is more likely to react positively to correct a mistake or poor performance. Someone with little confidence is likely to view the mistake as a further sign that they aren't very good. They may then be less likely to try to correct the mistake or improve in the future.

When we have negative **self-talk,** we start to doubt ourselves. Doubts can increase anxiety. They interfere with concentration and they can make someone indecisive or tentative. Sometimes loosing confidence in one part of a game can lead to a loss of confidence in other game skills. For example, a batter in cricket going through a run of low scores might then start to make mistakes when fielding. Keeping self-talk positive and realistic is the key to confidence.

Self-talk is what we say to ourselves.

Over to You

In a paragraph, define self-confidence in your own terms. Then, write a half-page description of a confident person you know personally. In a small group, share and discuss what you have written. Summarise similarities and differences in definitions and characteristics of the descriptions.

Managing Self-talk to Keep It Positive

As with managing arousal and anxiety, the first step in managing self-talk is be aware of the things you say to yourself in different situations. Think of a situation in which you felt really confident. Make a note of the situation and what you were saying to yourself. Now think of when you lacked confidence. Again, make a note of the situation and what you were saying to yourself. In the latter situation where you lacked confidence, there is a good chance you had some self-doubts. Maybe you were telling yourself 'I'm so useless', or 'I can't believe I'm playing *so* badly'.

Having built up a list of negative things we typically say to ourselves, we can then build up another list of positive statements to counter them. For example, 'Be calm and focused — remember all the good training you have done', 'Hang in there, one shot at a time'. These positive statements should be task-oriented; that is, they should focus on what you have to do. They should be focused in the present and encouraging.

When you find yourself thinking negatively, try repeating one of the positive statements to yourself to switch your thinking around. When you use the positive statements, say them to yourself with conviction and emotion, as if you really believe them. Recall your performance goals, as this can also be an effective reminder of what you are trying to achieve.

Over to You

Design an interview to investigate the negative things people typically say to themselves. Use this plan to interview your partner and then assist her or him to come up with positive counter statements. Imagining that you are a team-mate of your partner, how could you use this information to help him or her maintain confidence? Remember, it's important not just to note what your partner says, but also what the situation is.

CONCENTRATION

Concentration is the ability to focus on relevant cues at the right time and to maintain this relevant focus for the duration of an event.

Concentration is a vital factor in quality performances in any setting. When people are performing at their best, they seldom have difficulty with concentration. It seems to happen naturally and easily. However, when they are anxious or lack confidence, concentration can waver and the quality of their performance decrease.

There are several characteristics of good concentration. Concentration is selective. It involves paying attention to the right things at the right time. So it involves focusing attention on certain sources of information while ignoring others. For example, golfers attempting to sink a vital putt must focus on the task at hand and be oblivious to things that might distract them. Golfers thinking about other things cannot give their full attention to the putt.

Concentration involves the ability to shift between cues depending on the situation. For example, in football a player has to be able to make rapid shifts from a broad focus, scanning the pitch for the position of other players to a narrow focus when shooting. Concentration involves parking your mind in the present and nowhere else. The only thing you have control over is here and now. You cannot do anything about things that have already occurred, and you cannot do anything about things that might happen in five minutes' time. Thoughts about events that have already occurred or thoughts about the future are wasteful and distracting. If you are thinking What if I loose?, How could I have made that mistake? or What if I miss this basket?, then your mind is off task and you decrease the chance of performing well.

Improving Your Concentration

If you can develop a consistent mental and physical preparation routine, this will assist you to do your best more consistently. Softball players who do exactly the same thing each time they come to bat are more likely to be appropriately focused when the ball is pitched. For example, they may imagine themselves hitting the ball while waiting to bat. When they step up to the plate they always go through exactly the same routine: left foot in position, right foot in position, couple of easy swings, check balance and bat position, look at the pitcher, take a deep breath and use cue words such as 'target' to narrow in on the pitcher and the ball.

Such routines are effective because they help players learn to focus on task-relevant cues and avoid distracting ones. They also create a mental set. A mental set involves the idea that, by doing the same thing at the same pace every time, the player is ready to 'go'.

Finally, routines give you a familiar activity to return to after distraction. In free-flowing games such as hockey or rugby, routines may only be appropriate at set plays. However, you can use cue words to focus on what is happening. For example, in hockey you might use the words 'ball' and 'player' to focus your attention on where the ball is and where your opposition is. We have already noted how arousal and anxiety can affect concentration. So controlling your arousal and anxiety levels can help maintain concentration. Likewise, a focus on performance goals helps to maintain a focus on what has to be done here and now.

Over to You

Make a list of any mental and physical preparation routines you already use. Talk with other people to find out what routines they use. Now try out some of the routines in a selected activity and monitor your progress.

TEAM COHESION

The skills and techniques already discussed in this chapter apply to individuals. However, in team games how well the members of the group get on and share common goals can affect the overall team performance. It is often assumed that the best players go together to make the best team, but this relationship is not perfect. Simply summing the abilities of team members does not accurately describe team performance. Rather, it is necessary to consider team or group processes as well as individual ability.

An important group process is **team cohesion.** Team cohesion is the tendency for group members to stick together and remain united in the pursuit of team goals. There are two dimensions to team cohesion:

Team cohesion is about the tendency for group members to stick together and remain united in the pursuit of team goals.

Social cohesion refers to how much team members like each other and enjoy each others' company.

Task cohesion refers to the degree to which team members work together to achieve a specific goal.

The relationship between cohesion and performance depends on the amount of interaction required from team members in the sport being examined. Sports requiring a high level of mutual interaction are influenced by task cohesion to a greater degree than sports requiring little interaction between team members.

For example, basketball requires passing between players and the use of offensive and defensive team patterns. With basketball, task cohesion will be more important than in a sport such as rowing, where team members simply have to do the same thing at the same time. However, rowing will be influenced by task cohesion more than team events in archery or triathlon, where individual scores or times are added at the end of the event and no interaction is required during the event. Social cohesion appears to have little effect on performance although it can help an event be more enjoyable.

Over to You

In a group, make a list of 10 different sports, including at least 2 invasion games, 2 striking–fielding games and 2 net–racquet games. Position these sports along the continuum illustrated in figure 6. Discuss and make a note of differences in the positioning of each sport.

Team cohesion is important		Team cohesion is not important

Figure 6 Team cohesion continuum.

Although a positive relationship has been found between cohesion and performance, it is not clear whether increased cohesion causes improved performance or the other way around. At the moment, researchers think that it is a circular relationship with successful performance leading to a greater sense of cohesion, which leads to further success. Success leads to greater satisfaction and cohesion and consequently further improvements in performance and so on. Because of this circularity, sport psychologists suggest that when new teams are formed players should be given the chance to experience early success as a team in friendly matches, small-sided games and so on.

Developing Team Cohesion

There are many ways of developing team cohesion. Early and ongoing success has already been mentioned. Obviously, if having a commitment to a common goal defines team cohesion then involving team members in deciding what that goal is and how it will be achieved is an important step. In large teams where there are natural subgroups it can be useful to have performance goals for each subgroup that fit together to help the whole team reach their goal.

For example, in rugby union, the front row have a distinct job and can set goals for this job, whereas the back line have a different job with different goals. With each group setting relevant performance goals and taking pride in them, the overall team goal is more likely to be reached and cohesion increased. Remember that success is not the same as winning, so look for indicators of success and good performance, particularly after a loss. Displaying a team identity, by way of a uniform or on training T-shirts, can help a group feel more together.

■ ■ ■ ■ ■ ■ ■ ■ *Over to You* ■ ■ ■ ■ ■ ■ ■ ■ ■

Interview the coach of a local team or club. Write a one-page description of what he or she does to develop team cohesion.

SUMMARY

This chapter introduced psychological factors that influence performance. The material in the chapter was based around the idea that each performer has a particular mental climate associated with his or her best performances. This optimal mental climate is influenced by the levels of motivation, arousal and anxiety, concentration, confidence and team cohesion you experience. Each of these factors was described and you were asked to reflect on how they affect your own performance. Strategies for manipulating these factors were discussed.

Test Yourself Questions ■ ■ ■ ■ ■ ■ ■ ■ ■ ■

1. Define the following terms:

   Motivation

   Arousal

   Cognitive anxiety

   Somatic anxiety

   Self-confidence

   Self-talk

   Social cohesion

   Task cohesion

   Task orientation

   Ego orientation

2. Describe the mental climate associated with your best performance. Describe the strategies you might use to achieve this optimal mental climate.

3. Explain how attributions for success or failure might influence a performer's motivation for future participation.

4. Explain why a task orientation is viewed as motivationally adaptive.

5. Kelsey is a talented young swimmer who is looking to make the Olympic team in four years' time. However, the four years seems like a long, long time, and she is unsure whether she can make the improvements necessary to bring her times down. Explain why goal setting might help Kelsey and describe the steps involved in effective goal setting.

6. Robert is a mid-level tennis player. He reports to you that sometimes he feels 'physically really tight' before a game, but this doesn't seem to affect his performance once the game starts. However, on other days this tightness really worries him and he starts wondering why he's so tight; on these days his

performance seems to suffer. From your knowledge of the arousal–performance relationship, explain the reasons for this difference.

7. Explain the relationship between arousal, concentration and performance.

8. If an athlete experiences an overly high level of preperformance somatic anxiety, what techniques would you recommend to lower this level and why?

   If an athlete experiences an overly high level of preperformance cognitive anxiety, what techniques would you recommend to lower this level and why?

9. Explain how having a consistent mental and physical preparation routine would help a performer obtain or maintain concentration in a sport of your choice. Provide an example of a routine from this sport.

10. Self-talk is associated with an individual's confidence level. Describe a strategy for manipulating self-talk to enhance confidence.

11. Explain how the type of sport task influences the relationship between cohesion and performance.

12. Outline three strategies you would use with a junior hockey team to increase team cohesion.

PART 2

Biophysical Dimensions of Reflective Performance Physical Education

*T*he physiology and biomechanics of sport and exercise performance have traditionally occupied a large place in the study of physical education. The six chapters in this section provide key information and develop important concepts across the spectrum of knowledge in this field. In chapter 2.1 you can read about the functional anatomy of reflective performance, focusing on bone, cartilage, muscle and tendon. Chapter 2.2 is concerned with the molecular level of physiological knowledge and focuses on the ways in which energy is produced and used to make physical activity possible, from short-duration, high-intensity activity to longer, lower-intensity, endurance activity. Chapter 2.3 is concerned with the physiological processes that take place at the inter-face between the molecular and systems levels of the body. The focus in this chapter is on metabolic and cardiorespiratory capacity and oxygen transport use, and involves explanations of core concepts such as $\dot{V}O_2$max. A number of principles of training, including specificity and progressive overload, are explained in chapter 2.4, where the information from previous chapters is applied to the design of training programmes for sport performance and health. In chapter 2.5 you can read how the tools and concepts of biomechanics can assist you to describe motion. Chapter 2.6 further develops these tools and concepts to analyse forces and torques in physical performance.

Functional Anatomy and Reflective Performance

Chapter Overview

- Structure and Function of Bone
- Articular Cartilage, Ligaments and Intervertebral Discs
- Tendons and Muscles
- Summary
- Test Yourself Questions

Learning Outcomes

When you have studied this chapter, you should be able to

- ☑ describe the structure and function of bone, ligament, articular cartilage and intervertebral discs;
- ☑ describe the structure and function of tendons and muscles;
- ☑ describe the consequences of physical loading for anatomical structures and the implications for injury prevention.

STRUCTURE AND FUNCTION OF BONE

Bone is a composite material (like fibreglass) which takes advantage of the different mechanical properties of its components. Bone is made of organic collagen fibres embedded in an inorganic mineral matrix of calcium and phosphorous. The collagen fibres provide bone with strength in tension and give flexibility, allowing bone to bend and absorb energy when loaded; whereas the mineral matrix provides the bones with hardness and strength in compression.

Bone is a living tissue. The matrix contains bone cells, and these cells are responsible for bone formation and modelling, and remodelling which occurs in response to the load experienced by the bone.

Bones come in an extreme variety of shapes and sizes (figure 7) — from the tiny bones within the ears and the flat bones of the skull and pelvis to the long bones of the arms and legs. These bones all have very different mechanical characteristics and functions. In general, however, bone has both mechanical and physiological functions. The physiological functions of bone are red blood cell production in the marrow within long bones, and the storing of calcium and phosphorous. Mechanical functions include support and allowing movement (figure 8), and some bones (e.g., skull, pelvis, ribs) provide protection to sensitive internal organs. Others have a very specialised mechanical function (e.g., the patella, which serves to increase the moment arm of the muscles which extend the knee, thus increasing the turning effect, or torque, of the quadriceps muscles which extend the knee).

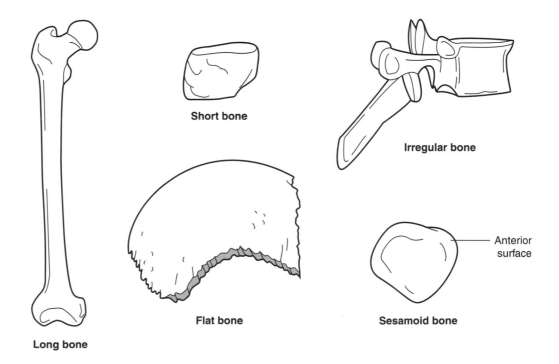

Figure 7 Bones of different shapes and sizes.
Reprinted, by permission, from Behnke, 2001.

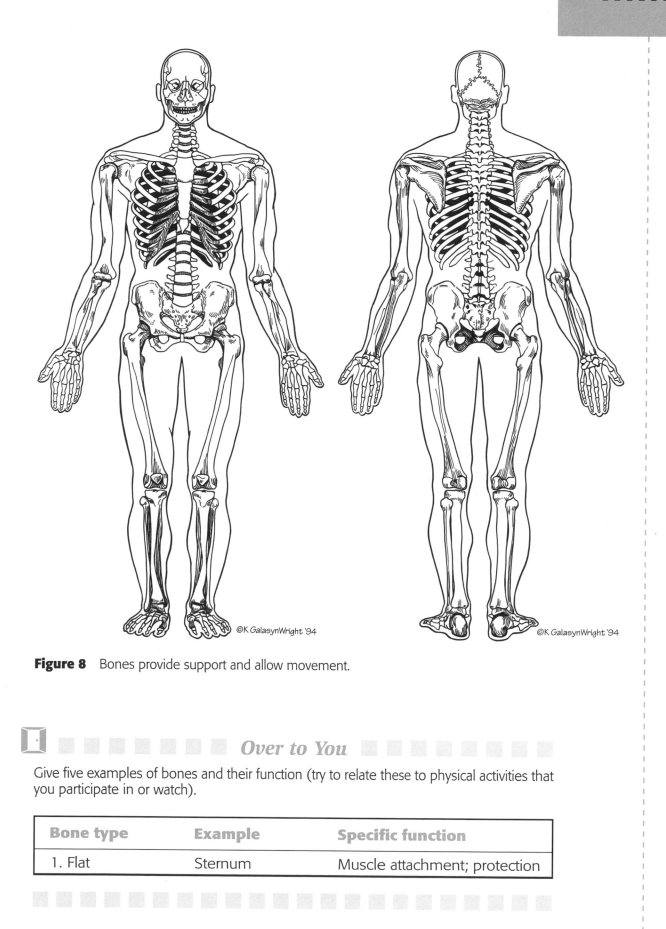

©K GalasynWright '94   ©K GalasynWright '94

Figure 8 Bones provide support and allow movement.

Over to You

Give five examples of bones and their function (try to relate these to physical activities that you participate in or watch).

Bone type	Example	Specific function
1. Flat	Sternum	Muscle attachment; protection

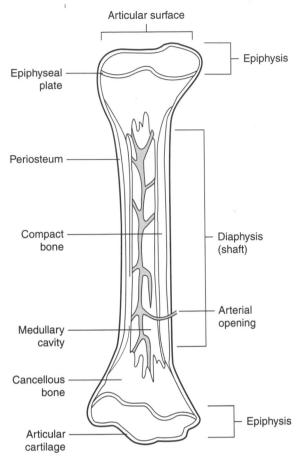

Figure 9 A typical long bone.
Reprinted, by permission, from Behnke, 2001.

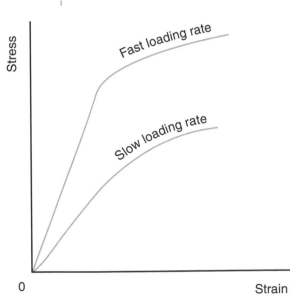

Figure 10 A bone's ability to withstand a load depends upon the load's direction.
Reprinted, by permission, from McGinnis, 1999.

Bone comes in two main forms. Compact cortical bone, typically found around the outside of bones, is very dense, stiff and strong. Cancellous bone, or spongy bone, consists of thin struts of bone (trabeculae) arranged in complex patterns inside bones, particularly inside the ends of long bones (figure 9), and the vertebral bodies. Cancellous bone is less dense and more flexible than cortical bone and allows significant energy absorption. The trabeculae are arranged to coincide with the normal stress distribution within the bone.

Strength of Bone

The strength of a material depends on its size. Consequently, the strength of a material is measured as the force per unit area (stress) that may be applied before failure occurs. The units of stress are Pascals (Pa), where 1 Pa is equal to 1 Newton applied over an area of 1 square metre. If cortical bone is compressed, a stress of 100–200 Mega-Pascals (Mpa) may be applied before failure occurs. This value is referred to as its compressive strength. (Steel has a compressive strength of about 370 Mpa.) Strength varies depending on the load direction and rate and the bone's age and health.

The ability of bone to withstand loads (its strength; see figure 10) depends on the direction of the applied load (a property known as anisotropy). Bone is better able to withstand loads that coincide with the long axis (such as the loads during locomotion). The strength of bone also depends on the rate at which loads are applied (a property known as viscoelasticity). Bones are stiffer and stronger when loads are applied at higher load rates (for example, in impact loading situations such as running and jumping). The mechanical characteristics of bone also vary with the age of bone. Young bones are less stiff and bend to absorb energy before failure. The consequence is that fracture of young bone is more likely to be incomplete (a greenstick fracture).

Bone Formation and Remodelling

The formation and growth of bone is influenced by genetic, nutritional and loading influences. Bones grow in length at the epiphyseal plates at the ends of long bones (figure 11) until ossification of the epiphyseal plates occurs in early adulthood. Whereas growth in length ceases with ossification of the epiphyseal plates and changes in bone density and shape occur most rapidly during childhood, bone remodelling continues throughout life. Bone continues to respond to the loads it experiences throughout life by changing shape and density. Reduced loading results in bone resorption and thus decreased density and strength; increased loading, up to an optimal level, causes increased bone deposition and hence increased density and strength. As a general rule, 'Use it or lose it' applies.

We don't know quite how this process occurs, but something like the following happens. Bones, and indeed all tissues, are continually experiencing a turnover of cells. Bone is continually being resorbed, and new bone deposited. The loading experienced by bone in daily living causes microdamage, and this microdamage is repaired as part of the normal processes. Additional bone is deposited where microdamage occurs, leading to increased density and strength. This is how bones get their characteristic shapes and how the trabeculae come to be arranged to coincide with the normal stress distribution of bone.

The reverse also occurs. Where less microdamage occurs, resorption occurs more rapidly than deposition, and a net loss of bone density (and hence loss of strength) results. The consequence is that any period of prolonged immobilisation or reduced weight bearing causes reduced skeletal integrity. Astronauts and people confined to bed through prolonged illness or to a wheelchair through injury are particularly at risk. Another implication is that regular weight-bearing exercise throughout childhood and young adulthood is essential to develop strong bones and reduce the risk of developing osteoporosis (reduced bone density) later in life, which leaves the person susceptible to fractures, typically hip fractures from falls and vertebral crush fractures.

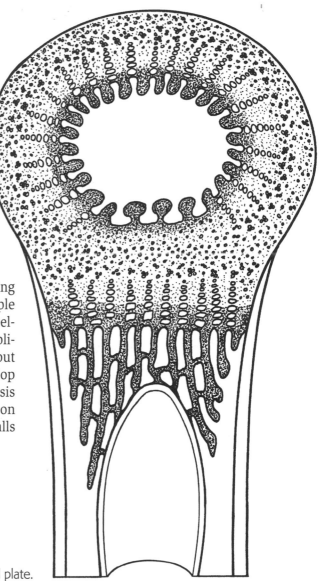

Figure 11   The epiphyseal plate.

Over to You

Using the diagram in figure 12, mark the actions in the following list:

Running (sprinting)
Hopping phase of triple jump
Push off the blocks in swimming start
Push phase in breaststroke
Batting action
Return of a tennis serve

Include an action from the two practical activities you have chosen to specialise in for this examination.

Heavy load   **Light load**

Figure 12   Load continuum.

Survey your peers or students in your establishment who participate regularly in extracurricular sporting activities or those you train or work out with to find out if they have sustained microdamage-related injuries. List the physical activities associated with the injury. Compare your list with others in your teaching group. In particular, compare male and female injuries. Can you draw any conclusions from your findings?

Using an activity that you are familiar with, draw a flow diagram to show the cycle of how microdamage is repaired.

It is possible to overload bone. If loading is excessive (high forces and prolonged exposure) and the rate of microdamage is too fast to be repaired, the microdamage will accumulate and a stress fracture can result. Such stress fractures are very common in the lower limbs of athletes training for endurance running events. They are even more likely if the mechanisms of bone deposition are impaired by hormonal dysfunction, in particular lowered estrogen levels that accompany absent or irregular menstrual periods (amenorrhoea or oligomenorrhoea). A classic example is the stress fracture to the tibia of a female endurance runner exposed to long periods of repetitive high-intensity impact loading while simultaneously experiencing hormonal disruption because of dietary restriction. Stress fractures can also occur in non-weight-bearing situations. For example, rowers commonly suffer stress fractures of the ribs. Here the forces exerted arise from prolonged exposure to repeated high-intensity muscular contractions.

Although mechanical loading is required to stimulate growth at the epiphyseal plates during childhood, excessive loading may cause premature closing of the epiphyseal plates. For example, excessive loading of the wrist during gymnastic events may lead to premature closure of the radius epiphyseal plate while the ulnar continues to grow, leading to a condition known as ulnar variance.

ARTICULAR CARTILAGE, LIGAMENTS AND INTERVERTEBRAL DISCS

Although limited movement occurs at other joints, most movement occurs at synovial joints (figure 13). Synovial joints are surrounded and supported by a joint capsule and ligaments, and contain synovial fluid. Articular cartilage and menisci provide cushioning, improve the fit of the joint and, in conjunction with the synovial fluid, reduce friction to extremely low levels. Intervertebral discs allow movement of the vertebral column.

Articular Cartilage

A thin layer of articular, or hyaline, cartilage covers the end of each long bone (figure 14). Think of the end of a chicken drumstick. The white bit that you can pull away from the bone is cartilage. Cartilage is a remarkable tissue that provides cushioning between bones, but, most importantly in conjunction with the synovial fluid in the joint, it lowers the friction to very low levels. Cartilage is much less strong than bone (about 5 Mpa) and has no direct neural supply and only limited blood supply. Nutrition of the cartilage is via the synovial fluid, and movement of joints is necessary both to allow this to occur and for the cartilage to remain hydrated.

If prolonged static loading occurs, the hydration of the cartilage is reduced and its capacity to withstand forces is reduced. Repetitive impact loading can cause damage to cartilage, and the rate of repair is slow because of a lack of direct blood supply.

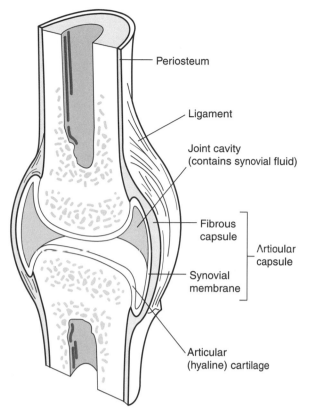

- Periosteum
- Ligament
- Joint cavity (contains synovial fluid)
- Fibrous capsule ⎤ Articular capsule
- Synovial membrane ⎦
- Articular (hyaline) cartilage

Figure 13 The synovial joint.
Reprinted, by permission, from Behnke, 2001.

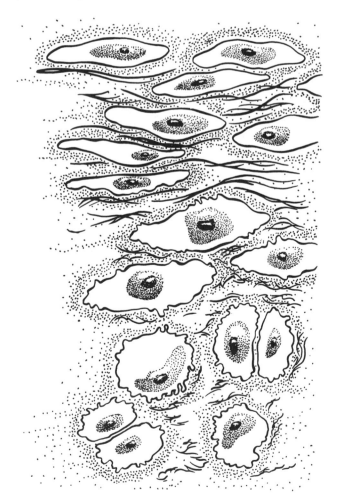

Figure 14 Articular cartilage covers the ends of long bones.

Over to You

Give a brief description of the structure and function of articular cartilage.

Draw on your experiences of physical activities as part of the school physical education curriculum and from extracurricular activities, and ask yourself where repetitive impact-loading injuries occur most frequently.

Give examples of injuries in sport that are associated with damage to cartilage. List the activities where these might occur.

Ligaments

Ligaments (figure 15) are composed of moderately stiff collagen fibres and more flexible elastin fibres. They join bones together, guide the movement of joints and have a protective function in limiting excessive motion. In some cases the range of movement is limited by ligaments (e.g., ankle inversion/eversion, knee inversion/eversion, anterior/posterior draw).

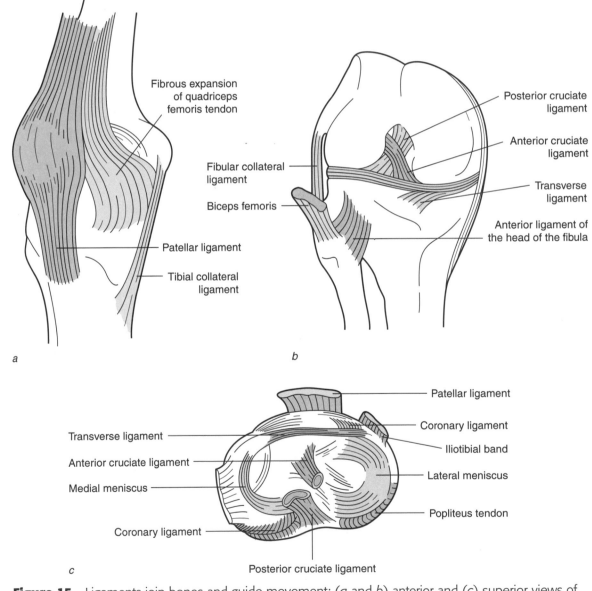

Figure 15 Ligaments join bones and guide movement; (*a* and *b*) anterior and (*c*) superior views of ligaments of the knee.

Reprinted, by permission, from Behnke, 2001.

The fibres within the ligament have a wave-like crimp at rest that gives the ligament a nonlinear force deformation curve (figure 16). Normal physiological loading is restricted to the 'toe' of the force deformation curve. Small forces are met with little resistance as the crimp in the ligament straightens, allowing some play in the joint. When larger deformations are caused, the ligament becomes stiffer and behaves as an elastic structure to resist deformation. If the forces are too great to be resisted, the ligament enters a plastic region where partial disruption of collagen fibres occurs before complete failure (see box 1). A single application of a sufficiently large force can cause partial or complete rupture of ligaments.

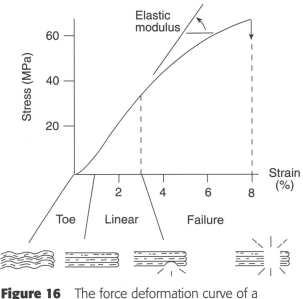

Figure 16   The force deformation curve of a ligament.
Reprinted, by permission, from Butler et al., 1978.

Box 1

Effect of Load History on Ligament Strength, Implications for Back Injuries

The behaviour of the ligament also depends on its load history (figure 17). The ability of the ligament to protect the joint can be impaired if the load event is preceded by a period of prolonged static loading. When you subject a ligament to prolonged static load, a force relaxation phenomenon occurs, and the resistance to deformation decreases over time. Consequently, if you apply a prolonged static load to a ligament, the ligament progressively stretches and, upon removal, it does not immediately return to its original length, leaving the integrity of the joint compromised for some time afterwards.

This phenomenon has particular implications for back injuries. The interspinous ligaments and posterior longitudinal ligaments that help protect the back are stretched when you are in a trunk posture involving full flexion (touching your toes). Consequently, a prolonged period of full trunk flexion reduces the protection afforded by these ligaments during subsequent activity.

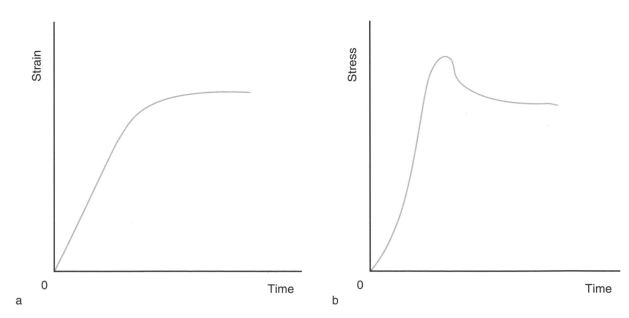

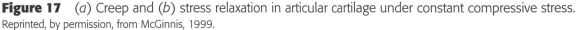

Figure 17   (*a*) Creep and (*b*) stress relaxation in articular cartilage under constant compressive stress.
Reprinted, by permission, from McGinnis, 1999.

🔲📡 ⬛ ⬛ ⬛ ⬛ ⬛ ⬛ *Over to You* ⬛ ⬛ ⬛ ⬛ ⬛ ⬛

Give a brief description of the structure and function of ligaments.

Are there other common injuries where a force relaxation phenomenon occurs? Draw a diagram showing the static load and the effect on the ligament(s), to illustrate your answer.

⬛ ⬛

⬛ Intervertebral Discs

Between each pair of vertebral bodies (figure 18) are specialised structures known as intervertebral discs which allow the spine to withstand large compressive loads while still allowing movement between adjacent vertebrae and hence flexibility of the whole spine. Structurally, intervertebral discs (figure 19) have an outer layer (annulus fibrosus) which consists of many layers of collagen fibres in many different orientations, providing resistance to tension in all directions. The centre of the intervertebral disc is the gel-like nucleus pulposus. The intervertebral disc is often attributed shock-absorbing properties, but the gel is incompressible (being a fluid), and the annulus does not normally bulge substantially. The intervertebral disc merely acts to transfer forces and allow movement of the vertebral column, while energy absorption occurs in the cancellous bone of the vertebral bodies.

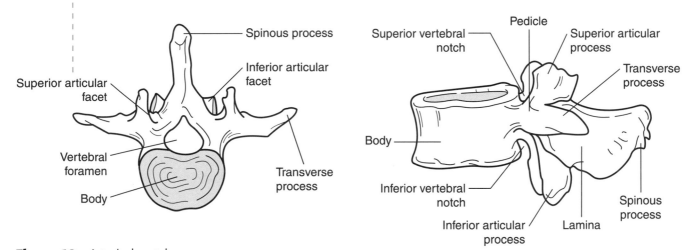

Figure 18 A typical vertebra.
Reprinted, by permission, from Donnelly, 1990.

A common, and serious, problem associated with the intervertebral disc is a prolapse (figure 20). Colloquially termed a 'slipped disc', this is a poor description of what actually occurs. The intervertebral disc, like cartilage, has poor vascular supply and, if damage to the fibres of the annulus occurs, it cannot be repaired rapidly. If damage to the fibres of the annulus continues, and full width ruptures develop, the gel-like nucleus begins to seep out through the rupture and impinge on the spinal nerve roots which lie immediately behind and to the side of the intervertebral disc, causing chronic back pain.

Degeneration of the intervertebral disc is an inevitable part of ageing but can be exacerbated by exposure to a number of risk factors. In particular, damage is likely to occur when the spine is loaded in full flexion, especially if this is combined with torsion (rotation)—for example, lifting from a fully flexed and rotated posture. Exposure to whole-body vibration, especially when in a seated posture (like that

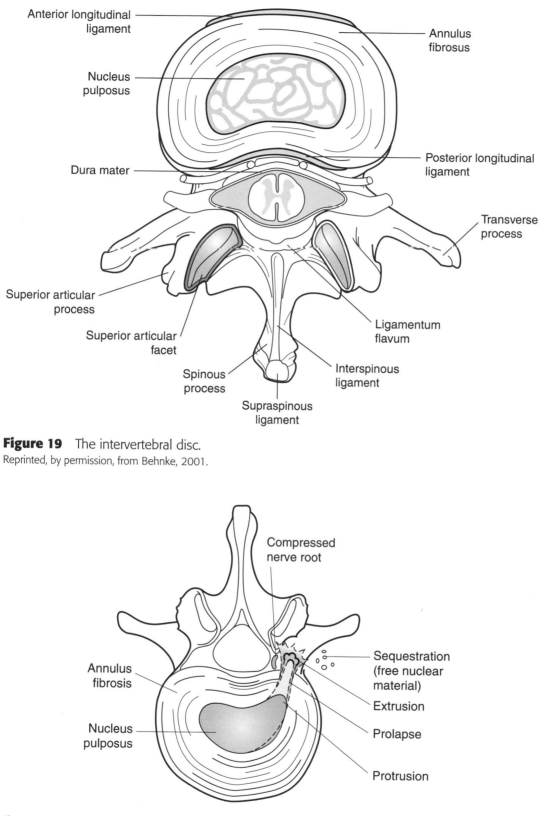

Figure 19 The intervertebral disc.
Reprinted, by permission, from Behnke, 2001.

Figure 20 A prolapsed disc.
Reprinted, by permission, from Schultz, Houglum, and Perrin, 2000.

which occurs in vehicles), is also associated with development of back pain, although here the pain may arise from any number of other sources in addition to the intervertebral disc.

Name sporting activities or specific actions where degeneration of the intervertebral disc may occur. Are these unavoidable, or could the participants change their movement in some way to avoid this damage?

TENDONS AND MUSCLES

Tendons join skeletal muscles to bones. Skeletal muscles cause movement by generating tension, which is transmitted to bone via tendons to cause joint torques, which in turn cause joint rotations.

Tendons

The mechanical characteristics of tendons vary with the tendon shape and size. Some long tendons allow forces to be applied a considerable distance from the muscle (for example, the long finger flexors in the forearm). In general, tendons are very strong and can act like springs, allowing some energy storage and return. The weak link is the attachment of the tendon to bone.

Single application of large forces to the tendon can cause rupture of the tendon or the tearing away (avulsion) of the tendon from the bone. In some circumstances this can be caused by a muscle contraction. Tendons respond to chronic loading in the same way as other tissues, but they don't respond as quickly as muscle. So if habitual activity levels are changed to include more high-resistance activity (such as strength training), the muscles gain strength more rapidly than the tendon. In these circumstances a muscle may be able to generate greater tension than the tendon can withstand and injury may result.

A more common injury to the tendon is degeneration as a result of cumulative microdamage. For example, the tendons running through the carpal tunnel (figure 21) are

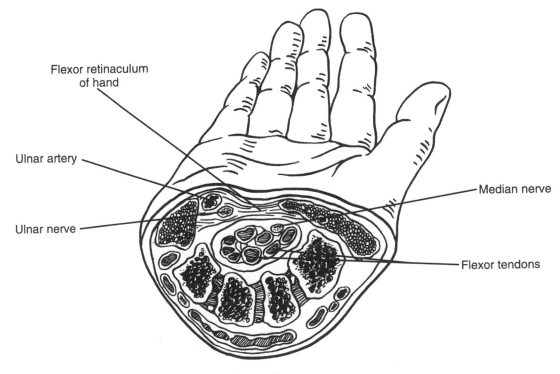

Figure 21   The structure of the carpal tunnel.
Reprinted, by permission, from Whiting and Zernicke, 1998.

compressed by extreme wrist extension and ulnar deviation. Prolonged or repetitive exposure to postures involving wrist extension (bent away from the palm) or ulnar deviation (bent towards the little finger) causes inflammation of the synovial sheath surrounding the tendons. Another example is lateral epicondylitis (tennis elbow), which is caused by repeated forceful elbow and wrist extension such as occurs in a tennis backhand.

Over to You

We have seen that high-resistance activities and cumulative microdamage both increase the possibility of damaging tendons. Name the activities that you and your peers participate in and train for and, more specifically, the movement where such damage could be a real possibility.

Skeletal Muscle

Skeletal muscles provide the forces that cause movement by developing tension within the muscle. These contractile elements are composed of overlapping actin and myosin filaments (figures 22 and 23). The theory is that cross-bridges between the actin and myosin attach and detach cyclically, pulling the fibres longitudinally and creating tension.

A consequence of the microstructure is that the tension-generating capability of each fibre at any time depends on the overlap between actin and myosin, which is a function of the length of the muscle. An optimal muscle length exists when there is an optimal overlap and tension-generating potential is maximised. If the muscle is shorter than this length, the increased overlap reduces the cross-bridge attachment sites available and consequently the tension-generating potential. Similarly if the muscle is longer, the reduced overlap also reduces the attachment sites available. The tension which can be developed by the muscle as a whole is also proportional to the cross-sectional area of the muscle (figure 24).

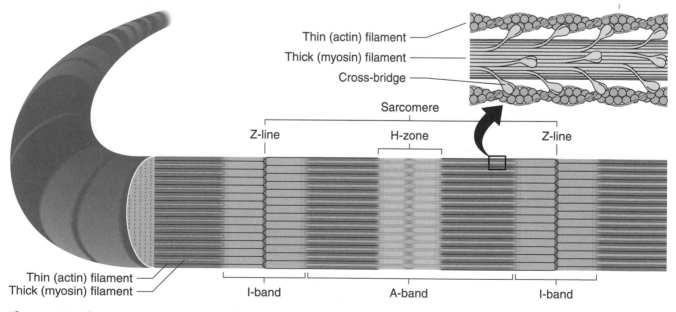

Figure 22   The interaction between actin and myosin.
Reprinted, by permission, from Behnke, 2001.

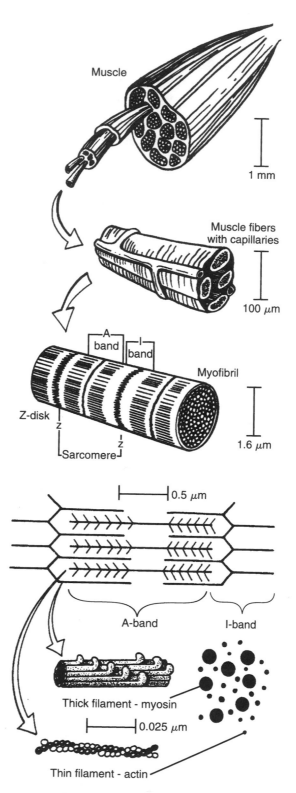

Muscle

1 mm

Muscle fibers
with capillaries

100 μm

A
band
I
band

Myofibril

Z-disk

Z

Z

Sarcomere

1.6 μm

0.5 μm

A-band   I-band

Thick filament - myosin

0.025 μm

Thin filament - actin

Figure 23   Actin and myosin filaments.

Within the whole muscle there are also passive connective tissues in both series and parallel with the contractile fibres, and these passive tissues act like nonlinear elastic bands. If stretched beyond their resting length, they contribute additional tension. A typical force–length relationship of whole muscle is illustrated in figure 25 for an isometric contraction (muscle produces tension while maintaining a constant length). When muscle is shortened, its tension-generating capabilities are impaired. At long lengths, tension is contributed by passive tissues, but less active tension is possible.

In addition to length, the tension-generating potential of muscle is also influenced by the velocity of muscle length changes (figure 26). During concentric contractions (muscle shortening while producing tension) the ability of a muscle to generate tension is reduced as the velocity of shortening increases. Greater forces are possible during eccentric contraction (when the muscle lengthens as it generates tension, typically involving working against gravity). We do not understood why, but we do know that unaccustomed repetitive forceful eccentric contractions lead to delayed onset of muscle soreness. For example, if you walk down 20 flights of stairs, the next day you will be hobbling. Figure 27 illustrates the major skeletal muscles.

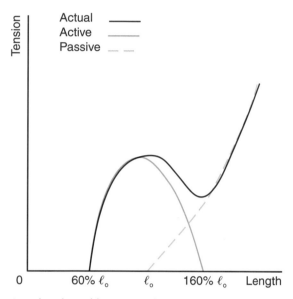

Figure 24   The tension developed by a muscle as a whole is proportional to the cross-sectional area of the muscle.

Reprinted, by permission, from McGinnis, 1999.

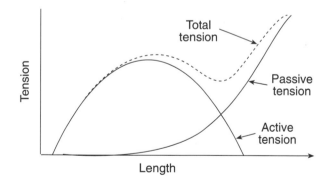

Figure 25   A typical force–length relationship in whole muscle.

Reprinted, by permission, from Whiting and Zernicke, 1998.

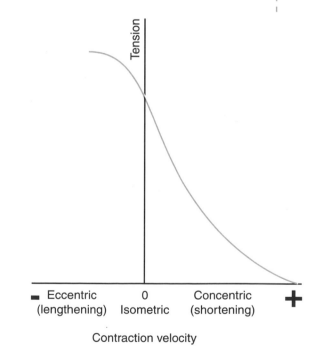

Figure 26   The velocity of muscle length changes influences a muscle's tension-generating potential.

Reprinted, by permission, from McGinnis, 1999.

Over to You

At what position of the wrist (flexed, neutral or extended) is your grip strength greatest? How is this determined by the length–tension relationships of the long finger flexors (e.g., flexor digitorum superficialis) and wrist extensors (e.g., extensor carpi ulnaris)?

Why doesn't a cyclist use low gears to pedal along a level road? How is this dependent of the velocity–tension relationship?

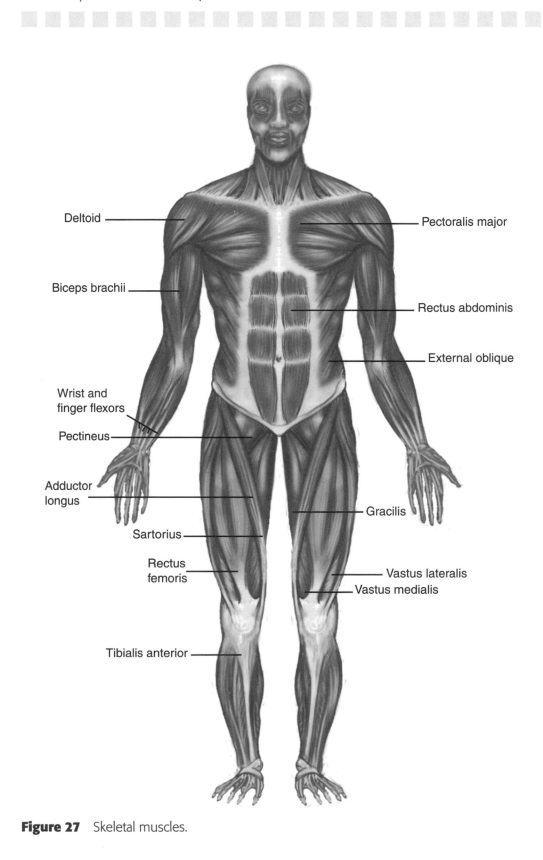

Figure 27   Skeletal muscles.

SUMMARY

This chapter describes the structure and functional consequences of the major musculoskeletal components of the body involved in movement. The body is an exceptionally versatile device, which has the ability, within limits, to change its structure in response to the loading experienced. This process occurs in all musculoskeletal structures. If loading on the body is reduced, the strength of tissues reduces; if moderate increases in loading occur, the strength of tissues increases. If the increase in load is too great, injury occurs.

Test Yourself Questions

1. What are three mechanical functions of bone? Give examples of bones which perform each function.
2. Bone is anisotropic and viscoelastic. What do these terms mean, and what are the functional consequences of these properties?
3. How is the process of bone remodelling believed to occur?
4. What is a 'stress fracture'? Give an example of a situation in which a stress fracture is likely to occur.
5. What are the functions of articular cartilage and menisci?
6. Draw the typical force deformation curve of a ligament, labelling the essential features.
7. Describe the structure and function of an intervertebral disc. What happens in the case of a disc prolapse?
8. Describe the sliding filament theory of muscular contraction. What are the functional consequences of this structure (draw length–tension and velocity–tension curves)?

Energy for Physical Activity

Chapter Overview

Learning Outcomes

When you have studied this chapter, you should be able to

- ☑ describe the role of ATP in muscle contraction,
- ☑ explain the three ways in which energy for movement is supplied to muscle and their characteristics,
- ☑ describe the characteristics of three nutritional sources of energy, and
- ☑ evaluate three nutritional sources of energy for specific physical activities.

ENERGY AND MOVEMENT

Movements such as running, jumping, dancing, swimming, throwing, lifting or swinging a racket to hit a ball occur because muscles exert forces on bones via tendons. The forces are created by parts of muscle fibres that contract and pull the ends of the muscle closer together. The contraction of these parts of the muscle fibres makes the muscle act like a tight elastic band, which then exerts force on the bones and may cause movement to occur. Generation of these forces requires energy, which the body gets from the food we eat. Energy is measured in joules (J) or kilojoules (kJ). An older unit of measurement, which is still used, is the calorie, or kilocalorie (kcal). 1 kcal = 4.184 kJ.

Large amounts of energy are stored in the body as chemical energy. These stores include fat, protein and carbohydrate in the form of glycogen and glucose. As we will see in chapters 2.3 and 2.4, when muscles contract, the chemical energy stored in the body is changed into mechanical energy in the form of elastic energy, kinetic energy and heat. One important factor that limits how fast and for how long we can move is how much energy can be made available to the parts of the muscle fibres that generate the forces. Another factor is the speed at which this energy is made available.

The energy that muscle fibres use comes from turning a molecule called adenosine triphosphate, or ATP for short, into adenosine diphosphate (ADP). An enzyme (ATPase) splits one of the three phosphate molecules from ATP. This action releases chemical energy, which the muscle fibre turns into mechanical energy. Figure 28 is a schematic description of this process.

Only a very small amount of ATP is stored within the muscle cells, about enough for a single weight lift, volleyball spike or golf swing. For movement to continue, other parts of the muscle cell then turn the ADP back into ATP, using energy obtained from other sources. The cycle is then ready to start again and can continue for as long as energy is available to turn the ADP back into ATP.

© Claus Andersen

Muscles cannot exert force when energy stores are exhausted.

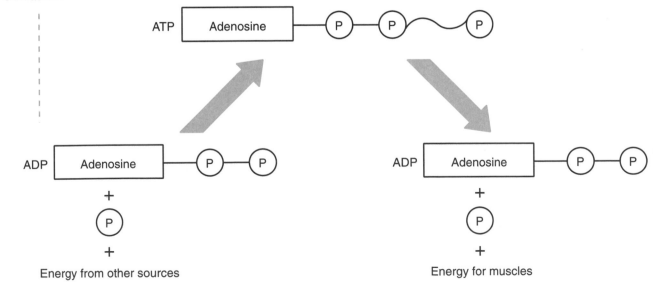

Figure 28 ATP = ADP + P + energy.
Reprinted, by permission, from Kirk et al., 1999.

ENERGY SYSTEMS

There are three sources of energy for turning ADP back into ATP. Although all three systems work at the same time, they differ in terms of the speed with which they can make energy available and the amount of energy that can be provided. The relative importance of each source of energy for any particular physical activity depends on the intensity and the duration of the activity.

▊ Creatine Phosphate

The fastest way of turning ADP back into ATP involves another molecule called **creatine phosphate** (CP), a process illustrated through figure 29. Small amounts of creatine phosphate are stored within the muscle cells and can be broken down very quickly by an enzyme (creatine kinase) to provide energy to turn ADP back into ATP. Although this system acts very quickly, it doesn't last long and provides enough energy only for about 10 to 15 seconds of maximum effort before the stores of creatine phosphate run out. Athletes competing in events of very short duration such as the 100 m, throwing and jumping in track and field, weightlifting or vaulting in gymnastics predominantly rely on the energy released from creatine phosphate. Replenishing the stores of creatine phosphate takes five to six minutes of recovery after the end of exercise. Performance will be impaired if another maximal effort is attempted before CP stores have been replenished.

▊ Anaerobic Glycolysis

The second-fastest way to obtain the energy to keep muscles contracting is called **anaerobic glycolysis** because it involves breaking down **glycogen** or glucose (glycolysis) without using oxygen (anaerobic). Anaerobic glycolysis is illustrated through figure 30. Glycogen stored in the muscles and liver and glucose stored in the blood are broken down in a complex process involving 12 enzymatic reactions. A by-product of this process is **pyruvic acid.** If sufficient oxygen is not available to the

Creatine phosphate is a molecule stored within muscle cells that when broken down releases energy which is used to rapidly rebuild ATP molecules.

Anaerobic glycolysis is the breaking down of glycogen or glucose without using oxygen.

Glycogen is a product of the breakdown of carbohydrates. It is stored in the liver and in muscle and is a key source of energy.

Pyruvic acid is a by-product of anaerobic glycolysis.

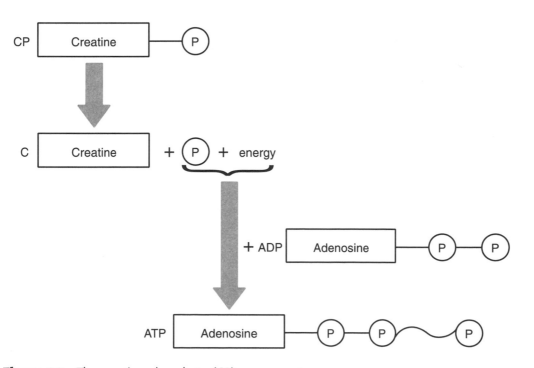

Figure 29 The creatine phosphate (CP) energy system.
Reprinted, by permission, from Kirk et al., 1999.

Lactic acid is a product that accumulates in muscle as a result of anaerobic glycolysis.

cells, the pyruvic acid is converted into **lactic acid.** If lactic acid accumulates, the anaerobic glycolysis process is slowed, resulting in fatigue.

Getting energy from anaerobic glycolysis takes a bit longer than from creatine phosphate, but it also lasts longer. Anaerobic glycolysis provides energy for up to three minutes of maximal effort before the build-up of lactic acid prevents further energy production by this system. Athletes competing in track events such as the 200 m to 800 m, 50 m to 200 m in swimming events or performing a competitive aerobics routine will run out of creatine phosphate before they are finished and end up getting most of the energy they need from anaerobic glycolysis. It takes about 20 to 60 minutes to remove the accumulated lactic acid after maximal exercise.

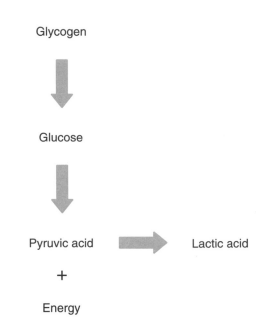

Figure 30 Glycogen utilisation (anaerobic glycolosis) energy system.
Reprinted, by permission, from Kirk et al., 1999.

■ Aerobic (Oxidative)

The aerobic energy system uses oxygen in the process of creating energy in the form of ATP from carbohydrates, fats and proteins.

A third way of obtaining energy does require oxygen, and so it is called the **aerobic system,** or oxidative system. As we see in figure 31, this system can take the pyruvic acid produced by glycolysis and turn it into more energy instead of turning it into lactic acid. The aerobic energy system also produces electrons and hydrogen ions, which are eventually turned into water and excreted through sweat and carbon dioxide, which is transported by the blood to the lungs where it is exhaled.

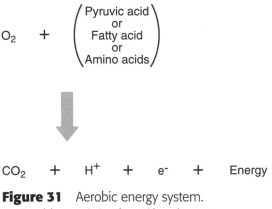

Figure 31 Aerobic energy system.
Reprinted, by permission, from Kirk et al., 1999.

In addition to using glucose or glycogen derived from carbohydrates, this system can also be fuelled by fatty acids which come from fat stores in the body or amino acids which come from protein stores.

The aerobic system is the slowest way of providing the energy needed to produce movement, but it can provide much more energy than the creatine phosphate or anaerobic glycolysis energy systems. If the heart and lungs can deliver enough oxygen, energy can continue to be supplied for as long as the on-board supplies of glucose and glycogen derived from carbohydrates, fat and protein last. Relative to the other systems, that is a long time. The aerobic system supplies most of the energy required in activities lasting longer than about three minutes.

Most exercise, sports and games involve all three ways of getting energy. Take a netball player for example (figure 32). While the aerobic system provides the majority of the energy required to move around the court, creatine phosphate and anaerobic glycolysis provide energy for short periods of high-intensity activity such as jumping for a ball or sprinting for a pass. When the player is not sprinting or jumping, the

Figure 32 Creatine phosphate (CP) supplies energy for high-intensity activities, such as jumping to defend a netball shot.
Reprinted, by permission, from Kirk et al., 1999.

aerobic system is working overtime to remove lactic acid created by the last sprint up court by turning it back into pyruvic acid and then into more energy. It also replaces the creatine phosphate to help the player to get ready for the next high pass.

Over to You

Select another physical activity and, as in the netball discussion, provide an example and explanation of how and when the three energy systems are used in that activity.

FUEL FOR PHYSICAL ACTIVITY

The energy the body needs for movement is supplied by the food that we eat. The energy in food comes in three basic forms: carbohydrate, fat and protein. At any one time the body uses a mixture of fuels, although some are used more than others. The relative contribution made by each fuel depends on what is available in the body and the intensity of physical activity being performed.

Once digested, carbohydrates such as grains, fruit, vegetables and sugar are mostly stored in the muscles and liver in the form of glycogen. To be used by muscles, the glycogen is first turned into glucose. The glucose is then used by the anaerobic glycolysis system, which provides energy to be used to synthesise ATP and produces pyruvic acid. The pyruvic acid can then be used by the aerobic system to provide more energy. For as long as sufficient stores of glycogen are available, most of the energy required during exercise of moderate to high intensity is provided by carbohydrates.

Carbohydrate, fat and protein provide the body with energy for movement.

The fat we eat in meat, dairy products and vegetable oils is stored as triglycerides in adipose tissues under the skin and around our body organs. The triglycerides are turned into fatty acids, which can then be used as fuel by the aerobic system. Fat provides most of the energy required at rest and during low-intensity exercise. Similarly, the protein in meat, eggs, dairy products and vegetables is stored in muscles and the liver. It can also be turned into amino acids and used as fuel by the aerobic system. Protein is not normally used as a major source of energy but may be used when supplies of glycogen have run out.

Imagine you are sitting around relaxing (figure 33). Your energy needs are relatively small—about 360 kJ/hr. This is supplied by the aerobic system. Most of the energy (about 70 per cent) is coming from fat. Fats are a high-energy food, providing 37 kJ/g (carbohydrate contains about 16 kJ/g). Sitting around watching TV uses about 7 g/hr of fat and about the same amount of carbohydrate.

Say you were to tire of sitting around and decide to go for a jog (figure 34). For the first few minutes, stores of creatine phosphate and anaerobic glycolysis supply the energy you need. Very soon, however, your rate and depth of breathing increase. The rate and volume of blood pumped by your heart also increase. If you continue jogging at a relatively slow speed, your rate of consuming oxygen will level out. That rate of oxygen consumption is sufficient to allow all the pyruvic acid produced by the anaerobic glycolytic system to be used as fuel by the aerobic system, and so no lactic acid is accumulating. If you are jogging slowly, the energy you need is normally coming from both glycogen and fat. However, if you were to use up all the glycogen, enough energy to continue jogging could still be supplied by fat and protein. If there were no other limitations, you could continue jogging at this pace for as long as your stores of fat last. This is what marathon runners and long-distance swimmers rely on.

Imagine, however, that instead of continuing to jog slowly, you gradually pick up the pace. Running faster involves taking longer strides and more strides per minute. To do this requires higher muscle forces and more frequent muscle contractions. More energy is required to keep turning the ADP back into the ATP which the muscles can use. Your muscles now require energy more quickly than before, and

Figure 33 Energy needs are small when you are relaxing.
Reprinted, by permission, from Kirk et al., 1999.

so the anaerobic system accelerates its production of energy using glycogen as fuel. This creates pyruvic acid, which the aerobic system then uses in preference to fat. This is good, otherwise the pyruvic acid would be turned into lactic acid, leading to fatigue. The result is that as the intensity of exercise increases by running faster or running uphill, glycogen supplies an increasingly higher proportion of the energy needs.

However, your supply of glycogen is limited. In a 65-kg person, about 110 g is stored in the liver and 250 g in the muscles. Glycogen supplies about 16 kJ/g, so these stores contain about 5,769 kJ. Running at 16 km/hr requires about 1.3 kJ/kg/min (85 kJ/min) for this 65-kg person. Assuming the person can consume enough oxygen to maintain this pace, the stores of glycogen will last about 70 minutes. Glycogen provides energy faster than fat and results in more energy per litre of oxygen consumed—about 21.2 as against 19.7 kJ per litre. So, when glycogen stores are depleted, the athlete will either have to reduce the intensity of exercise or increase oxygen consumption by increasing the volume of air breathed and blood pumped around the body. Endurance athletes refer to this as 'hitting the wall'.

Figure 34 As you run faster, glycogen supplies a higher proportion of your energy.
Reprinted, by permission, from Kirk et al., 1999.

NUTRITION FOR PHYSICAL ACTIVITY

The amount of glycogen stored in the body partially determines how long an individual can continue to exercise at moderate to high intensities. This length of time will be reduced if our diet contains an insufficient amount of carbohydrates or insufficient time is allowed between exercise sessions to allow glycogen stores to be replenished. Between 24 and 48 hours is required for completely depleted glycogen stores to be replaced.

Eating more carbohydrates can increase the amount of glycogen stored in the body. Athletes who train intensely for several hours each day should consume a high-carbohydrate diet. That is, 60 per cent or more of their energy intake should be carbohydrates. There is a limit to the amount that can be stored, however, and excess carbohydrate intake is stored as fat. Although an athlete's needs for protein may be slightly higher than a nonathlete, a normal diet typically supplies sufficient protein. Up to 15 per cent of the energy consumption is appropriate. High-protein diets or supplements are unnecessary and may lead to kidney problems. Adequate supplies of vitamins and minerals are essential for the body to function, and these are normally supplied by a balanced diet (figure 35). Supplementation to levels above normal will not lead to improvements in performance.

Whereas we have been concerned here with the use of energy to create movement, the body is not a very efficient machine, and the majority of energy

Increasing the amount of carbohydrates in your diet will increase the amount of glycogen stored in your body.

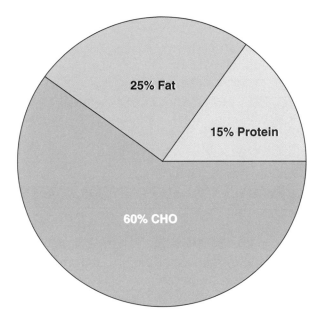

Figure 35   The recommended daily intake for fat, carbohydrates (CHO) and protein.
Reprinted, by permission, from Kirk et al., 1999.

liberated from the body's chemical stores actually ends up as heat. The body can only tolerate a narrow range of temperatures, and so another factor that limits performance is the ability of the body to get rid of this heat. The major way of doing this is through evaporation of sweat at the skin. Consequently, it is essential that sufficient water is consumed before, during and after exercise. A typical recommendation is that 500 ml of water should be consumed in the 20 minutes before exercise and 250 ml during every 15 minutes of exercise. Feelings of thirst lag behind our bodies' need for water. So, especially if you are exercising, drink more water than dictated by thirst. Adding a small amount of glucose to the water may be beneficial.

Over to You

Keep a diary of your food intake for a typical day. Using the dietary information provided on processed food labels, work out your total energy intake and the proportions produced by CHO, fat and protein.

SUMMARY

Chemical energy stored in ATP is converted into mechanical energy and heat when muscles contract. This energy in turn is supplied by three different systems. Energy stored in creatine phosphate supplies energy for very short durations. Anaerobic glycolysis, in which glycogen is broken down to produce energy and pyruvic acid in the absence of oxygen, is the second energy system. Oxygen is required for the third energy system, the aerobic system, in which pyruvic, fatty and amino acids are broken down into energy and carbon dioxide. Fuel for these systems comes from carbohydrates, fat and protein.

Test Yourself Questions

1. Describe the role of ATP and ADP in providing energy for muscle contraction.
2. Why might athletes take supplements containing creatine? What type of performance would be most likely to benefit from additional creatine stores?
3. Compare the characteristics of the anaerobic and aerobic energy systems.
4. What happens when an endurance athlete 'hits the wall'?
5. What diet should an athlete in heavy training have?

Physiological Capacity for Physical Activity

Chapter Overview

- Physiological Factors Affecting Performance
- Metabolic Capacity
- Cardiorespiratory Capacity
- Neuromusculoskeletal Capacity
- Physiological Capacity and Age
- Physiological Capacity and Sex
- Summary
- Test Yourself Questions

Learning Outcomes

When you have studied this chapter, you should be able to

- ☑ describe the physiological factors affecting performance;
- ☑ explain the short-term physiological changes which occur during physical activity; and
- ☑ predict the long-term physiological adaptations which occur in response to increased physical activity.

PHYSIOLOGICAL FACTORS AFFECTING PERFORMANCE

Performance of a physical activity depends on the ability of muscles to provide the forces required. Insufficient strength, power and endurance may limit the capacity for performance. In most cases, it is a combination of two or more of these capacities that determines the potential level of performance (figure 36). Many physiological capacities combine to determine strength, power and endurance. These capacities can be improved through training.

Human bodies are constantly changing, although the pace and nature of the changes vary across the life cycle. When people exercise, their bodies adapt to the demands placed on them and do so in ways that are very specific to the type of exercise involved. The parts of their bodies that are used get stronger and the parts that aren't used get weaker. This applies to the energy systems as well.

Some capacities change faster than others. Muscles are very well supplied with blood. Blood supplies energy and nutrients to muscles, so they respond quickly to changes. Ligaments and tendons are not as well supplied with blood, so they change more slowly. Bones also change slowly, but they also get stronger if used and weaker if not. The nervous system also adapts to exercise in specific ways.

METABOLIC CAPACITY

There are three systems that supply energy to the body—creatine phosphate, anaerobic glycolysis and aerobic. The capacity of each of the three energy systems to supply energy determines the limits of performance. The capacity of each is improved when specific forms of exercise place demands on that energy system.

Figure 36 Long-distance swimmers get most of their energy from their aerobic system.
Reprinted, by permission, from Kirk et al., 1999.

High-intensity, short-duration exercise such as strength training or short sprints requires energy to be rapidly obtained from ATP and CP stored in muscles (figure 37). This type of training leads to increases in the amount of ATP and CP that is stored in muscles. The consequence of this kind of training is an enhanced ability to generate quickly large amounts of energy to be used for force production.

Exercise of moderate to high intensity such as sprint training requires energy to be obtained through anaerobic glycolysis (figure 38). This leads to increased storage of muscle glycogen, increased activity of the enzymes involved in anaerobic glycolysis and an increased capacity of muscle to tolerate lactic acid accu-

Figure 37   High-intensity, short duration activities like putting a shot and spiking a volleyball require the body to rapidly obtain energy from stored ATP and CP.
Reprinted, by permission, from Kirk et al., 1999.

mulation. Together, these changes lead to an enhanced capacity to produce energy rapidly in the absence of oxygen.

Exercise of moderate to low intensity and long duration such as endurance training also causes increased storage of muscle glycogen. In addition, the activity of the enzymes involved in liberating the energy from pyruvic acid, fatty acids and amino acids is increased, as is the number and size of the parts of the cells, called mitochondria, where the chemical reactions take place. These changes lead to an increased ability to utilise energy from the aerobic system and to a consequential decrease in reliance on the anaerobic system for any given exercise intensity. Endurance-trained muscle also has an increased capacity to remove lactic acid from the blood and so delays the onset of fatigue because of lactic acid accumulation.

Figure 38   Running 400 m and playing Australian-rules football are moderate- to high-intensity activities that require the body to obtain energy through anaerobic glycolysis.

Orienteering is an example
of a moderate- to low-
intensity, long-duration
activity that will increase
the body's storage of
muscle glycogen.

© Sport, The Library/Michael Rayner

The aerobic energy system requires oxygen, and so the capacity of the body to utilise energy from the aerobic system is closely related to the capacity of muscles to obtain oxygen from the blood. The capacity to extract oxygen from the blood and to transport oxygen within the muscle cells is increased with endurance training. These capacities in turn rely on the ability of the heart and lungs to deliver oxygenated blood to the muscles.

CARDIORESPIRATORY CAPACITY

Imagine you are back relaxing with a friend. Your energy needs are small, and sufficient oxygen is usually easily provided by normal breathing and resting heart rate.

Say you decide to go for a jog again. The rate and depth of your breathing increase and the rate and volume of blood pumped by your heart also increase. If you continue jogging at a relatively slow speed, your rate of consuming oxygen will level out at a rate sufficient to metabolise all the lactic acid produced by the anaerobic energy system, as well as fatty acids to provide additional energy. In this situation the amount of oxygen consumed is a good measure of the amount of energy required to perform the activity.

If you pick up the pace, the rate at which you consume oxygen will increase to keep pace with your increasing energy needs. Eventually, your heart and lungs will no longer be able to deliver oxygen to the muscles any faster. The rate of oxygen consumption by the muscles at this time is the maximum rate of oxygen consumption, expressed as $\dot{V}O_2$max. The relationship of O_2 consumption over time is shown in figure 39.

$\dot{V}O_2$max refers to a rate of oxygen consumption, that is, a volume of oxygen consumed over a period of time, say 3 litres per minute. Because energy needs are related to body mass, $\dot{V}O_2$max is usually reported relative to the person's mass

When you are relaxing, your normal breathing and resting heart rate provide enough oxygen for your body.

The more intense the physical activity, the more oxygen the body requires.

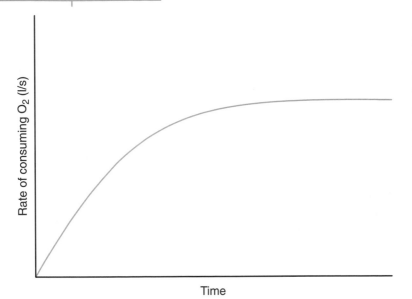

Figure 39 Oxygen (O_2) consumption versus time during submaximal running.
Reprinted, by permission, from Kirk et al., 1999.

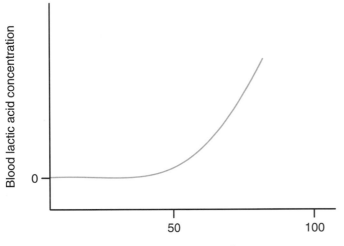

Figure 40 Lactic acid as a function of exercise intensity.
Reprinted, by permission, from Kirk et al., 1999.

as millilitres of oxygen per kilogram body mass per minute (ml/kg/min). If your maximum rate of consuming oxygen was 3 l/min and your mass was 60 kg, your $\dot{V}O_2$max would be expressed as 50 ml/kg/min. Typical $\dot{V}O_2$max values for untrained young adults are about 45 ml/kg/min, whereas elite distance runners may have $\dot{V}O_2$max of 70–80 ml/kg/min.

As you are increasing your running speed and rate of oxygen consumption, the rate of production of pyruvic acid by the anaerobic energy system is also increasing. As we saw earlier in this chapter, at low speeds the pyruvic acid can be metabolised by the aerobic system. However, as the intensity of exercise increases, the aerobic system cannot keep up with the amount of pyruvic acid produced by the anaerobic system, and the pyruvic acid is turned into lactic acid. Fatigue results rapidly if the intensity of exercise is increased above this level. This exercise intensity, above which lactic acid accumulates, is called the lactic acid threshold. In untrained people the intensity of exercise is equivalent to an oxygen consumption of about 60 per cent of their $\dot{V}O_2$max, but for endurance-trained athletes it might be 80 per cent of their $\dot{V}O_2$max. The relationship of blood lactic acid concentration and exercise intensity is illustrated in figure 40.

When you stop running and go back to watching television, although your energy requirements are back to what they were originally, your rate of oxygen consumption stays above resting level for some time. This oxygen is used, in part, to create the energy needed to replace the stores of creatine phosphate and glycogen you used up when you were exercising. Extra oxygen is also needed because the heart is pumping extra blood to return body temperature to normal, and respiration stays higher to clear the build-up of carbon dioxide from the blood. This phenomenon goes by the name 'elevated post-exercise oxygen consumption' and may last for several hours after high-intensity exercise of long duration.

Measurement of Oxygen Consumption

$\dot{V}O_2$max can be measured in a laboratory. The test typically involves the person exercising with gradually increasing intensity in terms of pace, gradient or resistance, while breathing through a mouthpiece and hose connected to a gas analyser. The average concentration of oxygen in the air breathed out each minute is measured and compared to the concentration of oxygen in the air breathed in. The difference multiplied by the volume of air breathed in that time is the volume of oxygen consumed.

As the intensity of exercise increases, the rate of oxygen consumption also increases. The test continues until the person can no longer increase the intensity of exercise, and the maximum rate of oxygen consumption (ml/min) is determined. As mentioned, oxygen consumption is related to body mass, and so we usually express $\dot{V}O_2$max relative to the person's body mass in terms of ml/kg/min.

Measurement of $\dot{V}O_2$max is useful for determining the intensity of exercise appropriate for an individual. An athlete may want to train at a high proportion of his or her $\dot{V}O_2$max (80 per cent or more), whereas intensities in the range of 50–80 per cent of $\dot{V}O_2$max are appropriate for an untrained person.

From Air to Muscle

For energy to be provided by the aerobic energy system, oxygen must be delivered to the muscles. Oxygen begins its journey to the muscles when air is drawn into the lungs (figure 41). The volume of air brought into the lungs each minute is known as minute ventilation. Minute ventilation is the rate of breathing in terms of breaths/ minute multiplied by the volume of air inspired in each breath expressed in terms of litres/breath. Both rate and volume per breath increase during exercise, and the minute ventilation may increase from about 10 l/min at rest to a maximum of about 160 l/min. Maximum minute ventilation increases with endurance training, leading to an enhanced capacity to excrete carbon dioxide.

Oxygen enters the blood in the alveoli within the lungs. This process is very efficient, and even in maximal exercise the blood leaving the lungs is almost saturated with oxygen. This means that the respiratory system is not the limiting factor for the rate at which oxygen can be delivered to the muscles.

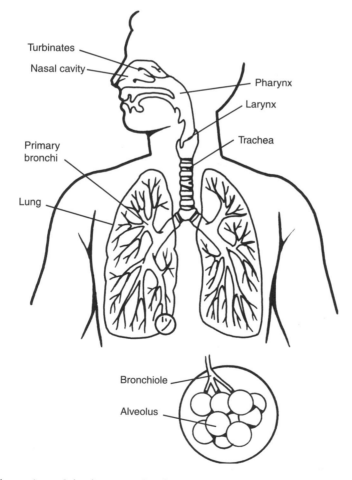

Figure 41   Illustration of the lungs and pulmonary circulation.
Reprinted, by permission, from Kirk et al., 1999.

The rate at which blood can be delivered to the muscles is the factor that limits the rate of oxygen consumption. Oxygenated blood returns from the lungs to the heart via the pulmonary veins and is then pumped to the muscles (figure 42). The rate at which the heart pumps (beats/min) increases during exercise from a resting value of about 70 beats/min for an untrained person to a maximum value that varies with age. The maximum heart rate is normally quoted as '220 beats/min minus your age', so a 17-year-old might be expected to have a maximum heart rate at or just above 200 beats/min, although this varies from person to person. The volume of blood the heart pumps each beat is known as the stroke volume. Stroke volume also increases from about 60 ml at rest to about 120 ml during maximal exercise.

The total volume of blood pumped to the muscles per minute is known as cardiac output. Cardiac output is the product of heart rate and stroke volume. On the figures just given, cardiac output would be increased from 4.2 l/min at rest (70 beats/min $\times$ 0.06 l/beat) to 24 l/min at maximum exercise intensity (200 beats/min $\times$ 0.12 l/beat).

Because the heart is a muscle, its size and strength increase with endurance training, leading to an increase in the stroke volume. The resting heart rate of trained athletes may consequently be much lower than normal, whereas resting cardiac

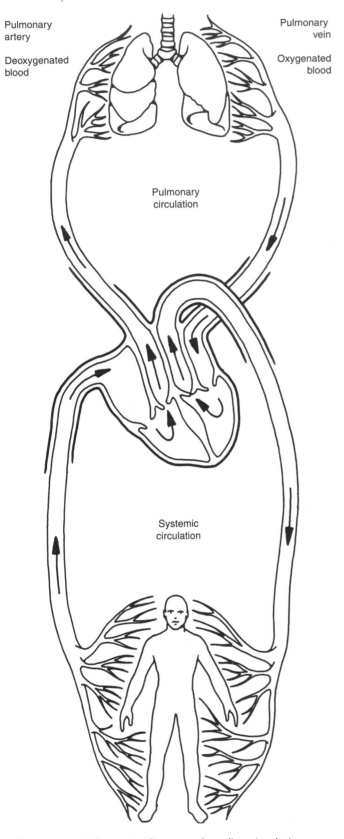

Pulmonary
artery

Deoxygenated
blood

Pulmonary
vein

Oxygenated
blood

Pulmonary
circulation

Systemic
circulation

Figure 42 Schematic diagram of cardiac circulation.
Reprinted, by permission, from Kirk et al., 1999.

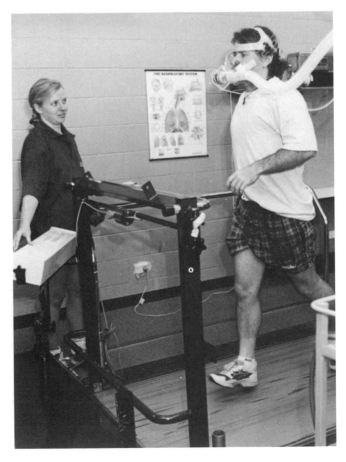

The $\dot{V}O_2$max test continues until the person being tested cannot increase the intensity of exercise.

output is the same. Maximum heart rate does not change with training but, because of the increase in stroke volume, the cardiac output of endurance-trained athletes at maximal heart rates is much larger, perhaps up to double that of untrained people.

Over to You

Analyse the effect of three different stroke volumes on the maximum cardiac output of 16-year-old high school students at rest and during maximum work. Assume Sam has a stroke volume at rest of 0.05 l/min and a resting heart rate of 80 beats/min, Jodie has a stroke volume at rest of 0.067 l/min and a resting heart-rate of 60 beats/min, and Ben has a stroke volume at rest of 0.09 l/min and a resting heart rate of 45 beats/min. Using these figures, calculate each student's resting cardiac output. Now calculate each student's maximum cardiac output, assuming that Sam has a maximum stroke volume of 0.1 l/min and a maximum heart rate of 204 beats/min, Jodie has a maximum stroke volume of 0.134 l/min and a maximum heart rate of 204 beats/min, and Ben has a maximum stroke volume of 0.18 l/min and a maximum heart rate of 204 beats/min.

The increase in cardiac output during exercise is not evenly distributed throughout the body. Figure 43 shows that at rest about 20 per cent of blood ends up in muscles, and the other 80 per cent goes to the brain and internal organs such as the stomach. When an individual begins to exercise, the blood flow is redirected to the muscles that are doing the work and to the skin. The redirection is achieved by narrowing the arteries which take blood to the internal organs and widening the arteries which take blood to the muscles involved. As well as carrying oxygen to the muscles, blood also delivers the fatty acids and glucose that fuel the muscles and removes carbon dioxide, lactic acid and heat from the muscles.

As well as receiving more blood during exercise, the muscles also extract a greater proportion of oxygen from the blood than at rest. About 25 per cent of the oxygen is extracted at rest, while this increases to up to 85 per cent during exercise. All these changes with exercise help to increase the rate at which oxygen is made available to the muscle cells, up to $\dot{V}O_2max$, so that energy can be produced by the aerobic energy system and the pyruvic acid produced by anaerobic glycolysis can be turned into carbon dioxide, hydrogen and electrons, rather than accumulating as lactic acid. However, fatigue rapidly develops if the intensity of exercise is such that the rate of

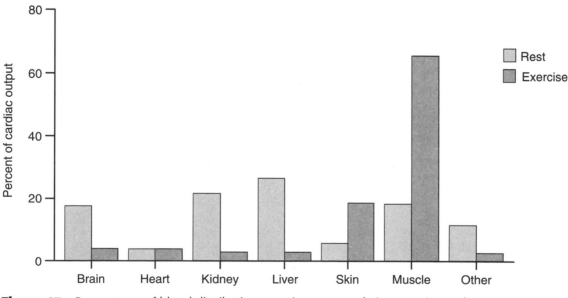

Figure 43 Percentages of blood distribution to various organs during exercise and rest.
Reprinted, by permission, from Wilmore and Costill, 1994.

pyruvic acid production exceeds the rate at which it can be metabolised. This exercise intensity is called the lactic acid threshold.

The maximum rate at which oxygen can be delivered to, and consumed by, the muscles ($\dot{V}O_2$max) and the lactic acid threshold (percentage of $\dot{V}O_2$max) determine the intensity of exercise that can be maintained for prolonged periods without fatigue occurring. As a consequence of the many adaptations that occur with endurance training, $\dot{V}O_2$max may be increased by 20 to 40 per cent. Endurance training also increases the lactic acid threshold.

NEUROMUSCULOSKELETAL CAPACITY

Muscle fibres supply the force that makes movement possible, but movement involves more than just muscles. Nerves deliver the stimulus to contract, and the forces are transmitted to the bones by tendons. Ligaments are also required to limit movement to particular directions. All these structures form the neuromusculoskeletal system. The capacity of these structures contributes to our ability to perform physical activity, and all respond to use and disuse.

Muscle Fibre Types

There are different types of muscle fibres that make up the skeletal muscle. The major distinction is between **slow-twitch fibres,** or type I, and **fast-twitch fibres,** or type II. Fast-twitch fibres are again divided into two types, IIA and IIB. Slow-twitch fibres have a high capacity for utilising energy via the aerobic energy system and do not fatigue rapidly. However, they are not as large and, as their name suggests, do not contract as rapidly as fast-twitch fibres. Fast-twitch fibres are large, contract faster than slow-twitch fibres, but fatigue rapidly. Fast-twitch fibres differ in the metabolic sources of energy utilised. Type IIB fibres have a high capacity for glycolytic release of energy, whereas type IIA fibres utilise both aerobic and glycolytic energy sources.

Type I fibres contract slowly and use energy from the aerobic process. Consequently, they are very useful for physical activities requiring low forces over long periods of time. The large type II fibres that contract quickly are useful for physical activities requiring large forces. However, because they obtain energy via anaerobic glycolysis they produce lactic acid. Type I fibres are smaller than type II and begin to produce force before the larger type II fibres. Only when more force is needed are the larger type II fibres used as well.

A typical muscle has about 50 per cent type I fibres, 25 per cent type IIA and 25 per cent type IIB, although the proportions differ for different muscles and different people. Muscles primarily used for posture have a higher proportion of type I fibres than the other types of fibre, whereas muscles used to produce large forces rapidly typically have more type II fibres than average.

If you are standing around waiting on the sideline to play a game of basketball, one of the muscles that continually has to produce low levels of force to keep you upright is a muscle called the soleus, which lies deep on the back of the calf. In normal standing, the soleus acts to stop you from falling flat on your face. The soleus is primarily composed of type I fibres, which means that you can stand around for long periods without getting tired.

However, if instead of standing around waiting you are now on the basketball court and about to perform a jump shot, your soleus doesn't help much. It can't generate forces very quickly, which is what you need to jump. Luckily, you have another muscle in your calf called the gastrocnemius, which is composed of a high proportion of type II fibres. This is exactly the kind of muscle needed to help you perform the jump shot.

Slow-twitch muscle fibres contract slowly and use energy from the aerobic process.

Fast-twitch muscle fibres contract faster than slow-twitch and use both anaerobic and aerobic energy systems.

These are extreme examples. Most muscles are general purpose, able to contract at low levels for long periods or generate relatively high forces for short periods. Most people do lots of different things, so it is an advantage to have different fibre types. It seems that some elite athletes have different distributions of fibre types from the average person. Elite endurance runners, for example, have large proportions of type I fibres, whereas elite sprinters and weightlifters have larger proportions of type II fibres. It is not clear whether fibre type changes in response to extreme exposure to either endurance or strength activities, or whether these fibre distributions are to some extent genetically determined, and that the performance of these elite athletes is a consequence of the abnormal fibre type distribution. Both may be true to some extent.

Responses to Training

Some parts of the neuromuscular system definitely do respond to training. One thing that changes with endurance training is an increase in the number of capillaries within muscle. This allows more oxygen to be delivered to the muscle cells and, in part, accounts for the increase in the ability of muscle to extract oxygen from the blood delivered to it by the cardiorespiratory system.

More dramatic changes occur in the neuromusculoskeletal system in re-sponse to strength and speed training. The initial gains in strength that occur in response to training are a consequence of changes in the functioning of the nervous system. In part, this is related to increased skill and coordination of muscle contraction, but there are also increases in the ability to activate muscle fibres.

Bodybuilders' muscles have larger proportions of type II fibres.

After the initial gains in strength as a result of neural changes, any further gains are a consequence of increases in the size or number of muscle fibres. Increase in the size of muscle fibres is called hypertrophy. Hypertrophy is the primary response to training, and the strength of a muscle is roughly pro-portional to its cross-sectional area. Which fibres increase in size depends on the specific nature of the training performed. Type I fibres will be increased in size as a consequence of endurance training, whereas the size of type II fibres will be increased in response to strength and sprint training. Type IIB fibres in particular, although having the greatest potential for hypertrophy, will only increase in size if near-maximal forces are involved in training. An increase in the number of fibres is called hyperplasia. Hyperplasia is less common than hypertrophy, but may occur in response to high-load and high-volume training.

PHYSIOLOGICAL CAPACITY AND AGE

Capacity for physical activity increases through childhood and early adulthood, and then decreases after about age 30. However, our bodies never stop responding to the demands placed on them, and training can reduce the inevitable decline.

Training can reduce decline in the body's capacity for physical activity

Maximum oxygen consumption declines after about age 30 in large part because of a decrease in the maximum heart rate and consequent decrease in maximum cardiac output, even though stroke volume may be maintained. There is also a decrease in number of capillaries and the ability of the vascular system to redirect blood to the working muscles, both of which reduce the amount of oxygen that can be delivered to muscle. Training may reduce the rate and amount of reduction in maximum oxygen consumption.

Strength appears to decrease by about 2 to 4 per cent per year in nonathletes, primarily due to a decrease in muscle mass. This decrease in muscle mass is predominantly the atrophy of the larger type II fibres, which are only recruited in high-force contractions. Training can slow the rate of loss of muscle.

PHYSIOLOGICAL CAPACITY AND SEX

Individuals differ in their physiological capacity for physical activity. On average, differences exist between females and males. $\dot{V}O_2$max, for example, is higher on average in males than in females, although the magnitude of the difference is small until after puberty. When trained female and male endurance athletes are compared the differences in aerobic capacity are small (<10 per cent). Of course, many females have a higher $\dot{V}O_2$max than many males.

In general, the differences between females and males in physiological capacity are small in children, and the differences are probably caused by differences in activity levels as a result of social rather than biological factors. After puberty, larger average differences are seen between females and males, especially in terms of muscle mass and, consequently, strength and power. Females and males respond similarly to training, and strength differences are reduced when similarly trained females and males are compared. We do not know how much of the average strength differences is a consequence of social factors affecting activity levels and how much is a consequence of physiological differences.

Until puberty, the differences in physical capacity between girls and boys are very small. During and after puberty, large differences occur, but the debate over whether these differences result from physiological or social causes continues.

Over to You

Carry out some library-based research and obtain world-record times for males and females in a variety of track events between 1960 and 1990, and draw some graphs to illustrate these trends. Describe any notable features of the graphs and try to explain these features.

A number of factors are specific to female athletes. The effects of menstrual cycle on performance are highly individual. Some women notice no differences, but others notice declines in performance during some or all of the flow phase. Some female athletes, up to 40 per cent in some sports, experience disruptions of their normal menstrual cycle. The likelihood of menstrual disruption increases with increased quantity and intensity of training, especially if combined with insufficient energy intake or psychological stress. It is important for female athletes to note that absence of menstruation does not necessarily mean absence of ovulation and, consequently, pregnancy still may be possible.

Osteoporosis is decreased density and increased porosity of bones and predominantly affects women after menopause. The loss of bone density leads to an increased risk of fractures, and fractures of the neck of the femur are especially common. This condition is a major public health concern. The most effective way of preventing osteoporosis later in life is to engage in regular weight-bearing exercise throughout childhood and adulthood, in combination with an adequate calcium intake and normal hormonal balance. Although regular weight-bearing exercise is essential for developing and maintaining bone density, some women who engage in large amounts of intense physical activity suffer hormonal disruption that is associated with disruption of the normal menstrual cycle. Hormonal disruption is also more likely if energy intake is restricted or the person is experiencing psychological stress. The consequence of this hormonal disruption is reduced bone density and an increased likelihood of developing osteoporosis in later life.

SUMMARY

Short-term and long-term changes occur in response to physical activity. Acute changes include increased heart rate and stroke volume, increased rate and volume of respiration and increased blood flow to muscle. Longer-term adaptations also occur in response to increased physical activity levels. Changes occur in the energy systems and cardiorespiratory and neuromuscular systems. The changes that occur are highly specific to the nature of the physical activity performed. Long-term physiological adaptations include increased glycogen storage, enzymatic activity and number and size of mitochondria. Neuromuscular changes include heart volume and strength, as well as increased skeletal muscle size and strength.

Test Yourself Questions

1. What is the lactic acid threshold? Why is it important?
2. Why is the rate of oxygen consumption elevated for some time after exercise stops?
3. What long-term changes will occur with high-intensity strength training?
4. Describe the functional consequences of different muscle types.
5. What physiological and neuromuscular changes occur in response to endurance training?
6. What sex differences exist in physiological capacity?

Improving Physiological Capacity for Physical Activity

Learning Outcomes

When you have studied this chapter, you should be able to

- ☑ describe four principles of training,
- ☑ apply the principles to design a training programme to achieve a specific goal,
- ☑ apply the notion of periodisation within a training programme, and
- ☑ explain some health benefits associated with exercise.

INTRODUCTION

If exercise is carried out in a haphazard or random fashion, then the changes that occur in the body will also be haphazard. On the other hand, if the exercise programme is planned, the capacity for physical performance can be developed systematically. The principles of specificity, progressive overload, reversibility and individuality can be applied to the design of a sound programme of training that will improve physical performance. We also need to consider the effects of the various types of training on physiological functioning and how training may be periodised to allow peak performance at the right time in a competitive sport season.

PRINCIPLES OF TRAINING

When you plan your exercise programme, keep in mind the factors that will affect your progress. By attending to the principles of training that follow, you can develop your most effective training programme.

Specificity

Specificity is a principle emphasising that training movements should be identical to those involved in the activity you are training for.

The most important principle of training is **specificity.** You can read in chapter 2.3 that the changes occurring in the body are very specific to the types of physical activity we engage in. For example, increases in strength that occur as a result of lifting weights will only affect the muscles used to lift the weights. Not only that, strength gains will be specific to the speed of movement. If the aim is to improve the ability to exert large forces very quickly — in training for shot put, for example — then not only is there little benefit to be gained by lifting light weights, there is also little to be gained by lifting heavy weights slowly.

To gain maximum benefit in terms of improved capacity for performance of any particular physical activity, training should involve movements that are, as far as possible, identical to the movements involved in the actual activity. The same joints and muscles should be involved, and the movements should ideally involve movements of the same force, speed and direction.

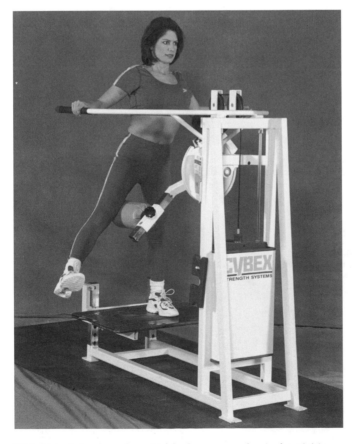

Weight training is only suitable for some physical activities.

Over to You

Select a resistance exercise that is designed to improve the height obtained from a jump when spiking in volleyball. Explain how your exercise achieves this outcome in terms of its effects on particular muscles and joint actions. Complete the same process for a component of a physical activity that you participate in regularly.

The changes that occur in the ability to utilise energy from each of the energy systems are also very specific to the demands placed on them. If the aim is to improve capacity to perform a specific activity, then training should be similar in frequency, duration and intensity to that of the physical activity. If the aim is to improve sprint performance, then training should involve short bouts of high-intensity exercise to promote improvements in the functioning of creatine phosphate and anaerobic glycolytic energy systems. There is less benefit to be gained in this case from long-duration, low-intensity sessions that improve cardiovascular functioning and the aerobic energy system. On the other hand, if the aim is to complete a marathon, then long-duration, low-intensity exercise sessions are the way to improve the functioning of the aerobic energy system that supplies most of the energy requirements of the activity.

Over to You

Draw a continuum with aerobic work at one end and anaerobic work at the other. Locate the following activities on the continuum in terms of the proportion of their aerobic and anaerobic work requirements for a trained adult athlete:

- 400-m sprint
- 1500-m swim
- A vault in gymnastics
- Rock climbing for 45 minutes
- A 60-second round of boxing
- A competitive aerobics routine lasting two minutes
- A complete hockey match for a goalkeeper
- A complete hockey match for a midfielder
- A single dive from a springboard

Progressive Overload

The body adapts to the demands placed on it in order to increase its ability to withstand those demands. When this is achieved, further improvements in capacity will not occur unless the demands also increase. For continued improvements in physiological capacity to occur, the programme of training must include progressive increases in the demands placed on the body. These demands can be increased by changing either the frequency, intensity or duration of the training. Which element or elements should be increased throughout the programme will depend on the specific requirements of the physical activity. For example, if increased endurance is the goal, then increasing the duration of exercise is appropriate. If, on the other hand, an individual wants to get stronger, he or she must lift heavier weights as formerly heavy weights become easier to lift.

To get stronger, when the weight you currently lift starts to feel lighter, increase the weight.

Reversibility refers to reductions in physiological capacity for performance when you reduce training demands on your body.

© Terry Wild Studio

Reversibility

The flip side of the principle of progressive overload is **reversibility.** The changes that occur in response to increased demands will remain for as long as the demands on the body remain. If the demands on the body suddenly reduce to much lower levels, then the changes in physiological capacity are reversed and reduce to match the new levels of activity. A dramatic example of reversibility is the astronaut who spends a long period of time in a weightless environment. The muscles that are normally used to maintain posture are not required, and these muscles consequently get very weak. Similarly, the astronaut's bones get weaker because they are not being loaded by bearing the astronaut's weight under gravity. The same sort of thing happens to anyone who is forced to remain inactive for prolonged periods.

Individuality

People differ — this is most evident in the different body sizes and shapes. People also differ in less obvious ways, such as the relative proportions of muscle fibre types they possess. It is important to realise that people will also differ in how quickly and to what extent they respond to a training programme. Consequently, any training programme and, especially the timing and extent of increases in exercise demands, must be flexible and be adapted to the individual. If training loads are too high or increase too quickly for an individual, then overtraining may occur.

Height is one of the many differences between people, but not all differences are so obvious.

Overtraining

It is possible to overload the body through training. The training load or frequency, intensity and duration of training, and increases in the training load must match the capability of the individual and the speed with which an individual responds to training. If the load is too high or increased too quickly the body becomes fatigued and is no longer able to respond to the demands placed on it. There is a reduced capacity for physical activity and, consequently, reduced performance levels and increased susceptibility to injury and illness. An athlete who has been exhausted by **overtraining** may require weeks, or even months, to recover.

Overtraining is the unintentional overloading of the body through excessive training.

TRAINING PROGRAMME DESIGN

Different types of training are appropriate to promote different types of changes in the body. The types of training may be broadly categorised as resistance, interval and continuous.

Resistance Training

Resistance training involves a low number of repetitions of high forces. The forces may be static, which means they are exerted without movement, or dynamic, which means they are with movement. Dynamic actions include the use of free weights and a variety of different mechanical devices.

Resistance training involves muscles working against a resisting load such as a dumbbell.

If the aim is to develop maximal strength, then a typical resistance training programme would consist of three to six sets of between one and eight repetitions of a load which is 80 to 100 per cent of the maximum load the person is able to lift. Lower loads and higher repetitions might be used if the aim was to develop health-related improvements in strength.

With free weights, the load or resistance remains constant through the whole movement while the body's ability to generate force changes. You can use mechanical devices to match the resistance to the strength of the body throughout the whole range of movement. You can also use isokinetic devices to maintain a constant speed of movement while the force exerted by the person varies as strength changes through the range of movement.

In dynamic actions, forces may be exerted while a muscle is shortening, as in concentric training, or lengthening, as in eccentric training. For example, during the upward movement in a bicep curl the biceps brachii shortens as it generates tension. This is a concentric muscle contraction. When the load is lowered, the same muscles provide the tension, but now they are lengthening. This is described as an eccentric contraction. Muscles are stronger when they are lengthening, and so eccentric training can involve higher loads, and theoretically this may lead to larger strength gains.

Another resistance training technique is to pre-stretch the relevant muscles just before exerting force in a rapid explosive movement, so involving both eccentric and concentric muscle contractions. This type of resistance training is known as **plyometrics.** An example of plyometrics is depth jumping, where the athlete jumps down from a height to the floor before jumping upwards with maximum effort. This type of training is ideal for developing the takeoff for blocking and spiking in volleyball, along with a range of other sports involving jumping. As the volleyballer's knees bend to absorb weight on landing, the quadriceps lengthen in an eccentric contraction. Once the landing force has been absorbed, the big muscles of the quadriceps shorten rapidly in a concentric contraction as the volleyballer jumps as high as possible.

Plyometrics is a particular type of resistance training that involves eccentric (lengthening) and concentric (shortening) muscle contractions.

Interval Training

Interval training involves a combination of high-intensity exercise interspersed with periods of rest. The changes that occur in the body will depend on the intensity and

Interval training combines periods of exercise with periods of rest.

duration of exercise bouts and the duration of rest. If the aim is to achieve maximum sprint performance, the training bout should be very high intensity, say 95 to 100 per cent of maximum speed, and short duration of up to about 30 seconds, with rest breaks of about 5 to 20 minutes to allow creatine phosphate stores to be replaced. If the intensity is reduced to about 60 to 80 per cent of maximum speed and duration of the exercise bouts increased to between 30 seconds and 2 minutes, the training will lead to improved utilisation of energy produced by anaerobic glycolysis, rather than from creatine phosphate. Longer-duration exercise bouts at even lower levels of intensity will primarily lead to changes in the aerobic energy system.

Continuous Training

Continuous training involves a steady level of easy exercise.

Continuous training involves low-intensity exercise, around 50 to 80 per cent $\dot{V}O_2$max performed for relatively long duration. The consequence of this type of training is improvement in the ability to utilize energy derived through the aerobic energy system. The appropriate intensity of exercise for continuous training depends on the individual and the aim of the training programme. Elite runners will train at a high proportion, possibly up to 80 per cent of their $\dot{V}O_2$max, while a lower intensity, perhaps about 50 per cent of $\dot{V}O_2$max, is appropriate for recreational runners exercising for health benefits.

If the aim is to improve strength, then resistance training is appropriate. If the aim is endurance, then continuous training is appropriate. If speed is what you are after, then short-interval training is the answer. Many physical activities require a combination of the three types of training. The emphasis that each form of training should receive will depend on the importance of each element.

Over to You

Design a training programme that will develop your cardiorespiratory endurance capacity for a sport or physical activity you participate in regularly. You should take into account factors such as any variations in cardiorespiratory endurance requirements during competition or active participation, variations at different phases in a season and the variety of methods you could employ to achieve specific effects.

Periodisation

Periodisation involves organising training into blocks that vary in frequency, intensity and duration.

Training is frequently planned in blocks that vary the frequency, intensity and duration of training activities and the types of activity. Breaking the training cycle up into blocks or periods of training is known as **periodisation.** The most common example of periodisation of the training cycle for team sports players is the off-season, preseason and competitive season. Different types of training may be undertaken during each period.

Varying the training in this way has a number of potential advantages. Reductions in training load are frequently planned to coincide with important competitions when maximal performance is desired. This process is known as tapering. Variation in training may also be desirable to develop different physiological capacities or to prevent boredom and maintain motivation or to reduce the risk of overtraining.

Many team sports, such as field hockey, netball and the various football codes, require a combination of general aerobic capacity, a capacity for frequent anaerobic efforts such as sprinting, as well as strength to perform specific skills such as hitting, throwing or kicking a ball. In these cases, you may address different aspects of the physical capacities and skills required at different stages of the season and off-season.

Warming Up, Flexibility and Stretching

Warming up before exercising elevates heart rate and breathing and reduces the risk of injury. For most activities involving running, between 5 and 20 minutes of stretching combined with low-intensity aerobic activity such as walking, jogging or striding forms an appropriate general warm-up. Finishing exercise with a cooling-down period of low-intensity aerobic exercise is also beneficial and reduces muscle soreness by speeding up the process of removing accumulated lactic acid.

The range of motion through which any joint is able to move is determined by the bony structure of the joint, the ligaments and the length of the tendons and muscles surrounding the joint. For some specific skills, such as many gymnastic skills, a large range of joint flexibility is necessary to successfully perform the movements. In many other cases, the performance of movements can be impaired and the risk of injury increased if the range of motion is abnormally small.

In both cases the range of movement or flexibility of a joint can be increased by stretching the muscles and tendons that surround the joints. Stretching before and after exercise sessions is also a useful way to reduce the risk of injury. Regardless of the reason for stretching, you should perform the stretching movements slowly, never involving rapid bouncing-type movements.

TRAINING FOR HEALTH

Improved physiological capacity for physical activity has many benefits for health, including preventing or reducing the risks of obesity, osteoporosis, heart disease and diabetes. A training programme appropriate for maintaining health in a normal adult population involves regular participation in a form of whole body exercise that you can maintain for a prolonged period of time. Walking, running, cycling and swimming are typical examples. The activity should be performed 3 to 5 times per week, for between 15 and 60 minutes. The intensity of the exercise should be between 50 and 70 per cent of $\dot{V}O_2$max. Resistance training should also form part of a general training programme for health. Sets of a relatively large number of repetitions, perhaps 15 to 25, of low loads of around 50 per cent of maximum, are appropriate to promote beneficial changes in muscular strength.

SUMMARY

The changes that occur in response to training are highly specific to the type of training. Progressive increases in training load are required for continued adaptations to occur. If training load is reduced, adaptations are reversed. Large individual differences exist in responses to training. Overtraining may occur if training load is increased too quickly. Training type may be characterised as resistance, interval or continuous. Periodisation involves altering the frequency, intensity and types of training to gain optimal adaptations.

Test Yourself Questions

1. Describe the four principles of training and the implications of each for training programme design.
2. What type of training would you design for a high jumper? How would this differ from a training programme for a hockey player?
3. Who might use plyometrics as a resistance training technique?
4. Why is tapering used before a competition?
5. What health benefits are associated with increased physical activity?

Biomechanics of Learning Physical Skills: Describing Motion

Chapter Overview

- Biomechanics and Learning
- Describing Motion
- Linear Motion
- Angular Motion
- Projectile Motion
- Centre of Mass
- Summary
- Test Yourself Questions

Learning Outcomes

When you have studied this chapter, you should be able to

- ☑ describe motion, using linear and angular kinematic terms;
- ☑ explain the distinction between linear and angular displacement and distance, speed and velocity;
- ☑ use examples from physical activity to illustrate Newton's Law of Inertia; and
- ☑ predict the consequences of this law for the motion of projectiles.

BIOMECHANICS AND LEARNING

The moving body obeys the laws of physics. Biomechanics is the use of these laws to understand the movement of the body. Understanding the biomechanics of a physical activity can be useful in improving performance and preventing injury.

Human movement is very complex, too complex to be understood completely. Biomechanics attempts to understand the moving body by using simplified physical models. We apply the laws of physics to the simplified model to predict the behaviour of the moving body in various circumstances. If the predictions agree with the behaviour observed, then we have enhanced our understanding of human movement. If the predicted behaviour does not match the observed behaviour, then one or more of the assumptions made in constructing the model must be inappropriate for that specific situation.

To talk about the movement of the body in physical terms, we must understand the language of physics. We use terms such as distance, displacement, speed, velocity, acceleration, inertia, momentum, work, energy, power and force in our daily language, but they have very specific meanings within biomechanics. The aim of these chapters on biomechanics is to explain each of these terms and their usefulness for understanding human movement.

DESCRIBING MOTION

Linear motion is movement in a straight line.

Angular motion is rotation about an axis.

Kinematics is a collective term for descriptors of motion, including distance, displacement, speed, velocity and acceleration.

The first step in understanding the movement of the body is to describe the movement. **Linear motion** refers to movement of the body or parts of the body in a straight line. **Angular motion** refers to rotation of the body or parts of the body. Rotation always occurs about an axis, and this axis can be inside or outside of the body. We can describe any movement of the body through a combination of linear and angular distances, displacements, speeds, velocities and accelerations. These values are collectively referred to as **kinematics.**

LINEAR MOTION

Movement occurs in time and space. Linear distance refers to the distance in metres (m) an object has moved during a time period measured in seconds (s), whereas linear displacement refers to the distance *and direction* which an object moves in a straight line during some time period.

Linear Speed, Velocity and Acceleration

Linear speed is the rate of change of distance during the time interval, or distance divided by time. Linear velocity is the rate *and direction* of change of displacement in some time period, or displacement divided by time. The units of speed and velocity are metres per second (m/s). Linear acceleration is the direction and rate of change of velocity in some time period, and the units are metres per second per second (m/s/s, or m/s^2). Linear displacement, velocity and acceleration all have both magnitude and direction, whereas distance and speed have magnitude only.

As an example, consider the movement of a sprinter from start to finish of a 100-m race. Assume the sprinter's time is 12 seconds. If the start is defined as 0 and the finish line 100 m away in a positive direction, then the displacement of the sprinter at the finish line is +100 m. The average velocity during this time period is the displacement/time (100 m/12 s) or +8.33 m/s.

© Sport, The Library/Darrin Braybrook

Average velocity is greater for sprinters than marathon runners.

Linear Displacement

Unfortunately, the average velocity over the duration of the race does not tell us anything very useful. It doesn't tell us what the velocity of the sprinter was at any particular time; nor does it tell us anything about the sprinter's maximum velocity, nor how she ran the race. How quickly did she leave the blocks? Was she easing up at the end? To answer these questions we would need to know the **displacement** of the sprinter at many more times throughout the race.

If, for example, we measured the displacement of the sprinter every half-second throughout the race, then we might be able to tabulate the information in a similar fashion to table 2. We could then proceed to calculate the difference in displacement between each half-second and divide by half to calculate the average velocity of the sprinter for each half-second of the race.

If we plot these numbers on a graph (figure 44), we now know something about the way the sprinter ran the race. We can see, for example, that she increased her velocity rapidly at the start, continued to increase velocity gradually until about seven seconds had elapsed, maintained this for a further two seconds, but then slowed down until the end of the race. Although more useful than knowing the average velocity for the race, these velocities are still only averages for each half-second, and they do not tell us exactly what the velocity of the sprinter was at any point in time, that is, her **instantaneous velocity** at any point.

If we wanted to know something about how the sprinter's velocity was changing during the race, her acceleration, we could estimate the sprinter's approximate **average acceleration** (m/s^2) during each half-second by calculating the differences between average velocities and dividing by half. To be accurate, we would need to know what the sprinter's actual velocity was at each point in time, not just her average velocity.

Displacement refers to the distance and direction an object has moved in a given time.

Instantaneous velocity is the velocity of an object at a particular instant in time, such as the moment of impact with another object.

Average acceleration is the rate of change of velocity during a given time.

Table 2 **Displacement, Velocity and Acceleration Versus Time for 100 m Sprint**

Time (s)	Displacement (m)	Velocity (m/s)	Acceleration (m/s/s)
0.5	0.5	1	2
1.0	2.5	4	6
1.5	6.0	7	6
2.0	10.0	8	2
2.5	14.0	8	0
3.0	18.0	8	0
3.5	22.5	9	2
4.0	27.0	9	0
4.5	31.5	9	0
5.0	36.0	9	0
5.5	41.0	10	2
6.0	46.0	10	0
6.5	51.0	10	0
7.0	56.0	10	0
7.5	61.5	11	2
8.0	67.0	11	0
8.5	72.0	10	−2
9.0	76.5	9	−2
9.5	80.5	8	−2
10.0	84.5	8	0
10.5	88.5	8	0
11.0	92.5	8	0
11.5	96.5	8	0
12.0	100.0	7	−2

Reprinted, by permission, from Kirk, 2000.

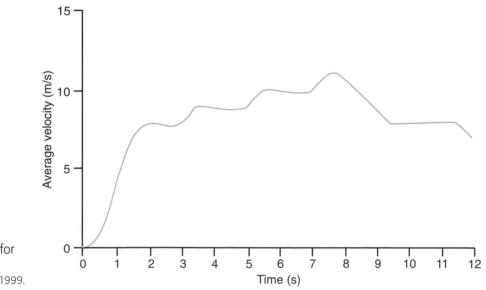

Figure 44 Velocity versus time for
100-m sprint.
Reprinted, by permission, from Kirk et al., 1999.

Over to You

Plot the numbers from table 2 for the acceleration of a sprinter on a graph of your own and note changes in acceleration at various points in the 100-m race.

ANGULAR MOTION

Not everything moves in a straight line. We are often interested in the rotation of an object, the body or limb. In this case we might describe the movement in terms of angular kinematics, using angular displacement, angular velocity and angular acceleration.

Remember that movement occurs in time. Angular displacement is the angular change that occurs during a specified time period and may be measured in degrees (°). One complete rotation equals 360° but, if an object has rotated back to its initial orientation, then the angular displacement is zero and the angular distance is the distance the object has rotated through during the time interval, in this case, 360°. Angular velocity refers to the rate and direction of change in angular displacement of a body in a time period, whereas angular speed is the angular distance divided by time. The units of angular speed and velocity are degrees per second (°/s). Angular acceleration refers to the rate and direction of change in angular velocity during some time period (°/s²).

Over to You

Consider the following activities and actions:

Cricket — batting
Hockey — striking a ball
Football — kicking a ball
Rounders — striking a ball
Basketball — set shot
Golf — hitting a ball

Address the following tasks:

- Using the information regarding angular displacement, angular velocity and angular acceleration, describe how this information can help players in these sports to improve their power, accuracy and precision.

- In pairs, choose one activity each. Set up a situation (e.g., a chip shot in golf). Relate the information in the previous task to a practical session with your partner.

Consider a chip shot in golf (figure 45). To describe the movement of the golf club during the downswing we could use angular kinematics. If we define the position of the club at the moment of impact as zero and the direction of the downswing (anticlockwise) as positive, then, in the swing illustrated, the angular displacement of the club during the downswing is 90°. If the duration of the downswing is 0.5 s, then the *average* angular velocity for the downswing is 90° divided by 0.5 s, or 180°/s.

This *average* angular velocity is not the angular velocity of the golf club at the moment of impact. If we were to measure the actual angular velocity of the club at the moment of impact, we would find that it was greater than the average velocity across the duration of the downswing.

Figure 45 For a chip shot in golf, the angular displacement equals 90° and the time of downswing equals 0.5 s. Therefore, the average angular velocity equals 90°/0.5 s, or 180°/s.
Reprinted, by permission, from Kirk et al., 1999.

 ■ ■ ■ ■ ■ *Over to You* **■ ■ ■ ■ ■ ■ ■ ■**

How can this information help a golfer understand how to improve the chip shot? Imagine that the chip shot landed in the bunker in front of the putting green, instead of landing on the green as the golfer had planned. What could the golfer have done differently? Discuss these questions and write down at least two or three solutions.

Newton's Law of Inertia states that the velocity of an object remains constant unless a force acts on it.

PROJECTILE MOTION

What would happen if a ball were thrown in space where there is no gravity or air resistance? The velocity of a body remains constant unless a force acts on it. This is known as **Newton's Law of Inertia.** So, in the absence of any forces, the ball would maintain constant velocity; that is, it would continue to travel in a straight line with the same speed.

What happens when we throw a ball on Earth? It doesn't maintain constant velocity. From the instant of release, the velocity of the ball changes and continues to change until it stops moving. This applies to any object in flight, such as a discus, javelin or ball, and includes the human body during the flight phase of activities such as jumping, diving, vaulting and running. The continual changes in velocity are caused by the resistance of air to the object passing through it and the gravitational attraction between the Earth and the object.

The gravitational attraction between the Earth and the object always causes acceleration vertically downwards. The magnitude of the acceleration may be considered to be constant, about 10 m/s². The accelerations caused by air resistance are not easy to predict. In many cases—for example, a shot put or high jump—the effects are very small and may be ignored. In other cases such as discus or badminton, the effects of air resistance are large and complex. We will discuss these effects of air resistance later when we consider fluid mechanics.

CENTRE OF MASS

All objects are composed of matter. **Mass,** measured in kilograms (kg), is the amount of matter in an object. The **centre of mass,** or centre of gravity, of an object is the point at which the force due to gravity appears to act. The location of the centre of mass of an object depends on the arrangement of mass within the body. If an object is a regular shape and its mass is evenly distributed, then the centre of mass will be at the centre of the object. Objects with irregular shape or arrangement of mass can have a centre of mass quite distant from the centre of the object, sometimes even outside the object, as we see in figure 46.

Mass is the amount of matter in an object, measured in kilograms.

Centre of mass is the point on which the force due to gravitational attractions appears to act.

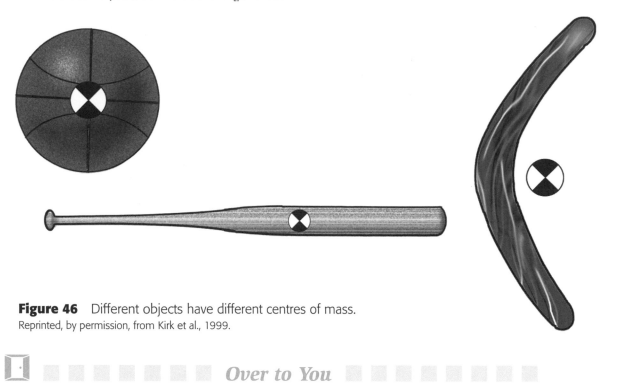

Figure 46   Different objects have different centres of mass.
Reprinted, by permission, from Kirk et al., 1999.

Over to You

Choose equipment from each of your chosen practical areas of study and draw a diagram showing the centre of mass.

If a body rotates during flight, it rotates about the centre of mass. Forget about air resistance for the moment, and assume that the only force acting on an object is that due to gravity. The centre of mass of the object in flight will travel in a particular curve **(parabola)** and continue on this curve until acted on by another force. The initial velocity of the object, as well as its initial position and the acceleration caused by gravity, determines the precise details of the curve.

A parabola is the curved path that the centre of mass of an object follows during flight.

The example shown in figure 47 illustrates how you can use this knowledge in a throwing activity such as shot put. The velocity of the shot at release and the height of release determine the horizontal displacement of a shot when it hits the ground. Increases in the height of release will increase the horizontal displacement at landing, as will increases in the speed of release. For any given height and velocity of release there is an optimal angle of release which maximises the horizontal displacement at landing.

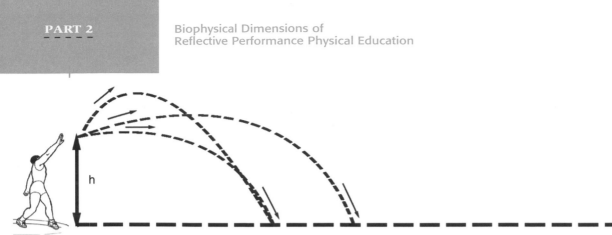

Figure 47 For any height at release (h), there is an optimal release angle to achieve maximum horizontal distance. The optimal angle is always less than 45°. Shown here is the relationship between release angle and horizontal displacement (distance) for a shot-putter.
Reprinted, by permission, from Kirk et al., 1999.

When the human body is in flight, its centre of mass also travels in a curve that cannot be altered during flight. However, unlike rigid objects, altering the arrangement of the body's mass can alter the location of the centre of mass of the human body during flight. Raising your arms, for example, raises the location of the centre of mass of the body relative to the trunk. Adopting a pike position or arching the spine backwards can, just like the boomerang, cause the centre of gravity of the body to move outside the body, as we see in figure 48.

Volleyball blockers sometimes seem to hang in the air 'forever'. But they haven't discovered the secret of flight. What they have learned to do is raise their legs by bending at the knees after takeoff and then lower their legs as they reach the peak of the jump. Lowering the legs has the consequence of lowering the centre of mass of the body relative to the upper body and arms. The player's trunk remains higher for longer than it would have if the legs had not been lowered.

Figure 48 The centre of mass in different postures; centre of mass passes under the body when performing the Fosbury flop.
Reprinted, by permission, from Kirk et al., 1999.

Another situation in which the location of the centre of mass within the body is changed during flight is in the high jump and pole vault events, where the body arches over the bar. At the moment of passing over the bar, the centre of mass of the body may actually be outside the body—perhaps even under the bar. But even though it is possible to manipulate the location of the centre of mass relative to the body, the flight of the centre of mass itself cannot be changed.

Over to You

In pairs, select an exercise from the list that follows. Observe your partner's angle of release in relation to displacement or accuracy of aim. It would be useful to employ a video camera.

Rugby — penalty kick

Hockey — penalty flick

Swimming — start

Netball — shooting

Basketball — shooting

Tennis — serving

Badminton — smash

Athletics — throwing an implement

Plot findings in the form of a diagram. Look at the optimal release angle to achieve either power, distance or accuracy in your chosen action. Teach another pair in your group your chosen actions, explaining the appropriate angle of release. Describe how angular motion affects the outcome of the skill performed.

SUMMARY

Biomechanics involves using simple models of the body to understand the physical influences on movement. Kinematics refers to description of movement in terms of linear and angular distance, displacement, speed and velocity. Displacement and velocity have directions as well as magnitudes. The velocity of a body remains constant unless a force acts on the body. This is Newton's Law of Inertia. The gravitational attraction of the Earth causes a constant change in velocity towards the Earth. In the absence of other forces, the centre of mass of a body in flight travels in a parabola.

Test Yourself Questions

1. What is the difference between speed and velocity?

2. How is average velocity calculated?

3. How would you describe the movement of a golf club during a swing?

4. In the absence of air resistance, would an arrow shot by an archer towards a target travel in a straight or curved path? Explain your answer.

5. What determines the location of the centre of mass of an object? Give two examples where the centre of mass is outside the object or body.

6. What can a volleyball blocker do after takeoff to influence the path of the trunk during flight?

Biomechanical Factors Influencing Performance: The Effects of Forces and Torques

Learning Outcomes

When you have studied this chapter, you should be able to

☑ describe the effects of forces;
☑ describe Newton's Laws of Action–Reaction and Acceleration;
☑ explain the conditions required for equilibrium;
☑ calculate impulse and momentum;
☑ predict the consequences of the conservation of momentum;
☑ calculate work, energy and power;
☑ predict the consequences of the conservation of energy; and
☑ explain the forces caused when an object moves through fluid.

INTRODUCTION

Forces cause, or tend to cause, changes in velocity. If a force is applied anywhere except the centre of mass, it causes rotation. The turning effect of a force is called its torque. Three important relationships provide useful ways of understanding the way forces cause movement: the relationship between force and acceleration, the relationship between the duration for which the forces act and the change in momentum that results, and the relationship between energy and the mechanical work done by a force. This chapter introduces force and torque and explores examples of how each of these three relationships can help in understanding the movement of the body.

FORCE

Force is the cause of change in the velocity of an object. Forces are measured in newtons and have both magnitude and direction.

Forces cause, or tend to cause, a change in the velocity of an object. Forces are measured in newtons (N) and have both magnitude and direction. Two examples of forces mentioned in chapter 2.5 were gravity and air resistance. Other examples of forces involved in physical activity are the forces exerted by muscles on bones via tendons and the forces that occur during contact between objects, such as friction, impact forces and reaction forces.

The application of force always involves an interaction between objects. Every action by a force is accompanied by an equal action in an opposite direction. This is Newton's Law of Action–Reaction. For example, when an object is resting on the ground it exerts a force on the ground vertically downwards which is equal to the object's mass multiplied by the acceleration due to gravity. The ground also exerts a force on the object that is equal in magnitude and opposite in direction, vertically upwards in this case. This force is called a reaction force.

If the line of action of all the forces that act on an object pass through the centre of mass of the object, then we can pretend that the object is a point located at the centre of mass of the object. If, for example, we are interested in the force applied to a softball when it is struck through its centre by a bat, then this is a reasonable assumption to make. In this case the only change in velocity caused by the impact force will be a change in linear velocity of the centre of mass of the ball. The moment before impact, the ball has a large linear velocity in one direction, towards the bat, and, after impact, the ball has a very different velocity as it speeds over a fence. The change in the ball's velocity occurred as a consequence of the force applied to the ball by the bat during the time they were in contact. The ball also applied an equal force on the bat, but in the opposite direction.

TORQUE

In many cases the object we are interested in cannot be usefully modelled as a point. Imagine another impact situation. This time it is a free kick in soccer, and the player taking the free kick is attempting to kick the ball slightly off centre so that it spins, causing it to curve in flight around the defensive wall (figure 49). The ball is initially stationary, so linear and angular velocity are zero. The force applied to the ball by the foot during the time they are in contact causes a change in the ball's linear velocity. It also causes a change in the ball's angular velocity.

The change in angular velocity occurs because the line of action of the force does not pass exactly through the centre of mass of the ball. The change in angular velocity depends on the 'turning effect', or **torque,** of the force. The torque caused

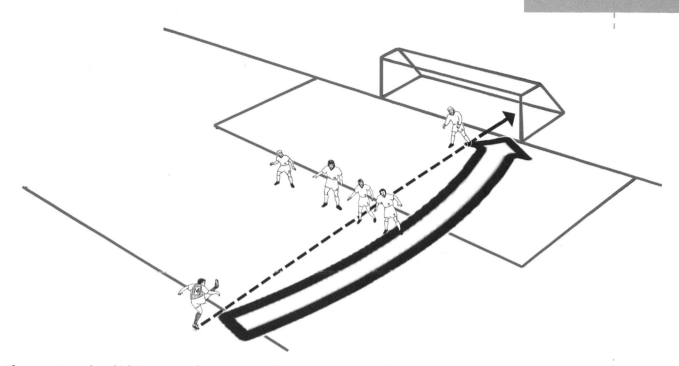

Figure 49 A free kick in soccer demonstrates the power of torque forces.
Reprinted, by permission, from Kirk et al., 1999.

by a force depends on the size of the force and the distance the force acts from the axis of rotation; in this case, the centre of the ball. The distance the force acts from the axis of rotation is called the moment arm. The torque of a force is equal to the magnitude of the force multiplied by the moment arm, expressed as Torque = Force × Moment Arm.

Another common situation in which the turning effects of forces are important is the movement of our limbs. The human body moves because muscles generate forces that cause rotation of limbs. The turning effect or torque caused by muscular contraction depends on both the size of the force produced and the distance the muscle acts from the axis of rotation; that is, its moment arm. Take for example the biceps brachii shown in figure 50. This muscle lies on the front of the upper arm, and, when contracted, a force is applied via the muscle's tendon to the forearm. This force tends to rotate the forearm up towards the upper arm. The size of the turning effect, or torque, is equal to the force multiplied by the moment arm.

Torque is the turning effect of a force.

F

Moment arm

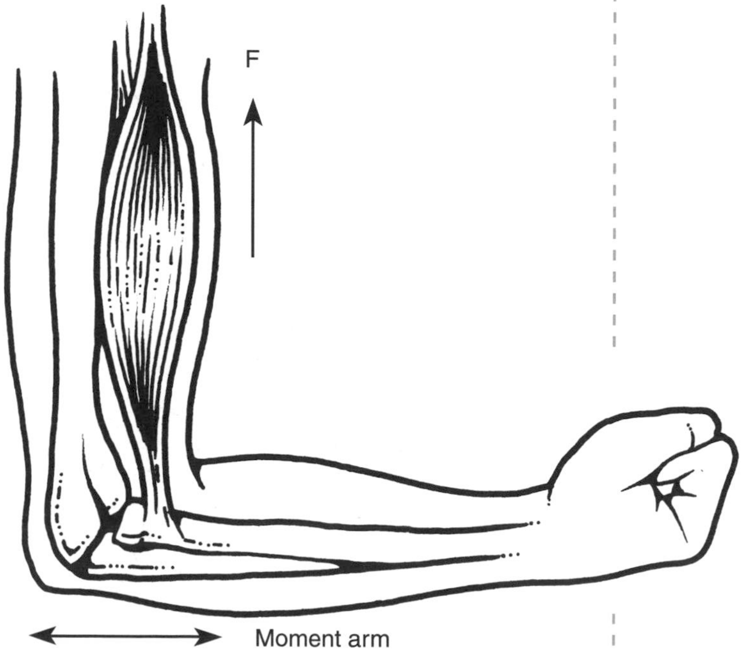

Figure 50 Moment arm of biceps brachii.
Reprinted, by permission, from Kirk et al., 1999.

MORE THAN ONE FORCE: RESULTANT FORCES AND TORQUES

If more than one force acts on an object at any moment in time, the effect of the combined forces is the same as if one equivalent force and torque, which is the sum of all the applied forces and torques, were applied. This equivalent force and torque is called the resultant force and torque.

For example, a rugby player jumping to catch a high ball is tackled simultaneously by two opponents, one from the left, in a tackle around the waist, and the other from the right, in a tackle around the shoulders. If the force applied from the left is 400 N and applied 0.1 m below the player's centre of mass and the force from the right is 600 N, 0.2 m above the player's centre of mass, then the effect of these two forces is the same as if a single force of 200 N to the left and a torque about the centre of mass of 80 N/m anticlockwise were applied (see figure 51).

■ Effects of Forces and Torques

The magnitude of the linear acceleration that occurs when a resultant force acts on the centre of mass of an object depends on the mass of the object. If the mass of an object is small, then the linear acceleration caused by a given force will be greater than if the mass is large. This relationship can be expressed as: Force = Mass × Acceleration, or Acceleration = Force/Mass. This is Newton's Law of Acceleration.

So, in the preceding example, if the player has a mass of 50 kg, the linear acceleration resulting from the tackle would have been 200 N divided by 50 kg = 4 m/s^2. If the player's mass were 100 kg, the linear acceleration would have been half as much (2 m/s^2).

The angular acceleration caused by a given torque is dependent on the resistance of the object to turning about the axis of rotation. This property of an object is called the moment of inertia, and it depends on the mass of the object and the way in which the mass is arranged relative to the axis of rotation. The moment of inertia increases when mass is located further from the axis of rotation.

If an object's resistance to turning is less — that is, the moment of inertia is less — then a given torque will cause a greater angular acceleration. In the same way as Force = Mass × Acceleration, Torque = Moment of Inertia × Angular Acceleration. In the example just given, the 100-kg player will have a larger moment of inertia than the 50-kg player, and, consequently, the angular acceleration as a result of the resultant torque will be less.

The relationship between moment of inertia and angular acceleration explains how the mass and distribution of mass within an object affect how fast a person can rotate the object. Imagine you are swinging a wooden tennis racket. If a different racket, made of aluminium, were the same length and shape, but lighter, the resistance of the racket to turning would be less. You could cause a greater change in angular velocity by exerting the same torque with your arms and body, and, if the duration of the swing were constant, the consequence would be a higher velocity of the racket at the moment of impact.

Changing the mass of the object is not the only way to change the moment of inertia. Suppose that you shift your grip up the handle of the racket; you would then change the arrangement of the mass of the racket relative to the axis of rotation, thus reducing the moment of inertia of the racket, and the same torque would produce a greater angular acceleration and, swing duration being constant, higher *angular* velocity of the bat at impact.

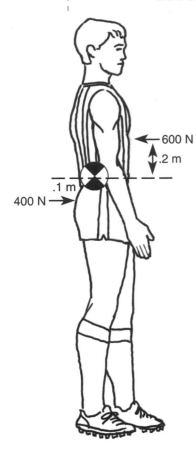

Figure 51 If the resultant force between front and back = 600 N − 400 N, then the net force = 200 N. Since acceleration is calculated as force/mass, for a person whose mass is 50 kg acceleration = 4 m/s^2. The resultant movement is 600 × 0.2 m anticlockwise − 400 × 0.1 m clockwise = 80 N/m.

Reprinted, by permission, from Kirk et al., 1999.

This same principle explains why field hockey players will sometimes drop their hands lower down the stick to hit the ball. If there is lots of time, then the way to hit the ball hardest is to grip the very end of the stick and use a large backswing. In this case, the moment of inertia is large, so the angular acceleration for a given torque is small. However, if applied for a long time, a large angular velocity results which, when multiplied by the length of the stick, gives a high linear velocity of the head of the stick at impact.

However, if an opposition player is close, a tackle could be made easily if the hit takes a long time. Instead, when the time available is small, the player reduces the moment of inertia of the stick about the axis of rotation by lowering the hands on the stick. This allows a greater angular acceleration to be produced by the same torque and allows a hard hit to be produced in a shorter time interval.

Over to You

Give another example from sport of a way in which a change in technique changes the moment of inertia. Back it up with an explanation of how this process works.

When Velocity Is Constant: The Concept of Equilibrium

Sometimes forces don't cause changes in velocity; they only tend to do so. Changes in velocity do not occur if other forces of equal size but opposite direction resist the forces. In this case the object is said to be in **equilibrium.**

Imagine you are standing still. There is no change in velocity, but are there no forces acting on you? On the contrary, as figure 52 shows, gravitational attraction is acting, tending to cause a change in velocity of approximately 10 m/s² vertically

> Equilibrium is the situation in which the linear and angular velocity of an object remain constant.

© Sport, The Library/Mike Larder

Reducing the moment of inertia of the hockey stick by lowering their hands lets hockey players execute a hard hit quickly before a tackle can be made.

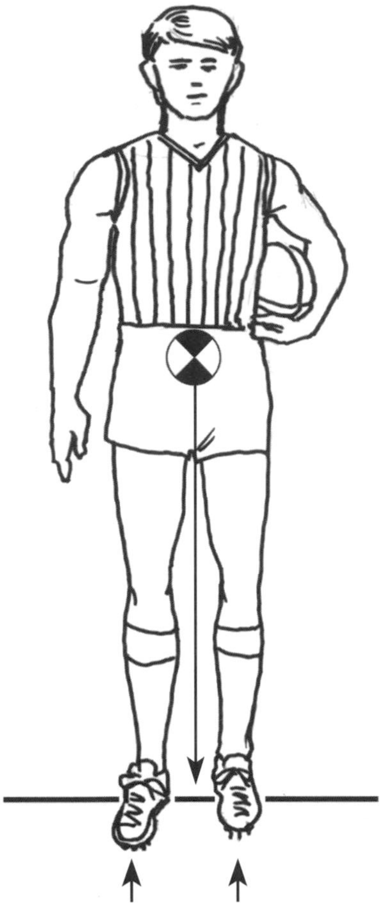

Figure 52 Equilibrium equals weight balanced by ground
reaction force, so Weight = Mass × Gravity.
Reprinted, by permission, from Kirk et al., 1999.

Weight/2 Weight/2

downwards. What is stopping you? The ground is exerting an equal and opposite force through your feet, often called a ground reaction force, and so the resultant force is zero and no change in velocity occurs.

Let's take a more complex example of a toddler and his mother playing on a seesaw (figure 53). The seesaw is stationary, that is, there is no change in velocity. But the mother has much greater mass than the toddler. How can the seesaw possibly remain stationary?

Remember how to calculate the turning effect of a force. The gravitational attraction between the mother and the ground is causing a force equal to the mother's weight, mass × gravity, to be exerted on the seesaw vertically downwards at a small distance from the fulcrum, or axis of rotation, of the seesaw. The torque caused by the mother is equal to the product of the mother's weight and the distance from the fulcrum. Similarly the toddler is causing a torque in the opposite direction equal to the product of his weight and his distance from the fulcrum. If the difference in distances from the fulcrum is just right, the resultant torque will be zero and the change in velocity will be zero.

In general, if the linear and angular velocity of a rigid object is constant, then we know that the forces and torques which are acting on the object cancel out, and the resultant force and torque is zero. Note that the velocity of an object does not need to be zero for the object to be in equilibrium, just not changing.

If a rigid body is experiencing a change in linear or angular velocity, then the resultant force and torque must be proportional to the angular and linear acceleration. This is only true for a rigid object. If the object's mass, or more likely its moment of inertia, is changing, then changes in velocity can occur in the absence of resultant forces or torques.

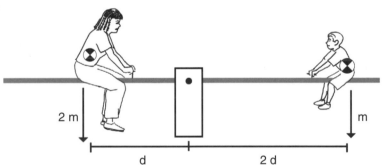

Figure 53 This seesaw is in equilibrium. The mass (m) and distance (d) are equal: 2 m × d = 2 d × m.
Reprinted, by permission, from Kirk et al., 1999.

IMPULSE AND MOMENTUM

Another way of thinking about the effects of force is in terms of the **impulse** applied to an object and the change in momentum that occurs as a consequence. If a force is constant, then the impulse is equal to the force multiplied by the time for which it is applied to an object. That is, Impulse = Force × Time. The momentum of an object is equal to the object's mass multiplied by its velocity, expressed as Momentum = Mass × Velocity. These quantities are related. When a force is applied to an object for a defined time period, the impulse is equal to the change in momentum that results.

Impulse is force multiplied by the time it is applied to an object.

The relationship between impulse and momentum provides one way of understanding, for example, the generation of high velocities. To propel a ball at high velocity we can apply a very high force for a very short period of time, such as hitting a ball with a bat, or we can apply relatively small forces for a longer period of time, such as pitching a softball or baseball.

The relationship between impulse and momentum also provides a way of understanding how a gymnast can prevent injuries during landing from a dismount or vault. When the gymnast first touches the ground, he has a large **linear momentum** equal to the product of his mass and the velocity with which he is approaching the ground. A short time later he is standing stationary. His velocity, and consequently his momentum, is zero. What caused the change in momentum? From the time his feet first touched the ground until the gymnast was stationary, a ground reaction force was exerted on the gymnast. These forces can be very large and cause injuries. What can the gymnast do to reduce the magnitude of these ground reaction forces?

Linear momentum is an object's mass multiplied by its linear velocity.

As we noted earlier, impulse equals change in momentum. Assuming that the gymnast's mass and initial and final velocities remain constant, then the impulse required to produce the change in momentum is constant. Impulse is force multiplied by the time period over which that force acts. So increasing the time period will allow a smaller force to produce the same impulse. Gymnasts can increase the time over which the force is applied during landing by bending their knees as they land. This will reduce the size of the ground reaction forces and the potential for injury. By increasing the time period, landing mats help prevent injury in the high jump and pole vault.

Angular momentum is an object's moment of inertia multiplied by its angular velocity.

Angular Impulse and Angular Momentum

A similar relationship holds for **angular movement.** Angular impulse is equal to torque multiplied by the time during which it is applied so that Angular Impulse = Torque × Time. Angular momentum is equal to angular velocity multiplied by the moment of inertia of the object about the axis of rotation, expressed as Angular Momentum = Angular Velocity × Moment of Inertia, and the impulse of a torque is equal to the change in angular momentum.

So when a discus thrower or hammer thrower rotates around and around before releasing the implement, he or she is increasing the time during which he or she can generate torque and, consequently, the angular impulse. An increased angular impulse means a larger change in angular momentum and a higher velocity of the implement at the time of release. Increasing the impulse applied by the body, either to an object or to the ground, is a common goal of many sporting techniques.

Conservation of Momentum

Another important insight arises from the relationships between linear and angular impulse and momentum. What if the resultant force or torque is

Landing mats help prevent injury by increasing the time over which force is applied.

© iPhotoNews.com/Brooks

zero? If there is no resultant force acting on an object, then the impulse is zero and there can be no change in momentum. Similarly, if there is no resultant torque acting on an object, then the angular impulse is zero and there can be no change in angular momentum. In other words, momentum remains constant when no resultant forces or torques are acting. This is **conservation of momentum,** another way of stating Newton's Law of Inertia.

If momentum is constant and the mass of the object is constant, then the velocity will also be constant. Similarly, if angular momentum is constant and the moment of inertia of an object is constant, then angular velocity must also be constant. However, whereas the mass of an object usually remains constant, there are many instances where the moment of inertia of an object, particularly the human body, does not remain constant.

Remember that the moment of inertia refers to the resistance of a body to rotating about a particular axis and is dependent on the object's mass and the distribution of the mass relative to the axis of rotation. The moment of inertia can be decreased by locating the mass close to the axis of rotation and increased by locating the mass further from the axis of rotation. If the arrangement of the mass of an object is changed, then the angular velocity of the object can change in the absence of any resultant torque (figure 54).

This principle is commonly encountered in physical activity. For example, the angular velocity of a springboard diver when she leaves the board is relatively small. During her flight to the water the only external force acting is the force due to gravitational acceleration. This force acts through the centre of gravity of the diver and causes no resultant torque. Consequently, the angular momentum of the diver during flight remains constant. If the diver is stretched out when she leaves the board, her mass is distributed a long way from her axis of rotation. Consequently, she has a relatively large moment of inertia about her centre of gravity.

For her to rotate fast enough to complete, for example, a double somersault before hitting the water, she tucks, bringing the mass of the limbs closer to the axis of rotation, reducing her moment of inertia. Her angular velocity increases to maintain constant angular momentum, and she is able to complete the required number of revolutions in the time available. The diver does not want to be rotating quickly when she enters the water, and so she straightens her body again before entry. This increases the moment of inertia again, resulting in a reduction of her angular velocity.

Another example where conservation of angular momentum is involved in determining techniques used is the long jump, illustrated in figure 55. When a long jumper leaves the board she is leaning forward, and the line of action of the reaction force that propels her into the air passes some distance behind her centre of mass and consequently has a rotational effect as well. Because of this torque, the jumper has some angular momentum in a clockwise direction during the flight. This presents the jumper with a problem. She would like to land in the sand with her feet ahead of her centre of gravity, which is following a parabola and cannot be altered. But, if she continues to rotate forward at the same rate, her feet will be a long way behind the centre of gravity at landing.

Figure 54   Divers change their angular velocity by changing their moment of inertia.
Reprinted, by permission, from Kirk et al., 1999.

Conservation of momentum occurs when no resultant forces or torques act on an object and both linear and angular momentum remain constant.

The various techniques of long jumping are each devised to cope with this problem in different ways. If the jumper uses a hang technique, she tries to minimise the forward rotation during flight by maximising her moment of inertia and hence reducing her angular velocity clockwise. In the last moments before impact she draws her legs and upper body forward to land.

Another alternative technique is the hitch kick (see figure 55a), in which the jumper rotates his legs as if he were pedalling a bicycle. This pedalling is in the same direction as the angular momentum that the jumper had at takeoff. However, the total angular momentum of the jumper must remain constant. Consequently, the angular velocity of the whole body is reduced.

A third way of dealing with the angular momentum during the long jump is illustrated by the jumper in figure 55b. This technique involved not reducing the angular velocity but increasing it by adopting a tucked position much the same as a diver. The aim was to perform a complete rotation in the form of a somersault during the time of the flight and extend the legs at landing. This technique was briefly popular before it was banned for safety reasons.

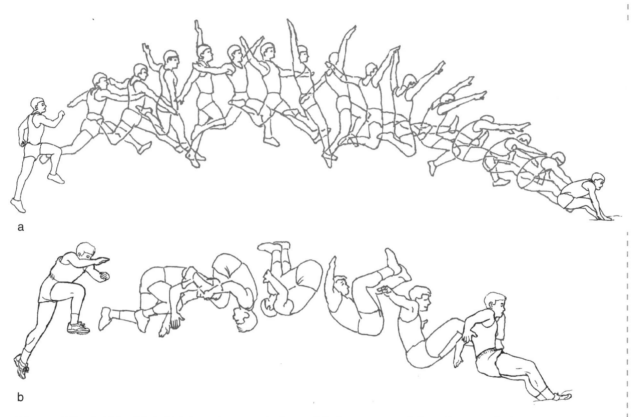

a

b

Figure 55 (a) The hitch kick long jump technique; (b) the somersault long jump technique.
Reprinted, by permission, from Kirk et al., 1999.

WORK, POWER AND ENERGY

The term 'work' is common in our ordinary language. In mechanics the term has a very specific meaning that is somewhat different from its normal use. Here, mechanical **work** is defined as the force applied to an object multiplied by the displacement through which the object is moved by the force, or Work = Force × Displacement.

This leads to some confusion for people used to more common meanings. For example, a person holding a very heavy box in their arms for a long time may get

Work is the force applied to an object multiplied by the displacement through which the object is moved by force.

very tired doing so, but in mechanical terms there is zero work being done because the object is not being moved. Even more confusing is the situation where the person lifts the box from the ground and then puts it down again in the same place. During the lifting phase, positive work is done on the box. However, during the lowering phase the work done is negative, and the total mechanical work done is still zero!

If we consider the lifting phase only, the force necessary to raise the load against gravity is equal to the mass of the load multiplied by the acceleration due to gravity. If we know the distance the load was lifted, then we can calculate the work done on the load as the force multiplied by the height the load was lifted. So, if a 30-kg load is lifted from the floor to a shelf at 1.5 m above the floor, approximating gravity as 10 m/s², the work done on the load by the lifter = Mass (30 kg) × Gravity (10 m/s²) × Displacement (1.5 m), or 450 N/m.

Power

In the same way that velocity is the rate of change of displacement, **power** is the rate of change of work. We can calculate the average power achieved by the lifter in the previous example if we know how long the person took to lift the load. If it was done very quickly, say in half a second, then the average rate of change of work was 450 N/m divided by 0.5 s, or 900 N/m/s. If the lift was done slowly, over a 2-s period, then the average power was 450 N/m divided by 2 s, or 225 N/m/s.

A similar calculation is used in simple measurements of power such as in the stair climbing test. In this situation the person being tested is instructed to climb a set of stairs as fast as possible. The total height of the stairs is known, and the time taken for the person to climb the stairs is measured as accurately as possible. The average power is then calculated as the work done (Mass of the person × Gravity × Height of the stairs) divided by time taken to climb the stairs.

> *Power is the rate of change of work during a given time interval, or the work done divided by the time interval.*

Over to You

Complete the stair climbing test. Use the procedure just described to calculate the average power.

Energy

To understand the usefulness of the concept of mechanical work, we need to also define **energy.** A fundamental law of physics is that energy is conserved. It is never created; nor is it destroyed. Energy can only be changed into different forms.

Energy comes in many forms. For the body to move, chemical energy stored in the body is converted to mechanical energy and thermal energy by the contractile elements within muscles. Where this energy comes from is the subject of another chapter. The muscles in turn transfer this energy into movement of the body and objects with which the body interacts. When transformed into movement the energy is called **kinetic energy.** The kinetic energy of a moving object depends on its mass, its linear velocity, its moment of inertia and its angular velocity.

Other forms that energy can take include gravitational potential energy, which an object possesses by virtue of its height above the ground, and elastic energy, such as when tendons or springs are stretched.

Considering the different forms of energy and especially how energy is transferred between different forms provides another way of understanding the movement of the body. A good example is the trampolinist. The trampolinist in figure 56 is flexing his knees and then jumping straight up with no rotation. The movement starts by

> *Energy is a dynamic quality that can never be destroyed. It can only be changed into different forms.*

> *Kinetic energy is energy inherent in movement.*

muscles turning chemical energy into kinetic energy as they cause angular rotations of the lower limbs. These angular rotations in turn cause the centre of mass of the body to have some linear velocity upwards as the trampolinist leaves the trampoline (time = t_1). If we define the height of the centre of mass of the trampolinist at this instant (h_1) as zero displacement, then all his energy at this instant is kinetic and equal to $1/2\, mv_1^2$, where v_1 is the velocity at the moment of leaving the trampoline and m is the mass of the trampolinist.

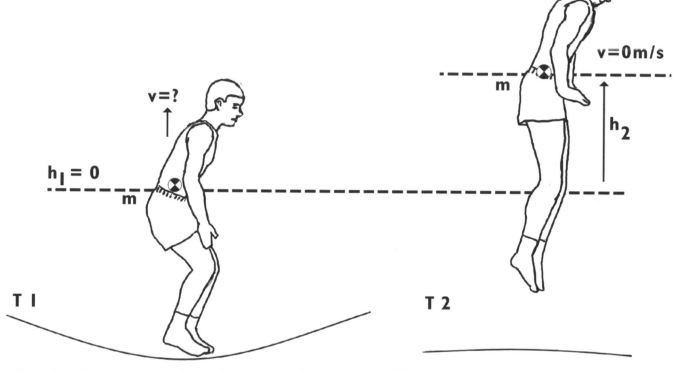

Figure 56   Energy $= 1/2\, mv_1^2 = mgh_2$. So $v_1^2 = 2gh_2$, then $v_1 = \sqrt{2gh_2}$. If $g = 10$ m/s^2 and $h^2 = 1$ m, then $v_1 = 4.5$ m/s.

As the trampolinist gains height he slows. His kinetic energy is reducing, but his potential energy due to gravity is increasing. When he reaches his maximum height (at time = t_2), his velocity is zero, all his energy is potential energy due to gravity and, if we ignore the effects of air resistance, equal to mgh_2, where h_2 is maximum height and g is acceleration due to gravity. All the kinetic energy possessed by the trampolinist at t_1 has now become potential energy due to gravity.

If we can measure the maximum height he reached, then we can work out what his initial velocity must have been. Regardless of the trampolinist's mass, the initial velocity is equal to the square root of two times gravitational acceleration times the maximum height of the trampolinist [$v_1 = v(2gh_2)$]. Assuming an approximate value of g of 10 m/s^2, if the trampolinist reached a maximum height of 1 m, then the initial velocity must have been the square root of 20, or approximately 4.5 m/s. With what velocity would he have to leave the trampoline to reach a height of 2 m?

The same logic may be used to discover that when the trampolinist again reaches zero height and gravitational potential energy is again zero, the velocity must be equal in magnitude but opposite in direction to the initial velocity.

What happens then? The trampolinist again slows as the springs holding the trampoline mat stretch and the jumper's height becomes negative. At the moment of lowest height, when the trampolinist is again stationary for an instant, all the energy he possessed is now stored as elastic potential energy within the springs of the trampoline, before being returned to the trampolinist as he jumps again.

The Relationship Between Work and Energy

Did you notice the similarity between the calculation of the work done by a person lifting a box and the change in gravitational potential energy of the trampolinist? Both were equal to mass times gravitational acceleration times the height through which the object moved. This is just one example of the equality between work done and changes in energy.

In the same way as the impulse of a force equals the change in momentum of the object, the mechanical work done by a force is equal to the change in energy.

The work–energy relationship provides another way of understanding the movement of the body and its interaction with the environment. For example, consider a cyclist struggling up a steep hill. The mechanical work done by the cyclist to reach the top of the hill is equal to the cyclist's mass times the acceleration due to gravity times the height of the hill. Because we know that work equals change in energy, then the mechanical work done to reach the top of the hill is equal to the additional gravitational potential energy gained in climbing the hill.

Where did this energy come from? Chemical energy stored in the body was converted into the necessary kinetic energy by muscles. However, energy was also needed to overcome friction within the bicycle, and the body also produces a lot of heat. If we were also able to measure, or estimate from heart rate, the oxygen consumed by the cyclist at the same time, we could also estimate the total amount of chemical energy needed to cycle up the hill. The ratio of mechanical work done to the total energy is a measure of the efficiency of the system.

FLUID MECHANICS

As the human body or an object propelled by the human body moves through air or water, the air or water exerts forces on the object. In some cases, such as shot putting or gymnastics, these forces are small and can be ignored. In other cases, such as discus, javelin, cricket fast bowling and golf, the forces are too large to be ignored and usually must be included in the analysis. In other cases, such as swimming, rowing and canoeing, these forces are the most important of all.

In general, we can divide the forces applied by air or water to an object passing through them into those that act in opposition to the direction of motion of the object, known as drag, and those that act at right angles, known as lift. Examples of **drag** forces include the frictional forces that act as a consequence of the contact between the object and the particles within the fluid. These forces always act to slow the movement of the object. In situations where these drag forces are significant, such as cycling, speed skating, swimming and rowing, considerable effort may be expended to try to reduce the magnitude of the drag in the form of helmet design and frame shape, full body costume, swimming costume material and boat hull design, respectively.

If the shape of an object passing through a fluid is asymmetrical in cross section perpendicular to the direction of movement or it is spinning, then **lift** forces act perpendicular to the direction of movement. If the object is asymmetrical, particles of the fluid on one side of the object travel further around the object in the same time and so have a higher velocity than particles on the other side. The increased velocity causes a decrease in pressure on that side, and the consequence is a lift force tending to cause a change in velocity towards the side of lower pressure.

As shown in figure 57, a discus is thrown so that the body of the discus travels at an angle relative to the direction of movement. Drag forces act to slow the discus,

Drag forces oppose the direction of motion of an object moving through a fluid.

Lift forces act at right angles to the direction of travel of an object moving through a fluid.

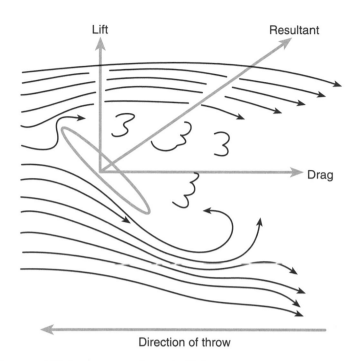

Figure 57 Drag and lift forces on a discus in flight.
Reprinted, by permission, from Carr, 1997.

but lift forces occur as a consequence of the asymmetrical cross section, and these forces prolong the duration of the flight by reducing the acceleration due to gravity.

A similar effect occurs with a spinning ball. On one side of the ball the spin opposes the direction of motion, increasing the fluid pressure on that side. The consequence is a lift force acting towards the side of lower pressure, illustrated in figure 58. The consequence of spin is to alter the trajectory of the ball.

In golf, the ball is usually hit with a large amount of backspin due to the backward angle of the club face. As figure 58 shows, the ball spins so that the bottom of the ball travels in the direction of flight. This causes higher air pressure on the bottom of the ball and a lift force to act in a direction that reduces the gravitational acceleration, prolonging the duration of the flight. As novice golfers quickly notice, it is also common for this spin to be not just backspin. If the club face is not exactly

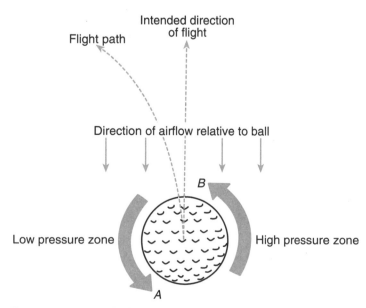

Figure 58 Effects of spin on a ball in flight.
Reprinted, by permission, from Hay, 1978.

perpendicular to direction of travel of the club at impact, then the spin will not be perfectly vertical. The consequence is that the lift force created acts to one side as well, causing the ball to curve sideways in flight. This is known as a hook or slice in the language of golf.

Over to You

Think about a ball sport such as tennis, table tennis, or volleyball. Topspin is commonly used. Provide a written explanation in about a paragraph of what forces act on the ball and what the advantage of topspin might be.

Lift forces are even more important in swimming. Until quite recently, we thought that propulsion in swimming was caused by drag forces produced as the hands moved backwards through the water. However, it seems likely that *lift* forces created by the hands moving sideways through the water are important, possibly more important than drag forces.

SUMMARY

Forces cause, or tend to cause, a change in velocity of an object. Torque is the turning effect of a force which tends to cause a change in angular velocity. The moment of inertia of a body is its resistance to changes in angular velocity. The magnitude of the change in linear and angular velocity is proportional to the magnitude of the force or torque and inversely proportional to the mass or moment of inertia, respectively. Equilibrium occurs if no resultant forces or torque act. In this case, linear and angular velocity remain constant. Linear and angular impulse is the product of the force or torque, respectively, and the time for which the force of torque acts. Linear momentum is the product of the velocity and the mass of a body, whereas angular momentum is the product of angular velocity and moment of inertia. In the absence of external forces, linear and angular momentum remain constant. When a force acts, the change in momentum that results is equal to the impulse applied. The mechanical work done by a force is the product of the force and the displacement through which the body travels in the direction of the force. Power is the rate of doing mechanical work. Energy is conserved but changes forms between chemical, mechanical, elastic and gravitation potential energy.

Test Yourself Questions

1. Summarise Newton's Laws of Inertia, Action–Reaction, and Acceleration.
2. How is the turning effect of a force calculated?
3. What conditions are necessary for a body to be in equilibrium? How do you know whether a body is in equilibrium?
4. Is the moment of inertia of a diver's body greater in a tucked or layout position? Why?
5. Define linear momentum and impulse. What is the relationship between them? How does the relationship help in understanding the different ways in which projectiles can be propelled by people?

6. Angular momentum is conserved in the absence of rotational forces. Describe the consequences of this for divers and gymnasts performing rotations in flight.

7. How is physical work defined? How much work is done to lift a 20-kg load from the ground to waist height and then lower it back to the same position? Explain your answer.

8. Describe the changes in the forms of energy which occur when a person performs a standing long jump.

9. What forces are produced when a spinning object moves through air? How does this explain what happens when a golfer 'slices' the ball?

PART 3
. . . .

Historical Dimensions of Reflective Performance in Physical Education

*I*n this section you will find six chapters about the history of physical education and sport development in Britain from the 1850s to the 1970s. In chapter 3.1 you can read about the earliest form of physical training in British schools for working class children based on Swedish gymnastics. Chapter 3.2 explores a contrasting example, based on games and sport, of the development of physical education in the schools serving the wealthy classes in British society. In chapter 3.3, you can read about the development of forms of physical education between the 1930s and 1960s that became closely associated with boys' education and girls' education and so contributed to the social construction of gender. Chapter 3.4 investigates the growth of a scientific approach to the study of physical education after the Second World War and how this approach influenced thinking about physical education. Chapter 3.5 shows how the government increasingly became involved in the provision of sport and recreation for the working classes and how they believed games could rescue working class youth from delinquency. In chapter 3.6, you can read about the development of sport-based physical education during the 1950s and 1960s, which is the form of physical education that currently dominates in British schools today.

Physical Training and the Health of Working Class Children, 1850–1933

Learning Outcomes

When you have studied this chapter, you should be able to

☑ describe Ling's system of gymnastics,

☑ list some early arguments for health-related physical training,

☑ summarise the debate on militarism or health as a focus for physical training,

☑ explain the impact of the 1909 and 1933 syllabuses on physical training, and

☑ analyse and describe how it might have felt to take part in physical training lessons during this period.

INTRODUCTION

For almost 100 years, from the mid-1800s until the 1930s, **physical training** in government elementary schools in Britain was aimed at improving the health of working class children. There were a number of systems of exercises in existence from the late 1700s. Each system competed for a place in the school curriculum. Eventually, in the early years of the twentieth century, the British government selected the Swedish system of formal, freestanding exercises developed by Per Henrick Ling.

The first professional physical educators in Britain, most of whom were middle class women trained in private colleges, also practised **Swedish gymnastics.** The female Swedish gymnasts championed the role of their system of gymnastics in promoting health. But, with the exception of the work of a few of their number as Inspectors and Advisers, their influence was limited to middle class girls' private schools. The Swedish gymnasts' objectives were also dramatically different from those of the elementary school teachers. In the girls' private schools, Swedish gymnastics aimed to develop elegance, poise and posture, and the sound physical functioning that was required to bear children.

In the elementary schools, the concerns were rather different, focusing instead on the role of physical activity in compensating for, and possibly remedying, inherited and acquired physical 'defects', as they were known at that time. There were other reasons for selecting Swedish gymnastics for working class children's physical training, too. Because of the formal teaching methods it employed, some people believed the Ling system taught discipline. There is evidence to suggest that teachers valued this system for precisely this reason. There was also an attempt around the end of the nineteenth century to use Swedish gymnastics for military purposes. But in official government policy it was health that formed the basis of physical training in elementary schools. Before examining the forces behind the development of this policy, we can take a brief look at what Swedish gymnastics involved.

LING'S SYSTEM OF GYMNASTICS

The British navy used the Ling system of gymnastics from the middle of the nineteenth century as the basis of its physical fitness programme, although Ling and his colleagues designed the system for health-related therapeutic purposes. The freestanding exercises were popular with institutions because large groups of people could perform them in small spaces. The exercises were based on systematic progressions of exercises that built on each other. The Swedish gymnasts claimed the progressions provided a general foundation for all-round, symmetrical physical development. The physical fitness, health and skill benefits provided a benevolent justification for the system. But Swedish gymnastics was attractive to education authorities because it also came with a formal pedagogy that required uniform activity from pupils and instant response to commands.

Swedish gymnastics lessons were set out in tables that dealt comprehensively with the major joints and muscle groups of the body. The tables were organised in a sequence that had to be followed to the letter, and arranged according to the age and experience of the pupils (table 3). The tables set out progressions, sequencing and age standards in minute detail.

Physical training was the term used between 1880 and 1950 to describe a form of physical education for working class children that comprised Swedish gymnastics and drill.

Swedish gymnastics was a system of freestanding exercises created by Per Henrick Ling in the late 1800s that sought to exercise the body systematically – sometimes referred to as 'callisthenics'.

Lessons were set out in a format that teachers had to adhere to strictly. There were eight categories of activities. Each lesson was constructed on the basis of a selection of exercises from each category. The categories were, in order of appearance in the lesson:

1. Introductory and breathing exercises
2. Trunk bending backward and forward
3. Arm bending and stretching
4. Balance exercises
5. Shoulder-blade exercises
6. Trunk turning and bending sideways
7. Marching, running, jumping, games, etc.
8. Breathing exercises

Teachers had to memorise the exact sequence of exercises for each lesson and deliver their instructions using such commands as 'head backwards — bend!', 'left foot sideways — place!', 'trunk forward and downward — stretch!' and 'knees — bend!'. As we can see from the example provided in table 4, these commands had a strong military flavour.

All pupils had to perform the exercises exactly as the teacher required. Also, the whole class had to perform the exercises together. The emphasis was on precision and complete obedience to the word of command.

Table 3 Training Program Based on Swedish Gymnastics

Series	Approximate age of the pupils	Years of work in physical exercises	TERM		
			First	Second	Third
A	7-8	First	1-4	5-8	9-12
	8-9	Second	13-16	17-20	21-24
B	9-10	Third	25-28	29-32	33-36
	10-11	Fourth	37-40	41-44	45-48
C	11-12	Fifth	49-52	53-56	57-60
	12-14	Sixth	61-64	65-68	69-72

Table 4 Example of the Beginning of a Lesson

1. Free running in large circle. Instant halt on signal.

   Double — march! Class — halt!

   Run to form one rank at wall; place leaders on marks; run to open ranks.

   Back to the wall — move! Leaders on markers — move! To your places — move!

2. (Astride) Trunk bending downward to grasp ankles.

   (With a jump, feet astride — place!) Grasping both ankles — down! Class — up! and etc.

   (With a jump, feet together — place!)

Over to You

Carry out some research on Swedish gymnastics and teach part of a physical training lesson to a small group of peers. Write down a description of what it felt like to teach the lesson. Write down a description of what it felt like to be a pupil in the lesson. With others in your group, make a list of some of the physiological and skill benefits of Swedish gymnastics.

It is easy to see why some teachers, education policy makers and politicians thought that the Ling system should be used to develop military discipline. But it was early arguments for health-related physical training that were most prominent from the 1850s to the beginning of compulsory universal elementary schooling in 1878.

EARLY ARGUMENTS FOR HEALTH-RELATED PHYSICAL TRAINING, 1850–1876

Concerns over the health and physical wellbeing of working class children arose out of a number of interconnected events from the middle to the end of the nineteenth century. As the factory system became more widespread by the 1850s and the cities began to grow at an accelerating rate, philanthropists directed considerable attention to the living conditions of the working classes and the effects of these conditions on their health. A number of surveys of slum dwellers revealed the extent of deprivation and squalor at the heart of Britain's great manufacturing cities. These surveys made a big impact on the middle classes in particular. During the second half of the nineteenth century, the middle and upper classes increasingly accepted the view that the physical condition of the British working classes was deteriorating.

The mid-nineteenth century also marked a new phase of imperial expansion in order to protect Britain's overseas trading interests. This expansion required a regular supply of fit manpower to fill the ranks of the army and navy. So the matter of **physical deterioration** was a cause for grave concern to capitalists and other members of the merchant classes.

By 1880, the effects of compulsory schooling itself, with pupils having to spend up to eight hours a day in a classroom, revealed that some working class children were not fit enough to benefit from instruction. So the focus in the late 1800s was on the notion of national efficiency and on the question of whether physical training should be made compulsory in government elementary schools.

Physical deterioration was a concern of the middle and upper classes in late nineteenth-century Britain, who believed that the British people were becoming physically inferior because of poor housing, factory work and malnutrition.

The Work of William Jolly, HMI

William Jolly, appointed to Her Majesty's Inspectorate in 1868, was a strong supporter of physical training. His various speeches and reports reflected the range of arguments for the inclusion of physical training in the elementary school curriculum that echoed the concerns just outlined. In a paper read to the British Association in Glasgow in 1876, he advocated a national system of 'rational physical education' as the basis for improving the health of school children.

> Systematic Physical Education should, beyond doubt, be carried on in all our schools, and, if any national improvement in health and physique among the masses of our people is to be effected, it can be achieved only by systematic physical culture in our Common schools. (Jolly, 1876, p. 19)

Jolly had been much impressed by the 'scientific physical education' of Archibald McLaren at Oxford, the writings of Dr Mathias Roth and the expanding literature on physical education and health from the United States. He used this information to identify four pressing problems that rational physical education could overcome: 'deteriorated physique'; 'organic defects'; diseases of the eyes, nose, throat, chest and spine; and 'misery and death' because of 'ignorance of the commonest laws of health'. He alleged:

> These formidable evils are largely produced by our present defects and errors in school buildings, furniture, and practice, and by the neglect of physical training in our schools. (Jolly, 1876, p. 20)

Jolly made three recommendations to remedy this neglect:

1. That grants be offered to schools for teaching physical training (under the system of payment-by-results)
2. That hygiene or 'the principles of health' be included as a specific subject and made compulsory
3. That physical education be made a compulsory part of teacher training

In putting his case, he was clearly aware that a broad range of people had an interest in physical education.

> With such evils to be cured and such advantages to national health and education to be gained by its means, surely it becomes not only our profit but our duty to do all we can to secure [physical training]. Ambition itself prompts us to efforts to prevent our being ignobly beaten by other nations in a matter of national advantage. Self-interest of the most utilitarian kind should urge its adoption, for any improvement in the health and strength of our people will raise the working power and skill of the artisan, and increase the value of his labour. Our Government should foster it, if only on the grounds of national defence, for it would furnish better recruits, and improve the national courage and endurance by its Spartan training. Our teachers and School Managers should encourage it, for if it did nothing more, it would improve discipline by its vigour-giving, cloud-dispelling effects, raise the mental work done, and increase even monetary results. (Jolly, 1876, p. 21)

Jolly's comments reveal the battleground that physical education was already becoming as a range of interest groups pursued their own advantage through the establishment of a form of physical training in the state elementary schools. It is also significant to note that, apart from staving off 'misery and death' for working class children, there was little suggestion in Jolly's arguments that health might be something of value to the working classes for their own wellbeing, rather than some one else's.

MILITARISM OR HEALTH, 1895–1908

From 1880, the start of compulsory elementary schooling, until 1895, the effects of the school itself on children's health had become an important topic of debate. The concern was that **'over-pressure'**, brought on by the rigours of school work, was a major cause of physical deterioration among poorer children. The fact that schooling badly affected some children's health or, more precisely, that some children were not fit enough to cope with schooling in the first place was readily conceded by all sides in the debate. The two main points at issue were how many children were actually affected and how the problem could be remedied.

Some saw the introduction of school meals as the key to improving attendance and performance at school. Others, such as Jolly, argued for exercise as a means of improving health. This latter claim was countered by the suggestion that, if children were in poor health in the first place, physical exercise would simply be another form of over-pressure.

Over-pressure was a term used in the late nineteenth century to refer to stressful situations experienced by children in schools.

Historian Ian Thomson has suggested that the argument was partially resolved in 1895 when the school codes in England and Scotland were altered to recognise physical training as eligible for a grant, a point recommended by Jolly years earlier. So schools were to be offered a financial incentive to provide physical training.

The next question to be resolved was what form physical training should take. Thomson suggests that the deciding factor in the government choosing to give grants to schools for physical training was to combat the poor discipline rather than promote health.

A number of shocking defeats for the British army in South Africa during the Boer War brought to a head the question of what form physical training should take. Sir Henry Craik, Secretary of the Scottish Education Department, was one of the major supporters of military drill. Craik used the full range of the powers of his office in his attempt to establish military drill in Scottish schools. A Royal Commission on Physical Training was appointed in 1902 'to inquire into the opportunities for physical training now available in state-aided schools and other educational institutions'. Craik intended to use the Royal Commission as a means of furthering his ambitions for military training in schools. In the event, he failed to achieve his goals.

The Commissioners were very impressed by the determination of teachers and headmasters to resist military drill. The larger school boards in Scotland simply ignored the important Circular 279, issued by the Scottish Education Board in 1900, that threatened to reduce school grants if they did not meet approved standards in teaching military drill. The Commissioners also accepted, after much consideration and a survey of the health of school children conducted by two Scottish medical researchers, Dr MacKenzie and Professor Hay, the contentious idea that exercise could not cure disease but, properly conducted, could have a beneficial effect on minor defects and deformities. The Commissioners also accepted that the wrong kind of exercise or exercise for undernourished children could have a detrimental effect.

> Militarism was the belief in the value of military action to solve economic and political problems.

Over to You

Discuss with a partner and then list how the wrong kind of exercise might affect undernourished children? Drawing on your knowledge of Swedish gymnastics, functional anatomy and physiology, list some reasons why MacKenzie and Hay may have believed properly conducted drill could have a beneficial health effect on children's minor physical disabilities.

The main impact of the Commission's recommendations was to encourage the government to empower the school boards to introduce regular and systematic medical inspections and school meals. In the process, the case for military drill had been thoroughly defeated. In February 1905, Lord Balfour, the Secretary of State for Scotland, commented: 'I am prepared to advocate ordinary physical drill as part of the general curriculum of education; I am not prepared to advocate to the same extent anything which seems to train the military side of human nature'.

So it was a health rationale that informed the selection of Swedish gymnastics as the form of physical training to be offered to government elementary schools in the early 1900s. Physical training was to be used to ensure the health of working class school children. It was regarded as a therapy that could be applied under medical supervision to improve minor physical 'defects' and deformities.

This doesn't deny that, in practice, physical training may have been used or viewed by school headmasters and teachers as a means of controlling and disciplining large numbers of children. Nor does it deny that governments might have believed there was still some military advantage to be gained from physical training. However, the official policy informing physical training in schools was concerned with health and defined in medical terms.

THE BOARD OF EDUCATION SYLLABUSES, 1909–1933

The medical definition of physical education was confirmed in 1908 through the establishment of the School Medical Service within the Board of Education, with Dr George Newman (later Sir George) as its Chief Medical Officer. Newman was a strong advocate of physical education, overseeing the publication of three Board of Education syllabuses between 1909 and 1933. However, he always believed that the real work in maintaining the health of school children was through medicine.

At first, the School Medical Service merely inspected children, but by 1912 the Board made available grants for treatment as well as inspection. By the end of the First World War, inspections had been extended from elementary to all State-aided schools. In tune with these developments, student teachers in training had to know 'the main principles of healthy living' and ensure the maintenance of 'hygienic conditions in every part of school work'.

The role of physical education as an arm of the School Medical Service altered little between the two world wars. Consecutive syllabuses issued by the Board of Education did reflect a broadening view of physical education subject matter. But the practical circumstances of government schools, lacking specialist teachers, facilities, equipment and playing fields, meant that there was little challenge to this role.

The 1933 Syllabus, the last to be published under Newman's direction, revealed the extent to which the health and medical rationale for physical training, which first emerged in Jolly's work in the 1870s, had been carried forward into the 1930s with only minor and relatively superficial alteration. According to the author of the Syllabus 'the ultimate test by which every system of physical training should be judged [is] to be found in the posture and general carriage of the children'.

Sir George Newman, in his Prefatory Memorandum to the Syllabus, confirmed that medical matters were the leading concerns in the use of physical education. Although he acknowledged that 'suitable nourishment, effective medical inspection and treatment, and hygienic surroundings' were essential to good health, 'a comprehensive system of physical training . . . is indispensable as much for the normal healthy development of the body as for the correction of inherent or acquired defects'.

Newman also carried forward in his preface the nineteenth-century preoccupation with physical deterioration among the working classes. He remarked that 'the Board wish to record their conviction that the development of good physique is a matter of national importance, vital to the welfare and even the survival of the race'. Conditioned by the events of the Depression years of the 1930s, Newman repeated the upper class philanthropists' views of the late nineteenth century on what was good for the working classes.

> In exceptional conditions of unemployment, poverty, or economic distress it is particularly necessary to safeguard mental and physical health by means of wisely directed physical education of the body, which will lay the foundations of wholesome out-of-door recreation as well as protect normal growth, health and strength. (Newman, 1933, p. 6)

> The conditions of modern civilization with its crowded locations, confined spaces, and sedentary occupations; the increasing need for study and mental application; and the many social circumstances and difficulties which restrict opportunities for natural physical growth, all require that children and young people should

receive physical training by well-considered methods devised in a broad catholic spirit to promote and encourage the health and development of the mind and the body. (Newman, 1933, p. 9)

Neither of these statements would have been out of place 30 or even 50 years earlier. Their presence suggests that the upper and middle classes' views of the health needs of the working classes had changed little in this time. The 1933 Syllabus did include an expanded version of physical education, adding games, swimming and dancing to Swedish gymnastics. But these additions did little to change the medico-health definition in which working class physical training was firmly set.

In this respect, the 1933 Syllabus was not a blueprint for the future of physical education but a backward-looking confirmation of the past, with its roots deeply embedded in the attitudes of the late 1800s. Four years after the publication of the 1933 Syllabus, in 1937, the Physical Training and Recreation Bill was enacted. This Bill confirmed that formal, mass physical exercises had come to be closely associated, in the words of historian Peter MacIntosh, 'with the playgrounds of the Board Schools, elementary schools and the military training of "other ranks"'. This positioning of physical education within a medical and health framework marked it as the curriculum for the working classes. As you can read in chapter 3.2, this was all to change after the Second World War as competitive team games were promoted within government secondary schools.

SUMMARY

This chapter investigates the development of physical training in government elementary schools between 1850 and 1933. From the early 1900s, physical training took the form of Swedish gymnastics. The government selected this version of gymnastics because it involved exercises aimed at improving the health of working class children. However, it is noted that there were other interests in physical training through this period, including a powerful lobby for compulsory military training in schools. Teachers also used physical training to discipline children. Regardless of these other uses of physical training, the health rationale was dominant until the 1930s.

Test Yourself Questions ▓ ▓ ▓ ▓ ▓ ▓ ▓ ▓ ▓ ▓ ▓

1. Why did some teachers in the late 1800s to early 1900s see Ling's system of gymnastics as a favourable form of physical training for working class children in elementary schools?

2. William Jolly (HMI) identified four pressing problems that rational physical education could overcome. Name the four problems and explain how Jolly believed these could be overcome.

3. Why was military style drill rejected? State the benefits that the Royal Commission believed ordinary physical drill would have on working class children.

4. What were the arguments for and against physical training to promote health?

5. Explain why there was little change in the content and rationale of physical education between the two world wars.

6. Contrast the ways in which the provisions of the 1933 Syllabus were different from those contained in previous syllabuses.

7. Why did the positioning of physical education within a medical and health framework mark it as the curriculum for the working classes?

The Rise of the Games Ethic in Schools, 1850–1950

Learning Outcomes

When you have studied this chapter, you should be able to

☑ define the games ethic,

☑ explain the process of social emulation and distancing and its significance among the middle and upper classes,

☑ summarise the development of games in government schools up to the 1940s,

☑ explain how the games ethic began to be associated with national as well as class identity, and

☑ describe the development of games playing in the public schools after the First World War.

INTRODUCTION

Team games occupied a central role in the education of boys of the wealthy middle classes from the mid-1800s. Later, schools serving middle class girls and boys from other, less wealthy members of the middle classes took up this practice. Participating in and spectating at competitive sports contests was a popular leisure-time pursuit across the social class spectrum in Britain. However, as chapter 3.1 reveals, games and sports did not form a substantial or significant part of physical education in government schools serving the working classes until the late 1940s.

By the end of the nineteenth century, powerful men from the upper middle classes strongly supported the idea that unique educational qualities could be gained from playing games. Games such as cricket and football had come to embody and symbolise their cherished ideals — virility, vigour, competitiveness, individualism and fair play. Part of the success of competitive team games among the middle classes was their symbolic value as a mark of social superiority. In a hierarchical society, games allowed the socially aspiring simultaneously to emulate their social superiors and distance themselves from their inferiors.

This chapter investigates the emergence and development of the public school games ethic. It briefly traces the roots of the public school games ethic and outlines the social and political conditions of its origin and development in the schools of the middle classes. It then describes the wider dissemination of the games ethic to private schools for girls and then to lower middle and working class society.

THE EVOLUTION OF THE GAMES ETHIC, 1850s TO THE EARLY 1900s

The cult of athleticism celebrated sporting prowess excessively.

The games ethic refers to a belief that the distinguishing qualities of an English gentleman, such as courage, loyalty and so on, could be developed through playing competitive team games.

The '**cult of athleticism**' and the '**games ethic**' were born in the public schools of the male middle classes in Victorian Britain. They were part of a powerful educational ideology that, over a century, was to become influential well beyond the boundaries of space, time and social class. Within the public schools themselves, team games and sports such as football, rowing, cricket, racquets and fives rose to prominence from 1850 to reach a peak around 1914.

As it developed during this period, the cult of athleticism was very much in tune with the needs of its creators. The civil and political unrest that had marked the first three decades of the nineteenth century gave way to a new prosperity and significant changes in the social structure along with developments in industrial capitalism. It was at this time, towards the mid-1850s, that a new, many-layered and diversely constituted class emerged, formed in part by an 'industrial aristocracy', a new middle class of managers and other professionals, and a range of other occupational groups centred on manufacturing. Together, these groups formed the middle classes. During this period, the English public school was resurrected from a less-than-illustrious past, and the cult of athleticism and games playing were at the centre of its reformation.

The merchant classes had been continuously invading and replenishing the English aristocracy from the sixteenth century. However, by the middle of the nineteenth century, industrial capitalism brought profound changes to the structure of society, including massive shifts in population from rural to urban areas, the development of the factory system and the creation of wealth. The new, powerful upper levels of the middle class that emerged from this upheaval set about consolidating their places in the social hierarchy at levels which reflected members' material wealth. The reformed public school was one of the institutions invented to fulfil this project, and the cult of athleticism was central to its success. Games satisfied a demand for leisure complementary to work. They also provided a way of disciplining the male youth of the middle classes to take their place in the social order and produced a sense of class identity and cohesion.

The ethos surrounding games playing came to symbolise the central values of the aspiring middle classes and later came to be seen by them as a way of uniting an increasingly divided nation. The games ethic came to express, according to historians John Hargreaves and J.A. Mangan, 'the quintessential **bourgeois** English qualities that were felt to make the English superior to foreigners' (Hargreaves, 1986, p. 75), involving a 'subscription to the belief that important expressive and instrumental qualities can be promoted through team games (in particular, loyalty, self-control, perseverance, fairness and courage, both moral and physical)' (Mangan, 1983, p. 315). At its height, games playing spawned a clutch of cliches such as 'play the game' and 'it's not cricket' which were later to become bywords of 'the British way'.

> Bourgeois is a word of French origin used in some forms of sociology to describe the emerging middle classes.

Over to You

With a partner, discuss experiences you have had as a performer when you have felt loyalty, self-control, perseverance and courage. Were you aware of these feelings being demonstrated by your team-mates and opponents? Write a summary of your discussion. Then write a brief note on the extent to which you think these qualities are characteristic of British citizens. Write down whether you think the British hold these qualities in high regard.

THE GAMES ETHIC IN THE EDUCATION OF MIDDLE CLASS GIRLS, 1880s AND 1890s

The games ethic infused the physical education of girls' schools in much the same way as it had done for boys, although the activities played were different and the same excesses did not always apply. Games such as netball and lacrosse were introduced into girls' schools by the 1880s and 1890s. These games emphasised the cooperative and therapeutic aspects of play rather than the physically vigorous and competitive character of the male games.

In the wider society, sport was challenging notions of the delicate female constitution and other practices concerning clothing and display of the body. However, games playing in the girls' schools remained focused on patriarchal notions of womanhood and motherhood. Women were not expected to become leaders in politics, the military or business, and so the characteristics and values that marked the male games ethic were seen to be unnecessary for females. And whereas women's participation in sport led to greater freedoms for some, old ideas nevertheless died hard.

Over to You

Discuss in a small group the following statement by Miss Conroy, a high school headmistress in 1922. Decide whether you agree with her statement. Then as a group, draft a one-page justification of your collective view, noting any significant differences of opinion.

Eighty per cent of gymnastics teachers [have] breakdowns . . . playing strenuous games develop[s] a flat figure with underdeveloped breasts . . . athletic women suffer from nerves, heart trouble, rheumatism, suppressed menstruation and displacements . . . they decry marriage . . . their confinements [are] always difficult . . . their children [are] often inferior, and . . . most athletic women seem to have stifled what is finest in women — love, sympathy, tact and intuitive understanding. (Adapted from: Miss Conroy, a High School Headmistress, published in *The Lancet* in 1922 — in McIntosh, 1952, p. 189)

Beliefs such as these were pervasive in British society at this time. They were enough to make games playing less popular among girls than boys. In addition, as you can read in chapter 3.1, the presence of trained women physical educators in the girls' schools meant that games playing was secondary to Swedish gymnastics.

THE GAMES ETHIC, SOCIAL EMULATION AND DISTANCING, 1890s TO THE 1930s

The cult of athleticism began to be imitated by other social groups in the lower sections of the middle classes. By the 1870s, excellence in games had become both a mark of the distinctiveness of public school education and a measure of the school's quality. The public schools were the training grounds of the upper middle classes for leadership in all of the major political, economic, military and legislative institutions in society. Games were considered by many of their advocates to be the ultimate testing ground of the qualities for a member of the ruling classes.

Before long, in the first decade of the twentieth century, games became a prominent feature in the schools serving members of the aspiring middle classes who existed outside the industrial aristocracy. Historian J.A. Mangan has argued that the grammar schools of the Victorian and Edwardian eras evolved with concerns for social status and prestige uppermost, and they therefore modelled themselves on their social superiors, the public schools. They also sought to simultaneously distance themselves from their social inferiors, and games played a key role in this process.

A grammar school education was an important means by which the aspiring middle classes could emulate their upper middle class 'superiors' and distance themselves from their lower middle class and working class 'inferiors'. In an accurate reflection of public school priorities, games and games fields were the expensive symbols of emulation, distancing, ambition and success. Mangan's historical research shows clearly that where schools rose in status and were successful — according to such criteria as admission of its headmaster to the Headmasters' Conference — they invariably included organised games, interhouse sports competitions, sports days and the awarding of school colours as central features of their curricula. Where schools were less successful, Mangan claims that lack of organised games almost always played a key role in their demise. So pervasive was the games ethic throughout the private schools system that, by the early twentieth century, games were 'no longer attractive, valuable adjuncts of the system; they were sine qua non of institutional existence' (Mangan, 1983, p. 336).

Over to You

You have read how public schools sought to market themselves through the games they played and the facilities available to them. As a class, discuss whether schools today do this. How does your school compare with other schools who use sport to attract students? Then write a paragraph summarising the main points of the discussion.

Mangan proposed three reasons for the widespread acceptance of games and the games ethic in both public and grammar schools between the 1890s and the 1930s.

1. Supporters believed games were an instrument of social control within the schools. They saw games as effective and practical instruments for creating enthusiasm, fostering team spirit and letting off steam.

2. Games provided private schools for the upwardly mobile with a visible and highly dynamic medium for the development of 'Englishness', of 'fair play' and 'the British way' that was unmatched by other curriculum activities.

3. The resources and facilities required to play games such as playing fields were prominent symbols of superiority.

The use of games in a process of emulation and distancing reveals the hierarchical nature of British society during the Victorian and Edwardian eras. It also reveals something of the dynamic nature of this hierarchy. Games playing and the schools themselves were a necessary means of obtaining the cultural credentials for entry into the upper echelons of society. The spilling of the games ethic over into the schools at the lower levels of the middle classes can be seen as a development of the original function of the games ethic in the public schools themselves. The consolidation of this ethic in the grammar schools, many of which achieved the status of 'public school' during the Victorian and Edwardian period, did much to perpetuate its key values in a living form within the upper level of the middle classes.

GAMES PLAYING IN GOVERNMENT SCHOOLS, EARLY 1900s TO THE 1940s

As early as 1906, the Board of Education introduced into government policy a version of physical education incorporating games. These regulations suggested that provision be made, in principle, for government school pupils to play sports and field games as part of their physical education. In practice, few working class children experienced competitive team games such as football, cricket, netball and hockey until much later.

A key reason for practice failing to match principle was a lack of playing fields and other specialist facilities in government schools. In addition, games playing did not fit easily into the health and medical rationale for physical training that was described in chapter 3.1.

Nevertheless, syllabuses produced by the Board of Education in 1919 and 1933 continued to develop the principle that government school children should play games in addition to participating in Swedish gymnastics. A number of factors helped this emergent view along.

1. The Fisher Education Act of 1918 had instructed local education authorities to provide playing fields for sport. The establishment in 1925 of the National Playing Fields Association added further emphasis to this requirement.

2. The extension of the school leaving age to 14 in the 1920s led teachers and policy makers to realise that young adolescents required activities that supplemented Swedish gymnastics.

3. The 1933 Syllabus represented a marked expansion in the kind of programme that could, potentially, be offered to the government school pupil. The 1933 Syllabus devoted an entire chapter to 'The Organisation and Coaching of Games' and recognised 'the value of Organised Games, as an adjunct to physical training in promoting health, moulding the character and developing team spirit in general'.

THE GAMES ETHIC, CLASS IDENTITY AND NATIONAL IDENTITY IN THE 1920s

The practical difficulties in providing the facilities for games playing in the elementary and post-elementary schools were not merely administrative or economic problems. Given the function of competitive games and sports in developing middle class identity, there was resistance to the lower middle and working classes gaining entry to particular sports. Many sports associations and clubs erected substantial barriers in the late 1800s to exclude them. A major barrier was the requirement of sports such as rugby union and athletics that players must be amateurs. Most of these amateur players were wealthy enough not to have to work for a living, and so were able to play for nothing. This ruling effectively excluded even the most talented of working-class men.

Running contrary to this exclusionary policy, there was a widespread belief among the middle classes during the last decade of the Victorian era that competitive games and sports could transcend class divisions and conflicts. However, the pressures for the development of class identity were the stronger in this period. It is not until the 1920s that this version of the games ethic became more prominent in the public sphere. An example of this is Peter McIntosh's description of a scheme aimed at overcoming class antagonism during the Depression years of the 1920s.

> Games were encouraged not only for their physical and moral value but as instruments of social policy in the hope that they would break down class barriers and mitigate the bitterness of industrial strife. . . . The most notable attempt to achieve this was the Duke of York's camp started in 1921 and held annually; 400 boys were invited, 200 boys from public schools and 200 working in industry. The common denominator was found in games. (McIntosh, 1952, p. 199)

Over to You

Write down a list of skills and values that the boys mentioned in this statement might have learned from each other. Now compare your list with the lists of several of your classmates. Discuss any similarities and differences. Then write a note of about half a page summarising the main points of your discussion.

The preceding McIntosh quote illustrates a shift in the use of games as a key aspect of middle class identity in the late nineteenth century to an aspect of national culture common to people from all social classes by the 1920s. Even when the hierarchical structure of games and sports are themselves taken into account, organised around the pivotal amateur/professional distinction, this notion represents a clear departure from the use of games as a medium for demonstrating class superiority. At the same time, we need to be aware of the political function of this transformation. The rhetoric of a national culture is consciously and deliberately conciliatory and unitary, an essential and desirable ideology during a period of class conflict and political unrest such as the Depression years of the 1920s.

Despite this shift in rhetoric, the practical reality for lower middle and working class children remained. They were unlikely in large numbers to have been playing games such as rugby union, cricket, athletics, rowing and netball because there were insufficient facilities. The gap between the rhetoric of games as a common denominator and the reality of lack of provision for the working classes was to remain an enduring problem up to and beyond the 1950s.

GAMES IN THE PUBLIC SCHOOLS, 1920–1940

After the First World War, the cult of athleticism began a long and gradual decline in influence within the male public schools. It was attacked on many sides by those critics from within who felt the value placed on games to be excessive and by pressures that affected the public school system as a whole — such as new political values and declining national prosperity. Nevertheless, such was the strength of the idealism it had generated, the games ethic continued between the wars to exert a powerful influence within private schools. For instance, describing the attitudes of Birmingham University students to physical activity in the 1940s, David Munrow remarked:

> Not only did the public schoolboys bring with them the games of their school days, but they brought also the climate of opinion and the traditions of behaviour in which these games were played. Briefly these were a tacit acceptance that some sort of exercise was good for you, but that it did not matter much what it was, that the moral effects of playing were more important than the physical, and that winning was pleasant but by no means essential. There was also a sturdy tradition of complete independence and self-government in the administration of the games by the students and undergraduates themselves. As a corollary there was relatively little interest in rules — provided somebody was in charge — even less in technique and, although physical virtuosity was admired (sometimes excessively), it was still a 'good thing' to play games, even for rabbits. . . . For many [students] it provided some opportunity for strenuous activity and a habit of mind which accepted games playing as a natural feature of youth and manhood. (Munrow, 1958, p. 2)

The mythology and symbolism associated with the games ethic as an educational ideology continued to infiltrate the policies of social reform and the education of the working classes, between the beginning of the decline of the cult of athleticism in the public schools and the advent of universal secondary education, a period of approximately 30 years. This is in some respects entirely unsurprising, as many of the policy makers were beneficiaries of a public school education and, whether they themselves were athletes or 'rabbits', by the 1950s the 100-year-old tradition of athleticism would have made its mark on them.

SUMMARY

This chapter traces the development of games playing and the games ethic in schools from the 1850s to the 1950s. In the second half of the nineteenth century, the major team games such as cricket and football were invented in the public schools serving England's male social elite. The ethos that developed around games became such a powerful symbol of social superiority in the hierarchical order of British society that games in the curriculum became essential to the prospects of aspiring grammar schools to move to a higher level of social status. The games ethic also spilled over into schools for girls, though it was not practised there with the same intensity. Although there were supporters of games for government school children from the early 1900s, this principle was not realised before the 1950s because of lack of facilities and the Swedish gymnastics form of physical training, whose health-related rationale could not accommodate games. Following the First World War, the games ethic lost some of its influence in the public and grammar schools. However, during the period between the wars, there began to emerge a shift in the games ethic, from its symbolic role representing class identity to national identity.

Test Yourself Questions

1. List four key characteristics of the games ethic.

2. Compare and contrast the games ethic as it applied in schools for boys and schools for girls.

3. Explain how the middle and upper classes used games as part of a process of social emulation and distancing.

4. List and describe three factors that encouraged the view that working class children should play games in school.

5. 'Games were encouraged not only for their physical and moral value but as instruments of social policy in the hope that they would break down class barriers and mitigate the bitterness of industrial strife' (P.C. McIntosh, historian). Discuss this statement.

CHAPTER 3.3

Gendered Physical Education, 1930–1960

Learning Outcomes

When you have studied this chapter, you should be able to

☑ identify the three versions of gymnastics and list their key features,

☑ summarise the key factors in the demise of Swedish gymnastics,

☑ summarise the key factors in the emergence of educational gymnastics,

☑ list the ways in which the male view of gymnastics is different from the female view,

☑ summarise the key points of the debate between females and males over skill competition,

☑ explain how and why physical education is gendered, and

☑ speculate on the significance of these events for your experience of physical education today.

INTRODUCTION

At the end of the Second World War, gymnastics formed the basis of school physical education programmes. However, before the introduction of universal secondary education through the 1944 Education Act (in England and Wales), there had been a growing feeling among sections of the physical education profession that physical education was broader than gymnastics. The 1933 Syllabus of Physical Training for Schools reflected this view with its inclusion of games, swimming and athletics.

The circumstances after the war were markedly different from those in which the 1933 Syllabus was written, as it had been prepared with mainly elementary school pupils in mind. The new secondary schools catered to older children. The problem for the profession was the extent to which gymnastics was likely to be able to hold the interest of these older pupils. The more mature physique of the adolescent created new possibilities for the kinds of activities — some demanding strength and speed — that could be offered.

With the arrival of universal secondary education, the demand for teachers grew, and, after 1945, men began to enter the physical education profession in large numbers for the first time. Until that time, from the 1890s until the 1940s, the physical education profession consisted mainly of women. Very soon, battle lines were drawn over which form of gymnastics should be taught in schools, and the two sides in the contest were distinguished almost entirely on the basis of sex. The women preferred the new, progressive educational gymnastics. The men preferred a form of gymnastics linked to skill acquisition and games.

What was significant about the debate that ensued over the next decade and a half was not so much the issue of what form of gymnastics should be taught but, rather, how physical education more generally should be defined. This definition depended, as one commentator at the time put it, 'on the sex of the individual'. This chapter shows how **gender** largely determined the type of physical education received in schools.

THREE VERSIONS OF GYMNASTICS, 1930–1945

By the end of the Second World War, three distinct versions of gymnastics were competing for teaching time in school physical education.

Swedish Gymnastics

Swedish gymnastics (or Ling gymnastics) had been the hallmark of the professional female physical educator between the late 1890s and 1940s. It was the version of physical education officially approved by the then Board of Education for use in its elementary schools. You can read more about the Swedish system in chapter 3.1.

In the 1880s, the Swedish system was promoted in Britain through the work of gymnasts appointed by the Board of Education to organise physical education in its elementary schools. One of these organisers was Madam Bergman-Osterberg, who in 1885 formed her own college of physical training for women. Swedish gymnastics formed the foundation of the women's professional training, which was supplemented by massage, remedial exercises and games. Its main focus was the physical and physiological effects of exercise on the body.

Olympic, or German, Gymnastics

A second form of gymnastics, which was witnessed in its modern form for the first time by British physical educators at the 1948 London Olympic Games, was German,

---

Gendered refers to the association of a form of physical activity with femininity or masculinity.

Swedish gymnastics was a system of freestanding exercises created by Per Henrick Ling in the late 1800s that sought to exercise the body systematically — sometimes referred to as 'callisthenics'.

or Olympic, gymnastics, now known as artistic gymnastics. **German gymnastics** had been around at least as long as Ling's system and involved work on apparatus such as the rings, parallel bars and pommel horse. At the beginning of the twentieth century it had vied with the Swedish system for selection as the official system of physical training by the Interdepartmental Committee set up by the Royal Commission on Physical Training (1903) to produce a Syllabus of Physical Exercises for British schools.

It lost that contest and, because of its German origins, after the First World War all but a handful of enthusiasts in Britain neglected it until the 1940s. It received a boost from the 1948 Olympics, however, which presented gymnastics as a competitive sport made up of the six activities of floor work, vaulting, rings, bars, beam and pommel horse. After the Olympics, there was an increasing level of interest in this version of gymnastics with a growing number of calls for its inclusion in schools from the early 1950s.

Educational Gymnastics

Educational gymnastics made a rapid and dramatic impact on women's physical education from the first appearance of Rudolf Laban's ideas on movement and dance in Britain in the 1930s. Modern dance was built on a radical critique of 'unnatural' movement patterns in industrial society that had, in Laban's opinion, much to do with the presence of mental illness and other personality disorders. Laban's philosophy argued for the release of dangerously pent up and inhibited energies through free, spontaneous movement.

Although Laban's main concerns were focused on the theatre and industry, female physical educators very quickly applied his ideas to gymnastics during the late 1930s and throughout the war years. Educational gymnastics borrowed from modern dance a concern for the qualitative dimensions of movement experience and selectively adopted some of the ideas of child-centred teaching.

German gymnastics, or *Turnen,* involved work on apparatus and became the basis for what is now known as artistic gymnastics.

Educational gymnastics was influenced by the work of Rudolf Laban and involved free-flowing movement that drew on children's creativity and emotional expression.

Educational gymnastics encouraged an experience of free and spontaneous movement.

THE DEMISE OF SWEDISH GYMNASTICS, 1940–1950

The Swedish gymnasts' fall from grace began in the 1930s, at a time when the Ling system was firmly established as the basis for the professional training of female physical educators. It had also begun to play the same role in the new specialist colleges for men that appeared during the 1930s at Glasgow, Leeds and Loughborough.

By the end of the Second World War, the Ling system was under siege on several sides. In the climate of national optimism that followed the war, the work of the Swedish gymnast seemed to have little place. The Swedish gymnasts failed to improve either the popularity or the public image of their version of physical education and had little success in attracting the attention of the press in the decade that followed the war. Criticisms of the formality of the Swedish system, and especially its unsuitability for young children, began to gain ground towards the end of the 1930s. Consider this description of Swedish gymnastics by Marion Wardle:

> One can have the type of lesson in which the children come into the gymnasium and go straight to their lines, where they either stand or sit cross legged, waiting for the teacher's directions. An introductory activity may be given, probably in a set formation, such as a ring or a double ring. Then back to files where they perform a series of static exercises. Then to their section places for the 'heave' where they sit cross legged while the apparatus is brought out. When this is ready, four, or possibly eight children stand and begin work at the teacher's command. This is followed by a 'balance' organised in the same way using either beams or forms — never both! After this back to files (or possibly wallbars) for abdominal and lateral exercises. Finally, section work, where the children again sit cross legged until the apparatus is ready, when the first four children begin to work at the teacher's or the leader's command. Throughout the whole period the children have had no single opportunity for moving freely and naturally and each individual has probably spent ten to fifteen minutes sitting cross legged on the floor. (Wardle, 1947, p. 8)

Over to You

In a small group, analyse this statement. Note the effects this kind of physical training might have had on children under the following headings: physical, social, emotional, cognitive.

By the end of the Second World War, an alternative form of gymnastics, drawing on Laban's principles of movement and already dubbed 'educational gymnastics', was making its mark among the female physical educators.

EDUCATIONAL GYMNASTICS AND CHILD-CENTRED TEACHING

Rudolf Laban did not commit his ideas on movement education to paper until 1948, when he published *Modern Educational Dance*. He had by then carried out research in industry and had become convinced of the detrimental effects of simple, repetitive movement sequences of many factory-based occupations on the worker's emotional and intellectual health. These ideas were eventually to find their way, in largely unaltered form, into the work of the female physical educators.

Laban's criticisms of modern industrial society were in tune with the sentiments of child-centred teaching popular in British primary schools during the 1940s and 1950s. In the 1930s, some of the key features of the child-centred approach had been set out for the first time in official policy. A key idea was that the primary school curriculum should be 'thought of in terms of activity and experience rather than knowledge to be acquired and facts to be stored'. Twenty years later, ideas such as this had become part of official government policy for primary school education.

So it is no surprise that Laban's theories found fertile ground among women physical educators during the war years. Indeed, historian Sheila Fletcher has suggested that Laban's views on movement and dance added a dimension to the educational gymnasts' version of child-centredness that increased its intensity.

> To move away from directed work and learning based on imitation, to teach the children rather than the subject, had become a broadly accepted goal; but could the history or mathematics teacher draw on such a radical ideology as the concept of movement developed by Laban? (Fletcher, 1984, p. 132)

The official patronage and enthusiastic endorsement by the Inspectorate and LEA Advisers gave the educational gymnasts' work additional support and resulted in the publication of the two curriculum guides *Moving and Growing* and *Planning the Programme* by the Ministry of Education in England. These guides appeared in 1952 and 1953 and were intended to replace the 1933 Syllabus for primary school physical education.

A key feature of educational gymnastics was that it dispensed with the military style and formal exercises of Swedish gymnastics. In their place, children were encouraged to explore space, to experiment with different ways of moving and to create their own ways of meeting challenges set by the teacher. In Swedish gymnastics, the quality of movement was judged by the extent to which all children performed the same movements together and in the correct way, as determined by the syllabus of the day. In educational gymnastics, the quality of children's movement was measured by the extent to which they displayed an understanding of dimensions such as time, weight, space and flow. In contrast with the 'old' system, the 'new' approach of educational gymnastics focused on individuals rather than the group and on 'natural' as opposed to 'contrived' movement.

Over to You

Teach part of an educational gymnastics lesson to peers or observe a Key Stage 1 or 2 class in a local primary school. Make notes on the following issues: How does the lesson differ from your experience of Swedish gymnastics? How do teaching styles compare? What cognitive, physical, social and emotional demands does the lesson make on the learner? Make a list of the learning outcomes demonstrated by the learners. Make a brief note on how this lesson compares with your own physical education lessons.

As you might imagine, the Swedish gymnasts were not impressed by the 'new' approach to physical education. From the beginning, the Swedish gymnasts were critical of educational gymnastics. Marion Wardle, although a supporter of educational gymnastics, was able to caricature the excesses of the new approach, just as many of her Swedish gymnast colleagues had done. Such classes, she said, involved 'a period of chaotic activity, in which children rush wildly about at their individual and group practices without apparently the faintest hope or intention of achieving good performances, and maintaining for most of the time a sort of monkey-house chatter' (Wardle, 1947, p. 8). A decade later, another critic of educational gymnastics was to remark that 'the aim of the physical education teacher should be to find out what children would do if left to their own devices, and then make a career out of it!' (McIntosh, 1957, p. 23).

Although both *Moving and Growing* and *Planning the Programme* were reasonably well received within the teaching profession, this achievement was not matched by a heightened public awareness or appreciation. A report in the *Times Educational Supplement* in September 1953 suggested that educational gymnastics still had to capture the public imagination: 'From old-fashioned gym, P.T. or physical jerks to the modern concept of physical education, the transition has been rapid and is not yet complete'. Despite the perception within the physical education profession that educational gymnastics was a radical alternative to the Ling system, the popular stereotypes of the drill teacher and of 'arm swinging and knee bending' persisted. The failure of the female physical educators to gain support and understanding for their work from a wider public was, in later years, to play a significant part in the marginalisation of educational gymnastics.

Just how radical the educational gymnasts were in terms of their child-centredness was open to question. Certainly, the idea of children moving on their own initiative would not have been acceptable to the Swedish gymnasts. But rather than displaying features of a radical child-centredness, the educational gymnasts' belief in the centrality of the teacher located them, along with their Swedish gymnast predecessors, firmly in a teacher-centred mode.

The debate continued among the female physical educators over the relative merits of Swedish and educational gymnastics until the mid-1950s. By this time, another challenge was beginning to emerge that was to generate much more acrimony and emotion, and to have a more profound effect on the future of physical education. This challenge did not lie in a return to the 'old way' of Swedish gymnastics but in the new knowledge derived from scientific measurement that was being produced in the university departments of physical education. It was at this point, from the early 1950s, that a distinctively male perspective began to emerge.

SCIENTIFIC MEASUREMENT AND THE MALE VIEW OF GYMNASTICS, THE 1950s

Before the 1940s, physical education was not as attractive a career for men as it was for women. Part of the reason for this was that the first male physical education teachers in government elementary schools were former army noncommissioned officers. Other teachers generally regarded these men as their social inferiors, a label that stuck with male physical educators for many years.

With the massive expansion of the secondary school system after the war, teachers in every subject were in short supply, but this was particularly true for male physical education teachers. Men very quickly made headway despite their status problem. In December 1945, 30 male and 20 female physical education teachers were appointed to the promoted positions of 'Principal Teacher' in senior secondary schools in Glasgow. This was acknowledged as a major breakthrough since it offered male and female physical education teachers the same prospects for advancement and salary that teachers of other subjects enjoyed.

Most male and female teachers of physical education were from the 1940s to the 1960s trained in single-sex institutions. Hugh Brown, Director of the Scottish School of Physical Education, expressed a common and widespread view about the importance of this single-sex arrangement.

> I believe . . . [that] the force of example in teachers is all important. In such things as speech, dress, personal cleanliness we are constantly under the keen scrutiny of that hypercritical section of the community—the school boy . . .

Constantly I am reminding myself that we are charged with the task of training men to teach boys. This is a purely masculine sphere. Training must at all times be strong, must be virile. (Brown, 1958, p. 93)

Over to You

In a small group, discuss this statement. Do you believe there is a distinction between the male and female approaches to teaching? Do the pupils have preconceived expectations? Write a summary of the main points of your discussion.

Within this context of single-sex training, the philosophy that lay behind the preparation of male teachers was at odds with the new ideas about educational gymnastics. For example, competitive games and sports were a key part of the men's philosophy of physical education. They also held in high esteem the new scientific knowledge that was beginning to emerge, particularly knowledge relating to the development of physical fitness and to the acquisition of physical skills. Drawing on the ethos of competitive sport and the new scientific knowledge of physical activity, the male physical educators began to develop their own perspective on gymnastics specifically and on physical education in general. They developed this perspective in direct opposition to the educational gymnasts.

David Munrow's influential book *Pure and Applied Gymnastics* was first published in 1955 with a second edition in 1963, and this book became the mouthpiece of male opposition to the progressive trend in physical education. The book was significant because of the distinctly alternative position it stated in relation to educational gymnastics. It was also significant because it was read by many of the educational gymnasts and so formed one of the few avenues of communication between the rival parties.

Munrow expressed his support for **scientific measurement** and explained how this new knowledge could be applied to physical education. It was during the 1930s that the departments of physical education at Edinburgh, Liverpool, Manchester, Birmingham and Leeds universities were producing this new knowledge. Their initial role was to provide recreational programmes for the students, but they soon added to this a research function. In 1949, physical education became an option within the BA degree at Birmingham, and this institution, and especially Leeds, appointed staff with research orientations. Many of these staff were male, and all of the directors of the university physical education departments were men.

Munrow argued that the university departments of physical education had an important role to play in the production of scientific knowledge of 'the body's mechanical and psycho-physiological behaviour in acquiring and performing intricate physical skills' as this was 'an area not being fully tackled by any other branch of learning'. On the basis of this view, he argued that 'the men could not at the moment subscribe to a general account of movement training' and 'doubted if movement training was capable of refining physical techniques'. By the middle of the 1950s, the stage was set for a debate between male and female physical educators over the nature of gymnastics which, in effect, was a general debate over the definition of physical education.

> Scientific measurement was a specific approach to physical activity based on physiology, biomechanics and skill learning.

Inside the Debate, 1950–1960

There were two major issues in the debate that unfolded through the 1950s and 1960s between the female educational gymnasts and the males with their competitive games and scientific perspective. The first was the controversy surrounding the level of specificity required for skill development and the problem of transfer of training. The second concerned the application of objective standards to gymnastic performance and the place of competition in the gym.

The Specificity of Skill Development. *In Pure and Applied Gymnastics,* Munrow suggested that in moving away from the Swedish system after the Second World War, male and female physical educators had reacted in different ways to the question of skill specificity.

> The men have made overt acknowledgement that other skills are as important and have 'diluted' the gymnastic skill content of gymnasium work so that now boys may be seen practising basket-ball shots and manoeuvres, carrying out heading practices or practising sprint starting . . . The women, in the main, have . . . 'diluted' the traditional gymnastic skills by a quite different device. They have ceased both to name and to teach them. Instead, a description is given, in general terms, of a task involving apparatus and individual solutions are encouraged. A much wider range of solutions is thus possible; some may include traditional skills but many will not. (Munrow, 1963, p. 276)

The problem with the female alternative to the Swedish system, as Munrow saw it, was that pupils rarely had the chance to consolidate their skills because no specific skill teaching took place.

The educational gymnasts' response to Munrow's challenge came from Marjorie Randall in 1961 in a book, *Basic Movement,* which was representative of the women's perspective. In the opening chapter of the book, Randall immediately went on the offensive to contest Munrow's functional definition of gymnastics, suggesting that 'the masculine approach. . . has become largely outmoded so far as women's work is concerned'. She claimed that:

> . . . women's gymnastics . . . have been emancipated from the restricted practices of stereotyped patterns of movements based upon anatomical classification. The physiological and anatomical ends . . . are incidentally served. (Randall, 1961, p. 12)

The major aim was the achievement of what Randall called body awareness, which included neural control combined with a higher level of kinaesthetic awareness that could be developed through experience into an intuitive control of movement. She added to this the need to engage the child cognitively in contrast with the male approach. She accused the men of stressing only the physical effects of exercise and consequently regarding intelligence as out of range. Her claim was this:

> The masculine approach to gymnastics separates content from method. Munrow's gymnastics exercises can be directly and formally taken or informally taken. Movement gymnastics requires the intelligent co-operation of the child, rendering command-response methods obsolete . . . this represents a big break-away from the traditional approach of the 'see this' and 'do it this way' school of thought. (Randall, 1961, p. 25)

Educational gymnastics was a holistic approach to physical education because it sought to integrate children's physical, emotional, creative and cognitive development.

Randall's response showed that behind the less formal methods of educational gymnastics lay an attempt to treat the pupil holistically, encouraging the simultaneous development of intellectual and creative abilities in a movement medium and relegating the physical effect of movement to a level of lesser importance.

However, the notion of body awareness, which lay at the centre of the women's scheme, suggested a theory of learning that ran directly counter to the new knowledge that the motor learning theorists were advancing. The educational gymnasts claimed, in much the same way as the Swedish gymnasts had before them, that the movement experience they had to offer was a general foundation upon which more specific skills could be built. The notion of body awareness expressed this idea as generalised kinaesthetic control.

As early as 1949, however, members of the Birmingham University staff including David Munrow and Barbara Knapp, questioned whether there was such a thing as generalised skill training. In her book *Skill in Sport,* which appeared in 1963, Barbara Knapp argued that transfer of training was most likely to occur when the tasks in question were similar, and so the best way to learn a specific action was to perform that action repeatedly over a period of time.

The main point of the motor learning theorists' criticisms, which the male physical educators championed vigorously, was that skill learning is specific. So, the best way to master any physical activity was to practise that particular activity repeatedly until it had been learned. The male physical educators took this principle to heart and developed an approach to teaching skills that consisted of reducing a skill to its component parts and learning these parts separately, before reassembling them gradually until the entire skill had been learned. All of this appeared to make nonsense of the females' claim that it was possible, indeed preferable, to develop a general body awareness as a foundation on which to build more specific learning.

Standards and Competition in the Gym. A second objection to the educational gymnasts' view related to the place of standards and competition in the gym. From the male perspective, it seemed unlikely that the educational gymnasts' child-centred approach could continue to stimulate pupils beyond the early stages of learning. Munrow argued that it could not challenge older boys or girls and it was for this reason, as a stimulant or incentive, that competitive activity was essential. In *Pure and Applied Gymnastics* he complained:

> Allied to a teaching philosophy which seeks actively to avoid confronting less able children with failure, is the belief that the child's own solution to the problem is always valid and right. This makes more sense with young children than with older boys and girls and with first efforts at a skill rather than with later ones . . . to leave children floundering to evolve their own technique when we could guide them is a neglect of our professional duties. (Munrow, 1963, p. 280)

Over to You

Decide whether you agree with Munrow's statement. Apply his argument to your experiences of physical education. Note some examples from your experience that support your view of Munrow's statement.

In response to Munrow's view that standards were a necessary and important means of challenging pupils to strive for excellence, Randall suggested that girls, particularly in adolescence, had quite different needs to boys. She argued that the growing boy 'derives considerable prestige and social prominence through physical advantage in competitive games which his increase in height, weight and strength gives him'. Girls, on the other hand, may have little to gain from competitive sport during the adolescent period.

> In the gymnastic lesson let her be free from all this competition and let her progress at her own rate and find joy and satisfaction in the slow but sure progress of controlling her body. Through her pride in the mastery of her body in the gymnasium will grow a certain independence, security and emotional stability . . . Teaching must be geared to the individual; it must be flexible and tolerant of a wide range in aptitude . . . no longer is her worth in the gymnasium measured by whether she can get over the box in long fly or whether she can put her head on her knees keeping her legs straight; but rather can she work to surpass her own standards without being harassed or harried because she cannot conform to a common one. (Randall, 1961, pp. 20 and 22)

The aims of independence, security and emotional stability contrast sharply with the desire to develop strength, endurance, flexibility and particular skills, and to use these attributes in competitive situations. These contrasts reveal starkly the contested issues that divided the male and female physical educators.

■ The Aftermath of the Debate, the 1960s

By the late 1960s, it was regarded as old-fashioned to think of gymnastics as the core of physical education. This is because the subject had expanded to include a wide range of other physical activities, particularly team and individual games, and outdoor pursuits. This new and expanded notion of physical education reflected a shift in the balance of power within the physical education profession, away from the female educational gymnasts towards the male perspective.

The shift was confirmed by the emergence of degree programmes in physical education by the mid-1960s. It was the men who took the lead in developing the degree programmes. They based these programmes primarily on the new scientific subdisciplines of exercise physiology, motor learning theory and biomechanics.

Another factor in this shift was the disappearance of the all-female colleges of physical education, which by the mid-1960s were in the process of being merged into other, larger co-educational institutions. Although this shift did not happen abruptly, between the 1940s and the 1960s, the influence of the women's perspective had moved from the centre to the margins of the field. In a subject that had been dominated by women for over 50 years, the rise of the male physical educators to power and influence during the decade and a half following the end of the Second World War was little short of dramatic.

One of the reasons for this sharp rise to power was the widespread popular acceptance of competitive sport in schools and its role in the promotion of national identity, as we will see in the next chapter. The great demand for teachers to meet the needs of universal secondary education was also a significant event for male physical educators. Tradition hindered women in ways that did not affect men. The universities and male teacher training colleges fostered scientific research, and this placed the men in a better position than the women to respond to contemporary challenges. The fact that educational gymnastics came to be associated with the physical education of girls and small children became a distinct disadvantage for the female physical educators. These factors helped the males to maintain a higher profile in relation to developments in the wider educational community and in society at large.

SUMMARY

This chapter shows how female and male physical educators between the 1940s and 1960s contested the meaning of physical education. We described the decline of gymnastics as the defining feature of physical education and the allied decline of a distinctively female influence in physical education. The debate over the merits of educational gymnastics and the male version of gymnastics linked to skill acquisition in games and scientific knowledge revealed basic differences in philosophy between female and male physical educators. The version of physical education that became dominant from the 1960s was a male version of the subject. The chapter reveals how the subject has been gendered since the 1940s.

Test Yourself Questions ▪ ▪ ▪ ▪ ▪ ▪ ▪ ▪ ▪ ▪ ▪ ▪ ▪

1. Explain the reasons why Olympic gymnastics largely failed in its acceptance in British school before the 1950s.

2. Compare and contrast the three forms of gymnastics.

3. Give at least three reasons for the demise of Swedish gymnastics.

4. What were the main criticisms levelled at educational gymnastics?

5. Munrow suggested in his book, *Pure and Applied Gymnastics,* that in moving away from the Swedish system after the Second World War, male and female educators had reacted in different ways to the question of skill specificity. Explain the main differences between the perspectives of the two groups of educators.

6. With reference to the teaching of educational gymnastics favoured by the female educators, explain what is meant by treating the pupil 'holistically'.

7. What did the motor learning theorists believe to be the best way to master a specific physical activity? How does this theory differ from the approach of the majority of female educators at this time?

8. From the late 1960s how and why did physical education change its emphasis?

The Emergence of a Scientific Base to Physical Education and Sport, 1946–1970

Learning Outcomes

When you have studied this chapter, you should be able to

☑ describe how the Second World War influenced developments in physical education,

☑ list the early developments in research that took place after the war,

☑ define the 'hard core' of fitness,

☑ summarise the application of scientific research to professional practice,

☑ explain what was new about emerging perspectives on fitness and health in the 1960s

☑ summarise the impact of scientific research on higher education, and

☑ speculate on the significance of these events for your experience of physical education today.

INTRODUCTION

You can read in chapter 3.1 that physical training in government schools had traditionally been concerned with the health of working class children. Until the 1940s, Swedish gymnastics was regarded as a form of therapy, with its main aim to promote health. When the word 'fitness' was used in relation to Swedish gymnastics, it referred to a general capacity for physical activity. The Swedish gymnasts thought strength was linked to balance, proportion and harmony of the body. They did not want to do anything in particular with their fitness. Their view was that physical education developed a general physical capability on which more specific capacities might be developed.

In addition, until the 1940s, health-related physical fitness was thought to be a *by-product* of participation in games and sports. It was only later that the pursuit of physical fitness became a goal in itself, following developments in the training of soldiers for active service during the war. The new definition of fitness was understood to refer to the capacity to perform specific physical tasks, such as the capacity to lift, throw, run, kick or strike. This meant that fitness had a number of specific dimensions, such as endurance, strength and flexibility.

The key concept that lay at the heart of these developments was **progressive overload.** Progressive overload involves systematically challenging the physiological and neuromuscular systems of the body with an ascending scale of physical work demands as these systems adapt to each new challenge. This idea was unfamiliar to physical educators before the 1940s and only became common knowledge by the early 1960s.

New research into skill acquisition and the mechanics of body movement began to appear in physical education journals by the early 1950s. However, it was the new knowledge of the physiological responses of the body to exercise that led the way in rethinking the relationship between physical activity and health.

The new concept of fitness was explicitly gendered. It was mainly men who pioneered the experimental research in exercise physiology. It was their definitions of fitness that dominated the new view of the relationship between physical activity and health. Within this view, strength and endurance formed the 'hard core' of fitness. The male physical educators' application of experimental science methods to investigate physical activity marked a distinctive break with their mainly female Swedish gymnastics predecessors. The outcome was the development of a scientific basis to physical education that was to play a key role after the 1950s, first in college and university programmes and later in schools.

THE INFLUENCE OF THE
SECOND WORLD WAR, 1939–1946

The Second World War played a significant part in developing new technologies, such as radar and the jet engine. One major success of the armed forces during the war is not usually thought of in the same light as these technological advances. But the development of a technology of fitness was nevertheless a major breakthrough. In 1946, Brigadier Wand-Tetley described in the *Journal of Physical Education* how the British army had used 'purposeful physical training'. He claimed that 'the science of body mechanics' had been applied to the development of 'dexterity and strength in the rifleman, to give him better neuromuscular control and consequently to develop those qualities essential to good shooting'.

Troops were trained to lift and carry and to vault from moving vehicles in full gear without injury. He did not use the term progressive overload in his paper. However,

Progressive overload involves systematically challenging the physiological and neuromuscular systems of the body with an ascending scale of physical work demands as these systems adapt to each new challenge.

Wand-Tetley's description of endurance training, specifically tailored to the infantryman's needs, described this process precisely. He explained how troops were gradually trained to accomplish 'great feats of endurance without undue strain' by walking, then walking with a pack, gradually covering greater distances, then progressing from flat to hilly ground.

Over to You

List the key features of progressive overload. With a partner, identify those features of Wand-Tetley's description of army training that match the features of progressive overload.

Wand-Tetley suggested that in peacetime 'skill and consequent enjoyment at games could be increased and the burden of industrial labour lightened considerably by the imaginative adaptation of purposeful training to sport and work'.

EARLY SCIENTIFIC RESEARCH IN PHYSICAL EDUCATION, 1946–1955

The influence of wartime developments in training were far-reaching in physical education. In addition to creating a technology of fitness, the armed forces generated new knowledge about how to learn specific physical tasks such as shooting a rifle and operating complex machinery and instruments. This work tapped an already existing and extensive body of experimental research on skill learning that physical educators eagerly developed after the war.

Peter McIntosh, also well known as an historian of physical education, carried out one of the first reviews of this literature and its application to physical education. He published a paper on 'Skill and Physical Education' in the *Journal of Physical Education* in 1948. This was followed four years later by a paper on 'Transference of Training' authored by his colleague at Birmingham University, David Munrow. Munrow argued that the topic of transference of training formed a highly appropriate field for investigation by experimental scientists in physical education.

Closely linked to this interest in skill learning was **'human kinetics'**, or kinaesiology. Human kinetics focused on the mechanics of muscle actions, the movement of limbs and the forces acting on the body in motion. During the 1940s and early 1950s, at least half a dozen books appeared on kinaesiology, most of them from the United States. In 1952, the first British book on this subject was published. *Human Kinetics and Analysing Body Movements* was written by T. McLurg Anderson, Principal of the Scottish Physiotherapy School and Director of the Institute of Human Kinetics.

Anderson claimed that human kinetics was a scientific approach to research on the body that had been in the process of development from the late 1920s at the Scottish Physiotherapy Hospital. In his book, he added a biomechanical analysis of human movement to an extensive knowledge of anatomy and well-established physiological material, creating his own terminology to analyse movement and effort. He also used slow-motion filming of sports performers to produce line drawings as illustrations of his analyses. Although his professional experience was mainly in remedial medical work, his analyses of a number of athletic events demonstrated the direct relevance of this kind of work to coaching sports performers.

These developments of experimental science research in skill learning and body mechanics made important contributions to the scientific basis of physical education. However, it was mainly through physiology and its applications to exercise that

Human kinetics, or kinaesiology, focuses on the mechanics of muscle actions, the movement of limbs and the forces acting on the body in motion.

experimental science was introduced most powerfully to physical educators. By the late 1940s, new research was emerging on the development of endurance and strength.

THE 'HARD CORE' OF FITNESS: STRENGTH AND ENDURANCE, 1955–1960

The American T.L. De Lorme developed the principle of progressive overload and its practical application through the idea of 'progressive resistance exercises' in the 1940s. De Lorme worked mainly in the field of exercise rehabilitation. Progressive overload was the key to developing both strength and endurance. De Lorme was reportedly critical of physical educators and sports coaches who neglected strength training on the grounds that, besides reducing the likelihood of injury, 'most activities will be performed more successfully and with less fatigue when greater strength and endurance are present'.

De Lorme's studies were widely cited by British researchers and his ideas were applied particularly to **circuit training** and to the use of weights in strength training, and later to intermittent running. Building on his work, one British researcher wrote in 1957:

> There is a realisation of the fundamental fact that man [sic] needs strength and endurance. Whether it be the housewife, typist, labourer, factory worker or professional man, all need strength, enough at least to perform their daily tasks economically and without undue fatigue — and a little extra in reserve for the emergency that may overtake each or all of us at some time throughout life. (McDonald, 1957, p. 33)

Over to You

In a small group, discuss the statement that all people need strength and endurance. Make a list of up to 10 current occupations. Then, on the basis of what we know today from functional anatomy, biomechanics and exercise physiology, assess the strength and endurance needs of each. Decide as a group whether the researcher in 1957 was on the right track and justify your decision in writing.

Another researcher made the connection between elite sports performance and strength training. In 1955, he suggested that Britain's failure to win a gold medal at the 1952 Olympic Games was because 'the British athletes had not the sheer strength reserve of their foreign rivals'. He also echoed De Lorme's comment that there would be fewer injuries and a higher level of performance among performers of modest abilities if they undertook strength training.

According to these writers, strength was considered to be essential to all sections of the population. The same methods based on progressive resistance exercises could be applied in each case to beneficial effect.

The publication of Morgan and Adamson's book *Circuit Training* in 1957 was an important British contribution to scientific research on fitness. It also provided male physical educators with a set of practical principles for fitness development in schools. Morgan and Adamson argued that strength and endurance were the 'hard core' of fitness.

> The hard core of fitness is the efficiency of the muscular and circulo-respiratory systems. These may be regarded as the engine which determines the work output

---

Circuit training involves different kinds of exercises arranged at stations designed to develop strength and endurance. You spend a set amount of time at a station before moving on to the next exercise.

of the body and their efficiency may be expressed in terms of strength, muscular endurance, circulo-respiratory endurance and power. (Morgan and Adamson, 1957, p. 14)

Morgan and Adamson developed circuit training based on experimental work at Leeds University. They were trying to discover a form of fitness training that would hold students' interest and improve their fitness at the same time. These experiments had been going on since the end of the Second World War. Their procedures involved pre- and post-tests, experimental and control groups, a limited and carefully defined set of variables, quantitative measures and correlational analyses. Based on this scientific research, they claimed that circuit training

> . . . will meet a definite need in the physical education of boys and young men. It satisfies the modern demand that pupils shall be treated as individuals and not in the mass, and that they shall pursue their activity with the minimum of direction from the teacher. It calls for their intelligent co-operation at every stage. It is based on principles which are biologically sound and its nature is such that performers are able to observe their own improvement. It has an undeniable recreative appeal. It is flexible enough to allow a bias towards one or another special aspect of fitness, while retaining the essential idea of all-round fitness for athletics and everyday life. (Morgan and Adamson, 1957, p. 5)

According to Morgan and Adamson, circuit training was scientifically, technically and educationally progressive. They stressed the point that participants could see their improvement in measurable terms and suggested that regular testing and the establishment of standards were a logical extension of the use of circuit training.

They set these advantages in the context of school physical education. They argued that, whereas the educational, social and psychological dimensions of physical education had been justifiably emphasised through the 1940s and early 1950s, physical educators had neglected to develop 'the power of the human machine'. They believed circuit training could redress this imbalance. They also went to some lengths to stress that circuit training

> . . . should not in any way supplant the training in skills which must be the supreme manifestation of physical education in schools [and that it] is not the whole of a boy's physical education, nor does it come early in his school career. (Morgan and Adamson, 1957, p. 67)

They intended circuit training to be put to best use in schools with boys aged 14 and older:

> It is at this age that boys become interested in their own development, physical as well as intellectual, and it is at this age . . . they begin to take part in pursuits which call for a high degree of strength and endurance. (Morgan and Adamson, 1957, p. 69)

Given that this new concept of fitness was gendered, it may come as no surprise to learn that girls are not mentioned in *Circuit Training*. Clearly, this kind of fitness training was not at this time considered appropriate for girls.

Over to You

In a small group, design a circuit that would develop aspects of strength and endurance specific to one of the physical activities you are studying. List the aspects of physical fitness that circuit training is best used to develop.

APPLICATIONS TO PROFESSIONAL PRACTICE IN PHYSICAL EDUCATION AND SPORT, 1955–1960

Circuit training achieved a high level of popularity among male physical educators in a relatively short period of time. In June 1955, *The Leaflet* (the journal of the Ling Association) contained a report from two teachers who conducted an experiment with circuit training in their schools. The next year, 66 men attended a conference on circuit training at Leeds University, and in 1957 the theme of the PEA Christmas Conference was 'The Place of Strength and Stamina Training in PE'.

Morgan and Adamson had emphasised that circuit training was not designed primarily for sports performers. They commented that 'we are not all ambitious seekers after maximum physical fitness, willing to submit ourselves to the inexorable increase in the intensity of training'. They strongly discouraged any attempts to make circuit training itself competitive. Nevertheless, they acknowledged that it was mainly sports performers who supported the circuits provided for students at Leeds University. The use of circuit training as preparation for competitive sport became more frequent by the late 1950s.

The Exeter-based St Luke's College rugby team reported on the beneficial effects of circuit training on their performances in *The Leaflet*, and several conferences on 'Fitness for Sport' were organised during 1958 and 1959. The enthusiasm for fitness training even partially overcame the gender barrier, with the Central Council for Physical Recreation (CCPR) organising a conference on 'Fitness Training for Sportswomen' in 1958. By the end of the 1950s, the success of circuit training in

© Human Kinetics

Circuit training develops strength and endurance as an individual rotates through the various stations.

promoting a new idea of physical fitness had also inspired a range of studies of the fitness of school pupils.

The significance of circuit training went far beyond its practical efficiency in developing physical fitness. It symbolised the major principles of the development of a scientific basis to physical education. It also signalled the power and potential of this way of thinking about physical activity to produce measurable results in relation to particular dimensions of sports performance and health. Circuit training marked a break with the old-fashioned pre-war view of the therapeutic purpose and effect of exercise on physical performance.

As a result of these developments of a scientific base to physical education, physical educators were one professional group among others responsible for stimulating social concern in the late 1950s over the less desirable effects of affluence and technological innovation. These effects were manifesting themselves in sedentariness and the resultant problems of obesity and coronary heart disease.

A NEW VIEW OF FITNESS AND HEALTH, THE EARLY 1960s

By the late 1950s, the idea was only just beginning to be understood by physical educators that people living in highly urbanised and industrialised areas were in need of regular health-related exercise. Most often, this was seen to be part of an inevitable evolutionary process, in which increasing affluence and technological advancement contributed to physical deterioration of the population. One writer in 1957 clearly expressed this perspective. He commented that 'somewhere along the road of progress' in physical education

> We have forgotten that our principal concern is with the physical. This is an omission, made all the more serious in this modern age of automation and sedentary living. Physically, man [sic] hasn't changed very much throughout the centuries — perhaps a little less surface hair, a narrowing of the jaws, not so much of the bent knee stance — but his way of life differs greatly from that of his more primitive ancestors. His muscles, for example, which thrive on movement, are today as a rule sadly neglected. (McDonald, 1957, p. 33)

This view of the relationship between exercise and health challenged the opinions of some of the medical profession. One physical education researcher wrote:

> According to Dr E Jokl, it would seem that health and physical fitness have nothing to do with each other. Those physiological adaptations which are affected by physical training are supposed to be unimportant for our health because the structural and functional changes involved in them are apparently useless under pathological conditions. (Schrecker, 1954, p. 51)

Over to You

In a small group, decide whether you agree with this statement. Write a paragraph justifying your decision.

However, although the researchers in physical education conceded that fitness 'bore no relation to resistance to disease' they promoted the idea, nowadays accepted as commonplace, that 'physical education could stave off degenerative diseases and the products of the unnatural stresses of urban life'. In 1957, Peter McIntosh supported this idea:

> Surely the old idea that you could survive the winter without a cold provided you did enough 'keep fit' exercises must be extinct by now. Health is a mental as well as a physical attribute. With more automation, urbanisation and mechanical transport, the need to encourage pride in physical efficiency and to demonstrate the well-being and pleasure that come through the exercise of physical skill becomes increasingly important. (McIntosh, 1957, p. 23)

Automation, mechanisation, urbanisation and sedentariness were the recurrent themes of the new view of the relationship between fitness and health. Researchers believed that physical education in schools had a key role to play in combating the unhealthy side effects of affluence. By the early 1960s news was beginning to reach physical education teachers that there was a relationship between obesity and coronary heart disease and between sedentariness and obesity. Regular exercise, they were told, had a part to play in preventing the onset of the so-called risk factors associated with coronary heart disease. But this exercise had to be of a type and of sufficient intensity and duration to substantially affect the relevant physiological systems.

However, the significance of this new relationship between exercise and health was more symbolic than practical at this time. The practical effect on school physical education of this news was, in the late 1950s and on into the 1960s, confined largely to male teachers and male pupils. And even among these teachers, competitive games and sports were now the major element of the physical education programme. Throughout the 1960s, circuit and weight training became established as indoor activities for older boys, taking up about 20 per cent of the physical education curriculum time of 15-year-old pupils.

The application of the new scientific knowledge of skill acquisition, the mechanics of movement and the technology of fitness could be applied to improving the performance of games players. In the late 1950s and on to the early 1970s, this became a major practical use of the new knowledge because of the interest in successful sports teams, rather than its use as a means of promoting the health of pupils.

THE IMPACT OF SCIENTIFIC RESEARCH IN HIGHER EDUCATION, 1960–1970

In 1955, David Munrow of Birmingham University argued that researchers in physical education needed to take responsibility for scientific and other research directly relevant to their interests. This was because 'the study of the body's mechanical and psycho-physiological behaviour in acquiring and performing physical skills is an area not being fully tackled by any other branch of learning'.

This idea was developed a decade later by Franklin Henry, Professor of Physical Education at the University of California at Berkeley. Henry argued that the time was ripe for the development of physical education as an academic discipline in higher education. He outlined what was to become, through the 1960s and 1970s, the accepted model for the development of degree courses in physical education based on a collection of subdisciplines. He suggested that physical education

> . . . considered as an academic discipline, does not consist of the application of the disciplines of anthropology, physiology, psychology and the like to the study of physical education. On the contrary, it has to do with the study, as a discipline, of certain aspects of anatomy, anthropology, physiology, psychology, and other appropriate fields. (Henry, 1965, p. 6)

He accepted that there was no clear-cut line between subject matter properly belonging to the subdisciplines or to physical education and suggested:

> The study of the heart as an organ is physiology, whereas determining the quantitative role of the heart action as a limiting factor in physical performance is perhaps more physical education than physiology. (Henry, 1965, p. 7)

Both Henry and Munrow supported the view that there was sufficient scientific knowledge of physical education to enable it to be recognised as a distinctive field in its own right. Although neither wished to exclude non-experimental research from this scheme, the momentum behind such an idea was coming, with few exceptions, from the experimental scientists. During the 1960s, the availability of degree courses in physical education grew in number. A decade later, higher education institutions in Britain were able to offer three- and four-year degree courses in physical education.

Over to You

In class, discuss the extent to which the view of the field of physical education emerging in the 1960s remains influential today with reference to your A-level course. Think about and note any alternatives to this way of thinking about the field of study.

SUMMARY

In this chapter, you can read about the emergence, after the Second World War, of new forms of scientific research in physical education. You can also read about the development of a new concept of physical fitness that referred to specific dimensions of physical performance such as endurance and strength. The new view of fitness was gendered and was developed by male physical educators and researchers. Developments during the Second World War in training soldiers for active service provided momentum for early research in skill learning, human kinetics and physiology of exercise. Morgan and Adamson's book *Circuit Training* was based on the findings of experimental research into fitness development. The book provided physical educators and sports coaches with practical methods to develop fitness. The research also assisted physical educators to understand the relationships between physical activity, sedentary lifestyles and coronary heart disease. During the 1960s, experimental science research formed the basis for the growth of degree-level programmes in higher education.

Test Yourself Questions

1. List the benefits of war-time 'purposeful physical training' for physical educators in peacetime.

2. Identify and describe the positive aspects of strength that T.L. De Lorme, in his work 'progressive resistance exercises', hoped to develop.

3. Explain what was meant by the phrase 'the hard core of fitness'.

4. State at least two reasons why you think girls may initially have been excluded from circuit training.

5. Despite the acknowledgement of the relationship between obesity and coronary heart disease and between sedentariness and obesity in the late 1950s, explain briefly why there was limited practical effect in school physical education.

6. Discuss the extent to which, after the Second World War, the development of a scientific base to physical education has impacted on physical education today.

Government Involvement in Sport and Recreation and the Rescue of Working Class Youth, 1920–1965

Chapter Overview

- Introduction
- The National Playing Fields Association, 1925–1965
- The Central Council for Physical Recreation, 1935–1965
- The Success of State Intervention: Opportunity or Regulation?
- Delinquency, Social Control and Games, 1925–1955
- The Wolfenden Report, 1960
- The Aftermath of the Wolfenden Report, 1960–1965
- Summary
- Test Yourself Questions

Learning Outcomes

When you have studied this chapter, you should be able to

☑ describe the role of the National Playing Fields Association (NPFA) and the Central Council for Physical Recreation (CCPR) and explain their significance for government intervention in sport;

☑ summarise the factors affecting government intervention in sport during the period being investigated;

☑ explain the idea that sport could 'rescue' working class youth from delinquency;

☑ analyse and explain the importance of the Wolfenden Report on thinking about young people, physical education and sport; and

☑ speculate on the significance of these events for your experience of physical education today.

INTRODUCTION

Over a period of 50 years, from the mid-1920s, the British government gradually became involved in funding and making policy for sport and recreation. This happened despite successive British governments actually resisting becoming directly involved in funding and organising sport, and so the Government's funding and policy commitments steadily increased after the Second World War.

By the 1960s, the government's direct funding support had led to the harnessing of competitive games and sports in schools and the community to the power structure and to the projects of ruling class interests. None of this was straightforward and obvious, especially to the people actually involved at the time. But, as sports sociologist John Hargreaves (1986) rightly emphasises, none of this involvement was uncontested either. It was the outcome of the co-existence of a range of diverse pressures, interests and forces.

In this chapter, the governments' growing and sometimes reluctant involvement in sport and recreation is investigated. A particular focus is the thinking behind their concerns to regulate the behaviour of working class youth through the provision of sport. You can read about a particular example of this thinking in an important report by the Wolfenden Committee in 1960. This report is significant because it drew heavily on the games ethic to justify its recommendations for State intervention in working class leisure time. The chapter begins with a discussion of two major avenues for State involvement besides government-funded schooling. These were the provision of playing fields and the work of the **National Playing Fields Association (NPFA)** and the promotion of mass participation in recreational physical activity through the **Central Council for Physical Recreation (CCPR)**.

The National Playing Fields Association (NPFA) was formed in the 1920s.

The Central Council for Physical Recreation (CCPR) was formed in 1935.

THE NATIONAL PLAYING FIELDS ASSOCIATION, 1925–1965

The NPFA was formed during the Depression years of the 1920s. Its formation was a direct response to philanthropic concern for the plight of the unemployed. The organisation's work was based on the middle class belief that participation in games and sports had a civilising effect. The NPFA was a voluntary organisation. From the beginning it was under royal patronage and was financed by public subscriptions and charitable donations.

By 1935, the NPFA had funded 908 projects at a cost of just under three million pounds. These projects represented significant progress. However, the provision of public playing fields and other sports facilities continued to be in short supply after the Second World War. In an address to the NPFA in 1951, the Honorary Secretary of the Amateur Athletic Association reported that of the 66 cinder tracks that existed in England and Wales, 37 were privately owned and another 21 were owned by the London County Council. This latter figure highlighted the disproportionate distribution of facilities around the country. Scotland had seven tracks and there were none in Northern Ireland. The availability of facilities varied between sports and regions, but the situation in athletics was representative of the general state of affairs.

The 1949 annual report of the NPFA, delivered by its President the Duke of Edinburgh, noted the acute shortage of playing fields for public use. This was to be a consistent message in subsequent annual reports throughout the 1950s. Funding had been and remained the key problem. A highly successful £250,000 fundraising campaign in 1951 as part of the Assocation's silver jubilee included £115,000 from a 'cinema appeal' and £15,000 raised at Butlin's holiday camps. Despite this

© Youth Sport Trust

Public playing fields have been funded in part by the NPFA.

fundraising success, the government came under increasing pressure during the late 1940s and 1950s to provide funds for playing fields.

The 1944 Education Act created a precedent for this pressure by allocating the functions of the defunct National Fitness Council's Grants Committee, which operated under the terms of the 1937 Physical Training and Recreation Act, to the Ministry of Education. According to historian Peter McIntosh, this involved 'the government more intimately than ever with the leisure pursuits of the community at large'.

THE CENTRAL COUNCIL FOR PHYSICAL RECREATION, 1935–1965

A decade after the establishment of the NPFA, the National Association of Organisers and Lecturers in Physical Education cooperated with the Ling Association to form the Central Council for Recreative Physical Training (CCRPT) in 1935. Community recreative physical training had reached the proportions of a 'movement' by the mid-1930s. The function of the CCRPT was to coordinate the diverse community physical recreation groups that had been growing steadily in number from the 1920s.

Like the NPFA, the CCRPT was under royal patronage from the beginning. Indeed, as John Hargreaves has noted 'the membership of the Council read like a roll call of the Establishment'. The use of physical training in the title of the Council was testimony to its origins in the keep fit movement and other forms of physical training. But in 1944 it changed its name to the Central Council for Physical Recreation to reflect a change of focus away from physical exercise to incorporate a wider range of activities including competitive sports and games.

The CCPR's responsibilities included coordinating the activities of its affiliated associations, clubs and groups. But its immediate concern after the Second World War was the provision of courses for recreation leaders and participants. In order to do this, the Council employed a number of officers and regionally based technical representatives and set up facilities to house their activities. Its first national qualification for leaders of physical recreation was in place by 1940, with over one thousand men and women successfully completing the course. Its first national recreation centre opened in 1946 at Bisham Abbey.

In his Presidential Address to the CCPR AGM in September 1949, Lord Hampden predicted that, as the local education authorities began to meet their responsibilities to provide facilities for physical recreation under the terms of the 1944 Education Act, the CCPR's role would shift from local to national level. This pattern began to emerge over the following decade. At the same meeting, a National Sports Development Fund was approved that was to help extend the influence of the CCPR and to set up recreation centres around the country.

Bisham Abbey offered 'training holidays' in its first year to males and females in the 16 to 25 age range. Two new national centres quickly followed. Glenmore Lodge was opened in Scotland as an outdoor activities centre in 1949. Lillieshall Hall opened in 1951. The South African government funded Lillieshall with a £120,000 gift, and Princess Elizabeth opened it in the presence of sports star Roger Bannister and administrator Stanley Rous.

These additional facilities allowed the CCPR to extend its services. By the end of the 1947–48 financial year, it had run 750 training courses, 1,450 lectures and demonstration classes, enrolled 19,000 students, and organised summertime rallies at seaside resorts. Over the next few years, it created a network of personnel and facilities that laid the ground for its continuing expansion through the 1950s and into the 1960s.

THE SUCCESS OF STATE INTERVENTION: OPPORTUNITY OR REGULATION?

Both the CCPR and the NPFA operated without the direct control of the government. According to Peter McIntosh both organisations

> . . . were in the mid-twentieth century pursuing an ideal of sport for all which broke down or took no notice of social and educational distinctions which had been such a feature of physical education and recreation fifty years earlier. (McIntosh, 1968, p. 280)

In one sense, McIntosh was correct. After the Second World War, the opportunities available to lower middle and working class people to participate in recreational physical activity improved greatly. Sports and games that had previously been restricted to the wealthy and privileged were opened up to a wider cross section of the population.

But was there a cost to pay for increased opportunity? Greater provision also meant a higher level of formalisation and regulation of the recreational and leisure-time pursuits of working and lower middle class people. At this stage, in the 1950s, the government's entry into sport and recreation provision was relatively uncoordinated. However, the patronage of aristocracy and the provision of indirect funding and other material assistance drew popular physical recreation into the State's sphere of influence and drafted it increasingly into the service of 'the national interest'.

Over to You

In a small group, identify and then list the main reasons why there was increased opportunity for lower middle and working class people to participate in sport and physical recreation. Then discuss whether this was a case of opportunity or social regulation for these people. Write a half-page summary of the main points of your discussion.

The association of the CCPR with prominent sports performers such as Bannister and administrators like Rous was significant. From the early 1950s onwards, the case for extending the provision of playing fields and other sports facilities to promote the national interest began to be more frequently heard in the public sphere. One supporter of increased government involvement argued:

> Improved facilities should result in improved standards of performance. Good facilities provided for secondary school, together with expert and enthusiastic teaching, will provide the means of improving standards of performance in our national games and athletics. (Presswood, 1954, p. 5)

Over to You

Decide whether you agree with this statement in general. Decide whether it applies to your school in particular. In a small group, give an oral presentation of no more than three minutes defending your view. While listening to others' presentations, make notes of their views. Finally, summarise how others' views compared with your own.

DELINQUENCY, SOCIAL CONTROL AND GAMES, 1925–1955

Concerns over a perceived increase in juvenile crime during the First World War led to the setting up of Juvenile Delinquency Committees (JDCs) and the publication of a Juvenile Delinquency Report by a Standing Committee of the Home Secretary. The report suggested that boys and girls who became members of youth organisations on leaving school were less likely to be involved in crime.

The work of the JDCs was transferred in 1937 to the short-lived National Fitness Council (1937–1939), establishing a direct and formal association between physical activity and the control of delinquency. The National Youth Committee (1939–1942) and the Youth Advisory Council that replaced it in 1942 continued this work throughout the war years. The term 'juvenile' was replaced by the word 'youth' because 'juvenile' had by this time come to be associated with delinquency, the courts and crime.

By the end of 1941 and two years into the Second World War, all 16- to 18-year-olds were required to register with a youth organisation. The main purpose for this was 'to reach those who had left school and were no longer under educational supervision and discipline'. Within the organisational framework of the youth services, the Board of Education issued a series of circulars on youth organisations during the war. Physical recreation was considered to play a key role in these organisations. A concern to maintain supervision and control over working class youth during the period of leaving school and becoming established in regular employment motivated these formal requirements. Up to 1947, membership of a youth organisation was not considered appropriate or necessary for grammar and public school boys and girls.

The raising of the school leaving age to 15 in 1947 relocated the so-called problem of working class youth from the youth organisations to the new secondary modern schools. Much was made of the effects of the new affluence of the post-war period on young working class adults. It was claimed that these young people had greater spending power and more leisure time to fill than ever before. Going to the cinema, gambling and other elements of popular leisure culture, such as the emerging rock 'n' roll music, were seen to be symbolic of a more egalitarian and materialist spirit among the working classes. In some cases, there was a belief that the activities of young people were antisocial and threatening to good public order.

One upper class commentator claimed that working class youth 'are getting completely the wrong idea of the purpose of life; making as much money as they do, they have got it into their heads that the things in life which are worth having can be bought'.

Schools, it was claimed, could do much to counteract this philosophy of 'I want: I see: I take'. By the end of the 1940s, the idea was becoming firmly established in ruling class circles that organised games and outdoor adventure activities could be used as a means of regulating and supervising the activity of working class youth.

From the point of view of members of the Establishment, delinquency was a relatively straightforward question of keeping working class youth occupied. The Duke of Wellington, reporting in his capacity as President to the AGM of the London and Greater London Playing Fields Association, suggested that there was an urgent need for playing fields to combat juvenile delinquency and that 'many juveniles became delinquent because of sheer idleness'.

In a House of Commons debate on juvenile delinquency in 1950, a similar comment was made by a Miss E. Burton, who was reported to have said:

> Unless something vigorous and attractive is done for our young people we have no right to complain if they go into activities of which we do not approve. While more playing fields are not the whole answer to juvenile delinquency they are part. Young people have nothing to do at night or on Sundays. (Reported in the *Times Educational Supplement*, 22 December 1950)

Most of these statements were concerned with the **social control** of working class youth. John Hargreaves has pointed out that this kind of thinking was an extension of the logic of the welfare state in which the working classes were to be provided for by a benign and caring government. In containing working class delinquency, the qualities to be gained from 'team games well played . . . loyalty, dependability, unselfishness, and above all, courtesy' were the values of the reconstructed middle class games ethic, discussed in chapter 3.2.

Social control refers to the process of maintaining law and order and proper behaviour morally. The ruling and middle class perspective was that the behaviour of young working class people could be controlled by involving them in games and sports.

■ The Contribution of the *Times Educational Supplement*

Throughout the late 1940s and the 1950s, the *Times Educational Supplement* (TES) was to the fore in reporting examples of the socially therapeutic power of games. The newspaper cited an instance in Harmondsworth, London, in 1949, where

> Hooliganism, which reared its ugly head last summer, was eliminated by employing two games supervisors after play centre hours to organise cricket, in which local boys' clubs have also taken part . . . particular attention was paid to Saturday morning activities by which it is hoped to break the cinema habit. (Reported in the *Times Educational Supplement*, 13 May 1949)

The *Times Educational Supplement* supported the ruling and middle class perspective in the construction of a sport-based form of physical education in the 1940s and 1950s.

Indeed, the TES was an important contributor to the reconstruction of the public school games ethic and an unashamed proponent of ruling class interests. Photographs and commentaries on sport, particularly male public school and elite sport, appeared frequently in the pages of the TES throughout the entire post-war period. Virtually no space was given to the version of physical education favoured by the female physical educators.

Not only did the TES report and highlight a selection of episodes and events relating to physical activity and sport, but it consistently under-represented what physical education actually consisted of for most teachers and pupils of the subject at that time. Many of the key themes of this era, reflecting the selection of particular aspects of sport and physical activity as worthy of serious concern, are illustrated in an editorial comment that appeared in the TES in June 1951:

> Sport in England remains under a cloud. The South Africans beat us at cricket; a United States golfer is Amateur Champion; an Australian tennis player is

supreme at Wimbledon. The tide may be about to turn in athletics, but it does not seem to have done so yet. In spite of a tradition and a comparatively large population to choose from, the record remains one of failure and defeat. Nor is this low standard of skill and prowess the only criticism. It is said that the British have become a nation of spectators, not sportsmen. Gambling is needed to stir enthusiasm. Bodily exercise and vigorous physical activities have long been succeeded by the sedentary enjoyment of expert entertainment. Professionalism has ousted the sportsman and made nonsense of the Englishman's love of games. 'Bodily exercise profiteth for a little time,' said St. Paul, possibly having in mind some of the muscle-bound athletes with enlarged hearts and fibrositis who do most to extol the animal aspect of games. But the need today is not so much physical fitness as the development of sound character and healthy interest — the war has shown that severe military training can turn the flabbiest civilian into a commando, if necessary. And if, incidentally, a certain sporting patriotism enters in, what of it? In England, every instinct would be against State intervention in sport, but private bodies have done and are doing much . . . with such bodies as the National Playing Fields Association, the CCPR is doing practical work to combat the evil of the passive circus-goer. And in the course of encouraging more young people to play sport instead of watching it, it may well, one day, enable England to win some international events. (Editor, the *Times Educational Supplement*, June 1951)

Over to You

Discuss this statement in a small group. Would it be possible for the Editor of the TES to make the same statement today? Make a decision as a group whether it would or would not be possible, and write a collective one-page defence of your point of view.

This statement displays all of the key elements of the ruling class perspective on physical education and reveals that the selective process had already reached an advanced stage by the early 1950s. Its dramatic listing of the evidence of 'failure and defeat' conveys the impression that the natural order of things has somehow been upset and hints, with the passing references to spectatorship and gambling, that problems in sport are indicators of deeper problems in society. The loss of a glorious past is nostalgically mourned, while the baser features of modern sport are vilified. Only six years after the war, there is still some symbolic mileage to be gained in recalling military success, and patriotism is mentioned in the same breath.

There is also an inescapable moral tone in the support given to groups such as the NPFA and the CCPR for their work in 'combating the evil of the passive circus-goer'. The final statement that as a result of their efforts 'England may win some international events' is deliberately understated, suggesting that it is not winning alone but winning with apparent effortlessness that reveals the superiority of the English. The editorial is also chauvinist, with no suggestion that women's sport may be worthy of consideration. One female reader who noted this omission wrote to the Editor the next week that England's female hockey team 'is still regarded as the greatest exponent of the game'.

The TES played an important role through the 1940s and 1950s in contributing to the reconstruction of the games ethic for use in the rescue of working class youth through games and sports. However, it was not the only active agent in promoting the patriotic and socially cohesive functions of competitive games and sports.

THE WOLFENDEN REPORT, 1960

The Wolfenden Report
published in 1960 further
promoted the ruling class
view of physical education.

The Wolfenden Report was commissioned in October 1957 by the CCPR to examine factors affecting the organisation of British sport. The Committee, which included David Munrow, interpreted its remit widely, reviewing the situation at that time across all sports and forms of physical recreation, including major and minor games, outdoor recreational activities, amateur and professional sports, and other matters such as facilities, coaching and the influence of the media. The Committee paid particular attention to 'the needs of young people'.

In a well-known and often-quoted statement, the Committee expressed the quintessential middle class view of the role of games and sports in meeting young working class people's needs:

> It is widely held that a considerable proportion of delinquency among young people springs from the lack of opportunity or the lack of desire for suitable physical activity. The causes of criminal behaviour are complex, and we are not suggesting that it would disappear if there were more tennis courts or running tracks: nor are we concerned to press for wider provision of opportunities for playing games just on the ground that it would reduce the incidence of those various forms of anti-social activity which are lumped together as 'juvenile delinquency'. At the same time, it is a reasonable assumption that if more young people had opportunities for playing games fewer of them would develop criminal habits. (Wolfenden Report, 1961, p. 4)

Such an assumption is only 'reasonable', of course, within a particular view of games playing based on the middle class games ethic. At the same time, the Wolfenden Committee was, in stating this view, merely confirming a widespread conviction that had been growing in strength since the end of the Second World War that games did have the power to rescue young working class people from delinquency.

The way in which this middle class view was treated in the Report reveals the extent to which the games ethic had become influential. In the early pages of the Report, the Wolfenden Committee went to some lengths to caricature what was intended to be understood as an obsolete and slightly ridiculous version of the games ethic. This stereotyping was done in order to make legitimate those elements of the games ethic the Committee wanted to retain. For instance, they commented:

> 'Character-building' is a description commonly applied to games, especially team games. It is easy to exaggerate (and to react from) this kind of claim. It is not in actual fact obvious that those who have been brought up on competitive team games are more unselfish, co-operative and self-sacrificing than those who have not; and we should not wish to press this particular argument too far. But within limits we believe that the playing of games or the sailing of a boat does at least provide the opportunity for learning this kind of lesson. Certainly it can be said that in Britain there is an ingrained respect for certain attitudes which have their roots in sport. The word 'sportsmanship' means something important and valuable; and the notion which underlies it is perhaps still one of the traits on which we customarily pride ourselves most. It is easy to ridicule the 'That's not cricket, old boy' attitude. But in its deeper (and usually inarticulate) significance it still provides something like the foundations of an ethical standard, which may not be highly intellectual but which does have a considerable influence on the day-to-day behaviour of millions of people. (Wolfenden Report, 1961, p. 5)

Over to You

Discuss in class whether you believe the values listed by the Wolfenden Committee are common in sport today, particularly for people your age. Are these values socially appropriate or do they have a more sinister side in terms of social control? Make notes of the main points raised in the discussion.

These sentiments express a version of the games ethic that is intended to have relevance and authority in the 1960s. The very idea that the values embodied in games playing form an ethical standard that is the measure of the everyday behaviour of millions of people reveals the extent of the influence of the games ethic by the end of the 1950s. It also shows how far these values had penetrated discussion of physical education and sport. This reconstructed games ethic formed the legitimating framework of the Wolfenden Committee's analysis of the problems facing British sport. It also led directly to the identification of 'The Gap' as one of the key difficulties requiring urgent resolution.

The notion of 'The Gap' was borrowed from an earlier report on youth and in the Wolfenden Report signified

> . . . the manifest break between, on the one hand, the participation in recreative physical activities which is normal for boys and girls at school, and, on the other hand, their participation in similar (though not necessarily identical) activities some years later when they are more adult. (Wolfenden Report, 1961, p. 25)

Identifying this issue as one of the leading concerns of their Report, the Wolfenden Committee strongly endorsed the role of organised physical activity in the Youth Service and greater linking between youth groups, statutory bodies, sports clubs and schools. In addition to arguing for a more cohesive approach to organisation, the Committee also expressed an optimistic view that the infrastructure of coaching, facilities and other services that would facilitate participation was on the way to being put in place.

However, the Committee members could scarcely conceal their puzzlement over the apparent reluctance of young working class people to take advantage of the opportunities being offered to them. The CCPR survey of secondary modern school leavers in the summer of 1960, showing that few working class adolescents had any desire to continue their involvement in organised sport and games, confirms that the Committee's concerns were not groundless. After giving some lengthy consideration to what was clearly to them a surprising and unexpected obstacle to mass participation, they speculated that the resistance of school leavers might be rooted in resentment to continuing regulation and organisation of their lives and an intrusion into their new-found freedom.

The Committee saw this problem as one of immaturity on the part of working class youth rather than as a symptom of broader social forces. Committee members expressed the view that intervention was for working class youngsters' own good. The tone of their recommendations was couched entirely in terms of providing opportunities for youth who might otherwise be deprived: 'We find it discouraging that so many fall away; and for their sakes we hope that something may be done urgently'.

This philanthropic tone is dominant throughout the Wolfenden Report. Other views were also expressed in the Report that reflect middle and upper class interests. Not only were the young missing out on the opportunity for 'healthy enjoyment', but there was a 'waste of the national investment in the provision of facilities for school games'.

Within the political and sports communities, 'The Gap' was less a problem of missed opportunity for wholesome personal development and more an issue of lack of supply of sportsmen and sportswomen who could excel in international competition. For the physical education profession, and especially for men, 'The Gap' represented an opportunity to confirm their importance to the development of British sport.

Running through these interests, 'The Gap' can be seen as an expression of concern about a perceived lack of control over working class youth. What the Wolfenden Committee was advocating was a very extensive network of supervision and surveillance during the post-school 'problem' years. The members of this

Committee were not engaging in a conspiracy to dominate the masses. Their sincerity and belief that games and sport were a power for good demonstrates how significant and influential the games ethic had, by the early 1960s, become.

Over to You

Organise a class debate with two teams and a chairperson. Set one team the task of defending the proposition that the Wolfenden Report's analysis is as pertinent today as it was in 1960. The opposing team should argue against the proposition. Make sure everyone in class contributes to constructing the arguments for their team, even though only a small number of team members deliver the arguments.

THE AFTERMATH OF THE WOLFENDEN REPORT, 1960–1965

The Wolfenden Report was generally well received and many of its recommendations finally acted upon. Its solutions to the problems afflicting British sport focused on more and better organisation, facilities and coaching, and these were based on the provision of funding from the British government. The establishment of the Sports Council in 1965 was the outcome of this and other pressure from the sports lobbyists, an event that continued the trend toward State intervention which began, as we noted earlier in this chapter, with indirect funding of sport through the Ministry of Education after the war.

The inevitability of this outcome of greater government intervention was signalled by the almost simultaneous publication of policy statements on physical recreation and sport by the Labour opposition and the ruling Conservatives in 1959, just before the release of the Wolfenden Report. Each party's policy statement differed only slightly in approach. Labour in particular made much of teenage delinquency and the lack of provision of sports facilities. However, their recommendations were virtually identical, both supporting the idea of a Sports Council of Great Britain.

This outcome was entirely consistent with the consensual politics of the 1950s and 1960s, and it may be significant that this heightened political interest in sport emerged at the same time that education became an election issue. The egalitarian rhetoric of the day influenced education and sport. The Sports Council's 'Sport for All' slogan had similarities with the ideology of comprehensive schooling and the notion of equality of opportunity.

In this respect, the reconstructed games ethic appeared as the ideal form of physical education for the new mass secondary schools. As we will see in chapter 3.6, it promised to supply the common denominator to unite divided social class groups, to overcome delinquency among working class adolescents, and to provide a cohesive focus for the development of national identity.

SUMMARY

This chapter examines the increasing involvement of government in funding and policy making for sport and recreation from the 1920s to the 1960s. Two nongovernment organisations, the NPFA and the CCPR, did much of the groundwork to establish public facilities for sport and recreation and training programmes for leaders. Although both organisations were independent of government, their link to ruling class interests was clearly established by their royal patronage and Establishment membership. These class-based interests were seen to be important as we investigated the uses of sport and recreation as a means of regulating the leisure-time behaviour of working class youth. The Wolfenden Report, published in 1960, is considered in some detail. This is because it brought together the thinking of the time among sections of the ruling classes that sport could rescue the working classes from delinquent behaviour, centred on a reconstructed version of the games ethic. It was also important in providing the impetus for a Sports Council of Great Britain, established in 1965. The establishment of the Sports Council was further evidence of increasing government involvement in funding and organising sport.

Test Yourself Questions

1. Why was there a need for the National Playing Fields Association?

2. Describe the NPFA's role between 1925 and 1965.

3. The 1944 Education Act led to the CCPR shifting its emphasis from a local to a national level. What did this new focus entail?

4. With greater opportunities for the working and lower middle classes came a form of regulation. List the disadvantages that came with regulation.

5. Explain why the government and juvenile delinquency committees believe that boys and girls who became members of youth organisations, on leaving school, were less likely to be involved in crime.

6. Between 1941 and 1947, membership of a youth organisation was not considered appropriate or necessary for grammar and public school boys and girls. Describe the situation as it affected working class youth. Why were the groups treated differently?

7. What were the main concerns raised in the Wolfenden Report? Discuss their relevance today.

CHAPTER 3.6

The Social Construction of Sport-based Physical Education, 1940–1970

Chapter Overview

Learning Outcomes

When you have studied this chapter, you should be able to

- ☑ list the forces behind the emergence of sport-based physical education,
- ☑ explain how sport-based physical education was gendered,
- ☑ summarise the early challenges to sport-based physical education,
- ☑ explain how physical education was influenced by its location in early comprehensive schools,
- ☑ describe how physical education developed in the 1970s,
- ☑ define the concept of the 'social construction of physical education', and
- ☑ speculate on the significance of these events for your experience of physical education today.

INTRODUCTION

- -

In 1951, the Editor of the *Times Educational Supplement* wrote about the **'two traditions'** in English education. These were represented, on the one side, by the schools serving the middle and upper classes and, on the other, by the schools serving the lower middle and working classes. In the next issue, the TES published a letter to the Editor from historian Peter McIntosh. McIntosh stated that physical education was one of the clearest examples of these two traditions. He noted that physical education for the 'haves' was represented by team games and for the 'have nots' by drill and gymnastics. McIntosh wrote:

> There was almost no mingling of the two traditions before the twentieth century. Indeed, there has often been antagonism between them: the public schools have looked down on physical training as mere pedantry, while the protagonists of physical training have decried games because they are neither systematic nor primarily designed to promote health. In spite of considerable intermingling of recent years the fusion is still far from complete. There will only be a single national tradition of physical education when the State's schools can provide adequate playing fields and facilities for all children and when the public schools realise and appreciate the value of scientific and systematic physical training. Apparently a deficiency of insight is as difficult to make good as are deficiencies of space and money. (Letter to the Editor, *Times Educational Supplement,* 26 January 1951)

It was lack of space and facilities for public use that was blamed for the continuing separation of the 'two traditions', beginning with the formation of the NPFA in the 1920s but accelerating after the Second World War. As we noted in chapter 3.5 this issue received much attention in documents such as the Wolfenden Report of 1960. Meanwhile, McIntosh's challenge to the public schools fell on deaf ears. Public schools did not change their version of physical education. On the contrary, from the 1950s to the 1970s, schools serving the 'have nots' emulated their version of physical education.

In a relatively short space of time, competitive team games and other sports became the core of physical education in schools serving the masses. In this chapter, we track the rise of sport-based physical education in government secondary schools from the late 1940s to the 1970s. This new form of sport-based physical education was centred on the public school tradition of games. A new version of the games ethic, which you can read about in chapter 3.2, provided the rationale for the development, and, in the process, the meaning of school physical education was reconstructed. Within a decade and a half, a version of physical education that had until the 1950s only been 'traditional' to the private schools in Britain became **'traditional physical education'** for everyone, for the masses as well as the wealthy.

In order to place the emergence of sport-based physical education in its broader context, we revisit briefly some of the issues presented in chapter 3.5.

FORCES BEHIND THE EMERGENCE OF SPORT-BASED PHYSICAL EDUCATION

- -

Three forces assisted in the establishment of games as the central feature of physical education for the masses after the Second World War.

1. There was increasing State intervention in sport and physical recreation outside the school system, a process that began to draw school and community physical education and recreation into the service of 'the national interest'.

The 'two traditions' in physical education refers to games for the wealthy members of British society and drilling and exercising for the working classes.

'Traditional physical education' was based on a version of the games ethic and was invented in the 1940s and 1950s by individuals and groups serving ruling class interests.

2. By the end of the 1940s, there was a view among the ruling classes that competitive games and sports were a unifying force and a means of promoting national identity: a common denominator in society that rose above class interests and politics.

3. There was public concern for social order. The growth of consumer culture, working class affluence and materialism, and the emergence of youth subcultures, particularly in relation to working class youth and their use of leisure time, promoted this.

These three forces together played an important role in forming public opinion and commonsense attitudes to the educational potential of games and sports. These forces were part of a self-conscious movement in society towards post Second World War social reconstruction in an era of Britain's declining influence as an international power.

THE GENDERING OF SPORT-BASED PHYSICAL EDUCATION

The introduction of universal secondary education through the Butler Education Act in 1944 and the raising of the school leaving age to 15 in 1947 meant that physical education needed to cater for older pupils. The resulting rapid development of secondary schools presented men with a much more attractive career path in physical education than was available to them before the war. The influx of males into the physical education profession had a profound impact on the gendering of the subject.

The emergence of **sport-based physical education** in secondary schools was sponsored enthusiastically by the newly arrived male physical educators, whose numbers relative to the female members of the profession increased dramatically after the war. Their appropriation of games playing and a version of the public school games ethic was an important means of enhancing their status, in relation both to their middle class female colleagues and other teachers.

In this, the educational press and other ruling class interests, who viewed games playing as a vehicle for solving a range of social ills, gave the male physical educators considerable ideological support. At the same time, there was a need to reconstruct the public school games ethic for use in the mass secondary school system in a form that could enlist the identification and support of working class pupils.

Sport-based physical education was gendered because it was based on masculine forms of physical activity such as competitive team games.

EARLY CHALLENGES, THE 1940s AND 1950s

Policy makers had suggested as early as 1919 that it would be desirable for older elementary and post-elementary pupils to participate in an expanded range of activities beyond gymnastics and drill. Pupils who attended the selective government-run or -aided secondary and grammar schools had played competitive sports and games in the private school tradition since 1900. But these schools catered for only a small number of pupils, and even then facilities were in short supply.

The introduction of universal secondary education and the raising of the school leaving age presented the Ministry of Education with considerable challenges. They had to provide new school buildings, specialised facilities within the schools such as science labs, workshops, gymnasia, swimming pools and playing fields. Specialist teachers were also in great demand. For physical educators, the challenge was how to adapt existing forms of physical education, based on Swedish gymnastics or educational gymnastics, to the needs of older pupils. These young people, unlike their grammar school peers, represented a wide range of academic and physical abilities. Poor facilities and lack of equipment made this task even more challenging.

A survey of physical education in government selective secondary schools for girls reported in 1946. The survey showed that gymnastics and games dominated the curriculum, with little time provided for dancing, swimming or athletics. In the schools for boys, apparatus and some freestanding (Swedish) gymnastics vied for time with major games such as cricket and football and other activities such as boxing. In the elementary schools, physical training in the form of Swedish gymnastics and drill were, as you can read in chapter 3.3, giving way to less formal methods and modified exercises such as educational gymnastics.

This was the situation that faced physical educators at the end of the war. Not surprisingly, their discussions at conferences and in professional journals in the years immediately following the implementation of the Butler Act were taken up with the problem of how to cater for the larger numbers of older pupils in the new secondary schools. The unanimous response was to provide older pupils with more freedom of choice of activities. While this idea was proposed with much qualification, it was to have far-reaching consequences for physical education. This was because choice assumed the existence of a range of activities from which to choose.

In responding to this challenge, female physical educators were influenced by tradition. Competitive sports and games had formed a part of the female Swedish gymnasts' work from the 1880s. But their professional body, the Ling Association, had followed a consistent policy of opposition to overcompetitiveness in games and sports from the late 1800s up to the 1940s. The Association was dismissive of the excesses of competition so evident in the public schools for boys.

At the Ling Association annual conference in 1925, 'professionalism in women's games and participation for children in Junior County Teams' was 'deprecated'. This point was restated forcefully at the 1932 gathering. The 1928 conference focused on the introduction of 'Competitive Athletics for Schoolgirls'. Although this innovation received a generally favourable response, the discussion at the conference was taken up entirely by concerns over whether toilet and dressing room facilities would be suitable for the schoolgirl athletes. As late as 1948, an editorial in *The Leaflet*, the Ling Association's journal, took a dim view of competitive gymnastics at the London Olympics held in that year.

However, the men were, from the beginning of their specialist courses, strong advocates of competitive games and sports. In the 1930s and 1940s, Swedish gymnastics complemented games in their college curricula. But this sharing of time did not last for long. Male physical education students from Loughborough and Carnegie Colleges performed at the 1949 Lingiad held in Stockholm, the stronghold of Swedish gymnastics. The *Journal of Physical Education* reported that 'their performances splendidly contrasted in type and presentation' with the activities of the host nation and left the Scandinavians 'not knowing what next to expect from the British'. The report went on to say:

> The Carnegie programme opened with quickening and strengthening activities all conducted competitively. It then gave four series of games skill practices and competitions. The games taken were cricket, basket-ball, soccer and rugger. Each series showed the separate skills of the game being practised and then applied the skills in a competitive phase. Twenty-five activities were packed into fifteen minutes and the work was a good test of stamina as well as a fine demonstration of speed and skill. Cricket greatly intrigued the audience and Rugby Touch brought them to their feet. (Reported in the *Journal of Physical Education*, 1949, p. 123)

During the late 1940s and early 1950s competitive games quickly became the staple of the male specialist college curriculum. At the Scottish School of Physical

Education (SSPE) based at Jordanhill in Glasgow, this enthusiasm for games extended beyond the curriculum. The college had first claim on all students in their chosen sport, exemptions being granted only to professional footballers. Students were also required to attend a Friday afternoon briefing before the match, regardless of whether they were in college on that day or in schools on teaching practice. Not attending incurred disciplinary action.

This system was established under Hugh Brown, Director of the SSPE between 1958 and 1974, who was an ardent advocate of games. Speaking at a conference in 1958, he commented:

> The curriculum in the Colleges of PE is ever-widening. This is something that I rejoice to be able to report, and my only comment is 'high time, too!'. We are British people — for which I can find no cause for apology — and we are a games-playing nation. It has always puzzled me, for instance, that gymnastics should be regarded as being synonymous with Physical Education. Gymnastics is a part — a very valuable part — of a vast subject, and in some countries it may have been looked on as being the main fraction of the whole. No longer is that so here. However good a system may be, the folly of adopting it in its entirety and foisting it upon people, unadapted to peculiar needs, is at last recognised. What may delight the Germans or the Danes, and what suits their national characteristics, does not necessarily make a similar appeal here. Now we are recognising this! (Reported in *Physical Education*, 50, p. 92)

Over to You

Analyse Mr Brown's statement in a small group. What is the link between being British and physical education? Brown implies there are differences in national characteristics reflected in games. What characteristics evident in games do you think he might have associated with being British? Now discuss the relevance of Brown's statement today. Could he reasonably make this statement now? List reasons to defend your view. Write a brief summary of your group discussion.

The notion that games playing was part of the national culture of Britain strongly influenced Brown's statement. As you can read in chapter 3.5, he was expressing a point of view that had gained widespread legitimacy by the end of the 1950s.

PHYSICAL EDUCATION IN THE COMPREHENSIVE SCHOOLS IN THE 1960s

By the end of the 1950s, team games formed the core of an expanded physical education curriculum that included a wide range of indoor games and other activities such as swimming and in some places, outdoor activities such as hill-walking and canoeing. The traditional role of games in the existing grammar and other selective secondary schools was consolidated between the 1920s and early 1950s and was quickly establishing itself in the new secondary modern and comprehensive schools.

In 1961, Vivien Jacobs, a teacher at a new comprehensive, explained the planning and organisation of physical education at her school. Holland Park School was a London comprehensive opened in September 1958 with an initial intake of 1,700 pupils. The school had new and extensive facilities for swimming, gymnastics and indoor games; outdoor court games such as basketball, netball and tennis; and space for jumping and throwing.

These facilities allowed the school to offer a wide range of activities on-site. However, as games formed the major part of physical education, pupils travelled by bus to London County Council playing fields 20 minutes from the school to play soccer, rugby, hockey, netball, cricket, tennis, rounders and athletics; to Wimbledon Common for cross-country; and to Putney Reach for rowing. As many as 500 pupils were taking part at any one time in physical education lessons.

Despite problems of discipline and organisation, Jacobs and her colleagues did not question the viability of this option of transporting pupils to various venues for their physical education lessons. One of the reasons for this was practical. The on-site facilities at the school could not accommodate team games, athletics and rowing. But the large amount of time spent on games was justified on a different basis than practicality. Jacobs explained:

> We are a Comprehensive School, and naturally we believe in the comprehensive system. In the Physical Education Department we felt that games was one subject, at least, in which we could carry out the system completely and beneficially. We were convinced that there would be an all-round improvement, and that lower intelligence groups would not debase the standards, the view held, unfortunately, by so many people. (Reported in *The Leaflet*, 1961, p. 45)

If they could not apply the principle of equality of opportunity to the academic work of the school, then perhaps games could provide the common denominator that would allow this ideal to be practised.

Jacobs noted that teachers were still coming to terms with older pupils who now had to remain at school until they were 15. These young people in the secondary modern and remedial streams were, she conceded, 'extremely difficult to manage' and that they were gaining little from playing games. She noted, however, that these 'problem pupils' participated more readily when streams were mixed, suggesting that this mixing of abilities had a civilising effect on the 'lower intelligence groups'.

Jacobs did not raise the issues of the disaffection of the pupils in the lower streams and their hostility to the school in general, the effects of streaming itself, and the imposition of cultural values that were foreign to the pupils. However, she implied that sport-based physical education could solve some of these problems of disaffection because games possessed properties that were common to all students, regardless of their social class or intelligence. Significantly, at Holland Park School, it was the physical educators who supported this common denominator view of games and claimed for themselves the role of integrating the various social class groupings among the pupils.

A survey of secondary modern schools conducted by the CCPR in the Eastern Counties of England in the summer of 1960 revealed that the Holland Park curriculum was not uncommon. On the basis of responses from almost 5,000 pupils surveyed, the study reported the most popular school physical education activities at that time of the year. These activities are listed, in order of preference, in table 5.

This survey suggests that the opportunity to play most major games seemed to be available to working class pupils in the south east of England by the early 1960s. Moreover, sport-based physical education now seemed to be well established in their schools. However, the survey showed that few secondary modern pupils wished to continue with these sports after leaving school.

Young people's apparent lack of willingness to take advantage of the range of activities now available to them was the unexpected obstacle to mass participation that baffled members of the Wolfenden Committee, as you can read in chapter 3.5. Although this response continued to puzzle policy makers for years to come, it did not arrest the rate of growth of sport-based physical education in government secondary schools.

Table 5 **Popular Physical Education Activities**

Girls	Boys
Tennis	Tennis
Swimming	Football
Netball	Swimming
Athletics	Cricket
Hockey	Athletics

PHYSICAL EDUCATION IN THE 1970s

Researcher Nick Whitehead's survey in 1969 of a range of secondary schools mainly in the north of England found that the 'national sports' of soccer, rugby and cricket for boys, and hockey and netball for girls and athletics for both now dominated school physical education. He also made two observations.

The first was that the traditional, national games were clearly the main priorities of physical education teachers, particularly males. However, schools were paying little or no attention to the physical activities adults actually chose to do in their leisure time. This observation is important because it contradicted the accepted opinion of the previous three decades that team games could fulfil this leisure-time function.

His second observation was that, whereas games were now the major part of school physical education in the post-war period, nonspecialist teachers often taught them. Paradoxically, only specialists were permitted by local authority inspectors to teach indoor lessons, particularly those involving gymnastic equipment. So, although the gymnasium continued to be the specialists' preserve, by the early 1970s, nonspecialists often taught the core of the physical education programme.

This suggests that the development of game skills in the gym was regarded as the physical education teacher's main responsibility. Meanwhile, games were not under their sole ownership and control but were the property of a wider section of the school community.

Over to You

Is this a good way to organise physical education? How might such a scheme impact on your ability to learn in, about and through physical activity? Prepare and deliver a two-minute presentation to a small group outlining your answer to this question.

As for Whitehead's view, he applauded the efforts and enthusiasm of the nonspecialists. Although he was prepared to concede that 'the coaching could be good' among nonspecialist teachers, he suggested that 'educational principles are not applied to the extent that they might be'. The educational principles of the games ethic were, according to one advocate, the 'basic themes of social life — success and failure, good and bad behaviour, ambition and achievement, discipline and effort'.

It would appear, at least in the schools surveyed, that young working class people were not particularly interested in playing team games in their leisure time, even though by the 1970s they had the opportunity to do so. It would also appear that some of the educational principles of the games ethic that formed a rationale for teaching games in physical education may not have been realised to the extent that policy makers had intended. By the 1970s, these values did not seem to have resonated with the working classes in the ways they had for the middle classes over the preceding 100 years. Sport-based physical education was apparently unable to merge the 'two traditions'.

Over to You

Carry out an informal survey of your parents or guardians, grandparents, uncles and aunts. Find out how many played organised team games after they left school, what they played, their age when they stopped, and the year they stopped. Pool your information in class and produce a class report. Then consider the extent to which your generation has followed the same trends or has adopted a different pattern of activity.

We know that female physical educators had resisted the excesses of the male public school games ethic from the beginning, and many educational gymnasts continued to do so throughout the 1950s and 1960s. However, there was dissent among male physical educators, too. Teachers were clearly aware from their own experience of the issues the surveys were reporting.

Teachers at a conference in Scotland in 1968 were concerned with 'The Place of Organised Games in the Curriculum'. They discussed the issue of the 'carry-over' between what is learned in games and other aspects of life. The conference report recorded that 'when considering competition in adult life in commerce, industry, the professions or anywhere else, [the group] completely agreed that the experience of children in game situations would be of no value whatever'.

In a paper presented at another professional gathering two years earlier, K.B. Start, a college lecturer in physical education, poured scorn on many of the educational benefits alleged to derive from participation in games. He argued that any literal interpretation of the games ethic was naive and that the values it was supposed to teach were meaningless to many working class pupils.

However, by the 1970s, sport-based physical education was established in official policy and school practice. The survey by Whitehead at the end of the 1960s and another by John Kane in 1974 confirmed that games occupied the majority of physical education curriculum time in secondary schools for both boys and girls.

It is worth noting that many physical educators benefited from the games ethic. It provided them with a respectable rationale for games teaching while they were drawn more and more throughout the 1960s into developing the base in the **pyramidal structure** for British sport. The function of servicing elite sport became a prominent but unstated purpose of physical education in many schools. In pursuit of this goal, physical education teachers were assisted by the new scientific knowledge of skill acquisition, exercise physiology and biomechanics discussed in chapter 3.4.

The pyramidal structure to sport development places sport-based physical education at the base of a pyramid of performance levels.

Over to You

Is this true of your school today? How does your school programme compare? Discuss in a group and summarise the key points.

SUMMARY

This chapter tracks the emergence of sport-based physical education in government secondary schools between the 1940s and the 1970s. Before the 1940s, it was noted that physical education reflected the 'two traditions' of education in England, with different provision made for the wealthy compared with the working classes. However, supported by an educational rationale formed by a reconstructed version of the public school games ethic, sport-based physical education developed rapidly in government secondary schools after the Second World War. Men who had entered the field in large numbers after the war promoted this form of physical education. Surveys in the 1960s and 1970s confirmed that sport-based physical education had established itself in secondary schools across England. However, these surveys also found that, contrary to the expectations of policy makers, young working class people were reluctant to grasp the opportunities given to them to play games and sports in their leisure time. Finally, it was noted that physical education teachers benefited from the development of sport-based physical education as it tied them into the structure of sport development in Britain.

Test Yourself Questions

1. Explain how physical education reflects the two traditions of education in England.

2. List the major factors that promoted sport-based physical education in secondary schools between the 1940s and the 1970s.

3. Despite the establishment and development of games in the physical education curriculum, why was there a lack of participation in these activities during the pupils' leisure time?

4. Discuss how far these reasons exist today.

PART 4

....

Policy Dimensions of Reflective Performance in Physical Education

*I*n this section you will find three chapters concerned with policy dimensions of reflective performance in physical education. In chapter 4.1 you can read about the developments in physical education during the 1980s, including co-educational physical education, teaching games for understanding and the emergence of health-based forms of physical education. Chapter 4.2 examines the effects of the introduction of a National Curriculum for Physical Education (NCPE) in 1988 and a subsequent revision in 1995. This chapter notes that physical education and sport were entering into a new relationship. In chapter 4.3 you can read about another revision to the NCPE under a different government in 1999 and separate developments in England and Wales. The focus of this section is on the forces of continuity and change and how they affect your experience of physical education.

The 1980s: New and Progressive Times in Physical Education?

Learning Outcomes

When you have studied this chapter, you should be able to

☑ have an understanding of a number of initiatives arising in physical education in England and Wales in the 1980s;

☑ be able to explain the *various* interests in physical education that each of these initiatives was associated with and their similiarities to and differences from established or 'traditional' curricula and teaching in physical education in England and Wales;

☑ appreciate the ongoing political interest in physical education having a *particular* form and focus and the role that the media can play in promoting particular images and understandings of the subject; and

☑ be able to explain the various examination and vocational courses that have been developed in physical education, their key characteristics and links to further education or employment opportunities.

INTRODUCTION

This chapter is the first of three chapters that address contemporary developments in physical education in England and Wales throughout the 1980s and 1990s and into the 21st century. Each chapter draws attention to important links between contemporary developments and past practices and traditions. Continuities and changes in both the form and focus of the subject and the ways in which it has been taught are therefore discussed. This first chapter outlines a number of initiatives that emerged during the 1980s that were labelled as 'new' and 'progressive' and explores the reasons why there was some opposition to these initiatives. The chapter then addresses the development of physical education as an examination subject in England and Wales and the growth in vocational courses associated with physical education. The reasons for, and benefits of, these developments are discussed. Many of the issues we address in this chapter are identified as ones that reappear when we move on to consider developments in physical education in the 1990s.

Previous chapters have described the historical development of physical education in Britain. We have seen certain characteristics established as defining features of the subject, with physical education emerging as a subject that is notably 'sport-based' and gendered. We have also seen that the increasingly prominent position of games in physical education has been linked to notions of 'national culture' and has come to be seen as the 'base' of the **pyramidal structure** for British sport. These associations are particularly relevant when considering contemporary developments in physical education in England and Wales. Many of the activities associated with physical education curricula in the 1960s should now be familiar to you. This chapter is therefore concerned not only with changes since those times but also continuities from them. It specifically outlines a number of initiatives that were labelled as distinctly 'new' and 'progressive' in the 1980s and explores the degree to which they can be regarded as challenging the values and practices of what by then was deemed 'traditional' physical education. These initiatives in the 1980s represent an important aspect of the context for the development of a National Curriculum for Physical Education (NCPE) in England and Wales that we discuss in detail in chapter 4.2.

The pyramidal structure refers to the foundation–participation–performance–excellence pyramid for sports development, discussed in chapter 5.2.

PHYSICAL EDUCATION IN THE 1980s: THE NEW AND THE OLD

It is important to realise that in many schools the provision of physical education in England and Wales in the 1970s remained essentially unchanged. The 1980s were notable for the emergence of a number of initiatives in physical education, but schools and teachers throughout England and Wales did not consistently or comprehensively adopt them. Development was instead very varied. We should not, therefore, regard the initiatives as 'transforming' physical education in England and Wales. It is more appropriate to see them as having *some* impact upon curricula and teaching in some schools and, to some degree, influencing thinking within the profession in relation to matters of curriculum design, groupings and teaching methods. The importance of the initiatives emerging during the 1980s was not so much their *actual* impact upon physical education in schools as what politicians and the media judged and also *portrayed* their impact to be. As Evans (1990) vividly documented, by the end of the decade physical education was deemed (by politicians and the media) to be in a state of crisis, caused at least in part by the spread of 'new' and 'dangerously progressive' practices that, it was claimed, constituted a threat to the nation's sporting identity and achievements, its economic future and the health of children.

In this chapter we take a closer look at some of the initiatives that generated such interest and concern. However we also need to acknowledge concerns over the provision of physical education and sport in schools at this time. Teachers' industrial action was associated with a decline in the provision of extracurricular physical education and school sport, and the increasing number of local education authorities selling school playing fields in order to generate income clearly threatened future provision (Evans, 1990). As you are probably aware, many physical education and other teachers devote a great deal of time, on a voluntary basis, to provide extracurricular physical education and school sport. As we discuss in chapter 4.3, initiatives currently being developed are directed towards other individuals (such as sports coaches and parents) playing a greater role in this provision. Meanwhile, the National Playing Fields Association and the Central Council for Physical Recreation (see chapter 3.5) continue to lobby against the sale of school playing fields. Thus, issues that were a source of concern in the 1980s remain relevant twenty years on. So, what was 'new' and (dangerously) 'progressive' about physical education in the 1980s?

Co-educational Education and Mixed-sex Grouping in Physical Education

In preceding chapters we have seen that physical education in England and Wales has a 'gendered history' and that the provision of different curricula for girls and boys, invariably taught respectively by female and male staff, was standard practice in many schools. Physical education is one of 'the most gender-segregated subjects in the school curriculum' (Green and Scraton, 1998, p. 272). As Green and Scraton (1998) have explained, schools recognised the problem and sought to establish equal opportunities for girls and boys via provision of 'the same curriculum'. In the 1980s **co-education** became the norm in other subject areas and in turn, responses arose in physical education. In particular, there was a trend towards mixed-sex grouping.

Scraton (1993) has emphasised that although mixed-sex grouping may have been seen as a critical step towards the development of co-education and equal opportunities in physical education, it was often introduced for pragmatic reasons (timetabling and staffing) rather than educational reasons. Furthermore, mixed-sex physical education cannot be assumed to be a context that provides co-educational experiences and equal opportunity for girls and boys. As we discussed in chapter 1.2 many mixed-sex lessons may fail to challenge stereotypical images and beliefs relating to the respective abilities of, and the activities and roles appropriate for, girls and boys. Instead, many mixed-sex lessons may see girls having a marginal role in activities dominated by boys, or girls, and boys working independently of one another in a mixed-group setting (see Green and Scraton, 1998; Scraton, 1993). Thus, moves towards co-educational physical education did not successfully or comprehensively address equal opportunities in the context of physical education. Nevertheless, in the 1980s, politicians and the media portrayed these moves as an integral element of the 'new physical education' that represented a threat to established and valued traditions in schools (Evans, 1990).

Teaching Games for Understanding (TGfU)

Teaching Games for Understanding was a new approach to the teaching of games that was developed by Rod Thorpe and colleagues at Loughborough University (see Thorpe and Bunker, 1986). It was an approach that appealed to *some* teachers in England and Wales, who therefore used it in their teaching. In addition, it was an initiative that attracted international interest. The influence of TGfU has been apparent in developments in physical education and junior sport in Australia and New Zealand in particular. In England and Wales it is still the case that the ideas and

Co-education was directly linked to equal opportunities in education and, in particular, the recognition that boys and girls should have access to the same educational opportunities.

Learning experience refers to tasks within lessons that are designed to develop particular learning.

Learning environment refers to the lesson context. 'Environment' encompasses physical and social dimensions. By using particular teaching styles, or using different grouping arrangements, teachers can affect the learning environment.

Skill development in traditional approaches typically takes the form of drills and practice focusing on a particular skill.

Game play in traditional approaches often focuses on the full-sided 'adult form' of a particular sport.

principles that TGfU presented have been variously (rather than consistently or uniformly) developed in physical education teaching.

So how was TGfU different to 'traditional' approaches to the teaching of games? As its name suggests, TGfU was concerned with developing pupils' 'understanding' and, specifically, their understanding of principles of game play, and therefore of what are appropriate and effective skills and strategies in particular game situations. TGfU differed from past approaches to games teaching in that it focused attention upon *similarities* between different games, identifying common skills, knowledge and understanding needed for effective performance in different games. Also, TGfU prompted teachers to consider how they could design **learning experiences** and create **learning environments** that would promote the gradual development of these skills, knowledge and understanding. There was therefore encouragement for children to experience increasingly more sophisticated game contexts in terms of rule structures, tactics and decision-making demands, and for the learning of skills to be integrated with (rather than separate from) experience of game settings. The aim was to promote understanding of what skills were effective in particular situations and thereby encourage the appropriate selection of skills in given situations. It sought to integrate the learning of skills with children's experience of game settings. With these aims in mind, it also emphasised that the 'adult form' of games was not an appropriate starting point for learning. Instead, TGfU encouraged the modification of the equipment, playing area and rules of adult sports, and developments that would enable children to play a more central role in the teaching and learning process (see Thorpe, 1992; Thorpe and Bunker, 1986).

In several respects, TGfU promoted the use of activities and approaches to teaching that contrasted with established practice. The move to different forms of games, and away from the distinct division of **'skill development'** and **'game play'** that characterised much games teaching, represented a notable shift from 'the traditional approach' to games teaching in physical education. As you will appreciate from your reading of this and other chapters, many people have passionate (but also differing) interests in physical education and in the skills, attitudes and behaviours that the subject may instil in children. Therefore mixed reaction would result from any development that signalled a shift from 'the norm' in attempting to achieve desired outcomes. Almost inevitably, TGfU would give rise to doubts and concerns not only among some teachers, but also among individuals outside the physical education profession who have particular interests in the subject. A key concern for some people would be whether TGfU would advance or threaten the development of games players with the potential to go on to represent their school, county or country. With children playing 'different games' in physical education and being encouraged to learn in 'different ways', were Britain's 'great sporting traditions' and international standing in sport being jeopardised by physical education?

These were the concerns of the media and politicians at the end of the 1980s. They were not directed solely at TGfU, but more generally at physical education curricula and teaching. Approaches that sought to emphasise *cooperation* between children, over and above a focus on *competition* between them, were particularly singled out for 'attack'. They were portrayed as failing to develop essential values and 'lessons for life' that children traditionally learned through competitive team games. In his commen-

Lessons for children involving modified versions of adult games are recommended by TGFU.

© Human Kinetics

tary on a BBC *Panorama* television programme that focused on these issues in 1987, Evans (1990) explained:

> The demise of competitive team games is singled out as a matter of general public concern, the process signifying not only a threat to tradition [the moral and social order], but also the dissolution of important elements of the hidden curriculum in schooling which foster the development of drive, ambition and a competitive spirit arising from the will, the longing, the desire to win . . . (p. 162)

As you can read in chapter 4.2., concerns for competitive team games to be the focus of attention in physical education re-emerged during the development of the National Curriculum in Physical Education. Once again, you see team games associated with the development of particular attitudes and values among children.

Over to You

In small groups, discuss your experiences of team games in physical education and school sport. What attitudes and behaviours do you feel that your experiences have instilled in you? Also consider other pupils in your physical education lessons and particularly those who are less able in team games. How do you think that their experiences of team games will have affected their attitudes towards sport and physical activity?

An interesting point about the debates in the late 1980s is that team games and, specifically, the emphasis of competition, was also linked to the development of fitness and health. In the *Panorama* programme broadcast in 1987, parents were informed that a decline in provision of school sport and a shift in attention from 'competition for the few' to 'participation for the many' represented a threat to the health of children (Evans, 1990). As we have discussed in other chapters, we can question the extent to which extracurricular physical education and school sport provide opportunities that encourage all children to adopt active lifestyles and become regular participants in sport. The link between the provision of competitive sport and the health of children is one that we need to explore further. Ensuring the active participation of *all* children seems crucial if physical education and school sport are to justify an association with health promotion. Importantly, such developments *can* retain a competitive focus. It is simplistic and inappropriate to talk of physical education, sport or games being about *either* 'competition' *or* 'co-operation'. Instead, we need to recognise that effective cooperation between players is critical to success in competitive sport and that one of the things that attracts children to sport is the opportunity for them to work cooperatively with friends (see chapter 5.2). If physical education and school sport are to succeed in addressing interests in *both* the development of sport performance and the development of active lifestyles, we need to provide competitive sporting opportunities for children of all abilities and for children whose main concern may be the enjoyment of taking part and who do not aspire to reach elite levels.

As indicated earlier, in many respects TGfU and other 'new initiatives' were portrayed as having a more widespread and consistent impact upon physical education curricula and teaching than was the case (Evans, 1990). Some of you may have experienced games lessons that you recognise as adopting a 'TGfU approach', but not all teachers will use this approach, nor did they in the 1980s! We can see some evidence that TGfU has influenced the development of the National Curriculum in the identification of different categories (net/wall, striking/fielding and invasion) of games within this curriculum, but we can also note that many games lessons remain firmly focused upon one specific sport.

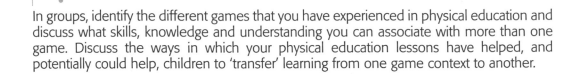

Over to You

In groups, identify the different games that you have experienced in physical education and discuss what skills, knowledge and understanding you can associate with more than one game. Discuss the ways in which your physical education lessons have helped, and potentially could help, children to 'transfer' learning from one game context to another.

PHYSICAL EDUCATION AND INTERESTS IN HEALTH

As well as the aforementioned developments associated with the teaching of games, the 1980s were notable for a growth in units within physical education that were labelled 'health-related fitness' (HRF) or, more latterly, 'health-related exercise' (HRE). The difference in the terms used is important. Although both HRF and HRE have lacked uniformity in the way in which they have been developed in schools, they can nevertheless be associated with two contrasting sets of learning objectives and activities. HRF has an explicit focus upon knowledge and understanding relating to various dimensions of fitness. It has often featured the testing of various dimensions of fitness (such as flexibility and aerobic fitness), and units have been designed to enable and encourage children to improve their fitness for sport or general health. HRE has been primarily concerned with the latter interest: general health and wellbeing, and the role that physical activity has to play in maintaining and improving general health. HRE units have therefore sought to promote awareness, understanding and behaviours that will enable and encourage children to adopt active lifestyles, featuring involvement in physical activity at appropriate levels of intensity and with appropriate regularity in order to achieve health benefits. HRE has also led to a number of popular 'health-related' leisure activities, such as aerobics, being introduced into curricula. Both HRF and HRE have also featured weight-training activities in some schools.

Like TGfU, HRF and HRE have attracted support, but also criticism. Critics of the early developments of HRF in physical education pointed to negative learning experiences for many pupils, in which they were left with feelings that they were 'unfit' compared with fellow pupils and that engagement in physical activity was painful and embarrassing. Teachers needed to use fitness testing selectively and sensitively, and ensure that there were clear educational merits to the inclusion of testing in physical education lessons (see Harris, 1997). HRE has been acknowledged as having important potential to provide learning experiences that may particularly appeal to adolescent girls, many of whom may find other forms of physical education not very interesting or sometimes threatening. However, on occasions the educational 'rigour' of HRE lessons featuring activities such as aerobics has been questioned. Critics have highlighted the need for physical education to retain its educational focus and ensure that it is addressing the notions of learning 'in, through and about' physical activity (see chapter 1.1). Whereas these concerns are important, it is not only in activities associated with HRE that the focus on *learning* may be neglected. Quality of teaching is crucial, irrespective of the particular activity context. Any activity has the potential to be notably *recreational* rather than *educational*.

Although we have emphasised the distinctions between HRF and HRE, it is also important to acknowledge similarities between the initiatives. In particular, both initiatives have tended to focus attention primarily, if not exclusively, 'upon the *physical* dimensions of health, with little acknowledgement of the potential of teaching and learning in physical education to address mental and/or social aspects of health' (Penney & Waring, 2000, p. 22). In addition, both have adopted a somewhat uncritical approach to matters of health and physical activity. Pupils are rarely encouraged to consider the ways in which particular forms of activity and patterns of participation may constitute a *risk* rather than benefit to one's health or acknowledge that the body shapes that have become associated with achievement in particular sports may be ones that are neither feasible nor healthy for many of us to aspire to (see chapter 6.1). As we identify in chapter 6.4, (comparative) physical education curricula in some other countries devote far more attention to these issues.

Over to You

With a partner, discuss what types of physical activity you would associate with maintenance of mental health and wellbeing. Identify ways in which physical education curricula may address these dimensions of health in practical contexts. This could involve the introduction of new activities into the curriculum, such as forms of yoga or some of the martial arts. As a group, discuss how you would feel about such activities being introduced in physical education.

THE GROWTH OF PHYSICAL EDUCATION AS AN EXAMINATION SUBJECT

In parallel to the initiatives just discussed, the 1980s also saw physical education become established as an examination subject in schools. Since then, there has been a growth in the range of qualifications that can be gained in the area of physical education, an increase in the number of pupils choosing to take physical education or a related subject as an examination subject, and in the numbers of pupils taking vocational qualifications relating to physical education, sport and leisure. These developments reflect two issues in particular. Firstly, establishing examination courses in physical education has been regarded by many teachers as a key means of raising the status of physical education in schools. The development of CSE, then GCSE and A-level and A/S-level courses means that physical education can be seen as an academic subject, rather than merely a 'release' or break from academic studies. However, these course developments have not totally eradicated the misconceptions about the nature of physical education. Physical education may still be seen as 'an easy option' by some teachers and by many people outside of schools. The growing number of pupils taking the courses offered and their successes in examinations are now leading to a greater understanding of the nature of studies in physical education and an appreciation of their value for many pupils. An added benefit of the development of these courses is that many physical education departments have consequently been able to purchase new resources for use by all pupils, not only those taking examination courses.

The second issue with which we can associate the growth of examinations and qualifications in physical education is the increasing further education and employment opportunities in physical education, sport and leisure. The sport and leisure industry remains an area of expansion, with career paths emerging not only in facility management but also in sports development and coaching, fitness training, sports marketing, leisure, tourism and health promotion. The growth in number and diversity of employment opportunities has meant more courses in higher education (degree studies) and further education (diploma courses, General National

Vocational Qualifications and National Vocational Qualifications), as well as in schools. There are currently GCSE courses in physical education, game, and dance, and A-level or A/S-level courses in physical education, sports studies, and dance. Also, schools and other education institutions offer a range of other courses and qualifications, including National Governing Body awards, National Coaching Foundation courses and CCPR Leadership awards (see chapter 5.1). Increasingly, these qualifications are becoming linked into the formal structures of National Vocational Qualifications.

This growth in physical education as a focus for examination and qualifications is an important development, but we also need to look in more detail at the nature of some of the courses developed. What have the **syllabuses** incorporated and therefore defined as essential knowledge in the subject? And how do examination courses relate to the physical education that all children experience as the National Curriculum for Physical Education?

As indicated, a *diversity* of courses has been developed. One of the reasons for this was that until 1995 the various examination boards throughout England and Wales were free to develop new syllabuses as they saw fit. That situation has now changed, with the examination boards required to construct their syllabuses with reference to criteria established by the Qualifications and Curriculum Authority. But alongside the diversity of early developments, we can note some common characteristics. The GCSE and GCE A-level courses have all featured *distinct* 'theoretical' and 'practical' components. Theoretical components included many of the areas of study addressed in this book, relating directly to the content of higher education courses in sport science, sport studies or physical education. Practical components have required pupils to show evidence of attainment in specific activities. Personal performance in sport has been a key reference point for assessment in the practical component. What the balance between the theoretical and practical components of physical education courses should be and how attainment in a practical context should be assessed have been issues of debate. The development of the National Curriculum (see chapter 4.2) has highlighted the need for assessment to address the processes (knowledge and understanding) underpinning performance in sports and not merely constitute measurement of performance according to the criteria (such as speed or distance) that we would see in sporting, rather than educational, contexts. However, many courses still feature quite distinct 'theory' and 'practical' lessons. A challenge for physical educationalists is to address the ways in which teaching and assessment can better integrate these elements.

Syllabuses refers to the official requirements and frameworks that have been established by government, curriculum authorities or examination boards for schools to refer to when developing their curricula.

Over to You

For a chosen activity and referring to other chapters in this book, design *practical* tasks that could assess knowledge, skills and understanding relating specifically to (1) different components of fitness; (2) levels of arousal and their effects on performance in sport; and (3) equity issues in physical education and sport.

Whereas GCSE and GCE A or A/S levels have generally been directed towards entry to higher education, the growth in vocational courses has been directed towards employment opportunities in sport, leisure and recreation. The theoretical and practical components of these courses have therefore had a more specific focus, and courses may also require completion of work experience in an appropriate employment setting.

As you will be aware, physical education curricula that are not linked to examination or optional studies do not usually involve 'theory lessons'. The inclusion of a distinct theoretical component has been one of the characteristics that has distinguished examination courses from 'core physical education', and it is the component that has often been regarded as the key to the subject being 'taken seriously' or being recognised as 'an academic subject'. As you can read in chapter 4.3, the latest revisions to the NCPE and recent modifications to examination syllabuses are now encouraging teachers to develop pupils' understanding of 'theoretical aspects' in the context of practical lessons. Also, the latest revision to the NCPE has involved changes designed to encourage children to develop skills, knowledge and understanding in relation to a variety of roles in sporting contexts, including leadership and coaching. In the future, therefore, we can anticipate closer links between the NCPE, examination and vocational courses. Many schools already offer the CCPR sports leadership courses at Key Stage 4, and some schools provide opportunities for pupils to gain other qualifications, such as the Bronze Medallion Lifesaving award. In addition, it is now a requirement that new examination syllabuses are consistent with National Curriculum requirements.

Over to You

In groups, discuss what you think the focus of attention should be in core (non-examination) physical education? Specifically, what skills, knowledge and understanding should core physical education be seeking to develop? What aspects of knowledge and understanding (if any) that you currently regard as 'theoretical' do you think should be included in core physical education? How do you think these aspects can be addressed in the context of practical activity, rather than being indoor 'desk-based' lessons?

SUMMARY

In this chapter you can read about a number of developments in physical education in the 1980s that have variously featured in the curricula of schools in England and Wales since that time. You can see the range of different interests that these initiatives reflected and explained: that they relate to different views about what the central focus and knowledge of physical education should be, the activities that should feature in the curriculum and the ways in which they should be taught. We have explained that practices and emphases that are seen as different from 'traditional' or established practices may give rise to concerns, particularly in central government. The chapter has highlighted the contrast between the physical education curriculum provided for all pupils and the curriculum followed by pupils choosing physical education as an examination subject, and the way in which 'theoretical' and 'practical' components of courses are often seen as separate aspects of physical education. Finally, the issues arising in physical education in England and Wales in the 1980s are highly relevant to our investigation and understanding of developments in the 1990s and beyond.

Test Yourself Questions

1. Explain why a mixed-sex group setting cannot be assumed to be a co-educational learning environment.

2. Describe ways in which Teaching Games for Understanding is different from traditional approaches to teaching games in physical education.

3. Explain why the media described the various initiatives in physical education in the 1980s as 'dangerously progressive'.

4. Identify differences and similarities between HRF and HRE.

5. Identify the various examination and vocational courses that have been developed in physical education, and explain what the benefits of these developments have been for physical education departments.

CHAPTER 4.2

From Crisis to Reform: The Introduction of a National Curriculum for Physical Education

Learning Outcomes

When you have studied this chapter, you should be able to

☑ describe the framework established for the National Curriculum and National Curriculum for Physical Education (NCPE);

☑ explain changes in the requirements for the NCPE that relate to the breadth and balance of the physical education curriculum;

☑ outline specific views that the government had in relation to the nature of physical education and the activities that should be included in the NCPE;

☑ identify issues that received limited attention in the development of the NCPE;

☑ explain ways in which, in the second half of the 1990s, relations between physical education and sport were changing; and

☑ identify key developments giving rise to the change in these relations.

INTRODUCTION

In many respects the NCPE can be regarded as the single most important development in physical education in England and Wales in contemporary times (Penney & Evans, 1999). However, the development of the National Curriculum was not straightforward. Rather, it highlighted very vividly that developments in physical education in Britain are inextricably bound up with political interests and agendas relating to both education and sport (Penney & Evans, 1999). Furthermore, it demonstrated that one of the most notable characteristics of the physical education profession in Britain is the *diversity* of interests that it seeks to embrace. As we have shown in other chapters, at different points in time various interests (such as interests in creative movement, fitness, health, sport performance and games) have come to the fore to shape and 'define' physical education. There are 'other interests' at play in curriculum developments, albeit 'in the background'. Any curriculum will be something of a compromise between different views of what form physical education should take, what activities it should feature, what learning it should be seeking to develop in children and how it should be taught.

Talk of compromise is almost always accompanied by talk of conflict or contestation, and contemporary developments in physical education in England and Wales are no exception. In this chapter you will gain some insights into the contestation that has accompanied the development of the NCPE. When you have read this and the following chapter, you will appreciate the very rapid pace of educational change in the 1990s and into the year 2000. The scope and scale of these changes mean that our sense of history may also have shifted. As time goes by it may become increasingly difficult to think of there *not* being a national curriculum in place and to appreciate the relevance of events before its introduction. We hope that you will be able to see the influences of past practices and long-standing traditions in the contemporary developments that we address here. You should also see that the initiatives and the issues considered in chapter 4.1 are as relevant and potentially controversial now as they were in the 1980s. Matters such as the grouping strategies that teachers should employ in physical education, how to teach games and how to address health issues in physical education are things that the introduction of the National Curriculum has yet to achieve. Rather, they continue to be a focus of debate and, furthermore, constitute areas in which we can identify differences in provision and practices between different schools and within individual schools.

Over to You

With a partner, identify and discuss

- differences in the activities provided for girls as compared with boys in physical education in your school;
- different grouping arrangements that you have experienced for various activities in physical education (specifically, mixed sex, single sex, mixed ability, setted by ability);
- different approaches used by different teachers in teaching games in physical education; and
- activities that have been associated with health-related fitness or health-related exercise in physical education.

From the outset it is important to realise that the introduction of the National Curriculum did not signal the introduction of 'the same curriculum' for all pupils in all schools. As we will discuss, this was not its intention. Rather, the aim was to establish a standard *framework* for curricula and to ensure a *minimum* entitlement for all pupils. The framework was intentionally 'flexible', enabling **statutory requirements** to be met in different ways in different schools. It allowed for various issues, including the professional judgement of teachers, but also differences in the resourcing of physical education, such as facilities or staff expertise, to shape what the required minimal entitlement would look like in practice.

THE 1988 EDUCATION REFORM ACT AND THE DEVELOPMENT OF A NATIONAL CURRICULUM

In 1987 the Conservative government was preparing for a general election and had identified education as a key voting issue. There were clear benefits for the government to portray education as in urgent need of attention and at the same time show itself to be addressing identified 'problems' in education. The government introduced the Education Reform Act of 1988 as a response to something of a 'crisis' in education, with questions raised about standards of provision and learning, and the efficiency of the education system. As you can read in chapter 4.1, it was also argued that the 'crisis' was there to be seen in physical education.

The Education Reform Act (1988), or 'ERA' as it became known, legislated for the development and implementation of a National Curriculum for all State schools in England and Wales. In addition, the ERA introduced policies that changed the structure and organisation of education in England and Wales. The introduction of Local Management of Schools (LMS) involved many financial and management responsibilities being transferred from local education authorities to individual schools. LMS also linked funding of education directly to schools' intake of pupils. Under LMS, head teachers and school governing bodies would have to ensure the school operated within budgetary constraints and sometimes make harsh decisions about, for example, how many staff they could afford to employ or what new resources could be purchased for particular departments. The ERA also introduced the policy of Open Enrolment. On the one hand this policy aimed to give parents freedom of choice as to which school they would send their children. On the other, it sought to create a situation in which schools would have to prove that they were effective in order to continue to attract pupils (and in turn funding). Open Enrolment effectively created a situation in which schools would compete for pupils in a marketplace. If they failed to attract pupils, they might ultimately be forced to close.

Since the introduction of these policies, we have seen some teachers made redundant, some schools close and a growth in the 'marketing activities' of schools anxious to promote an attractive and successful image to prospective parents. As Penney and Evans (1999) have explained, both LMS and Open Enrolment are important to our understanding of the ways in which physical education and the NCPE have been developed in different schools. Physical education is not always a subject that is a priority when decisions are being taken about how resources are to be allocated within schools. Other subjects (and particularly those defined as the **core subjects** in the National Curriculum) will often be selected as areas of investment in preference to physical education. However, school sports facilities may be seen as having the potential to generate valuable income for schools. Also, achievements in school sport may well be something that is highlighted in school prospectuses and in school reception areas. It is invariably the achievements of a few pupils outside the physical education curriculum, rather than the provision for and achievements of *all* pupils within the curriculum, that have a high profile in schools. Although there may be support for 'school sport', physical education may still be regarded as a 'marginal' subject within the curriculum. As you can read in chapter 4.1, the development of examination courses has been a way in which some

Statutory requirements refers to the legal requirements established in the National Curriculum for curriculum provision in all State schools in England and Wales.

Core subjects in the National Curriculum were English, mathematics and science, and in Welsh-speaking schools in Wales, Welsh. Foundation subjects were technology, history, geography, music, art, physical education, a modern foreign language and, in non-Welsh-speaking schools in Wales, Welsh.

departments have tried to raise the status and profile of physical education. Achievements in GCSE physical education and other courses, such as the Junior Sports Leader Award course, are another issue that might be drawn to the attention of prospective parents.

Over to You

Study a local school prospectus and school reception area. Note the ways in which physical education or school sport are presented to prospective parents and visitors. What aspects of the subject receive particular attention?

The National Curriculum

The National Curriculum was designed to ensure the provision of a 'broad and balanced' curriculum for all pupils. It was decided that this should comprise certain 'core' and 'foundation' subjects, with physical education identified as one of the foundation subjects. The ERA also established a common framework for the requirements relating to each subject and a timescale for the development and implementation of the new curriculum in schools. 'Attainment targets' and 'programmes of study' were to be developed for each of four 'key stages' in education, for all subjects. Attainment targets referred to groupings of objectives that set out the knowledge, skills and understanding that pupils of different abilities and maturity were expected to develop within each subject area. Programmes of study identified the 'matters, skills and processes' which must be taught to pupils during each key stage in order for them to meet the objectives set out in the attainment targets. The key stages related to different phases of education, with Key Stages 1 and 2 covering the primary school years; and 3 and 4, secondary education (see DES, 1989).

Although this framework of attainment targets (ATs), programmes of study (POS) and key stages has been the same for England and Wales, differences in the curricula have then developed in these countries. An obvious difference is the inclusion of Welsh as a subject in the curriculum for schools in Wales. In some schools in Wales, Welsh is also the main medium for teaching. However, the differences extend beyond language. The Welsh language adjective 'Cymreig' (meaning 'concerned with Wales') has been used in referring to the 'whole curriculum' (incorporating the National Curriculum) in Wales. 'Curriculum Cymreig' has been a focus for the development of the requirements for all National Curriculum subjects. In physical education, the requirements established for the National Curriculum for England and Wales allowed for cultural differences (and, therefore, a Curriculum Cymreig) to be expressed in teaching and learning. Guidance issued by the Curriculum Council for Wales (CCW) explained:

> Through some of the programmes of study it is possible to be given an insight into the culture and traditions of the local Welsh community. For example, in dance, pupils could study the history and evolution of Welsh dance and perform a selection of Welsh dances. When hill walking or on nature trails, an appreciation of the Welsh landscape could be fostered. (CCW, 1992, p. 8)

As we go on to explain, the CCW also issued guidance that indicated some dissatisfaction with the statutory requirements issued by the government based in London. In chapter 4.3 you can read about structural changes in government, particularly the creation of the Welsh Assembly, that have enabled Wales to establish quite different statutory requirements for the NCPE from those in place in England.

© Youth Sport Trust

The Curriculum Cymreig allows for viewing the Welsh landscape through programmes of hill walking.

Furthermore, in the development of the National Curriculum, not all subjects were considered at the same time. Instead, the National Curriculum developed subject by subject, and physical education was one of the last subjects to be addressed. This reinforced the image of physical education as a low priority subject in schools. Also, pressures emerging in the whole curriculum as more subjects were introduced constrained the development of the NCPE. Schools were finding it increasingly difficult to manage the growing number of new requirements. Timetables became 'overloaded', and it became clear that requirements for the subjects being introduced last would have to be minimal (see Penney & Evans, 1999). One way in which these pressures were reflected in the requirements for physical education was the decision that there should only be *one* attainment target for the subject. However, the problem of how to fit everything into the limited time available in schools has not gone away. Your school may have reduced the length of lessons from, say, 60 to 50 minutes or reduced the length of break times in an attempt to accommodate the growing requirements of the National Curriculum. Any reduction in lesson time is a particular concern for physical education, where changing time is needed. Reductions in the length of a lunchtime break may mean that it is not possible to offer extracurricular activities during this time. This is a particular concern in rural schools, where a school bus may be the only way for many children to get home, meaning that they cannot stay for activities after school.

So, What Did the National Curriculum for Physical Education Look Like?

Developments at different points in history and in other countries show us that the form and content of physical education can vary (see chapter 6.4 and part 3). In considering the curriculum that was established as the National Curriculum in

England and Wales, decisions had to be made about what knowledge and interests within physical education would be the focus of attention and what would receive less attention. These decisions are ones that continue to attract political interest. The government has kept a tight hold on the development of the National Curriculum and it has openly expressed its view of what the requirements for physical education should be. The NCPE therefore needs to be acknowledged as reflecting the interests and agendas of the government of the time.

One of the interesting aspects of the development of the National Curriculum is that, although it was part of the 'reform' of education, before its creation, much of its form and content was already recognisable. This takes us back to government interests and, specifically, the fact that the Conservative government viewed 're-establishing' a 'traditional curriculum' as the solution to the crisis that it had identified in the education system. The curriculum as a whole and the requirements developed specifically for physical education were modelled on past practices. In the case of physical education it appeared that the curricula established in independent (public) schools, where competitive team sports have a particularly high profile (see chapter 3.2), were the key reference point for the development of the NCPE.

We do not have the space in this chapter to detail all aspects of the development of the NCPE. Instead, we will address *some* of its major characteristics and, in so doing, try to draw attention to the ways in which we can see continuity from the past, some prompts for changes in physical education curricula and teaching, and political intervention in physical education. The framework for the National Curriculum, comprising attainment targets, programmes of study and related assessment requirements, provides a useful focus for our discussion.

As already explained, attainment targets referred to 'groupings of objectives setting out the knowledge, skills and understanding that pupils of different abilities and maturity are expected to develop within the subject area' (DES/WO, 1991). In the early stages of the development of the NCPE, the working group appointed by the government to advise it on requirements for physical education recommended that three attainment targets be established for physical education. The three ATs identified focused on planning, performing and evaluating. The working group acknowledged that these elements were interrelated, but wanted to draw attention to the need for teaching to explicitly address skills, knowledge and understanding relating to *each* of the three elements. Underpinning these proposals was a desire to emphasise that physical education is about more than 'simply doing'. The three attainment targets could help distinguish physical education from physical activity or recreation.

The framework of three attainment targets was not acceptable to the government for two reasons. Firstly, politicians' understanding of physical education did not match with the group's proposals. The Secretary of State for Education specifically directed the working group to revise their proposals so as to emphasise the 'active element' and 'practical nature of the subject' (Penney & Evans, 1999). Secondly, the government associated more attainment targets with a need for more curriculum time, which was not available in schools. The working group was therefore forced to modify its proposals and establish a single attainment target for the NCPE. The group attempted to retain its emphasis of an 'educational process' while also accommodating the government's views of the subject. It stressed the interrelated nature of the dimensions of planning, performing and evaluating, and emphasised that planning and evaluating should be addressed within *active* learning contexts (Penney & Evans, 1999).

The NCPE provided only general guidance in terms of how teachers should develop knowledge, skills and understanding relating to the three inter-related dimensions. The 'programmes of study' identified the 'matters, skills and processes' which must be taught to pupils during each key stage in order for them to meet the objectives set out in the attainment target (DES/WO, 1991), but left it for teachers to decide upon the most effective way of achieving these objectives.

One of the notable characteristics of the framework for the programmes of study was that it was clearly recognisable to teachers. This familiarity of the structure is important in relation to the degree to which the NCPE was likely to prompt changes in physical education in England and Wales. The programmes of study for the NCPE were outlined in relation to six areas of activity: games activities, dance forms, gymnastics activities, athletic activities, swimming and water-based activities, and outdoor and adventurous activities. As Penney and Evans (1999) have stressed, because this was the existing format of most physical education curricula, it seemed an entirely natural framework for the NCPE. As it was also the only framework that many people were familiar with, it was difficult to imagine alternatives. As you can read in chapter 4.3, this remains the situation today and it reflects the extent to which a particular format for physical education has become so firmly established in schools in England and Wales.

The familiarity of the activity area framework also meant that many teachers saw the areas — and in turn the NCPE more generally — as 'what they already taught'. In many schools, therefore, implementation of the NCPE did not involve major changes to curricula and teaching, just minor adaptations to well-established curricula to ensure fulfilment of the statutory requirements (Penney & Evans, 1999). In some schools, there was a need for a change in the range of activities within physical education. The working group advising the government had been keen to prompt teachers to address the 'breadth and balance' of physical education curricula and to consider the range of activities within their curricula and the time devoted to various activities. The National Curriculum would specify a minimal entitlement for all children in all schools, and there was a desire to ensure that this featured a broad range of activities. Initially it was proposed that in each of Key Stages 1, 2 and 3 children should experience all six of the identified areas of activity and, in Key Stage 4, at least three areas, including games and either gymnastics or dance. However, once again, the government rejected the group's proposals. Firstly, the government was concerned about the practicality of these requirements. In particular it questioned whether there were the facilities, time and teaching expertise to address the range proposed. In addition the government did not necessarily share the group's concern that physical education should include a broad range of activities. The government did not view all of the areas of activity as of equal worth or priority, and it saw some areas as impossible to resource. Changes to the working group's proposals reflected these views. When the statutory requirements were finally published in 1992, the 'minimal entitlement' looked very different from the original proposals. 'Breadth and balance' was redefined as requirements were reduced and priorities were established for which areas of activity children should experience at the various key stages.

The requirements were for the curriculum in Key Stage 1 to include the five areas of games, dance, gymnastics, athletic activities and outdoor and adventurous activities plus, if desired, swimming, and for all six areas to be addressed in Key Stage 2 unless the programme of study for swimming had already been completed in Key Stage 1. More substantial changes were made to the requirements for curricula in secondary schools. Swimming was removed as an area of activity in its own right. Instead it was now identified as an activity that could be pursued in the context of the remaining areas so that, for example, competitive swimming would be regarded as an athletic activity and water polo as a games activity. For Key Stage 3 it was then stipulated that games should be included in *each year* of the key stage and at least three other areas should be experienced during the key stage. In Key Stage 4 pupils who were not following GCSE physical education would be required to follow two activities from either the same or different areas (DES/WO, 1992; Penney & Evans, 1999).

In secondary schools particularly, there was the scope for children to experience a relatively *narrow* range of activities in their NCPE. Statutory requirements could not specify the time to be allocated to particular aspects, and there also seemed little guarantee of 'balanced' curricula. The requirements seemed to support a 'games-dominated' physical education curriculum. The tendency to devote a disproportionate amount of time to this area was certainly not challenged by the NCPE. Rather, its requirements were likely to see this 'imbalance' continue in many schools. The requirements specified the need for teachers to address three different types of game: invasion (such as netball or rugby), striking/fielding (such as cricket and rounders) and net/wall (such as tennis, squash and volleyball). This categorisation of games reflects the influence of work in the area of Teaching Games for Understanding (see chapter 4.1), but in many curricula the focus may still be on specific games. Units of work are identified as 'hockey' or 'soccer' or other specific sports. In contrast, you might envisage units identified with, for example, 'invasion games'. Within such units, pupils could experience more than one invasion game context, which might help encourage the transfer of skills, knowledge and understanding across different sporting contexts. In the next chapter you can read about the issue of transfer of learning across different activities within physical education.

The CCW issued its own recommendations to teachers in Wales that encouraged them to go beyond the statutory minimum entitlement and specifically extend the breadth and balance of the NCPE. The CCW recommended that, during Key Stage 3, pupils should experience *five* areas of activity; that in *each year* of the key stage they should experience *at least four areas,* including games and either gymnastics or dance; and in Key Stage 4 that the minimum two activities should be from *different* areas (CCW, 1992).

Over to You

Undertake an audit of the activities included in the Key Stage 3 curriculum of a secondary school and the time devoted to each. Critically address the 'breadth and balance' of the curriculum.

Although many of the debates focused on the required coverage of particular areas of activity, you also need to note other aspects of the requirements. Throughout the 1980s some schools created units of work focusing on health (see chapter 4.1). Given the ongoing association of physical education with the promotion of active and healthy lifestyles and the government's expressed concerns relating to the nation's health, we may have expected health-related exercise to be a major focus of the NCPE. Instead, the National Curriculum requirements left teachers uncertain about how they could and should address 'health-related' aspects of physical education in the NCPE. Aspects of learning associated with HRF and HRE were incorporated in some of the text of the NCPE, but there were no programmes of study for them. There was the potential for health issues to be a focus in teaching but, without detailed requirements for coverage, there were also dangers that the links between fitness and health would be marginalised (Fox, 1992; Penney & Evans, 1999). It was unclear whether there was a legitimate place for units of HRF and HRE within the NCPE framework; whether, instead, teachers should be addressing skills, knowledge and understanding relating to health in an 'integrated' manner, in the context of one or more of the activity areas; or whether they should be developing distinct units and also integrating 'health' into units of work in various areas of activity. The statutory requirements represented a minimum that schools could choose to 'go beyond' if they wished. There was also flexibility in relation to how they chose to design their curricula. 'Health', HRF or HRE could be a major focus in the NCPE, but not all teachers would pursue this potential. This 'positioning' of health in the NCPE reflected the government's view that other aspects of knowledge in physical education were more important. Performance in sport, rather than matters of health and active lifestyle, was the government's main focus in the development of the NCPE.

The NCPE also addressed equal opportunity in physical education. Draft proposals from the working group particularly drew teachers' attention to the fact that access should not be equated with opportunity in contexts of physical education (see chapter 1.2). However, ultimately the advice relating to equal opportunities was non-statutory. The ways in which equal opportunity developed in the implementation of the NCPE were dependent upon the responses of individual teachers, the importance that they attached to this issue and their knowledge and understanding of equal opportunities in contexts of physical education.

The statutory requirements were particularly notable for the 'flexibility' that they offered schools and teachers to choose the specific activities to be included in curricula, how these should be taught and by whom. This meant that sex-differentiated teaching could continue in physical education in England and Wales. In some instances this has also meant that stereotypical gendered images and attitudes relating to physical education and sport may go unchallenged and continue to be reinforced in schools. The introduction of the NCPE did not change the fact that in many departments male teachers teach boys rugby, soccer or cricket, and female staff teach girls hockey, netball and rounders. In some departments it is still assumed that female staff should be responsible for teaching dance to both girls and boys. In other schools, dance has remained an activity that is only included in the curriculum offered to girls.

With practices such as these continuing, you might question the degree to which the introduction of the NCPE had created reform in physical education. In many respects, little had changed. Physical education still had low status in many schools and might be a low priority in resource allocations. The National Curriculum had not prompted any change in the basic form of physical education. To many people, physical education was still a 'collection of activities'. Games also remained the dominant activity. The NCPE reinforced the strong association between physical education and sport, and, in the **'education marketplace'** of the 1990s, school performances in sport might well have been the key criteria by which the quality of physical education provision would be judged. Also, and perhaps most importantly, the National Curriculum had not altered the fact that differences in the facilities available for physical education, in the time allocated to the subject and in the individual interests and expertise of physical education teachers would mean that the physical education curriculum in one school might be very different from that in a neighbouring school.

To a great extent the introduction of a National Curriculum represented a *continuation* of historical and established practices in physical education in England and Wales. This reflected the particular interests of the Conservative government, whose visions of 'reform' centred on a strengthening of the past traditions and practices that you can read about in earlier chapters. In the next section, you can read about the ways in which the government made a number of changes to the NCPE that further emphasised the importance of 'traditional team games' and the view of physical education as the base of the pyramid of sports development.

Education marketplace draws our attention to the fact that, following the introduction of Local Management of Schools and Open Enrolment, schools had to attract pupils in order to support themselves financially and faced possible cuts in staffing or ultimately closure if they failed to attract sufficient numbers of pupils.

1995: REVISION AND REDUCTION OF THE NATIONAL CURRICULUM FOR PHYSICAL EDUCATION

Even before the NCPE had been introduced for all of the key stages, there was talk of changes to the requirements. As schools had introduced the National Curriculum subject by subject, they had found it increasingly difficult to manage the whole curriculum. The government faced demands for reductions in requirements and it therefore commissioned a review of the requirements for all subjects. Making reductions necessitated making decisions about the relative importance of different types of knowledge. In physical education, it meant that attention again focused upon what activities should be retained within the curriculum. Again the government had a particular interest in specific activities, namely games, and was concerned that the National Curriculum requirements should reflect what it was realistic for all schools to provide. Irrespective of the reasons for the changes, the result was that the 'new NCPE' identified some activities as more important than others as an educational experience for all pupils. From September 1995, schools in England were required to include games, gymnastics and dance in each year of Key Stage 1. If they wanted, they could also include swimming in Key Stage 1. The Key Stage 2 curriculum still had to feature all six areas of activity unless the programme of study for swimming had been completed in Key Stage 1, but only games, gymnastic activities and dance had to be included in each year of the key stage. Effectively, the National Curriculum was identifying these three areas of activity as of greater importance than athletics, outdoor and adventurous activities and swimming at Key Stage 2.

Over to You

With a partner, develop a list of what you regard as basic movement skills that should be developed in physical education in primary schools. Identify the activities that you feel would be the most effective contexts in which to develop these skills.

In Key Stages 3 and 4, the revised requirements reinforced the image of games as the single most important area of activity in physical education. Games were now the only area of activity that schools were required to include in each year of Key Stage 3. At some time in the key stage they would also have to address three other areas of activity, with one of these being gymnastics or dance. In Key Stage 4, the requirements were changed so that at least one of the two activities included in the curriculum must be a game. If you compare these revised requirements with those initially proposed by the working group, you can see the changes to the notion that the NCPE should be 'broad and balanced'.

As in the debates in the 1980s (see chapter 4.1), claims were made about the particular qualities and attitudes that 'traditional team games' would instil in pupils. On behalf of teachers in Wales, the Curriculum Council for Wales argued that there should be an unrestricted choice of activities at Key Stage 4. However, the Conservative government had a different view, and the requirement that one activity in Key Stage 4 must be a game therefore stood. These revisions to the National Curriculum need to be seen as part of wider government interests relating to the role that physical education could play in the development of sport in England and Wales.

1995–1999: CLOSER RELATIONSHIPS BETWEEN PHYSICAL EDUCATION AND SPORT

The revision of the NCPE coincided with a major policy initiative directed towards the development of sport: *Sport – Raising the Game* (DNH, 1995). As discussed in chapter 5.2, 'Raising the Game' identified a specific role for schools and physical education in the future development of sport in England. Many of the initiatives proposed in Raising the Game were mirrored in policies issued in Wales, Scotland and Northern Ireland. These policy developments signalled the prospect of stronger and more direct links between physical education and sport throughout Britain. They reaffirmed the long-standing view of physical education as the foundation for sport participation and performance, but made this more explicit than had previously been the case. At the same time they demonstrated the government's interests in particular sports and in particular forms of participation. Many of the proposals in the policy seemed directed towards the development of elite performance in a selected few sports, and there were a number of proposals designed to encourage schools to direct their provision of physical education towards these particular objectives. For example, there were proposals for Sportsmark and Sportsmark Gold awards to be introduced in schools (see chapter 5.2).

In its revised form and particularly with its increased focus on games, the NCPE seemed to match very obviously with the agendas set out in *Sport – Raising the Game*. The mid-1990s also saw other developments that have had a very significant impact upon physical education and particularly the relationship between physical education and sports development. In 1994, the Youth Sport Trust (YST) emerged as a critical 'new player' in the development of physical education and school sport in Britain. The resources and associated training programmes developed by the YST have supported curriculum development in many schools in England since the mid-1990s. The YST developments came at a time when there was a notable absence of any other investment in physical education. They have been invaluable to many schools, especially primary schools. These programmes were designed to support the teaching of the NCPE and the development of a 'sporting pathway' for children, from an age of 18 months to 18 years. As you will see, the programmes for 7- to 11-year-olds focus on the various areas of activity within the NCPE. They have also addressed ways to design physical education and sport to better meet the specific needs of children with disabilities and ways to improve the links between primary schools and secondary schools. TOP Link is a programme encouraging secondary school pupils to develop leadership skills and experience by planning and organising a sport or dance festival for pupils from feeder primary schools.

Importantly, the YST has stressed that its programmes and resources are intended to support the curriculum, as there were fears within the physical education profession that the YST programmes (and thus 'sport') would replace physical education in primary schools. Once again, you can see some tensions between different interests (and interest groups) associated with physical education.

The YST Programmes

The YST programmes are designed to support the development of a 'sporting pathway' for children from age 18 months to 18 years.

TOP Tots is designed to help parents, childminders and nursery staff to introduce children aged 18 months to 3 years to physical activities and games.

TOP Start is designed to enable nursery or playgroup staff to encourage 3- to 5-year-olds to learn through physical activity.

TOP Play is designed to support 4- to 9-year-olds in acquiring and developing 'core skills'.

BT Top Sport is designed to provide 7- to 11-year-olds with opportunities for skill development in a range of sports, including basketball, football, netball, squash, cricket, hockey, Gaelic football, swimming, tennis and hurling. British Telecom have sponsored this programme.

TOP Gymnastics, TOP Athletics and **TOP Outdoors** are designed to provide 7- to 11-year-olds with opportunities for skill development in gymnastics, athletics and outdoor and adventurous activities.

Medisport Fit for TOPs is designed to address aspects of fitness and health relevant to 7- to 11-year-olds' participation in a range of physical activities.

SportSability is designed to create opportunities for young disabled people.

Ecclesiastical Insurance TOP Link is designed to enable 14- to 18-year-olds to take a lead in the organisation of sport.

The YST resources have been used in various ways in schools, and the training that teachers have received in various local education authorities has played a key part in shaping this use. In the development of resources and the provision of training, the YST has sought to work with a range of 'partners' (see chapters 5.1 and 5.3). It has secured sponsorship support from commercial organisations and other charitable trusts and, in the development and delivery of training, has worked with professional associations, local education authorities, private physical education consultants, national governing bodies and sports development officers. Particularly in England, the YST can now be seen as the key link between physical education and sport and the key partner in initiatives that seek to address both physical education in schools and junior sports development. This influence is extending, as YST programmes are now being introduced in Northern Ireland and Scotland, with the YST working in partnership with the Sports Council for Northern Ireland and **sport**scotland, respectively (see chapter 5.1 for discussion of the national sports councils).

In Wales, the Sports Council for Wales has launched 'Dragon Sport' with the aim of introducing children of primary school age to sport. The programme is focusing on athletics, cricket, football, hockey, netball, rugby and tennis and on the development of new after-school clubs for children. Dragon Sport is one of several programmes developed in response to the Sports Council for Wales' *Young People First* strategy (see chapter 5.2).

Throughout the United Kingdom, the relationship between physical education, school sport and junior sport outside of school, was close. As you can read in the next chapter, the relationship remains a matter of government interest and a key point of reference in considering future developments in physical education.

SUMMARY

This chapter described and analysed one of the most notable developments relating to physical education in England and Wales: the NCPE. The National Curriculum is one element of a package of policies incorporated in the Education Reform Act of 1988. Performance in sport, and particularly in team games, gradually became the dominant and defining characteristic of the NCPE, while other interests were relegated to a marginal position. A number of developments in the second half of the 1990s indicated a shift in the relationship between physical education and sport, with sport emerging as the dominant partner in this relationship.

Test Yourself Questions

1. Define 'attainment target' and identify the three attainment targets originally proposed for the NCPE. Explain the issues influencing the decision to establish a single attainment target for physical education.

2. Define 'programmes of study'. Identify the six areas of activity that provided the framework for programmes of study in the NCPE. Outline key changes to the programmes of study for Key Stages 1, 2, 3 and 4 during the initial development of the NCPE and in its revision in 1995.

3. Explain how health (and health-related exercise) was positioned in the NCPE.

4. Outline the ways in which the National Curriculum and the NCPE in Wales were different to that in England.

5. Briefly explain why the NCPE would 'look different' in different schools.

6. Explain the possible impact that other policies within the Education Reform Act of 1988 might have on the provision of physical education and school sport.

7. Identify the developments in sport in the second half of the 1990s that are particularly relevant to future developments in physical education in England and Wales.

Physical Education in England and Wales in the Year 2000

Learning Outcomes

When you have studied this chapter, you should be able to

☑ outline the latest changes to the National Curriculum for Physical Education (NCPE) in England and in Wales,

☑ identify differences and similarities between the requirements established for schools in Wales and those established for schools in England,

☑ describe the new framework for monitoring and reporting progression in learning in physical education and discuss issues associated with making judgements about learning and attainment in physical education, and

☑ describe ways in which changes in the NCPE have addressed links between teaching and learning in various areas of activity.

INTRODUCTION

This chapter is concerned with physical education in the year 2000. It addresses the further changes that have been made to the NCPE following a change of government and considers 'what is new' and 'what is old' in the requirements established for physical education in schools. It also draws attention to the fact that the NCPE in Wales is now distinctly different from that in England. This chapter revisits issues considered in chapters 4.1 and 4.2, of how the subject of physical education is being defined, what aspects of knowledge are the focus of attention and what is recognised as achievement and progression in physical education. You can also read about the latest requirements for the NCPE in relation to the relevance of physical education for pupils' adult lives. You should note throughout the chapter the ongoing political, social and cultural significance of physical education and school sport.

A CHANGE OF GOVERNMENT AND FURTHER CHANGES TO EDUCATION

In the general election of 1997 the Conservative government was defeated and a Labour government came to power. Education was one of its identified priorities for development and investment. Changes to the National Curriculum were somewhat inevitable. On the one hand changes were acknowledged as necessary. Schools (and primary schools in particular) were still struggling to fit all of the National Curriculum requirements into their timetables. On the other hand, the government wanted to be seen to be addressing these problems and initiating developments that would achieve the 'raising of standards' in schools that it had promised when elected.

In 1998 the government announced measures that would immediately reduce the statutory requirements for the curriculum in primary schools and enable primary schools to focus attention on the development of literacy and numeracy. Although schools were still required to teach all of the National Curriculum subjects, they were no longer required to cover the full **programmes of study** in history, geography, art, music, design and technology and physical education at Key Stages 1 and 2 (QCA, 1998). Schools were given the freedom to decide the way in which they would address these subjects, with one notable exception in physical education. The requirement to fulfil the programme of study in swimming was retained. The government had signalled that some subjects were of greater importance than others and, in relation to physical education, had identified swimming as the single most important element of the curriculum for Key Stages 1 and 2. Swimming was clearly identified as 'an essential life skill'.

The effect of these changes was dramatic in primary schools. Placing the emphasis on the raising of standards in literacy and numeracy meant a reduction in the time and resources for other subjects. Professional associations and other organisations with interests in physical education (see chapter 5.1) recognised the potential threat to teaching and learning in physical education. They lobbied head teachers and the government to recognise the importance of physical education. The British Association of Advisers and Lecturers in Physical Education (BAALPE) stated that 'It remains critical to the wellbeing of every child and the Nation's health generally, that there is an entitlement to a rigorous physical education programme' (BAALPE, 1998, cited in Penney & Chandler, 2000). Sir Rodney Walker, the Chairman of the English Sports Council, stressed that 'The contribution of the PE curriculum to a child's education and as an integral element of Sport for All at grass roots level should not be underestimated' (Walker, 1998, cited in Penney & Chandler, 2000). The state-

Programmes of study refer to the matters, skills and processes which must be taught to pupils in order for them to meet the objectives set out in the attainment target for the subject.

ments illustrate two of the key interests, health and sport, that are associated with physical education in schools.

Although there was a relaxation of these National Curriculum requirements, a review of the National Curriculum was undertaken with the aim of introducing revised requirements in September 2000. Policy and curriculum developments always involve compromises between different interests. The revision of the requirements for the National Curriculum had to accommodate contrasting interests and objectives. After the stream of policy developments in the 1990s, schools and teachers would not welcome major changes to the National Curriculum. However, the government was also anxious to pursue its aims for the development of education. It had ambitions to

> . . . create a nation capable of meeting the challenges of the next millennium; [to] raise the level of educational achievement for all young people, enabling them to fulfil their potential and to make a full contribution to their communities; [to] help young people to develop spiritually, morally, culturally, mentally and physically; [and to become] healthy, lively and enquiring individuals capable of rational thought and discussion and positive participation in our ethnically diverse and technologically complex society. (Blunkett, 1999)

The review had to somehow address these ambitions while avoiding placing undue demands on schools for changes to curricula. The review recommended the development of new National Curriculum requirements that would improve clarity and manageability for schools and that would create the space for schools to focus their attentions on the government's priorities of numeracy, literacy and the development of citizenship and personal, social and health education. In some areas this would mean reductions in requirements. For all subjects, it meant working to a common framework. Consequently, several changes were made to the NCPE.

THE NATIONAL CURRICULUM FOR PHYSICAL EDUCATION 2000

The development of new requirements for the National Curriculum was focused on clarifying, improving and making some reductions to what had been established, rather than making any radical change to existing requirements. New requirements were to be informed by and compatible with current practice in schools. Much in the 'new' NCPE appeared to be very familiar. However, there were also elements that would be notably new.

Before taking a detailed look at these new elements, you should be aware that this revision of the National Curriculum saw the development of an NCPE for schools in Wales that was notably different from that in England. In England the Qualifications and Curriculum Authority (QCA) has been the agency responsible for developing the new requirements. In Wales, In Awdurdo Cymwysterau Cwricwlym Ac Asesu Cymru (ACCAC; the Qualifications Curriculum and Assessment Authority for Wales) has had this responsibility. There are now some important differences between the two countries. In both England and Wales the new requirements for Key Stages 1, 2 and 3 took effect in September 2000, and the requirements for Key Stage 4 were to come into effect in September 2001.

▮ The National Curriculum for Physical Education in England

The revision of the National Curriculum sought to improve the clarity of requirements. Statements describing the 'distinctive contribution' of each subject to the school curriculum were included in the new National Curriculum texts.

Over to You

Develop a statement to describe the 'distinctive contribution' of physical education to the school curriculum. Compare your statement with those developed by others in your group. Discuss the differences and similarities in your statements in relation to what you have identified as the contribution of physical education to the curriculum. Finally, compare your answers with the following statement of 'the importance of physical education' that is included in the National Curriculum for Physical Education.

The importance of physical education

Physical education develops pupils' physical competence and confidence, and their ability to use these to perform in a range of activities. It promotes physical skilfulness, physical development and a knowledge of the body in action. Physical education provides opportunities for pupils to be creative, competitive and to face up to different challenges as individuals and in groups and teams. It promotes positive attitudes towards active and healthy lifestyles. Pupils learn how to think in different ways to suit a wide variety of creative, competitive and challenging activities. They learn how to plan, perform and evaluate actions, ideas and performances to improve their quality and effectiveness. Through this process pupils discover their aptitudes, abilities and preferences, and make choices about how to get involved in lifelong physical activity. (DfEE/QCA, 1999, p. 15)

In addition, for all subjects there had to be written programmes of study to a common format that identified 'key aspects' of the subject. Collectively the aspects would define the knowledge, skills and understanding to be taught. They would thereby provide reference points for curriculum planning and for identifying progression in the subject. The following four aspects were identified for physical education:

1. Acquiring and developing skills
2. Selecting and applying skills, tactics and compositional ideas
3. Evaluating and improving performance
4. Knowledge and understanding of fitness and health (DfEE/QCA, 1999, p. 6)

Each of these aspects had to develop through a range of activities. The new requirements defined the range (i.e., the 'breadth of study') of activities for each key stage. There were pressures for reductions in requirements and greater flexibility for schools in their implementation of requirements. There were further debates about the respective importance and feasibility of particular areas of activity in physical education (see chapter 4.2).

Key Stage 1 required schools to teach the four aspects through dance activities, games activities and gymnastic activities. Schools could also choose to include swimming in this key stage, and a non-statutory programme of study was provided for this purpose. In Key Stage 2, five areas of activity were now required: dance activities; games activities; gymnastic activities and two areas of activity from swimming activities and water safety, athletic activities and outdoor and adventurous activities. Swimming had to be included unless pupils had already completed the Key Stage 2 requirements for swimming (i.e., via additional study in Key Stage 1). In Key Stage 3, the requirement was for games activities and three areas of activity from the remaining five, with at least one of the three being dance or gymnastic activities. Games therefore remained the area of activity with a secure place in the curriculum from Key Stages 1–3. Coverage of other areas might vary greatly between schools. The resources in any one school would continue to be important in determining the 'breadth and balance' of the physical education curriculum.

Games activities are used in Key Stage 1 to teach the four aspects of physical education.

However, it was in relation to Key Stage 4 that controversy about new proposals arose. The Qualifications and Curriculum Authority (QCA) proposed that all pupils should still pursue two activities, but felt that it was appropriate to remove the existing requirement that one of these two activities must be a game. The proposed change was designed to ensure that physical education at Key Stage 4 would appeal to more girls, for whom other activities may be more enjoyable and relevant to their adult lives. It would also give schools flexibility at this key stage, enabling them to select two areas of activity that in their view were most appropriate in the light of pupils' interests and the facilities and staff expertise available in their school.

The reactions to the proposal from some of the media showed the strength of feeling attached to the inclusion of games in physical education. The *Daily Telegraph* described the proposal as 'alarming', reflecting the view that games have a key role to play in developing certain attitudes and behaviours among children, and that physical education has a particular responsibility to address the team sports that have a high profile nationally. However, despite the media criticisms, professional associations and sporting bodies supported the QCA's recommendation, and it was retained.

Part of the framework for the programmes of study for the new NCPE was familiar (the areas of activity), but now the emphasis was that teaching in the various activity contexts should focus on the four aspects of knowledge, skills and understanding that had been identified. The new programmes of study identified points to be addressed relating to each of the four aspects and then specific points to be taught in the context of particular areas of activity. The relationship between the areas of activity and aspects was perhaps not as clear as it could have been in the programmes of study. It remained to be seen how the aspects would be developed in teaching in the various areas of activity and, in particular, the extent to which they prompted greater coherence in teaching and learning across the physical education curriculum as a whole.

Over to You

Reflect upon your experiences of different areas of activity in physical education. Write a brief paragraph in response to the following questions. Do you see the various areas of activity as very different from one another? What connections can you think of between learning in the context of one area (such as games activities) and learning in another (such as athletic activities)? Did your teachers emphasise links between your learning in different activities or areas of activity?

The change made to the National Curriculum framework in 2000 was notable for establishing knowledge and understanding of fitness and health as one of the four aspects of knowledge, skills and understanding. It seemed a clear prompt to address issues associated with fitness and health in the context of various areas of activity. However, as previously, there was still the scope for schools to also include specific HRF or HRE units in their curricula. A combined approach that addresses fitness and health in distinct units of HRE and HRF, and which is then reinforced and extended in the context of other 'area of activity' units, may prove the most effective way of approaching this aspect of physical education.

Over to You

There follows an extract from the programme of study for Key Stage 2. It shows the way in which the four aspects have been developed to guide teaching and learning across the various areas, and then the specific points to be addressed in the area of games. Discuss with a partner the extent to which you feel teaching in games will address and extend learning relating to each of the four aspects of knowledge, skills and understanding in physical education.

Programme of study: Key Stage 2

Acquiring and developing skills

Pupils should be taught to

- consolidate their existing skills and gain new ones, and
- perform actions and skills with more consistent control and quality.

Selecting and applying skills, tactics and compositional ideas

Pupils should be taught to

- plan, use and adapt strategic, tactical and compositional ideas for individual, pair, small group and small-team activities;
- develop and use their knowledge of the principles behind the strategies, tactics and ideas to improve their effectiveness; and
- apply rules and conventions for different activities.

Evaluating and improving performance

Pupils should be taught to

- identify what makes an effective performance, and
- suggest improvements based on this information.

Knowledge and understanding of fitness and health

Pupils should be taught

- how exercise affects the body in the short term,

■ to warm up and prepare appropriately for different activities,

■ why physical education is good for health and wellbeing, and

■ why wearing appropriate clothing and being hygienic are good for their health and safety. (DfEE/QCA, 1999, p. 18)

For each area of activity, specific teaching requirements are then provided. For example, for games activities, it is stated:

Pupils should be taught to

■ play and make up small-sided and modified competitive net, striking/fielding and invasion games;

■ use skills and tactics and apply basic principles for attacking and defending; and

■ work with others to organise and keep the games going. (DfEE/QCA, 1999, p. 19)

■ Level Descriptions and Exceptional Performance in Physical Education

In addition to these changes to the framework for the programmes of study in physical education, there was a change to the format of the attainment target. Previously, 'end of key stage descriptions' had been the reference point for planning for progression in learning and for reporting pupils' achievement in physical education. The revised NCPE established eight level descriptions for physical education and a description for 'exceptional performance' in the subject. The level descriptions set out progression in knowledge, skills and understanding and provided a basis for making judgements about pupils' attainment. They also brought physical education in line with other curriculum subjects that had been working with levels for some time. This was important for the status of physical education in schools.

The level framework may help develop a better understanding (among other teachers and parents) of the knowledge, skills and understanding that are addressed in physical education. However, there may still be a long way to go before people view the gymnasium or the playing fields as sites of teaching and learning and thus as 'classrooms', rather than as sites for recreation and a break from academic work.

Over to You

Referring to the four aspects of knowledge, skills and understanding identified for physical education, develop a statement that you feel would describe 'exceptional performance' in the subject. Compare your statement with one written by another member of your class. Discuss the differences in your statements in relation to the expectations you have about achievement in physical education and the type of learning that you value. Finally, compare your answers with the following statement for exceptional performance included in the NCPE:

> Pupils consistently use advanced skills, techniques and ideas with precision and fluency. Drawing on what they know of the principles of advanced strategies and tactics or composition, they consistently apply these principles with originality, proficiency and flair in their own and others' work. They evaluate their own and others' work, showing that they understand how skills, strategy and tactics or composition, and fitness relate to and affect the quality and originality of performance. They reach judgements independently about how their own and others' performance could be improved, prioritising aspects for further development. They consistently apply appropriate knowledge and understanding of health and fitness in all aspects of their work. (DfEE/QCA, 1999, p. 42)

One of the difficulties that teachers may face in using the eight-level framework is how to make an overall judgement of pupils' attainment in physical education. Often, we view achievement in physical education in very specific terms, relating to particular areas of activity or even individual sports, and there is a tendency to use measures of 'sporting excellence' in making judgements about ability and achievement in physical education. Boys and girls who excel in a particular sport may be looked upon as 'good at physical education'. They have sporting talent, but we cannot assume that they have reached levels of excellence in all aspects of learning in physical education. The identification of the four aspects of knowledge, skills and understanding highlights that we cannot rely upon simplistic measures of performance when we wish to assess learning in physical education. However, teachers face a difficult task in trying to make judgements that take into account the four aspects in the varied area of activity contexts incorporated within the NCPE. The NCPE stated that 'In deciding on a pupil's level of attainment at the end of a key stage, teachers should judge which description best fits the pupil's performance' (DfEE/QCA, 1999, p. 42), but it did not explain how teachers should reach 'best fit' decisions.

Over to You

Make a list of your strengths and weaknesses in physical education. Refer to the four aspects of skills, knowledge and understanding, and consider how your descriptions of strengths and weaknesses reflect each aspect of learning. Compare these with the list made by another person in your class. Discuss the basis upon which you judge your own and others' achievements in physical education.

Key Stage 4: Extending Learning in Physical Education

At Key Stage 4, the new NCPE presented clear opportunities for pupils who are not necessarily the most talented performers to pursue their abilities and interests in physical education. The programmes of study encouraged the development of knowledge, skills and understanding relating to 'other roles' in activity settings, such as coaching or officiating, and the development of leadership skills. This meant that courses such as the CCPR Sports Leader Award schemes (see chapter 5.1) could become an integral part of the NCPE at Key Stage 4.

Information and Communications Technology. One of the other issues addressed in this revision of the National Curriculum was information and communications technology (ICT). In all subjects there was now a statutory requirement for teachers to seek to develop pupils' ICT capabilities in their teaching. In physical education this requirement applied to teaching in Key Stages 3 and 4. Teachers in secondary schools therefore have to consider the ways in which learning in physical education can be enhanced via ICT and instances in which physical education may provide a context to develop children's ICT capabilities (DfEE/QCA, 1999).

Over to You

With a partner, discuss in what ways, and in what activity contexts, ICT can enhance teaching and learning in physical education. Consider your ideas in relation to the time and resources available for physical education at a local school. When do you feel that it will be possible and most appropriate to use ICT in physical education?

To assist teachers in planning, opportunities for using ICT are identified in the text of the NCPE. For example, in addressing the aspect 'knowledge and understanding of fitness and health' it recognised that 'Pupils could use heart and pulse rate monitors and a variety of other measuring and recording devices to collect, analyse and interpret data' (DfEE/QCA, 1999, p. 20). Opportunities are also identified in specific activity contexts. For example, in relation to games, it stated that 'Pupils could use data-recording and analysis software to analyse patterns of play and individual contributions' and that they could '. . . use stopwatches with lap recorders linked to data-collection devices to analyse and evaluate performance" (DfEE/QCA, 1999, p. 21). In some schools, the data gathered from such analysis are then used in cross-curricula work, such as learning of statistical techniques in mathematics.

Inclusion. The final feature of the new National Curriculum in England is something that relates to all subjects. It is also a matter that the government has attached particular importance to in its policies in education and in other areas of public service provision, such as health. The government has stated that it is committed to ensuring inclusion in education, health and also sporting provision. In the forward to the revised NCPE the Secretary of State for Education and Employment emphasised:

> An entitlement to learning must be an entitlement for all pupils. This National Curriculum includes for the first time a detailed, overarching statement on inclusion which makes clear the principles schools must follow in their teaching right across the curriculum, to ensure that all pupils have the chance to succeed, whatever their individual needs and the potential barriers to their learning may be. (Blunkett, 1999, in DfEE/QCA, 1999, p. 3)

In all subject areas teachers were now required to pay 'due regard' to the following three principles for inclusion:

1. Setting suitable learning challenges
2. Responding to pupils' diverse learning needs
3. Overcoming barriers to learning and assessment for individuals and groups of pupils (DfEE/QCA, 1999)

One of the initiatives discussed in chapter 4.1, Teaching Games for Understanding, may be an approach that is particularly valuable in addressing these principles. The principles point to the need for further development of differentiation in physical education to enable all children to progress in their learning, whatever their level of learning. However, in the discussion of equality, equity and inclusion in chapter 1.2 you can read that adaptation of activities and tasks may fail to embrace important aspects of equity. If they are seriously committed to greater equity, people must recognise that what constitutes a 'suitable' learning challenge will vary according to pupils' social and cultural beliefs. If you rely on adapting challenges that reflect the dominant social and cultural values, then you may be restricting your view of inclusion to 'inclusion into the dominant culture'. Instead there is a need to develop inclusive practices that celebrate the rich cultural diversity of modern-day societies in Britain.

There is also need to consider social and cultural, as well as physical, factors in approaching the principles relating to 'diverse learning needs' and 'barriers to learning'. Clothing, or the physical setting of the activity, such as whether other people can see into a swimming pool or gymnasium, may represent a barrier to participation for some pupils. Teachers need to ensure that learning environments as well as activities are 'inclusive'.

The National Curriculum for Physical Education in Wales

When the National Assembly for Wales took over responsibility for educational developments in Wales, there was the scope for the new National Curriculum in Wales to be quite different from that in England. This latest revision saw far more obvious differences arise in the NCPE in the two countries.

Whereas the documentation in England prompts schools and teachers to address 'inclusion', in Wales it emphasised that provision must ensure '*access* for all pupils' (National Assembly for Wales/ACCAC, 2000, p. 4, our emphasis). It required schools to select material to suit pupils' age and experience, enabling all pupils to progress and achieve, and yet still challenge particularly talented or gifted pupils. You can reflect on the degree to which this selection and adaptation of learning tasks represents a move towards greater equity in physical education (see chapter 1.2).

Cross-curricula Concerns. As in the previous NCPE in Wales (see chapter 4.2), teachers are required to address the way in which physical education can reflect a 'Curriculum Cymreig' and so 'develop and apply knowledge and understanding of the cultural, economic, environmental, historical and linguistic characteristics of Wales' (National Assembly for Wales/ACCAC, 2000, p. 5). Other cross-curricula issues that teachers need to address through physical education are communication skills, mathematical skills, information technology skills, problem-solving skills, creative skills, and personal and social education.

 Over to You

Select one of the cross-curricula issues just mentioned and identify ways and contexts in which physical education can address learning relating to the issue that you have selected.

As a group, share your ideas about the ways in which physical education can contribute to learning relating to each of the cross-curricula issues. Do you see some activities as better suited than others to address particular issues such as creative skills or problem-solving skills? In a single area of activity (such as games) can we address all of the issues?

A Focus for Teaching and Learning. Rather than identifying aspects of learning to be pursued in the context of the various areas of activity, the NCPE in Wales includes a 'focus statement' for curriculum design and teaching at each key stage. For example, at Key Stage 3 it is explained:

> Pupils should be given the opportunity to build on the knowledge, understanding and skills acquired at Key Stage 2. Activities should build on previous experiences, extend skills and challenge pupils to refine and apply them in new situations. Pupils should be taught how to analyse their own and others' performance in order to improve effectiveness and quality. They should be placed in problem-solving situations and taught how to plan, make appropriate decisions and evaluate outcomes. They should be taught the rules of activities and how to apply them. Their growing awareness of others' strengths and limitations of performance should be used constructively when working together and in competition. Pupils should be taught to exercise safely and appreciate the value of regular exercise. (National Assembly for Wales/ACCAC, 2000, p. 10)

Over to You

Compare this focus statement with the four aspects of knowledge, skills and understanding identified for the programmes of study in England. Does the focus statement address all of the aspects? Can you divide the statement into sentences associated with each aspect?

Health-related Exercise. A further difference in the structure of the NCPE in Wales as compared with England is that, in Wales, specific requirements have been developed for health-related exercise. These requirements sit alongside requirements relating to areas of activity. At each key stage the curriculum must cover HRE and particular areas of activity. For example, at Key Stage 1 it states that pupils should be taught health-related exercise and games, gymnastic activities and dance. Also, schools may choose to teach aspects of the Key Stage 2 programme of study for swimming in Key Stage 1. At Key Stage 2, pupils should be taught health-related exercise and games, gymnastic activities, dance, swimming and either athletic activities or outdoor and adventurous activities. At Key Stage 3, pupils should be taught health-related exercise and four areas of activity: games, plus at least one of gymnastic activities and dance, and the remaining area(s) chosen from swimming, athletic activities, and outdoor and adventurous activities (National Assembly for Wales/ACCAC, 2000).

The stated requirement within the NCPE in Wales for pupils to be taught HRE *and* certain areas of activity may encourage teachers to develop (or extend existing) *distinct* HRE units of work. However, there is also still the potential for at least some of the requirements relating to HRE to be met in the context of units associated with particular areas of activity, such as games or athletics.

Over to You

Study the requirements for health-related exercise in Key Stage 3 in Wales. Working with a partner, identify how these requirements could be met in Key Stage 3 physical education, taking account of the accompanying requirement to address four areas of activity (games, plus at least one of gymnastic activities and dance, and the remaining area(s) chosen from swimming, athletic activities, and outdoor and adventurous activities) at this key stage. Address the following questions:

■ Will you seek to meet some of the HRE requirements in the context of a distinct HRE unit? If so, what activities might feature in this unit?

■ What requirements will you seek to meet in the context of units associated with a particular area of activity? Identify the specific areas of activity that you are referring to.

■ What requirements do you feel are best addressed through a combined approach, in which they are taught in a distinct HRE unit and then revisited in units that focus upon a particular area of activity?

Health-related exercise: Key Stage 3

Throughout the key stage, pupils should be taught

■ to monitor a range of short-term effects on the cardiovascular system (e.g., changes in heart rate) and the musculoskeletal system (e.g., changes in muscular strength/ endurance and flexibility); improved muscle tone; the long-term effects of exercise on physical health (e.g., reduced risk of heart disease, osteoporosis, obesity, improved management of health conditions such as asthma);

■ to adopt good posture when sitting, standing and taking part in activity;

■ relevant and safe warm-up and cool-down routines (e.g., mobility exercises, whole-body activities and static stretches), and how to take responsibility for their planning and execution;

■ the differences between whole-body activities that help to reduce body fat and conditioning exercises that improve muscle tone;

■ that appropriate training can improve fitness and performance;

■ the value of exercise to social and psychological wellbeing (e.g., increased confidence and self-esteem, decreased anxiety and stress); and

■ the range of activity opportunities at school, home and in the local community and ways of incorporating exercise into their lifestyles (e.g., walking or cycling to school or to meet friends).

Pupils should adopt safe practices and procedures when taking part in physical activities that might require the wearing of protective clothing, the removal of jewellery to avoid injury, the supervised use of equipment or response to specific weather conditions. (National Assembly for Wales/ACCAC, 2000, p. 11)

Key Stage 4. At Key Stage 4, further differences arise between the curricula in England and Wales. The NCPE in Wales has used a different categorisation of activities. Instead of the familiar six areas of activity, there are four areas of experience for this key stage:

1. Sport (competitive focus) — for example, games, forms of gymnastics, trampolining, athletics, swimming, diving, rowing, canoeing

2. Dance (artistic and aesthetic focus) — for example, folk dances of Wales and other countries, historical dance (minuet, pavanne), theatrical dance (jazz, contemporary) and social dance (ballroom, square dance)

3. Adventure activities (outdoor learning focus) — for example, hillwalking, climbing, living outdoors and water-based activities

4. Exercise activities (non-competitive forms of exercise) — for example, step aerobics, jogging, weight training, cycling, circuit training and skipping (National Assembly for Wales/ACCAC, 2000, p. 12)

At Key Stage 4 pupils must be taught health-related exercise and two practical activities selected from one or more of these areas of experience.

Over to You

With a partner, discuss the categorisation used for Key Stage 4 in Wales. Do you see any problems with specific activities being identified with one particular focus (competitive, non-competitive, etc.)? Can you identify activities that could be placed in a different category to the one that they have been associated with?

This categorisation may lead to particular activities being associated with one form of experience. In contrast, it may be that an activity can offer various experiences. For example, cycling is presented as an example of a non-competitive exercise activity. Many people participate in cycling as a recreational activity with a focus upon everyday exercise. However, competitive cycling is also a well-established sport, nationally and internationally. More recently, mountain biking has established itself as a popular outdoor activity. Cycling could be an activity in which 'outdoor learning' was the focus of teaching and learning. We could develop similar arguments for other activities to be identified with more than one 'area of experience'. If there is an interest in increasing levels of participation in particular sports, we need to recognise that people may choose to participate in a sport for different reasons. Arguably, a challenge for sports development is to demonstrate that a sport can provide whatever experience any individual is seeking. Individuals may be seeking performance in formal competitions, recreation, personal health, exploring areas of natural beauty, or pursuing creative or artistic interests through movement activities.

CHANGE AND CONTINUITY IN CONTEMPORARY PHYSICAL EDUCATION

The revision of the National Curriculum represented a difficult compromise between the government's concern to give the National Curriculum a distinctly new look and focus and the need to avoid introducing changes that would demand significant changes in schools. The new NCPE clearly reflected this compromise. Also, some of the changes in the requirements in both England and Wales could be seen as very significant for future curriculum planning and teaching in the subject. The identification of the four aspects of knowledge, skills and understanding in England together with the focus statements in Wales prompted teachers to review the coherency of the physical education curriculum 'as a whole'.

The introduction of the eight-level framework for assessment and reporting of learning and planning for progression was also a notable development that encouraged teachers to review how they make judgements about pupils' attainment in physical education and the criteria that they use in making these judgements. Changes at Key Stage 4 in both England and Wales also prompted teachers to consider the appeal of physical education to older pupils and its relevance to pupils' later lives. Greater choice of activities and exploration of other roles, such as leadership in sport, may help to make physical education a meaningful and positive experience for more pupils at this key stage.

However, alongside the changes, important characteristics of the NCPE remain unchanged. The new proposals may seem largely familiar to many teachers so that, with limited time for curriculum planning and little support for implementation of the new requirements, there may be only a few changes made to existing curricula and teaching approaches. The only thing that can be said with certainty is that there will still be differences in the physical education curricula and experiences in different schools. There is a common framework, but the activities that feature in physical education and the ways in which physical education is taught will vary. In this respect the situation in 2000 is the same as it was in 1992 when the NCPE was first introduced.

SUMMARY

This chapter has provided a critical analysis of the latest policy and curriculum developments relating to physical education and school sport in England and Wales. It has illustrated that the government and the media retain a strong interest in physical education and school sport. It has shown ways in which these interests in the development of excellence in sport and in encouraging more people to participate in regular physical activity for health and wellbeing have been reflected in further changes to the NCPE in England and in Wales. It has identified differences between these two curricula, their similarities to one another and to past practices, and challenges for physical education teachers to address.

Test Yourself Questions

1. List the four aspects of knowledge, skills and understanding established for the NCPE in England.
2. Identify changes to the breadth of study at Key Stage 4 in England and explain why the changes were controversial.
3. List the three principles for inclusion in the NCPE in England.
4. Describe how the NCPE in Wales differs from the NCPE in England in relation to (1) requirements for health-related exercise and (2) requirements at Key Stage 4.

PART 5

Policy Dimensions of Reflective Performance in Sport Provision and Development

*I*n this section you will find three chapters on the policy dimensions of reflective performance in sport provision and development. In chapter 5.1 you can read about the key national organisations who together provide sport and leisure opportunities for children and adults across Britain. Chapter 5.2 examines some of the major policy documents and initiatives to emerge from these organisations in the past decade. In chapter 5.3 you can read about the local organisations who are involved in providing sport and leisure opportunities.

Key National Organisations in Sport Provision

Learning Outcomes

When you have studied this chapter, you should be able to

- ☑ outline the contemporary structure and organisation of sport in Britain nationally,
- ☑ identify key sites of policy making and provision of sporting opportunities at a national level,
- ☑ analyse the role of each organisation in relation to developing and providing sport opportunities, and
- ☑ use a range of resources (including the Internet) to access information relating to the changing structure of sport in Britain and latest policy developments.

INTRODUCTION

This chapter outlines the key policy makers and providers of sporting opportunities at a national level. It explains recent changes in the frameworks and organisations established to support and develop sport in Britain. The complexity of the 'sporting structure' in Britain and the many organisations with interests in, and influence on, provision will be readily apparent. The chapter begins with an overview of the major government departments that have responsibilities for the provision of sport and physical education and concludes with information on private organisations and charities.

THE DEPARTMENT FOR CULTURE, MEDIA AND SPORT

The Department for Culture, Media and Sport (DCMS) identifies its overall aim as 'to improve the quality of life for all through cultural and sporting activities and through the strengthening of the creative industries' (DCMS, 2001).

Sport is one arena in which these aims are pursued. In this process, the DCMS promotes the Government's policy for 'sport for all', aiming to widen access to sport and recreation. Reflecting the dual agendas of promoting participation and performance, the DCMS also supports the development of excellence in British Sport through national and international events and competitions.

The government influences the development of sport through policy statements and funding for sport. Implementing policy is then in the hands of other organisations. Some of these organisations have a direct link to government, but many are independent of it, including voluntary and commercial organisations. You can see immediately that there is a formal and an informal dimension to the organisation of sport. The central government's influence is both direct, in terms of supporting some specific organisations and initiatives, and indirect through encouraging others to adopt particular directions in their developments. Central government investment and influence in sport in Britain are therefore limited but nevertheless very significant.

In relation to direct support for sport, the DCMS funds UK Sport (formally the UK Sports Council) and Sport England (formally known as the English Sports Council) through grant-in-aid funding. In 1999/2000 Sport England received £34.5m and UK Sport received £12.6m from the DCMS to foster, support and encourage the development of sport and physical recreation. The other Sports Councils in Britain have historically been accountable to government departments in Wales, Scotland and Northern Ireland, and have received grant-in-aid from their respective governments. The new national assemblies in these parts of the United Kingdom represent new forums for the discussion of sports policy matters at a national level. All of the sports councils are accountable to the DCMS for the allocation of the lottery funds that they are accorded responsibility for distributing.

THE SPORTS COUNCILS

Following publication of the Wolfenden Report in 1957, which you can read about in chapter 3.5, an Advisory Sports Council was established in 1965. In 1972 the Sports Councils for Britain, Wales and Scotland were established and the Sports Council for Northern Ireland was formed two years later. Regional sports councils were also established in England. Over the years, the sports councils gained status and recognition as key sites for policy development and the promotion of initiatives for the development of sport and Britain's sporting infrastructure. A long-standing characteristic of the sports councils is their reliance on partnerships for the translation of national policies into local initiatives. One attraction for various organisations to establish a partnership with the sports councils has been an opportunity to access funding.

In 1997, the British Sports Council was disbanded. A new organisation, the UK Sports Council, was created to take responsibility for issues requiring attention at a UK level, such as doping-control in sport. The English Sports Council was established to take responsibility for the development of sport in England, in a similar way to the existing sports councils in Scotland, Wales and Northern Ireland. Each of these sports councils has its own administrative structures, policies and initiatives. There is some commonality in the general aims and functions of the sports councils, with all seeking to lead the development of sport in their respective countries. There are also some differences in structures and focus for developments.

In its role as the coordinating body for UK-wide developments, UK Sport has established itself as a distributor of Lottery funds. It has earmarked £20.5m from the Lottery Sports Fund to support the development of top UK medal hopes and to attract and stage major sporting events in the UK.

Sport England

The English Sports Council changed its name to Sport England in 1997. The objective of Sport England is 'to lead the development of sport in England by influencing and serving the public, private and voluntary sectors', with the aim of 'more people involved in sport, more places to play sport, more medals through higher standards of performance in sport' (Sport England, 2000). These aims have been translated into the 'More People, More Places, More Medals' programmes.

A number of advisory panels direct the work of Sport England. The panels deal with various aspects of Sports Council work, including the lottery, local authorities, women and sport, disability, racial equality and governing body investment. Sport England has a head office in London and ten regional offices across England. In all areas of their work, Sports Council staff are involved in collaborating with an extensive network of partners and contacts across the private and public sectors. These include local authorities; sports governing bodies; and national and regional organisations concerned with sport, recreation, education and the environment, including the Countryside Commission and national and local waterways organisations.

Sport England's grant-in-aid funding from the DCMS is directed towards maintaining the infrastructure of sport in England. In addition, Sport England is responsible for distributing **National Lottery** funds earmarked for sport development. It does this through its Sport England Lottery Fund. Across the United Kingdom, sports now receive around £300m per year from the lottery. As well as supporting national developments and events, lottery funding is a major factor in financing local initiatives. In chapter 5.2 you can read about some of the national projects developed with lottery funding.

The National Lottery has become a major source of funding for sport in Britain. Lottery grants are now critical for many national and local sport development projects.

Over to You

If you attend a school or college in England, find out where your nearest regional sports council office is. Identify ways in which the regional sports council disseminates information about lottery funding opportunities. Identify a development project locally that has received lottery grant funding and what organisations are involved in the development. Write a short (two-page) report on your findings.

If you attend a school or college in Wales, find out the ways in which the Sports Council for Wales disseminates information about lottery funding opportunities. Identify a development project locally that has received lottery grant funding and what organisations are involved in the development. Write a short (two-page) report on your findings.

The Sports Council for Wales

The Sports Council for Wales (SCW) has four aspects to its mission:

1. Increasing participation in sport — in terms of numbers of people involved and frequency of activity
2. Raising standards of performance and excellence in sport
3. Improving provision of sports facilities
4. Providing information and advice about sport and recreation (SCW, 1999)

In this mission you can see the dual aims of the SCW. On the one hand, the aim is to further the development of performance and excellence. On the other hand, the aim is also to increase participation. Like Sport England, the SCW has produced a strategy and initiatives directed towards the new millennium. *Young People First* was intended to provide direction for the future development of sport in Wales and prioritised the development of sport for young people.

The policy was developed at a time when the government in Wales was particularly concerned with health and lifestyle issues. You can read more in the next chapter on the ways in which SCW policy reflects this focus.

Sportscotland and *Sport 21*

Sportscotland is the national agency in Scotland. **Sport**scotland is 'dedicated to promoting sporting opportunities for all Scots at all levels, whatever their interest and ability' and claims that the development work it undertakes is driven by three visions:

1. Widening opportunities — creating a country where sport is more widely available to all
2. Developing potential — creating a country where sporting talent is recognised and nurtured
3. Achieving excellence — creating a country achieving and sustaining world class performances in sport *(Sport 21)*

These three visions arise from *Sport 21: Nothing Left to Chance,* Scotland's national strategy for sport. *Sport 21* was launched in 1998 and is now the reference point for not only **sport**scotland's own planning, but also that of agencies and organisations throughout Scotland at a national and local level. Many Scottish governing bodies of sport have now published or drafted development plans based on *Sport 21,* and Scottish local authorities are also leading the development of local plans for sport with reference to the priorities and targets established in *Sport 21*. As is the case with the policy developments that we consider in detail in the next chapter, *Sport 21* is notable for establishing formal targets for the future development of sport, linking directly to the three visions.

Sportscotland also recognises the way in which sports policy developments need to be planned with reference to other areas of policy development nationally and locally. You can see the links drawn between sport policy and issues of social inclusion and health at the **sport**scotland website (**www.sportscotland.org.uk**).

Over to You

Visit the **sport**scotland website to find out further information about *Sport 21* and, in particular, what targets have been established for sport in Scotland. Make a list of the targets. With a partner, compare the targets to those set by one of the other national sports councils and write a brief note of any differences and similarities.

Sports Council for Northern Ireland

The Sports Council for Northern Ireland (SCNI) describes itself as 'a lead facilitator in the development of sport', working with partner organisations to

- increase and sustain committed participation, especially amongst young people;
- raise the standards of sporting excellence; and
- promote the good reputation and efficient administration of sport. (SCNI, website)

In 1995, the SCNI commissioned a strategy for sport 'to bring together major partners in pursuit of increased participation and enhanced performance'. The strategy is based on the premise that involvement in sport has a natural cycle comprising 'starting well — learning about sport and how it feels to participate; staying involved — acquiring competence and wider understanding'; and 'striving for excellence — developing quality and deeper insights' (SCNI, website).

The SCNI identified key strategic themes for the future. Many of these are similar to the focus and approaches evident in the work of the other sports councils. The SCNI identified a need to

- increase support for **volunteers** involved in sport and to strengthen the contribution of volunteers,
- provide young people with a sound start in sport,
- improve coordination and cooperation in provision,
- facilitate movement within sport in order to encourage more people to stay involved in sport, and
- increase the support for the development of excellence. (SCNI, website)

Volunteers have a key role to play in supporting the provision of sport throughout Britain. They are involved in the organisation and administration of many national organisations and national sporting events, in running local clubs and in providing coaching for participants of all ages.

THE CENTRAL COUNCIL FOR PHYSICAL RECREATION

The Central Council for Physical Recreation (CCPR) was formed in 1935. You can read about the history of the CCPR in chapter 3.5. The CCPR has had a long-standing role in developing leadership courses, and some of you may have taken a CCPR Sports Leader award. The CCPR remains a key national organisation in relation to the development of sport in Britain.

When developing policy, the government is selective in terms of who it consults and involves in committees. The government clearly cannot involve representatives from each of the many national governing bodies of sport. The CCPR has the advantage and appeal of representing a range of sporting interests and organisations, including the governing bodies for sport, organisations representing sport for people with disabilities, for school sport, and for the armed forces.

The CCPR has been particularly active in developing sports leadership training programmes and associated awards. In the context of the National Curriculum for Physical Education, at Key Stage 4 many pupils are being encouraged to take the Junior Sports Leader Award (JSLA). These pupils may then progress on to take the Community Sports Leader Award (CSLA).

Over to You

Identify the skills that the CCPR Junior Sports Leader and Community Sports Leader awards aim to develop in sports leaders. In a small group, discuss what sports leaders can do to challenge inequities in sport (see chapter 1.2).

NATIONAL GOVERNING BODIES OF SPORT

One of the notable characteristics of the infrastructure of sport is the large number of governing bodies representing various sports in Britain. As Houlihan (1997) has noted, their structures vary in a number of respects. In some cases, these structures have undergone significant changes in recent years that relate to increased pressures to address equity issues in both sport and its organisation. Some of these pressures also stem from the increasing commercialisation of sport and issues of professionalism, which you can read more about in chapter 6.2.

As a result of these pressures, there have been some **mergers** of previously separate organisations for men and women. Also, some governing bodies have adopted a more commercial structure and practices. The governing bodies vary in their infrastructures and wealth. All rely to some degree on the sports councils for funding. National governing bodies of sport (NGBs) typically have a number of professional administrators and a network of volunteer officers and coaches.

A further characteristic of the vast majority of NGBs is their adoption of a 'pyramidal structure with individual clubs at the base supporting county/regional bodies and national organisations' (Houlihan, 1997, p. 165). NGBs vary in the particular interests that they pursue in their development of the sport and whose interests they can cater for. The pyramidal structure tends to direct funding and other resources towards the development of elite sport. This structure may provide well for elite performers, but may not adequately address the needs and interests of other participants.

This tendency means that some NGBs are clearly associated with a certain type of participant or level of performer, whereas other parallel organisations seek to cater for the needs and interests of other participants. For example, the British Cycling Federation attracts and serves members who compete in formal cycle road racing; whereas the Cycle Touring Club provides services for recreational cyclists. In recent years NGBs have been required to establish development plans in order to access funds from sports council and lottery funds. By studying these plans you will be able to explore what priorities are being pursued by particular NGBs and whose needs and interests are addressed in developments.

Hockey provides an example of the merging of two separate national governing bodies of sport (one for women and one for men) to form a single new organisation for both men and women.

Over to You

Identify the governing body or governing bodies associated with a particular sport. Find out about organisational structures and development priorities. Find out whether the structures and priorities have changed in the last three years. If so, note whether the changes have been made in response to new strategies established by the government and the sports councils.

For this task you may want to contact the governing body directly, a sports council office, or use the Internet.

THE BRITISH OLYMPIC ASSOCIATION

The British Olympic Association (BOA) is responsible for sending British teams to the Olympic Games and managing the team during the Games. The Association represents 35 NGBs, who are members of the National Olympic Committee, and the athletes from these sports. The BOA thus claims to be 'the largest independent sporting body in Great Britain in terms of the size, diversity of representation and the scope of services it provides' (BOA, website).

Among the services provided are coaching and team management programmes, the setting-up of working parties to address specific issues, the organisation of pre-Games preparation and warm-weather training camps, and the accreditation of training centres. Support for British athletes is also provided by the British Olympic Medical Centre, which has doctors, physiotherapists, psychologists, physiologists and nutritionists on its staff. The BOA provides some financial assistance to elite athletes to cover some of the expense of elite training.

Over to You

For one of your chosen sports, identify the specific types of support that the governing body may seek from the BOA for athletes seeking to participate at an international level. In a small group, share what you have found for different sports and write a short note describing your findings.

THE NATIONAL COACHING FOUNDATION

The **National Coaching Foundation** (NCF) is a registered charity, founded in 1983. In 1987 it amalgamated with the UK Sports Council. The main source of funding is grant aid from Sport UK and Sport England. Other funding comes from earned income such as membership fees and sales, and other grant aid and donations. The principal aim of the NCF is to work towards improving the quality of coaching, with the idea being that better coaching means better sport at all levels. It sets out to achieve this aim by providing coach education courses from introductory level for the novice coach through to courses for the experienced national coach. The courses address many issues that you will explore in your studies, including mental training for sport and sport nutrition.

Coaches from any sport can become members of the National Coaching Foundation as well as belong to their own sport's national governing body.

Increasingly the NCF courses are being integrated into the sport-specific coach education conducted by national governing bodies. Although it is a national organisation, the NCF has established a regional network for the coordination of coach education development. Regional officers work with a variety of organisations and individuals, including national governing body representatives, local authority leisure departments, sports development officers and regional sports council staff, to ensure meeting local needs.

The NCF is also helping to develop a national register for coaches and works to raise the profile of coaching through its information services. Coachwise is the trading arm of the NCF, retailing many sports-related publications and products.

THE YOUTH SPORT TRUST

The TOP programmes are also discussed in chapter 4.2.

Founded in 1994, the Youth Sport Trust (YST) is a registered charity. The YST has a mission 'to develop and implement, in close partnership with other organisations, quality physical education and sport programmes for all young people aged 18 months to 18 years in schools and in the community' (YST, website).

To achieve this mission the YST has developed the TOP programmes. These programmes cover the developmental spectrum starting with TOP Tots which introduces physical activity and games to children aged between 18 months and 3 years and finishing with TOP Skill and TOP Link which extend the skills learned at earlier age groups and provides leadership opportunities for those aged between 14 and 18. The YST also offers a programme called SportSability that is directed towards providing activity and sporting opportunities for young disabled people.

Taken together, the various TOP programmes are designed to offer opportunities to participate and progress in sport at any age or ability up to 18. The delivery of the programmes provides a working example of partnerships in sport, with the YST working with a range of agencies to maximise programme effectiveness. These agencies include local education authorities and schools, local authority sports development officers and community groups, NGBs and sports clubs, and the Early Years development and Childcare Partnership and their associated groups. The YST is funded through trusts and foundations, events and individual donations.

THE NATIONAL COUNCIL FOR SCHOOL SPORT

The membership of the National Council for School Sport (NCSS) comprises national schools' sports associations, NGBs and other national organisations providing sport in schools and federations of local schools' sports associations.

The aims of the NCSS are to promote the cause of school sport and to encourage the mental, moral and physical development of pupils through the medium of sport. The NCSS also aims to represent the views of school-based sports organisations to a variety of parties and to encourage the promotion of sport in schools. The NCSS encourages and supports the activities of local and area school sport organisations. Equity is a key concern of the NCSS as it encourages the provision of sport for all young people, regardless of race, creed or gender or disability (NCSS, website).

OTHER ORGANISATIONS

These are by no means the only organisations contributing to the development of sport in Britain. Others include, for example, the British Universities & Colleges Physical Education Association (BUCPEA). BUCPEA is the professional association for those people working in sport, recreation and physical education at British universities. There are also organisations specifically concerned with provision for people with disabilities, such as the British Wheelchair Sports Federation.

You can begin to appreciate the complex web of relationships that make up the organisational infrastructure of sport in Britain. You can now see why partnerships are an important feature of sport development. To gain funding, sports organisations have to establish that they are committed to partnerships with a range of agencies to ensure that different interests and different sections of communities will benefit from developments. You can read more about how these partnerships work at a local level in the next chapter.

THE HEALTH EDUCATION AUTHORITY
AND *YOUNG AND ACTIVE*

It is not only sports organisations that have an interest and involvement in sport. At the national level, the Health Education Authority (HEA) has had a high profile in developments related to sport. In 1998 the HEA launched a policy framework entitled *Young and Active* directed at educational institutions, organisations concerned with sport and recreation, health services, the media and government. The policy framework was concerned to increase the numbers of young people regularly participating in physical activity. The HEA identified three main reasons for encouraging young people to take part in regular physical activity:

1. To optimise physical fitness, current health and well-being, and growth and development
2. To develop active lifestyles that can be maintained throughout adult life
3. To reduce the risk of coronary heart diseases in adulthood (HEA, 1998, p. 3)

The HEA suggested regular physical activity has multiple beneficial health outcomes. These include improved psychological wellbeing and reductions in obesity. They also drew attention to potential negative effects of exercise, such as musculoskeletal injuries associated with over-training.

The HEA recommends that

- all young people should participate in physical activity of at least moderate intensity for one hour a day,
- young people who currently do little activity should participate in physical activity of at least moderate intensity for at least half an hour per day, and
- at least twice a week, some of these activities should help to enhance and maintain muscular strength and flexibility and bone health. (HEA, 1998, p. 3)

Over to You

For a week, keep an activity diary. Chapter 2.4 may help you with this. Once you have completed the diary, assess whether you are doing less or more activity than the HEA recommend. Identify ways in which you could increase your daily physical activity. Identify barriers to yourself and others in your class increasing the physical activity that you do. Discuss ways in which your school could help to address these barriers. For example, does your school have identified safe walking or cycling routes to the school? Does your school have secure bicycle sheds? Does your school have areas in which pupils can be physically active during breaks and lunchtimes?

The HEA also reported current levels of participation and noted differences in participation across various sections of the community. Not for the first time, specific population groups were identified as targets for future initiatives. As you may be aware, throughout the 1980s, the Sports Council initiated various programmes directed towards specific groups. On this occasion, the HEA identified these target groups:

- The inactive
- Girls aged 12–18
- Young people of low socioeconomic status
- Older adolescents (16–18 years) (HEA, 1998, p. 6)

In 2000, the Health Education Authority was disbanded. The newly formed Health Development Agency has taken on much of the work previously undertaken by the HEA.

According to the HEA, the likelihood that a young person will lead an active lifestyle is determined by both psychological and social and environmental factors. Of the psychological factors, the HEA highlighted enjoyment as important. Social and environmental determinants include friends and family, where you live and income (HEA, 1998, pp. 5–6).

The HEA is an example of a national organisation which may not appear to be directly involved in sport. However, you can see from the *Young and Active* framework that this organisation is also having an influence on the development of sport for young people. The HEA's interests in regular participation and enjoyment of sport among the whole population have been taken up by some of the organisations and agencies that you read about earlier in this chapter.

Over to You

With a partner, use the World Wide Web to identify other organisations that influence sport for young people. Write a paragraph noting the key interests of each organisation and also how they influence sport and physical activity.

SUMMARY

The purpose of this chapter was to outline the key policy makers and providers of sporting opportunities at a national level. We identified a number of key organisations and described the range of their responsibilities on a national scale. Together, these organisations form a complex infrastructure for sport organisation, development and provision.

Test Yourself Questions ▦ ▦ ▦ ▦ ▦ ▦ ▦ ▦ ▦ ▦ ▦

1. Name the government department that is the focal point for the development of sport in Britain and the key agencies that it funds to implement policies.

2. Identify partner organisations that the sports councils work with.

3. List the four aspects of the mission of the Sports Council for Wales.

4. List the three visions for sport in Scotland that have been identified by **sport**scotland.

5. Outline the services provided by the British Olympic Association.

6. Explain the role of the National Coaching Foundation and its relationship to national governing bodies.

7. According to the Health Education Authority there are three main reasons why young people should be encouraged to take part in physical activity. What are the reasons?

8. What target groups were identified in the *Young and Active* policy document?

National Policies for Sport Provision

Chapter Overview

- Introduction
- *Sport – Raising the Game*, 1995
- *England the Sporting Nation*, 1997
- *Young People First: A Strategy for Welsh Sport*, 1999
- Scotland and Northern Ireland
- Summary
- Test Yourself Questions

Learning Outcomes

When you have studied this chapter, you should be able to

☑ name and describe recent policy initiatives at a national level in England and Wales;

☑ critically evaluate recent policy initiatives at a national level;

☑ discuss the compatibility of, and tensions between, interests in the development of performance and participation sport; and

☑ use a range of resources (including the Internet) to access information relating to the changing structure of sport in Britain and latest policy developments.

INTRODUCTION

In chapter 5.1 you can read about the major organisations that have a role in development of sport in the United Kingdom. This chapter reviews three major sport policy initiatives relating to sport development in England and Wales. The first policy is *Sport – Raising the Game,* which was produced by the Conservative government in 1995. The second is the Labour government's policy *England the Sporting Nation,* which appeared in 1997. The third is the Welsh policy *Young People First,* which appeared in 1999. Each of these policy statements has provided frames of reference for sport development in England and Wales. They also, more subtly, attempt to frame the ways in which we think about sport. As you read about these policies, you are encouraged to think critically about them and whether they ensure equity in the provision of resources for sport at both participation and performance levels.

SPORT – RAISING THE GAME, 1995

Sport – Raising the Game made recommendations regarding the future development work of a variety of agencies and organisations. At a national level, funding schemes were established and were to be administered by the English Sports Council. These included 'challenge funding' directed towards the development of formal links between schools and clubs or governing bodies of sport. The 'sportsmatch scheme' was established to encourage more **private sector sponsorship** of local sport development. By directing specific funding to schemes such as these, and by establishing particular criteria that applications for funding have to adhere to, the government is able to encourage non-government organisations to adopt its plans and priorities for the development of sport.

Schools and an increased involvement of governing bodies, clubs and coaches in school sport were a major focus of *Sport – Raising the Game*. In the document, regional sports councils were identified as having a key role to play in developing links between various sport providers at the local level and particularly between schools and sports clubs. Governing bodies of sport were also encouraged to do more work with schools. They were asked to indicate in their business plans what they would do to develop their work in the area of school sport, including, for example, providing coaches to work with pupils in physical education and school sport.

In relation to the development of sport in schools, the policy also stated that 'alongside teachers, clubs have an important role to play by expanding the range of sports on offer and providing coaching to the most talented' (1995, p. 9). You should note a particular emphasis in this proposal. Provision of coaching is associated with 'the most talented', giving the impression that the interest underpinning the initiative is the development of only a select few pupils and, specifically, those with the potential and interest to perform at high levels in sport. This emphasis, linking resources with elite performance, was also apparent in other aspects of the policy.

The requirements that the policy established for future teacher training also reflected a desire to increase the amount of specialist coaching in schools and to create closer links between teaching and coaching. The document drew attention to the need for training to provide opportunities for teachers to gain coaching awards and also to specifically equip them to teach games.

Private sector sponsorship refers to the increasing involvement of local and national businesses in sport development, via investment in clubs or facilities, or specific development programmes for sport.

✴ *Over to You*

In a small group, consider these points of emphasis in *Sport – Raising the Game*. Assess how they may or may not meet requirements for equity of provision and opportunity. Discuss the issues raised in your assessment and make a note of the main points of the discussion. Chapter 1.2 may assist you in this task.

■ ■

Sport – Raising the Game encouraged schools to increase the numbers of children actively involved in sport, as well as improve their achievements in sport. The policy laid the foundations for the introduction of new awards for schools called Sportsmark and Sportsmark Gold. These awards have encouraged more schools to provide more and better quality opportunities for sport.

■ ■ ■ ■ ■ ■ *Over to You* ■ ■ ■ ■ ■ ■ ■

Find out if your school has been awarded or has applied for Sportsmark awards. Study the criteria for the awards. In groups, discuss the aspects of provision that you think your school needs to address and list them.

■ ■

The Sportsmark and Sportsmark Gold awards criteria focus on the following areas of physical education and sport provision:

- Time devoted to physical education and sport in the core curriculum
- Breadth and balance within the core curriculum programme
- Opportunities for students to develop their interests outside the core curriculum
- Planned development routes for talented performers
- Links with sports organisations and other schools
- Community activities
- Leadership development and opportunities
- Opportunities for further training and updating qualifications

Sport – Raising the Game directed attention to the development of sport in universities and other institutes of further and higher education. It also recommended the introduction of more university sports scholarships, designed to enable talented athletes to successfully combine their training and competition with their academic studies. Bath, Loughborough and Stirling are examples of universities offering such scholarships.

Sport – Raising the Game proposed the development of a British Academy of Sport as a specialist centre to support the development of excellence. Ultimately, opinions were divided as to the most desirable form for such an academy and, as you can read later in this chapter, the Labour government took this proposal forward with a different emphasis, focusing attention more upon a 'network' of regional centres rather than a single national centre. They also used the term 'institute' instead of 'academy'.

■ The Context of *Sport – Raising the Game*

Sport – Raising the Game was produced within a particular political context and so reflects a number of values and priorities that the then government in power considered important. The comments of John Major, who was prime minister at the time the policy was being formulated, provide a useful illustration of the government's values and priorities for sport.

The policy was described by John Major as 'the most important set of proposals ever published for the encouragement and promotion of sport' (in DNH, 1995).

Some of Major's comments in his introduction to this policy highlighted sport's political significance, but also the government's particular interest in particular sports and particular aspects of sport. It is apparent in this document that not all sports were valued equally by the Major government, nor were all forms of participation. For example, Major stated:

> We want to sustain the place of minor sports that bring much enjoyment. But I am determined to see that our great traditional sports — cricket, hockey, swimming, athletics, football, netball, rugby, tennis and the like — are put firmly at the centre of the stage. (John Major in DNH, 1995)

You can see that sports with an aesthetic emphasis, for example, were not among Major's priorities. In this next comment, he clearly focused attention on the development of elite sports performance:

> Together I want us to bring about a sea change in the prospects of British sport — from the very first steps in primary school right through to the breaking of the tape in an Olympic final. (John Major in DNH, 1995)

Other comments made by Mr Major may be open to challenge in terms of both their accuracy and their relationship to equity. He commented:

> Sport is open to all ages — but it is most of all open to those who learn to love it when they are young. Competitive sport teaches valuable lessons that last for life . . . above all, it produces pure enjoyment for those who play and those who watch. (John Major in DNH, 1995)

As you will be aware, not everyone has an equal opportunity to access sport. And for those children who do, some experience sport and physical education negatively. *Sport – Raising the Game* has little advice to offer young people who cannot access sport for a variety of reasons beyond their control or whose experiences of sport have been discouraging or unpleasant. Indeed, on the issue of funding for the policies identified in *Sport – Raising the Game,* Mr Major commented that 'people will, as ever, ask where the resources will come from. I do not believe every problem needs a financial answer' (John Major in DNH, 1995). So, whereas the government was outlining a comprehensive range of recommendations for many providers, it was relying on those providers to adopt, implement and resource the provision in large part by themselves.

ENGLAND THE SPORTING NATION, 1997

England the Sporting Nation was published in 1997. It was set up by the Labour government as a starting point for taking sport in England into the new millennium. This report incorporates a concern for both participation and performance sport. It highlights the right that everyone should have to play sport for enjoyment and health. It also states that striving to do one's best and continuous improvement are important at all levels, including national and international levels.

England the Sporting Nation emphasised many of the same values as *Sport – Raising the Game.* However, it also attempted to provide equal opportunities for all people to 'follow a lifestyle which includes active participation in sport and recreation' (ESC, 1997, p. 4). Schools and teachers were identified as having a critical role to play in the realisation of these aims.

It was also notable that *England the Sporting Nation* uses the sport development continuum, moving from foundation, through participation and performance, to excellence, that has featured in Sports Council initiatives throughout the 1990s. Performance at elite levels was a key concern in this policy development. One way that *England the Sporting Nation* attempted to move forward the agenda initiated in

Sport – Raising the Game was by stating specific targets for sport development. It established targets for four aspects of development work:

1. Young people and sport
2. Active participation throughout life
3. Performance development
4. Achieving excellence

Some of the targets set to be achieved by 2001 were

- a 10 per cent increase in the numbers of boys and 20 per cent increase in the numbers of girls who are members of sports clubs;
- a 10 per cent increase in the numbers of boys and 20 per cent increase in the numbers of girls 'who strongly enjoy doing sport in their leisure time'; and by 2002
- a 20 per cent increase in the numbers of adults, aged 16 plus, taking part in regular sporting activity; and
- a 10 per cent increase in the numbers of adults, aged 16 plus, who have received sports tuition, from an instructor or coach, to improve their performance.

Targets for 2004 included

- in netball — to win the World Championships in 2003;
- in hockey — the men's and women's teams to reach the Commonwealth Games finals in 2002;
- England to top the medals tables at the 2002 Commonwealth Games; and
- the Football Association to secure the hosting of the 2006 World Cup.

Over to You

In your class, identify 1) the percentage of boys and girls who are members of sports clubs; 2) the percentage of parents/guardians who take part in sport regularly; 3) the percentage of parents/guardians who receive coaching in a sport. Discuss and make notes on the following topics:

- Any differences in the percentages for girls and boys, and for men and women
- Some reasons why more people are not members of sports clubs
- What sports clubs need to do to attract more young people as members
- What type of clubs you would like as after-school sports clubs

The targets established by the government could not be achieved without action from a range of providers and, in particular, support from schools and teachers. Like *Sport – Raising the Game, England the Sporting Nation* identified the provision of resources as a local rather than national responsibility.

The English Sports Council, now known as Sport England, took the lead in directing and coordinating responses to *England the Sporting Nation* by launching a new programme of policy initiatives called More People, More Places, More Medals.

More People

In relation to the first element, More People, the Sports Council stated its determination to involve the entire community in sport, as spectators, participants or volunteers. In June 1998, three new programmes were launched: Active Schools, Active Sports, and Active Communities. Many of the initiatives established within the National Junior Sport Programme (NJSP) that arose as a response to *Sport – Raising the Game* were integrated into Sport England's 'Active' programmes (figure 59).

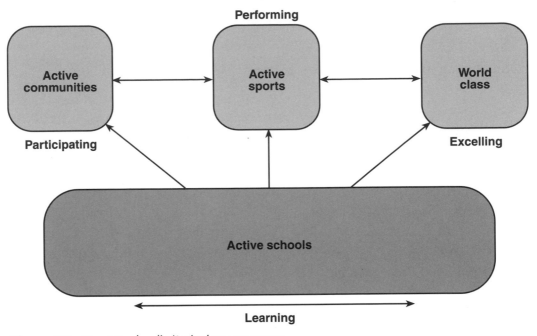

Figure 59   Sport England's 'Active' programmes.
Reproduced with permission of Sport England.

Specific initiatives developed within the NJSP included the Youth Sport Trust's TOP schemes for school, club and community sport development; the Challenge Funding scheme; Coaching for Teachers; the Sportsmark and Sportsmark Gold awards; and development of the Community Sports Leadership and Junior Sports Leader award schemes. Some of these programmes may have been developed in your school or local community. The Challenge Fund scheme aimed to help schools strengthen their existing links with sports clubs or develop new links and was relaunched as Sportslink in 1999. Coaching for Teachers was developed to enable teachers to extend their knowledge and experience of particular sports, or of sport for people with disabilities.

Active Schools. The Active Schools programme was designed to build on the initiatives in the NJSP and to promote the development of these initiatives in schools. The NJSP set out a range of training opportunities for young people. These opportunities were organised around the sport development continuum, a pyramid that imagines lots of young people at the base and only a few at the pinnacle. This structure inevitably means that fewer and fewer young people are able to succeed at higher and higher levels of performance. Even though a newer form of this model presented by the Active programmes is not a pyramid, some of the initiatives that have developed within this structure may reflect a similar way of thinking.

Over to You

Discuss the ways in which this structure for the Active programmes is similar to, and differs from, the pyramid structure for sport development. Make notes on some of the strengths and weaknesses of this way of thinking about sport development. Consider whether it accurately portrays your own and your friends' interests and pattern of involvement in sport.

One of the new initiatives to emerge from *England the Sporting Nation* is the Sporting Ambassadors scheme. This sought to establish national sportswomen and sportsmen as role models who would visit schools, help to develop school-club links and promote the value of sport and physical activity as a part of everyone's lifestyle. Sport England was specifically concerned to attract more girls and young people from ethnic populations to become active participants in sport.

There are mixed opinions on whether the use of talented sports performers achieves this goal. In contrast with Sport England's view, the Health Education Authority suggest that if celebrities are used to promote regular physical activity among young people, non-sport role models should be used. This is to avoid the stereotyping that sometimes occurs, associating elite performers with appearance, beauty and muscularity. In Germany, researchers have found that neither sportsmen nor sportswomen featured among the role models identified by girls. For girls, individuals from the world of music were most frequently role models.

Over to You

Discuss as a class who would be your chosen sport ambassadors and why? Who are appropriate role models to attract all young people to participate in sport and physical activity? What characteristics and behaviours identify someone as a 'good role model' to promote participation in sport and physical activity among young people? Make notes on your discussion.

Two accreditation programmes are key elements of the 'Active Schools' programme: the Sportsmark and Sportsmark Gold awards already established for secondary schools and new **Activemark** and **Activemark Gold** awards for primary schools.

As well as continuing to expand the 'Coaching for Teachers' scheme, Sport England has developed further support for teachers and others involved in the provision of school sport. *Running Sport for Schools* includes workshops and booklets on how to establish links with clubs and how to apply for lottery grants. The Active Schools programme has been designed to link with the other Active programmes and the World Class initiative.

Further information about the Activemark and Activemark Gold awards can be found via the Sport England website. These schemes have been developed by Sport England in partnership with the British Heart Foundation.

Active Sports. The Active Sports programme is directed towards nine sports: athletics, basketball, cricket, girls football, netball, hockey, rugby union, swimming, and tennis.

The emphasis was on national coordination of a programme delivered at the local level through sports partnerships and local action groups for particular sports. Local clubs were central to the development, but local authorities, education services, schools and governing bodies of sport also featured in the partnerships. Each action group had a remit to provide participation, competition and coaching opportunities, working to new development frameworks designed by the governing body for a particular sport.

Active Communities. Active Communities is a programme that aims to promote lifelong participation in sport through sustained provision of opportunities at local levels. Sport England notes that Active Communities will be directed towards ensuring that as many members of society as possible are given an opportunity to participate, so addressing the current inequalities that exist in English sport. Local community leaders and local authorities are key partners in this programme, and Sport England plans to expand the professional infrastructure of sports development officers working with the community. Investment is also being directed towards providing sports-related training for community agencies and related organisations, such as youth workers, community and social services workers and volunteer sports leaders in the community.

More Places

The More Places programme was established in recognition of the need for well-planned, well-designed and well-managed facilities for sport. Sport England developed a facilities planning model as a template for the provision of major sports facilities in local communities and a database of facilities throughout England. These developments are directed towards more strategic planning and development of sports facilities than has previously been the case in England.

One aspect of Sport England's work is distribution of lottery money, and many facility development projects have been funded by lottery funds. By providing advice to governing bodies, local authorities and other groups with interests in facility developments and by advising central government on development issues, Sport England seeks to facilitate the development of 'high quality facilities that are accessible to everyone' (ESC, 1998, p. 10). Like the Sports Council for Wales, Sport England is committed to the principles of **sustainable development** and also works closely with countryside agencies. In addition, a quality scheme for sports and leisure facilities, known as QUEST, has been established to address management of facilities.

Sustainable development refers to the concern to ensure protection of the environment in order that it can continue to be the context for sport and leisure activities.

More Medals

The More Medals programme comprises a series of schemes funded through lottery revenue:

Performance Funding aims to assist performers with the potential to win medals in significant international competitions and events within the next six years.

Potential Funding aims to assist the development of talented performers with the potential to win medals in significant international competitions and events within the next 10 years.

Start Funding aims to identify and nurture those performers with the necessary characteristics to achieve future World Class success within the next 10 years.

This funding links directly to the World Class programmes established by Sport England to

help national governing bodies develop a comprehensive system through which talented athletes can be identified and supported, in order to achieve consistent success in significant international competitions such as the Olympics and Paralympics. It aims to systematically develop the best performers in the world. (Sport England, 2001)

World Class Start will

- help to identify and nurture a specific number of English athletes who have the necessary characteristics to achieve future World Class success; and
- assist the development of talented athletes with the potential to win medals, or equivalent, in significant future international competitions and events within the next eight years. (Sport England, 2001)

World Class Performance will

- support the training and preparation programmes for elite athletes who have the potential to win medals, or equivalent, in significant international competitions and events such as the Olympics and Paralympics, now and within the next four years. (Sport England, 2001)

World Class performance was launched in November 1996 and by 2000 had awarded £30m to over 30 different sports.

Over to You

Find out a sport that has received World Class Performance funding, and make a list of the ways in which elite performers have benefited from the scheme.

Sport England is also working to establish a network of regional centres and institutes in England that will link to the UK Sports Institute and represent centres of excellence for sport in England. Sport science support, training facilities and coaching will be among the services provided at centres.

Over to You

Find out the location of your nearest regional centre. Write a one-page bulleted-point description of the services it provides.

In chapter 5.3 you can read about some of the ways in which these policy initiatives have been translated into new schemes and opportunities in local settings.

YOUNG PEOPLE FIRST: A STRATEGY FOR WELSH SPORT, 1999

This strategy document was developed at a time when the government in Wales was particularly concerned about health and lifestyle issues. The document *Young People First* drew attention to the health benefits of sport and physical activity and the need to encourage more people to participate regularly in sport and physical activity. In addition, the SCW identified potential social benefits of more people, but particularly 'socially excluded people' becoming involved in sport. Sport was claimed to be 'an effective tool for reintegrating all socially excluded people, especially young people, into mainstream community activities. . .' (SCW, 1999, p. 4).

As you can read in chapter 1.2, it is important to take a critical look at matters such as what are regarded as mainstream activities and what and whose values are reflected or, equally, excluded through the acceptance and promotion of particular activities. Are policies inclusive of the values held by various social groups or only one dominant group in society?

'Sport for all' is restated as a commitment in *Young People First*. The document also states a commitment to equity in sport. In addition, the writers of *Young People First* believe in 'fair play', explaining that fair play is about ensuring that all those taking part in sport adhere to the rules of sport and that the benefits of this, including the development of social bonds and friendship, are emphasised.

In relation to the environment, *Young People First* draws attention to the increasing demand for access to countryside areas and explained that its approach was 'access for all, but not access to everywhere' (SCW, 1999, p. 9), with a concern to promote responsible use while retaining a concern for sustainability. You may be aware of local areas where overuse may be leading to the deterioration of a recreation area. For example, in recent years, several long-established footpaths in National Park areas have been destroyed by the ever growing number of walkers using them, and mountain biking has been an activity seen as potentially damaging to countryside areas.

The final principle of the *Young People First* strategy is devolution. The policy writers emphasise that variations in participation across Wales mean that sport development needs a more localised approach than has been the case in the past. Partnership is the key means by which policies are taken forward, with implementation the responsibility of a variety of organisations.

Like *England the Sporting Nation, Young People First* sets targets for sport development. These relate to each of the aspects of work identified in the mission of the Sports Council for Wales, and included the goals of

- increasing sports participation by 15- to 24-year-olds to 85 per cent by the year 2005;
- halving the gap between men's and women's participation (in 1997/8: 53.5 per cent men and 41.2 per cent women) by the year 2005;
- increasing sports club membership;
- increasing extracurricular participation in sport;
- increasing the number of Welsh individuals achieving British representation to 350 by the year 2005 and the number of British champions to 150;
- monitoring unmet facility demands and encouraging provision where developments are identified as sustainable; and
- providing up-to-date, high-quality information for all involved in sport in Wales.

The programmes presented in *Young People First* represent component parts of a development structure that as figure 60 shows takes the form of a pyramid, with development focused on elite Welsh squads.

At the base of the pyramid is Dragon Sport, a programme specifically designed to introduce primary age school children to sport, with opportunities for them to feed into development programmes in clubs and the community. Development of club opportunities then links with the scheme Club Cymru, from which children will be able to access coaching opportunities in Centres of Local Development and Centres of Regional Excellence. Elite Cymru is then designed to provide support services for the elite and potential elite among young Welsh sportspeople, with, for example, access to sports medicine, sport science support services and accommodation at the Welsh Sports Institute.

This pyramid of programmes is accompanied by a number of support programmes

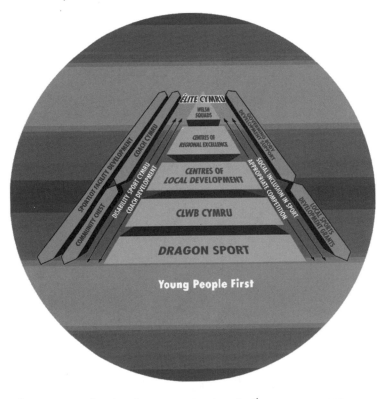

Figure 60   The development structure to the programmes presented in *Young People First.*

Reprinted, by permission, from "Young People First: A Strategy for Welsh Sport."

directed towards the funding of facility development, coach education development, and support for the development of governing bodies in Wales. The two Welsh Sports Council centres, the Welsh Sports Institute in Cardiff and Plas Menai on the Menai Straits are also linked into the development of the UK Sports Institute.

SCOTLAND AND NORTHERN IRELAND

Important policy documents were issued in Scotland and Northern Ireland that addressed very similar issues to *Sport – Raising the Game*. Scotland's *Sporting Future: A New Start* (Scottish Office, 1995) and *The Future of Sport for Young People in Northern Ireland* (Department of Education, Northern Ireland, 1995) stressed the importance of sport and particularly the provision of sport in schools. They also addressed matters such as the provision of extracurricular physical education and school sport, the need for development of school-club links, the introduction of awards for schools and the provision of coaching courses for teachers.

SUMMARY

This chapter describes and comments on recent policy initiatives in England and Wales that contain strategies for sport development. It is noted that there are tensions between the stated commitments to both participation and performance sport. These initiatives have a common concern to form partnerships for sport development. Whereas the policies provide national frameworks in England and Wales, they express a commitment to deliver sport services at local levels involving many agencies and organisations.

Test Yourself Questions

1. Name the titles of the policy documents discussed in this chapter.

2. Identify the issues relating to the provision of physical education and sport that are addressed in the Sportsmark and Sportsmark Gold awards.

3. Name the three linked programmes developed by Sport England in response to *England the Sporting Nation*.

4. In *England the Sporting Nation*, targets were established for four areas of development work. What are the areas?

5. Name the three 'Active' programmes developed by Sport England.

6. Name the three linked funding schemes within the 'More Medals' programme. Explain what each scheme is directed towards and identify the 'World Class' programme that each scheme links with.

7. Name the programme within the pyramid development structure outlined in *Young People First*.

Local Provision of Sport and Recreation

Learning Outcomes

When you have studied this chapter, you should be able to

☑ outline the contemporary structure and organisation of sport in Britain at the local level,

☑ identify key sites of policy making and provision of sporting opportunities at the local level and understand their respective roles in provision,

☑ describe and critically evaluate local responses to recent national policy initiatives, and

☑ use a range of resources (including the Internet) to access information relating to the changing structure of sport in Britain and latest policy developments.

INTRODUCTION

This chapter explores the relationships between the various agencies and organisations that feature in local structures and networks. It illustrates some of the ways in which the national policies and initiatives described in chapters 5.1 and 5.2 are shaping local development and retains a particular focus on developments directed towards young people. As in the case of national policy making, the developments described in this chapter highlight that you cannot look at sport in isolation from other areas of policy and planning.

In local authorities particularly you will see that issues relating to sport development can be linked to various areas of public service administration and that wider political and economic contexts will shape policies and provision relating to sport, leisure and recreation. You also need to consider commercial as well as publicly funded agencies and organisations. Finally, it is important for you to remember that the structures, organisations and policies that are described are not static. The 1990s featured some notable changes in local government structures, boundaries and remits, and further changes can be expected in the years ahead.

THE RELATIONSHIPS BETWEEN NATIONAL AND LOCAL INITIATIVES

There is great diversity in the provision of sport in different parts of the United Kingdom. It is possible to identify key providers. But their respective roles, the scope of local networks or structures for provision and the particular initiatives that they are involved in will vary. The national policy developments outlined in chapters 5.1 and 5.2, and the funding opportunities associated with the National Lottery, provide some common reference points for local providers and initiatives.

The national sports councils, and in England the **regional sports councils,** seek to play an advisory and supporting role in the development of sport locally. They also seek to guide strategic planning by various agencies and facilitate partnerships in the development and provision of sport. Partnerships between various agencies and organisations at a local level are the focus of more and more developments.

In part this is because collaboration in developments has become a requirement if bids for funding (for example, to the National Lottery) are to be successful. The sports councils are increasingly seeking more integrated sport development and provision, particularly in facility planning and the provision of training for sports development officers, sports leaders and coaches. More formalised and extended local sporting structures and networks may well emerge in the years ahead.

The government's recently published strategy for sport, *A Sporting Future for All* (DCMS, 2000), refers to a need for reconsideration of the ways sport is organised and funded. Alongside proposals for a change in the relationship between the government and national governing bodies are plans that clearly establish **'specialist sports colleges'** as a key site in development structures and networks. There is also recognition of the role that professional as well as amateur clubs have to play in providing opportunities for young people and a commitment to the development of a United Kingdom Sports Institute network.

LOCAL AUTHORITIES

Local authorities take several forms and include county, district, borough or city councils. Historically, they have been key providers of sport, recreation and leisure

Details of the location of the regional sports councils in England are available via the Sport England website.

Specialist sports colleges are discussed later in this chapter.

at a local level, dedicating funding to the development and running of facilities and to subsidising participation opportunities through, for example, low entry fees to facilities. In many respects, local authorities can be regarded as the key agency in promoting notions of 'sport for all'. Houlihan (1997) has suggested that the sports councils' funding for the development of sport 'is dwarfed by the volume of investment in sport allocated by local authorities' (p. 99).

In recent years, the structure and funding of local government have undergone major changes, with the result that local authority departments and services are now subject to many of the same financial pressures and demands as operators in the private sector. However, sport and recreation remain key, even if reduced, areas of local government investment, and local authorities continue to play a significant part in translating national sports policies and initiatives into real opportunities.

Local authority-owned and -managed facilities are key arenas for participation and for the hosting of local, regional or national sporting events. In recent years, many local authorities have also funded or contributed towards the funding of sports development officers. Local authorities have also played a key role in the implementation of initiatives relating to physical education and school sport, including 'Coaching for Teachers' and training for the development of the Youth Sport Trust's TOP programmes in school and community settings.

A further area in which local authorities have played a lead role in developments is in the community use of school-based sports facilities. In many respects, shared use of facilities seems desirable and very logical. However, developments have varied in their success and much potential use remains undeveloped. In some instances, schemes have failed to take adequate account of the different needs of school and community users. Although the basic facility such as a sports hall may appear to have ideal potential for use by the community outside of school hours, the support facilities such as reception and changing areas, management and maintenance arrangements may be lacking.

The TOP programmes are discussed further in chapter 4.2.

Over to You

In a group, discuss what facilities at your school are currently used by the community, or could be. Identify and make a note of the issues that would need to be addressed to facilitate community use and to avoid conflict between school and community users. You will need to consider parking, security of facilities and personal belongings, booking arrangements, changing facilities, timetabling of school and community activities, maintenance of facilities (including cleaning) and hire of equipment.

Local authorities vary considerably in structure and size. In some places, unitary authorities are responsible for all local government services. In other places, the local structure has two tiers. For example, a county council may have a number of district councils, and responsibilities for services are then divided or shared in various ways. In many places, there are specialist leisure services departments with responsibility for the development of sport and the development, management and maintenance of leisure facilities. In local government, as in national contexts, sport can be related to various aspects of policy, including health, transport, education, leisure and tourism.

Over to You

Find out the structure of your local authority. Which departments have responsibility for sport development and provision locally? Note all major sports and leisure facilities within the authority. These may include parks and countryside areas as well as pitches and sports centres.

As well as varying in structure and size, local authorities also differ in their social and economic characteristics. You may have heard some areas referred to as areas of social deprivation and be aware of local areas that are sites of widespread poverty or, in contrast, clear wealth. The extent and nature of facilities for sport, recreation and leisure may well reflect these differences. In several areas of government policy, including education and health, specific areas are being targeted with specific development initiatives and investment.

Certain areas in England are now identified as Education Action Zones and Health Action Zones. A recent addition to this targeted development approach is the identification of Sport Action Zones. Areas identified as most in need of sport development will be prioritised for investment. All of these target-based policy developments can be associated with broader political agendas and, in particular, the government's commitment to fight social exclusion and promote social inclusion.

Although differences between authorities are important to acknowledge, you also need to note significant points of commonality. The structure and resources of local authorities mean that they provide an obvious central point of contact for various organisations within their boundaries. Their boundaries also serve to define the scope of local sporting structures and networks. Local authorities feature centrally in Sport England's 'Active Communities' programme described in chapter 5.2.

In relation to school sport, the National Council for School Sport encourages the development of federations of the various school sports associations within one or more local authorities, creating a forum that can represent school sport and develop links with the local authority and other organisations within it. In addition, irrespective of their relative wealth, as we discuss in the next section, all local authorities have had to respond to changes in local government funding and operation that have impacted upon their provision of community services, including sport and leisure services.

■ Local Authorities: Pressures to Perform

In 1992, leisure services felt the effects of wider policy developments relating to the structure and operation of local government. Various services provided by local authorities, including leisure services, became subject to Compulsory Competitive Tendering (CCT). Houlihan (1997) explains:

> The essence of CCT within the leisure services policy area was that while the local authority would retain ownership of the facility, its management would be subject to a process of competitive tendering with contract periods running for four to five years. (p. 135)

Although many local authorities successfully submitted tenders to retain management responsibility for facilities, commercial contractors sometimes won the tendering process and assumed these responsibilities. A key implication of these changes in local government was that financial issues and efficiency in operation have become a key focus of attention. There is now the potential for tensions to arise between service to the community and profit-making by commercial organisations. Local authorities may consequently be unable to offer the same levels of support for particular forms of participation or participation groups as they have previously. A consequence of CCT may be a reduction in the choice of participation opportunities locally.

Over to You

Find out and make a list of the range of activities offered at a sports or leisure centre locally. Is it possible to identify programming priorities? Identify which participation groups are advantaged and disadvantaged as a result of programming arrangements and write a brief analytical report of your findings.

CCT has now been superseded by new measures and systems associated with the drive for improved efficiency and accountability in local service provision. Local authorities are being called upon to demonstrate that they are providing Best Value in their operations and have to develop Best Value Performance Plans outlining their proposals for improvement of services. The plans are intended to allow members of the public to judge an authority's performance and have a say in future developments locally. Plans include details of the authority's objectives in providing services for its local communities, how it intends to achieve the objectives, information about past service provision and targets for improvement.

Best Value Performance Plans

You should be able to obtain a copy of your county or city council's Best Value Performance Plan from your local council offices, library, or on the Internet. Leicestershire County Council provides one example of a Best Value Performance Plan.

Leicestershire County Council has established six key objectives for its service provision, concerned with

1. advancing lifelong learning,
2. building a healthier community,
3. protecting and enhancing the environment,
4. improving economic wellbeing,
5. promoting better government in Leicestershire, and
6. reducing crime and antisocial behaviour. (Leicestershire County Council, 2000)

It is in the context of the second objective that the development of sport and active lifestyles features in the plan. The County Council is committed to improving the personal health and wellbeing of the people of Leicestershire. The actions that the Council has planned in order to achieve this objective include the promotion of walking and cycling by creating new and improved routes, and supporting the development of sport and recreation for all the community. From our discussion of the national dimension of governance we can anticipate that such action will necessarily involve a number of departments within the Council and also needs to involve several other agencies and organisations.

Some councils have a two-tier structure for the provision of services with, for example, borough or district councils operating within a county structure. The responsibilities and resources available in this second tier vary. Usually some provision is made for sport, recreation and leisure. Increasingly this investment is subject to scrutiny in terms of realisation of targets and value for money in service provision.

So, for example, within Leicestershire, the Borough of Charnwood is a second-tier authority that has also recently established a performance plan and set targets for the improvement of services. The Borough Council has two leisure centres within its boundaries. Performance measures and targets have been established in relation to sports, leisure and cultural activities within the Borough. These targets include increasing the opportunities for young people and disabled people to become involved in sport (Charnwood Borough Council, 2000).

In anticipation that local authorities are reviewing and developing their sport and leisure provision in the light of Best Value, Sport England has developed new information, guidance and services for local authorities. They have taken a 'tool kit' approach, offering a range of advice and services to support local authorities that relate to the four Cs of challenge, consult, compare, compete (Sport England, 2000). This is a good example of the way in which the sports councils play a strategic role, advising and supporting the actions of local agencies and organisations that are central to the realisation of the sports councils' own aims, objectives and targets.

THE PRIVATE SECTOR

Recent developments in local authorities show that they have had to adopt management structures and systems the private commercial organisations use. During the 1990s, new partnerships were established in the provision of sport and leisure locally. The private sector needs to be recognised as a key provider of sports facilities and opportunities.

Private organisations have been behind the development of many sports and leisure facilities, including health and fitness clubs, tennis centres and golf courses. These facilities often provide a base for sports clubs, as well as offering opportunities for casual participation. Pricing policies may mean that these developments provide opportunities for *some* rather than *all* people in local communities. However, tensions between commercial interests and service provision are no longer confined to the private sector.

The sports councils have emphasised that national and local strategic plans should embrace private sector facilities. With reduced public funding for sport development it is inevitable that the private sector will have an increasingly important part to play in meeting development targets. The sports councils will continue their efforts to influence private as well as public developments and provision. In addition, the private sector is an important source of sponsorship for sport, relating to specific events, facilities, clubs and development initiatives. As such it must be acknowledged as a key, even if indirect, link in the structures for the governance and development of sport in the UK. This has been vividly illustrated in the growth of the Youth Sport Trust whose programmes have been underpinned by funding from a range of commercial companies.

SPORTS CLUBS

Sports clubs feature in many local communities and are a key dimension of the governance of sport in the United Kingdom. They are the place where many people enjoy participation in sport. They are often the key site for the implementation of initiatives and directions for development that have been established nationally. Sports clubs are the target for many national policies and for support and advice for the implementation of these policies.

Sports clubs are encouraged by the sports councils to enter into partnerships with other providers locally, particularly local authorities and schools. Many sports clubs are physically located at facilities owned by these organisations. Schools and local authority or private sector leisure centres are frequently a base for clubs. However, some clubs have their own facilities, and lottery funding has enabled many to develop or improve facilities. Whereas new developments are to be welcomed, the critical issue is sustainability of facilities. The sports councils are now demanding that clubs generate income for maintenance before the approval of a development.

Facility and club development feature in national governing body plans. Many sports clubs are affiliated to a particular NGB. As part of ongoing efforts to improve the provision of junior sport, the sports councils are encouraging NGBs to establish or improve junior club development plans. These plans should identify pathways for both participation and performance sport for young people through a programme of coaching, play and competition.

An important aspect of junior club development plans is improved links between the clubs and local schools so that young people can easily move between the two

Sports clubs provide opportunities for young people to participate and develop their performance.

sites of provision. Club coaches are encouraged to work more closely with physical education teachers in schools and to develop after-school sessions that can introduce pupils to the sport and to the club opportunity. Club coaches offering coaching at schools provide a tangible and familiar link for young people to transfer to adult club sport. Such links are a particular focus of Sport England's Active Sports programme, which you can read about in chapter 5.2. They are also a focus of other sports council initiatives directed towards the development of better pathways for continued participation beyond compulsory schooling and for talent development.

Equity issues are central to these developments of sporting opportunities for young people. More developments to cater for young people with different levels of ability and with different reasons for wanting to participate in the sport are important if the targets set by sports councils and NGBs for increased club membership are to be achieved. Clubs need to consider what types of activities will appeal to all young people. Many young people are made to feel that they are 'not good enough' to join a club or that a club will not provide the type of experience that they are interested in. It remains to be seen if the latest policy initiatives can achieve the dual aim of extending performance achievements and increasing participation for a broad range of young people.

 *Over to You*

For one of your chosen sports, visit your local club. Does it have a junior club or section? Find out whether it has a junior development policy and what structures or links it has established to encourage new members. Make a note of the type of sessions that the club provides. Are there opportunities to receive coaching and for participation in competitions within the club or against other clubs? Are all members able to participate in such competitions or do you have to be selected to do so? Are there opportunities for casual or recreational play? Write a brief report dealing with these questions. Consider also the equity issues your report raises.

Sports vary in the extent to which they develop a junior club network and in the resources that they have available to do so. Whereas many sports clubs are concerned with amateur sport participation and competition, there are also professional sports clubs. Links between amateur and professional arenas are important in relation to a number of issues.

Government interests in national sporting achievements and events and Sport England targets relating to these aspects of sport development relate to professional as well as amateur arenas. Increasingly, the sports councils and other agencies and organisations have recognised that strategies for sport development need to embrace rather than exclude the professional sector and that professional clubs may have an important role to play in supporting initiatives and particularly those relating to junior sport development.

The benefits of the involvement of professional clubs in junior sport development are mutual. As well as helping to meet targets, the clubs themselves have interests in fostering future players. Their future success depends on young people being motivated to participate in a sport and having opportunities to do so. Several of the clubs in the football league now have junior development sections, but football is by no means the only sport in which nationally recognised clubs are involved in junior sport development. Rugby union is another sport providing some good examples of clubs investing in the development of the junior participation and in so doing seeking to develop community sport and also establish links with schools.

The Leicester Tigers run coaching courses for girls and boys during the school holidays and have a youth squad. The club is also supporting the development of **tag rugby** in local schools. This initiative has benefited by support from Sport England's Sportsmatch funding scheme, in which investment by private companies is matched by a Sportsmatch grant. In this example, the Alliance and Leicester Bank provided the private sponsorship. The scheme involves 360 primary schools and features coaching programmes for teachers, school visits, rugby days and a tag rugby festival.

In Bristol, Bristol Rugby Football Club established a partnership with a company called Sanderson Recruitment to develop a scheme that introduces 9- to 11-year-olds to rugby. Other examples of Sportsmatch projects include Buxton Mineral water sponsorship of the MCC's cricket development scheme and sponsorship by Darthaven Marina and Philip Limited enabling Dart Sailability to put together a three-year programme to provide people with disability access to sailing. A Sportsmatch award of £9,000 helped fund specialist equipment and modified boats. Information about the **Sportsmatch scheme** and projects supported is available at the Sportsmatch website.

One of the notable features of Sportsmatch and other initiatives directed towards the development of community and junior sport is that they demonstrate the way governments view sport: namely, as a means to address social issues such as deprivation and crime. Sport development is seen as a means of making progress towards a better quality of life for many people and many communities. In Kent, Railtrack has sponsored a football development scheme being run in partnership with Charlton Athletic that is intended to play a role in reducing vandalism on housing estates and trespass on railways.

Tag rugby is a modified form of rugby in which a 'tag' replaces the tackling that occurs in the full adult version of the game.

The Sportsmatch scheme arose from *Sport – Raising the Game* (see chapter 5.2) and was established to encourage more private sector sponsorship of local sport development, with grants awarded that matched investment provided by private companies.

Over to You

For one of your chosen sports, investigate the ways in which private sponsorship has aided development and, specifically, has helped in club and junior development.

The Sportsmatch scheme highlights the role that the commercial sector plays in the development and provision of sport, both nationally and locally. You can read more about the commodification of sport and leisure in chapter 6.2.

In this context of commercialism, it is important to note that volunteers run the majority of sports clubs. A few clubs have some paid administrators or coaches. But it is volunteers who run sports clubs, individuals who give their time and money to help others. Most coaches and club officials are not paid, and their involvement is on the basis of goodwill, reflecting their commitment to sport.

Volunteers are recognised as crucial to the continued development of sport. Sport England estimate that in excess of 1.5 million volunteers keep sport running in England. In recognition of the vital contribution that volunteers make to sport, they have initiated the Volunteer Investment Programme. This programme aims to encourage good practice in the recruitment, motivation and retention of volunteers and provide guidance to help volunteer coordinators manage networks or groups of volunteers.

The British Sports Trust has initiated various regional projects that aim to increase the number of volunteer sports leaders and ensure that the work of sports leaders matches the needs of local community groups. Central in the British Sports Trust projects is the CCPR Sports Leadership Award training. The projects demonstrate that the role of volunteers in sport in the United Kingdom is by no means confined to club settings, but extends to more informal community-based provision and is critical to school-based sport. A Northwest project highlights a further crucial role that volunteers play in sport in running sports events. In this instance, 15,000 volunteers are needed to work at the Commonwealth Games in Manchester in 2002 (The British Sports Trust, 2000).

In junior sport, many volunteers are parents, motivated to assist in providing opportunities for their children to participate, compete and progress in sport. Parents may well become involved in club committee work, officiating and coaching. One of the main ways in which they assist is by transporting children to training sessions and competitions. Parents who begin coaching in an informal way may find that they enjoy the role and wish to learn more about sports coaching.

The National Coaching Foundation Coach Education programme and sport-specific national governing body award courses offer opportunities for parents and others to develop their coaching skills and knowledge. However, you should note that not all parents will have the time to follow coaching courses or be able to afford course fees. Although many clubs have relatively limited resources, one of the ways in which they can make a clear investment in their own future development is to provide funding to enable people to attend coaching courses. In addition, there is a need for clubs to recognise and value the many other ways in which parents support junior participation. As well as providing transport and assisting in club administration, parents also often initiate fundraising activities. You can begin to see the way in which a key arena of sport in Britain is highly reliant upon goodwill and has relatively fragile foundations.

Teachers represent another important part of this fragile foundation. Physical education and other teachers often become involved in running sports clubs, either at school or based in the community. Teachers are invariably key figures in encouraging children to progress from participation in sport at school to involvement in club sport. The National Coaching Foundation's **Coaching for Teachers** scheme has enabled many teachers to follow NGB courses and update their knowledge of sport and sports coaching.

Coaching for Teachers was developed to enable teachers to extend their knowledge and experience of particular sports or of sport for people with disabilities.

OTHER LOCAL SPORT PROVIDERS

Sports clubs are not the only place where young people can play sport. Sport is one of the activities offered by many youth organisations, and several of these organisations provide opportunities for young people to become involved in competitive sport. Scout and guide organisations, for example, frequently run regional tournaments for particular sports. Church groups may also organise sporting events. These and other organisations such as the Red Cross offer training that can assist people to play an important role in sport — for example, providing first aid in clubs and at sports events.

Schools are a key site in the provision and development of sport. This is increasingly being recognised in national policy statements issued by the government, the sports councils and individual NGBs. The facilities at schools and the provision made by schools are both critical, particularly in relation to junior sport. Furthermore, schools are acknowledged as the most accessible and, in some instances, the only accessible site for involvement in sport.

Community use of school facilities has been developed to varying degrees and with varying success in different areas. Ideally, schools can be a focus for the development of community sport, featuring adult and junior provision, and can encourage easy transition from junior to adult clubs or sessions. Government strategies and the sports councils' responses to community use have highlighted the need for coherent provision and closer links between schools' extracurricular physical education and sport and junior sports clubs.

As increasing numbers of sports development officers and club coaches become involved in after-school provision, the boundaries between these two arenas is becoming blurred. On the one hand, the involvement of individuals other than teachers in the provision of physical education and school sport is a key means of extending opportunities. On the other hand, as you can read in chapter 4.1, community use has also highlighted differences of opinion about the form school sport should take. Some organisations may have very limited interests in school sport and young people because they are concerned with elite sport performance. Nevertheless, recent policy developments point towards further links between physical education, school sport and junior clubs. These links are some of the most significant in the sporting structure of the United Kingdom.

The government's strategy for sport *A Sporting Future for All* established its commitment to the appointment of 600 school sports coordinators to develop opportunities for participation and competition (DCMS, 2000). These coordinators will be based in 'specialist sports colleges' and will work with local primary schools. These colleges are emerging as a significant new hub for local sport development, involving local primary schools, other local secondary schools and local sports clubs.

The development of specialist sports colleges is a Department for Education and Employment initiative, administered by the Youth Sport Trust. The publication of the government's strategy for sport signalled the Department of Culture, Media and Sport's interest in specialist sports colleges. Significantly the DCMS have a twofold interest in specialist sports colleges. On the one hand, there is a stated desire to improve the quality of provision to all young people. On the other hand, the DCMS is committed to establish such colleges as a focal point for elite sport development, linking the colleges to the **UK Sports Institute** network.

The UK Sports Institute is being developed to support the development of elite sport and will comprise a network of regional centres.

Over to You

Find out the location of your nearest specialist sports college. Draw a map of the 'family of schools' and external clubs or other organisations associated with the college.

Sport England is by no means alone in directing attention towards sport development in schools. The other sports councils in the United Kingdom are similarly establishing schools as a central focus for investment and future sporting networks. For example, in Scotland as in England, newly appointed school sports coordinators are regarded as having a key role to play in establishing improved links between school and community sport.

SUMMARY

The governance of sport locally is a changing scene. Some changes can be regarded as arising from government policies and national initiatives, but national strategies and organisations have also had to respond to changes in local structures and local sites. New partnerships are arising and new structures emerging. With the continuing importance that policies are placing on participation and provision for young people, schools are identified as the hub of local networks for development and provision and for the development of excellence.

Test Yourself Questions

1. Briefly explain the implications of the introduction of Compulsory Competitive Tendering for local authority leisure provision.
2. Name the policy that has now replaced CCT.
3. Identify ways in which links between junior clubs and schools can be enhanced.
4. Describe ways in which professional clubs are becoming involved in the development of junior sport.
5. Apart from sports clubs, what other organisations provide sporting opportunities in local communities?

PART 6

Social and Cultural Dimensions of Reflective Performance in Physical Education

*I*n this section you will find four chapters concerned with the social and cultural dimensions of reflective performance in physical education. In chapter 6.1 you can read about the social construction of the body and the implications of this process for your own body image. Chapter 6.2 focuses on the commodification of various aspects of physical culture, including sport, exercise, recreation, leisure and lifestyle. In chapter 6.3, you can read about the social construction of gender in and through sport and physical education, and how your femininity or masculinity influences your performance. Chapter 6.4 provides comparative information on the organisation of sport and physical education in seven countries from the continents of Australia, Africa, Europe and North America. This section will assist you to locate your own learning and performance in social and cultural contexts.

The Body, Culture and Physical Activity

Learning Outcomes

When you have studied this chapter, you should be able to

☑ recognise a naturalistic view of the body and a constructionist view of the body,

☑ list some key features of a constructionist view of the body,

☑ describe how the social construction of bodies has changed over time,

☑ define body image,

☑ explain how advertising works to construct bodies,

☑ analyse some social and scientific practices in relation to the regulation of bodies, and

☑ understand how your own body image is a social construct.

INTRODUCTION

- -

The social construction of bodies is a process of attaching social values to particular body shapes and sizes.

Whenever you make a connection between how someone looks or how they move and a personality trait or social value, this process can be described as the **social construction** of bodies. For example, you see a teenage boy in the street with orange-coloured spiky hair, a nose ring, Dr Marten boots, black skintight jeans and T-shirt. What thoughts go through your mind as that person walks by? Or how about the well-groomed, thirty-something woman who comes along two minutes later in a short skirt, suit jacket, smart shoes and with a slender briefcase under her arm? Or how about the guy in his early twenties with a short haircut, dressed in a vest and tight shorts and revealing very muscular shoulders, arms and thighs?

If your mind remained blank as these people walked past, then you haven't constructed anything. But most of the time, you connect the way people look and the way they move with various personal and social attributes. Depending on your values and lifestyle and the sort of person you think you are, you might have assumed that the orange-haired youth was either very cool or a deadhead punk. You might have decided that the thirty-something woman was a power-dressed, go-getting executive. And you might have guessed that the young muscular man was a hunk or a show-off, most definitely healthy or else ruining his health by taking steroids.

Immediately, you can see how complex this process of our socially constructing bodies can be. Your own personal life experiences and the values and attitudes you share with friends play a big part in how bodies are socially constructed. Your own and your friends' body images affect how you connect other people's body shapes, movements and the ways they dress with personal and social values.

This process is called the social construction of bodies because it involves making connections between the physical features of bodies and social values that are shared or prominent among groups in British society. Being female or male also plays a major part in influencing our views of the shapes and sizes of bodies that we might describe as normal or ideal.

Over to You

In a group, discuss and then describe what you think is an ideal body and identify who or what has influenced your views. Note the major characteristics of your descriptions. Then discuss, describe and note the main features of the ideal body for participating in the following roles and activities:

- Rugby union prop forward
- Netball goal attack
- Football wing back
- Downhill skier
- Weightlifter
- Golfer
- Artistic gymnast

Does it matter whether the sports performers listed are male or female? Add your own favourite sport to this list if you wish. Then discuss the similarities and differences you have identified for these sports. In a paragraph, write down what your results tell us about the social construction of bodies.

NATURALISTIC AND CONSTRUCTIONIST VIEWS OF THE BODY

- -

Until recently, social scientists have neglected the human body. Many researchers have acknowledged the individual within society, but relatively few have extended their analyses to include the part people's bodies play in producing and reproducing social practices. Part of the reason for this neglect has been the success of the biological sciences in providing explanations of the structure and function of the body. We tend to take for granted that bodies are flesh, blood and bones. The relevance of biological explanations of the body seems self-evident. The success of biological science has contributed to a **naturalistic view** of the body, a view that sees the body as a mainly biological phenomenon.

On the occasions when social scientists have turned their attention to the body, their theories have tended to reflect this naturalistic view. This view has led, for example, to claims that differences in sport performance between females and males can be explained solely in terms of biological factors such as strength ('men are stronger') and psychological factors such as motivation ('men are more aggressive'). Similar arguments are made to explain racial differences in sport performance. Researchers who agree with a naturalistic view of the body assume that biological differences explain variations in behaviour. In other words, differences in sex, colour, size and other physical attributes of bodies are seen to be the cause of how people behave and what they believe.

A problem with the naturalistic view is that it is too deterministic. An example of determinism would be where a social behaviour, such as being 'masculine', is thought to be dependent on and determined by biological factors such as muscularity and physical size.

However, the more recent work of sociologists, historians and cultural theorists has challenged this naturalistic view of the body. Many of these researchers have argued that people's understanding of their bodies is shaped by the society they live in. They claim that bodies are social at the same time as they are biological. To put this another way, the body is in nature and in culture simultaneously.

A **constructionist view** of the body suggests, in contrast, that biology does not determine social behaviour. In the case of **masculinity,** constructionists would point out that there are different forms of masculinity and different behaviours are associated with being masculine. It may be the case that some groups in society consider a large, muscular physique to be an essential quality of masculinity. But many men who are neither physically large nor muscular nevertheless are considered to be masculine.

From a constructionist point of view, bodies are important to understanding how and why people as individuals and in groups behave in the ways they do. The body transmits messages. Sometimes this process is called **'body language'.**

Social and biological factors interact in all of these cases and examples. A naturalistic view of the body stresses only one side of the process and presents social behaviour as 'naturally' connected to biology. A social constructionist view of the body allows us to analyse how bodies are constructed at different times in history. It shows how **body image** interacts with self-esteem. It helps us recognise the part the media plays in attributing social values to bodies. And a constructionist perspective helps us understand how bodies are implicated in the regulation of behaviour.

A naturalistic view of the body proposes that we can understand bodies solely in terms of muscle, bone and tissue.

A constructionist view suggests bodies are both biological and social, and that they exist in culture and nature simultaneously.

Masculinity involves associating values such as aggression and physical strength with bodies with male sexual characteristics.

Body language describes the use of the body to communicate information, either consciously or unconsciously.

Body image is a combination of the picture people have in their heads and the values they and others attach to body shapes and sizes.

Over to You

Draw up two columns on a piece of paper. Head one column with 'Naturalistic View' and the other with 'Constructionist View'. Under each heading, list the key features that describe each perspective on the body.

CHANGING CONCEPTIONS OF THE BODY AND PHYSICAL ACTIVITY

When we think about what might be a normal or ideal body, we can see that this is a more complex issue than it may at first appear. The ideal body for participating in a particular sport is just one example of how people with very different shapes, sizes and abilities to move in particular ways can still be considered to have normal or ideal bodies.

There are many other factors that influence our interpretations of bodies and their social construction. We have already mentioned femaleness and maleness. Age and stage of development are other key factors, as is lifestyle.

A naturalistic view of the body encourages the idea that the human body has remained constant across time and that bodies were pretty much the same in the past as they are now. As soon as we recall the process of evolution, however, we can see that this hasn't been the case. It is also true that people of different races have some slight physical differences such as skin colour, facial features, length of limbs, and so on. Even within racial groups, such as Caucasians, there have been important differences. For example, the knights in shining armour of the fourteenth and fifteenth centuries were often no more than five feet tall. More recently, there is evidence to suggest that people in developed countries such as Britain are becoming taller and heavier.

Bodies have not only changed physically across time. The ways in which bodies are socially constructed have also changed. What this means is that, as the values shared by groups in society change, so do our constructions of bodies. One very obvious way we can find evidence of this is to look at the history of fashion. At different times in recent British history, women and men have worn different kinds of clothes to those we wear today. Changes in the styles of sports attire, such as the differences in women's tennis outfits or differences in swimming costumes over the last century, provide a very clear example of changing constructions of bodies. For more see *Over to You* at the top of the next page. Another good example of the ways bodies are constructed is to look at what people in different cultures think is attractive or beautiful.

BODY IMAGE AND PHYSICAL ACTIVITY

An image is something that portrays, reflects or mirrors an idea or a way of thinking. Body image is a combination of the picture that you have of your body and the values that society links to body shape and size. Body image is personal to each of us. At the same time, people reveal something of their body image in the ways they move, dress and decorate themselves — for example, with make-up and jewellery. So although body image is personal, it includes our values and those of others around us.

Body image influences how people construct other people's bodies. Just as there are different and changing constructions of bodies across time and across culture, so, too, body image changes as people grow older and their bodies change over time.

Recent research has linked body image and self-esteem. The findings of this research suggest that poor body image is likely to be a major contributing factor to low self-esteem among adolescents. This combination of poor body image and low self-esteem can lead to an individual being reluctant to participate in physical activities, and so denying themselves access to a healthy and active lifestyle. However, poor body image is often based on incorrect assumptions about normal body shape and size.

Over to You

Examine the photographs of female tennis players below. Discuss in a small group the changes to their clothing. Look especially at the emergence of different kinds of clothing and accessories such as headbands, coloured shirts and briefer clothing. Note the changing social values that are reflected in these changes.

a   *b*   *c*

© Sport, The Library

© Sport, The Library

Female tennis players: (a) 1905; (b) 1970s; and (c) 2001.

Can you think of another sport where clothing has changed? Write down the changing social values that you think these changes reflect.

Research suggests that a major factor contributing to incorrect assumptions about normal and ideal bodies is media representations of the body.

MEDIA REPRESENTATIONS OF THE BODY

Open just about any magazine or turn on the television and you are confronted regularly with bodies on display, usually in clothing that shows off the model's body shape to best effect. Much of the time, these images of bodies appear in advertisements as a means of selling a product. Sometimes, the body that appears on the television screen and the product being sold might have some obvious connection, as in the ads for sports clothing or shoes.

However, sometimes there is no obvious connection between the image and the product. The bodies in these cases are used to attract our attention to the ad. They also link the values associated with particular body shapes to the product. An example might be the image of a fit and muscular athlete in an advertisement for an insurance company. In this case, the advertisers may be trying to link to the insurance company the values we associate with a fit, successful, powerful and talented body.

Something happens to bodies when they appear in this form, as a means of selling a product. All of the social values that are connected with various shapes and sizes of bodies as a matter of course in everyday life get mixed up together and then repackaged, or reconstructed, in order to sell the product. It is this process of making new associations between bodies and social values that we can refer to as **representation.**

In consumer societies, our sense of ourselves in relation to society is only possible through the continuous activity of making choices and decisions. Researchers argue that we are compelled into active self-formation by a lack of fixed traditional roles. The acts of acquiring, consuming and throwing away are at the centre of a complex process of self-formation. Advertising is crucially placed to give substance to this process because it stimulates desire and offers apparent alternative personae and lifestyles from which to choose.

The material the media supplies is not passively absorbed. Each of us actively appropriates this material to make sense of ourselves and our place in the social world. The media also manufactures our hopes and expectations of the future and provides a means of expressing our experiences. Media in consumer culture plays a crucial role in the formation of our self-identities. Visual representations of the body offer important resources in the process of self-formation. Advertising, in particular, not only establishes bodily norms, but also stimulates desire around these norms for the ways of life the body is being used to signify.

Advertisements do ideological work at a submerged or implicit level through the association and linking of otherwise unrelated ideas. Advertisements create structures of meaning and they achieve this through their more obvious function to sell products. Advertisements reassemble or reconstruct already existing pieces or chains of information. These chains consist of a series of already meaningful elements that are attached to other already meaningful elements to create a new chain of meaning.

It is possible for each of us to interpret an advertisement differently. However, if the advertisement is to be effective at selling products, then it must be interpreted in a particular way. The image is a puzzle that we need to decode before it can be understood. The creators of advertisements attempt to reduce the possibility of a reader *mis*understanding their intentions by targeting the advertisement at a specific group of readers. Moreover, for advertisements to work, it is important that they are not believed literally. For instance, you don't have to believe that 'Persil Washes Whiter' or that 'Coke Is The Real Thing!'. Advertisements work instead at the level that researchers call the signifier, at the meeting point of associations of already established chains of meaning.

Framing refers to what is selected for inclusion in an advertisement and what is left out. Advertisements are put together in this calculated way in order to target particular groups of people who are potential customers for the product. Advertising can have such a powerful influence on our body image because advertisers target specific groups of people by including in the advertisement information, ideas and images they know that group of people will recognise.

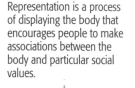
Representation is a process of displaying the body that encourages people to make associations between the body and particular social values.

Framing is the inclusion of some material within an advertisement and the exclusion of other appropriate but non-favoured material.

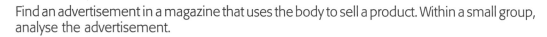

Over to You

Find an advertisement in a magazine that uses the body to sell a product. Within a small group, analyse the advertisement.

1. Describe
   who is in the advertisement;

what they are doing;

how they are dressed;

how they are posing;

whatever else is in the ad;

where the ad appeared; and

any other features.

2. Who is the audience for this? Whom is the ad aimed at? Who is the target group for this advertisement?

3. What is the message of the ad? How is it conveyed to us? How does it work?

4. How does the message make you feel? Can you associate yourself with the message?

5. How is it intended to make a member of the target group feel?

Media representations of bodies are, in a sense, reconstructing bodies by repackaging the associations that are made between bodies and values in our everyday lives. Researchers who support a naturalistic view of the body argue that this makes these constructions 'artificial'. Social constructionists say that the media are just one site among others in which bodies are socially constructed, and that the ideas about bodies that are prominent in British society are the outcomes of the interaction of many sites.

The Commodification of Bodies

When the body is used as a means of selling products through advertisements, it is drawn into the process of commodification. The social consequences of body commodification take at least two forms. Both forms turn the body into an object.

The first form of commodification involves a concern for body maintenance, where bodies require regular care and attention to preserve their efficiency and looks. In this respect, bodies become a site of consumption in themselves, particularly of the services of the beauty, cosmetics, clothing, exercise and leisure industries. Researchers suggest that this process has led to an increasingly widespread view of the body as a project. As a project, the commodified body is an object to be worked on according to the lifestyle choices you make, including what you eat and how you exercise.

In the second form, bodies are a focal point of the commercial process. Then, the everyday meanings attached to bodies are reconstructed to make new associations with commercial products. Bodies are used to sell products by linking these products to particular values; for example, linking muscularity and slenderness with fitness, health and social success to a product such as low-fat milk.

SOCIAL REGULATION OF THE BODY THROUGH PHYSICAL ACTIVITY

The way in which the human body is structured biologically and biomechanically sets some clear limits on how we might move. Within these constraints, there are some movements that are reflexes, such as the reflex that occurs when the doctor taps the patellar tendon with a rubber hammer and the knee involuntarily extends. Within the constraints provided by the musculoskeletal system, most movements are voluntary and learned. The process of acquiring new skills through learning contributes to the social construction of the body and to the regulation of social behaviour.

Anthropologists have provided evidence of **social regulation** of the body through their research in different cultures. In some cases, people are able to do things as a

Social regulation is a process of controlling bodies involving the acquisition of skills and competences that permit individuals to behave in ways valued by their social group.

matter of course that most of us living in Britain could not, such as climb trees to collect fruit or hold their breath for extraordinary lengths of time underwater to collect oysters. These techniques of the body, as one anthropologist has named them, including walking, running, climbing, sleeping and sexual activity, have to be learned.

Particular groups within British society value these physical competences and skills regarded as basic to a normal existence. Most people are not aware of learning to move in some ways and not others. This is because a lot of movements considered to be basic, such as learning to walk, run, wash and clean our teeth, even learning how to use the toilet, happen in the course of everyday life as children. Some activities are more complex than this, such as the specific skills needed to operate machinery such as a car or to play a sport, and usually we need to be assisted to master these skills.

In the process of learning physical skills, we are engaging in the social regulation of our bodies. Learning to play a game such as basketball is a good example of this process. All games are rule-bound activities, and their characteristic forms are created by their rules. As soon as we agree to abide by the rules, we immediately accept the regulation of our behaviour. So, for instance, we agree to certain rules about where and how our bodies might move in space. We can only play the game inside the boundary lines of the court, and we must control the ways in which we move in relation to other players.

We learn where to move on court to our advantage, for instance, in terms of being in a good position to shoot. Learning the skills of basketball is part of the regulating process. People learn to dribble, pass and shoot the ball in some ways rather than others because these are considered to be most effective within the context of the rules and strategies of the game.

Any activity in which we learn to move in prescribed ways is a form of social regulation of the body. Sometimes, we may resent this body regulation. Children often protest at being told to walk, not run. In other cases, submitting ourselves to learning to move in particular ways is necessary for the achievement of certain goals, such as being a good basketball player. All of these activities contribute to the social construction of the body in which the values of groups in society shape the ways in which people learn to move.

Bodies are regulated by a whole array of social factors, such as media images of bodies, peer pressure, self-identity and self-esteem. Currently, these social factors combine to encourage some females and males to participate in activities that maintain a slender body shape. Eating a sensible diet and taking regular exercise will help most of us to maintain an appropriate and healthy body weight and shape. However, when the pursuit of slenderness involves eating and vomiting or not eating at all, the individual may become bulimic or anorexic. Other practices that may reduce someone's weight or produce a slender body include use of diuretics or even surgical techniques such as liposuction.

Rather than trying to achieve slenderness, some young males and females may try to increase their body shape, size, weight and muscularity by working out with weights. There have been reports of this practice being taken to dangerous extremes when individuals have tried to supplement their weightlifting exercises by taking drugs such as anabolic steroids. In these cases, we begin to see bodies being regulated through scientific developments and related social practices such as commercial pressure on elite athletes to succeed in their sport.

SCIENTIFIC REGULATION OF THE BODY

Bodies can be described as being regulated if scientific processes or knowledge shapes the ways in which people behave. In this respect, it is hard to imagine a situation in British society where science or technology does not regulate our bodies to some extent. Even the simple act of crossing the road is influenced by the existence of motor vehicles and the knowledge of what can happen if they collide with the human body. People adapt their movements to the use of technological innovations in all aspects of everyday life. This is also true of the impact of science and technology on sport.

The scientific regulation of bodies is a very specialised dimension of the broader process of body regulation. One way this process takes place in sport is through the various training regimes players participate in to prepare them for competition. Some sociologists and historians have pointed out that these regimes are increasingly reliant on scientific information derived from biological, neurological and biomechanical research on the body.

Recreational exercisers also engage in the scientific regulation of their bodies. A good example of this is the treadmill machines now common in gyms that compute the exerciser's weight and provide information on heart rate, walking or running speed, and the amount of calories used in a session. If someone wants to improve cardiorespiratory endurance, knowledge derived from scientific research on the effects of training on the body will suggest that we could run, row, cycle or swim. This research would also stipulate that we should move at a particular speed appropriate to our current level of fitness and for a set period of time. We could reasonably describe this entire process as the scientific regulation of the body, as information obtained from scientific research shapes our movements.

This notion of the scientific regulation of bodies sounds reasonable and indeed essential to the improvement of sport performance or health enhancement through exercise. But is there a more sinister side to this idea that science regulates the body? Perhaps there is if we consider the use of drugs as a means of improving performance in sport. Once again, scientific research shapes the body and its capacities to some extent, but this time in ways that may meet with social disapproval.

Over to You

Organise a class debate with two teams and a chairperson. Set one team the task of defending the proposition that 'The use of drugs under proper medical supervision is acceptable because it is simply an extension of scientific knowledge applied to improving performance'. The opposing team should argue against the proposition. Make sure everyone in class contributes to constructing the arguments for their team, even if only a small number of team members deliver the arguments.

Surgical techniques such as liposuction that reduce body fat might also be considered to illustrate a sinister side to the scientific regulation of bodies. Perhaps the ever-diminishing fractions of time used to measure performance in some sports such as track running and speed skating provide another example of the scientific regulation of bodies.

There are, without question, misuses of scientific information that may shape and regulate the body and movement. It seems that some degree of regulation is unavoidable. Some regulation may be desirable and necessary to the conduct of everyday life and, particularly, to leading an active and healthy life. Social regulation of bodies is a key dimension of the social construction of bodies and an inevitable consequence of living with other people in groups and communities.

SUMMARY

Researchers in physical education have poorly understood the social construction of the body. A naturalistic view suggests that human bodies are biological. A social constructionist view suggests that social values are added to the biology of body shape and size. The significance of the constructionist's view is illustrated in this chapter in a number of ways. The social values linked to body shape and size have not remained the same but have changed over time. Body image is constructed through our perceptions of our physical selves in a range of social contexts. One of the most powerful influences on body image is the media. The media plays a large part in sending out messages about desirable and normal bodies. Bodies are constructed by media representations when social values are linked to body shapes and sizes and we learn to take these associations for granted. The chapter concludes with a brief discussion of the social and scientific regulation of the body.

Test Yourself Questions

1. Compare and contrast naturalistic and constructionist views of the body.

2. Historically, how has social construction of women's bodies changed? Use a sport as an example.

3. Define body image.

4. Explain how the body is commodified and describe some of the less desirable effects of this.

5. Identify and describe some of the ways in which bodies are regulated scientifically.

6. Explain how advertising and other media representations of bodies contribute to the social construction of the body.

The Commodification of Physical Culture

Learning Outcomes

When you have studied this chapter, you should be able to

- ☑ explain what is meant by the term 'physical culture';
- ☑ define sport, recreation, leisure and lifestyle;
- ☑ describe the process of commodification;
- ☑ apply your understanding of the process of commodification to sport, exercise and leisure;
- ☑ describe how technology influences sport; and
- ☑ define globalisation and explain its influence on sport.

INTRODUCTION

Dramatic changes to sport, exercise and leisure have taken place over a short period of time. These changes have accelerated during the 1980s and 1990s and show few signs of slowing down. Many of these changes are associated with the massive infusion of money into each of these areas of physical activity, but into sport in particular. Changes are also due to the influence of televisual media, beginning with terrestrial television but now linked to video, and cable and satellite television.

In addition, some sports have witnessed dramatic power plays between the owners of big media conglomerates who have attempted to outbid each other in an effort to gain control over sport and the wealth that can be generated from sport. These media barons also have control over news and information services. This gives them the ability to influence public opinion and potentially to fuel the growth of their own business empires.

We should not underestimate the extent to which money and the media are now important considerations in understanding sport in contemporary Britain. But sport is not the only arena of physical activity affected by **commodification.** This process also influences leisure and lifestyle, and the area of exercise for health and fitness.

In order to understand how these recent and sweeping changes are impacting on sport, exercise and leisure, we need to consider the commodification of physical culture. You also need to consider sport, exercise and leisure as industries primarily concerned with wealth generation and profit-taking, and how techno-logical development has been part of this process of commodification. Also fuelling the commodification of physical culture is the process of globalisation. Shifts in physical culture in Britain are linked to similar changes in other parts of the world.

This chapter is concerned with the commodification of the physical culture of British society. It begins with a definition of the concept of physical culture before going on to look separately at the commodification of leisure and lifestyle, exercise and sport.

A DEFINITION OF PHYSICAL CULTURE

Physical culture is an umbrella term for thinking sociologically about sport, exercise and leisure as three highly organised and institutionalised forms of physical activity. To think sociologically about sport, exercise and leisure is to understand that they are social practices. As such, they provide resources for making sense of yourself and the world around you. In particular, sport, exercise and leisure are three forms of social practice that are centrally concerned with the social construction of the body, which you can read about in detail in chapter 6.1. The term 'physical culture' allows you to think sociologically about the whole range of overlapping and interrelated physical activities that contribute to the social construction of embodied identity.

Not only are the three primary components of physical culture interdependent, they are also constantly reworking themselves. Analysis of the commodification of physical culture is therefore a complex process. It should be remembered that physical culture impacts on everyone at an individual and personal level, even people who are not interested in sport, exercise and leisure. Because physical culture is concerned with making sense of your embodied self, it touches everyone in some way or other. As a reflective performer, it is essential that you are able to identify the

Commodification is the process of turning something into a commodity that can be bought and sold.

Physical culture is an umbrella term for thinking sociologically about sport, exercise and leisure as three highly organised and institutionalised forms of physical activity.

effects of the commodification of sport, exercise and leisure on individuals as well as at the societal level.

Over to You

Draw a diagram that provides a visual representation of the concept of physical culture. Share your drawing with others in a small group. Decide together the best visual representation and write a brief paragraph explaining why your group thinks it is the best.

THE EMERGENCE OF RECREATION, LEISURE AND LIFESTYLE

The terms 'recreation' and 'leisure' have a long history, but until recently have generally tended to be associated mainly with a privileged and wealthy minority of British society. Along with the idea of **lifestyle,** leisure and recreation are notions that have only come to prominence for the general public in the past 40 years. This is because of their relationship to changing work practices that in turn have been influenced by our uses of increasingly sophisticated technology in our everyday lives.

A bewildering array of so-called labour-saving devices that we now regard as commonplace and essential were just beginning to make an impact in the home and the workplace 20 or 30 years ago. For example, as recently as the early 1960s, it was not unusual for women to have to do the family wash by hand, with the aid of a scrubbing board and a mangle. Washing machines became household items whose existence could be taken for granted only by people born in the late 1950s. The same is true of other electrical appliances such as the vacuum cleaner, refrigerator, and the electric heater and fan. Even more recent innovations, the microwave oven and the tumble drier, seem to have been there always, but these appliances were not common in homes until at least the mid-1980s. Before the late 1950s, a television set in the home was rare. Now, it is commonplace to have a set in several rooms in the house. And most recently, new technology such as the computer has impacted dramatically on every sphere of people's lives: at work, at home, in the bank, at the supermarket and so on.

At work in particular, increasing mechanisation of labour-intensive tasks has also had an enormous impact. Technological innovations have reduced working hours (table 6), but the downside is that they have also required workers to develop new skills and have rendered some people unemployed as their skills became obsolete, such as the trade of making moulds for products in the steel industry. Despite these disadvantages, in general terms, there were reduced working hours over the 30-year period from the end of the Second World War until the end of the 1970s and increased wages in real terms. These developments provided ordinary people with more time for leisure than previous generations and more money to enjoy it.

Recreation refers to activities that are undertaken for pleasure and in order to relax.

Leisure is a term used to describe the time that is available to individuals when they are not engaged in work.

Lifestyle is a term that suggests that our everyday lives can be 'styled' or designed.

Table 6 **Average Weekly Hours of Work in the UK, 1937-2000**

Year	Average full-time hours per week
1937	48.6
1951	45.6
1955	45.9
1960	44.7
1964	43.8
1968	42.2
1973	41.4
1984	38.2
1990	39.1
1995	39.5
2000	38.7

Sources: 1984-2000, National Statistics. 1984-2000, Labour Force Survey, Historical Supplement. London: The Stationary Office, and 1937-1973, Mitchell, B.R. (1988) *British Historical Statistics.* Cambridge University Press.

Table 7   **Participation by Female and Male Adults in Selected Physical Activities, 1996-7**

Activity[1]	Females (%)	Males (%)
Walking	42	50
Cue sports	6	18
Cycling	10	16
Swimming	16	14
Football	0	12
Weight training	4	10
Keep fit/Yoga	17	8

[1]By adults aged 16 and over in the four weeks prior to interview.
Source: National Statistics, Social Trends. No. 31, 2000 Edition. London: The Stationary Office, p. 230.

By the end of the 1960s, social theorists had yet to realise the extent to which television would affect the uses of leisure time, but they were confidently predicting nevertheless that Britons would have much more leisure time than they had ever had before. This pronouncement prompted physical educators to assert that active physical recreational activities should fill this free time. At the same time, government and local authorities developed policies for sport and recreation that focused mainly on the provision of facilities in which to play competitive team sports and other individual sports.

Over to You

In a small group, make a list of your most popular leisure activities. Then compare the list with the leisure patterns shown in table 7. Make a brief note of any notable differences between your group and the wider population and provide an explanation for any differences you see.

It was during the 1960s and 1970s that we started to develop our current understanding of notions such as lifestyle, leisure and recreation. Recreation is the earliest of these notions to make an impact on everyday life and refers to our ability to recreate or regenerate through activities that are alternatives to work, whether this be the domestic work of running the home or wage labour. The notion of leisure was the next to have an impact on everyday life during the late 1960s and into the 1970s. Although recreation can of course refer to a broader range of activities than sport and exercise, leisure has generally meant all of the time available to individuals when they are not engaged in work. We can see that leisure is a broader notion than recreation, but at the same time it lacks the idea of the healthy regeneration of energy that is suggested by recreation. If anything, leisure began to suggest non-vigorous forms of activity, such as going to the cinema, hobbies, and just about anything else that doesn't relate to work.

Lifestyle is the most recent of these three concepts to impact on everyday life and it appeared in the late 1970s. The notion of lifestyle assumes that people have some degrees of freedom from the responsibilities to work, family and other commitments, plus the time, self-discipline and money to shape their lives in particular ways. Implied in the notion of lifestyle is the idea that individuals can be in control of their lives and that they have a range of alternatives to choose from. So it should be possible for most people to choose to lead an active lifestyle or a sedentary lifestyle. This idea of choice of lifestyle has been a key assumption underpinning many health promotion campaigns in Britain and elsewhere.

Recent research by social scientists has suggested that some of these assumptions associated with the notion of lifestyle are too simplistic, as were some of the early theories about the 'leisure society' that some people in the 1960s predicted would result from the increasing impact of sophisticated technologies on the home and workplace. Indeed, far from having abundant leisure time in which to engage in physical recreation or having the freedom, time and money to choose a lifestyle from a range of alternatives, the reality is that people today may have less freedom due to a range of new social pressures. They may also in many cases have less leisure time than their parents and grandparents.

In contemporary British society, the notion of lifestyle subsumes both leisure and recreation, and also work and other everyday activities. One of the helpful things about lifestyle as a concept is that it allows us to talk about all of these aspects of everyday life in relation to one other. So we often hear about leading a 'balanced lifestyle' or an 'active lifestyle'. For instance, the idea of leading an active lifestyle has implications for our use of leisure time, taking regular exercise, our diet, the quality of our work or school environment, and a host of other everyday matters.

So the notion of lifestyle can be useful. But it can also be misleading. There is a danger of slipping from a point of view that quite correctly says we should take some responsibility for, and have some control over, our everyday lives to a mistaken view that assumes we can choose whichever way of life we wish. This latter view is encouraged through the commodification of lifestyle.

THE COMMODIFICATION OF LEISURE AND LIFESTYLE

The commodification of leisure and lifestyle takes place when we are 'sold' the idea that particular ways of life can be constructed through the commodities and services we buy and, along with this, a corresponding self-identity. Usually this process of commodifying lifestyle involves the acquisition of objects such as cars, boats, backyard tennis courts or sports goods and services. Typically, vendors attempt to convince people that the acquisition of the object will automatically provide the way of life they want. So, for example, busy and well-to-do businessmen may be targeted as a group likely to buy a boat or yacht so that they can 'escape from it all' on weekends. Older men are targeted as people susceptible to the idea that a holiday home close to good fishing will provide the tranquillity they are looking for in retirement. Young people may be sold all manner of brand-name sports gear that advertisers tell them they need to have to feel good about themselves or to be acceptable to their friends.

This idea that we can buy a particular way of life and a ready-made identity to go along with it draws heavily on leisure activities, as this is one area of people's lives where they are most likely to have some degree of freedom to choose between alternatives. Studies have shown that the lifestyles formed through these leisure-time pursuits can spill over into all other aspects of everyday life as people begin to form self-identities in relation to these activities. For example, recreational physical activities such as surfing and snow skiing show how the commodification process can construct particular lifestyles around leisure activities by accentuating through advertising their brand-name clothing and equipment and other products and services, already existing cultural activities, forms of dress and behaviours associated with these activities.

Over to You

The following sports have become highly commodified through the use of brand-name clothing, equipment and products. What brand names do you associate with merchandise from the following sports?

- Surfing
- Basketball
- Football (soccer)
- Mountain biking
- Tennis
- Aerobics

Now look at your favourite sports. What brand names are associated with these sports? If there are no brand names readily associated with your sports, why do you think this is?

There are few areas of recreational physical activity where commodification is not already well advanced. You need only think of bungee jumping, white water rafting and parasailing to see how far the commodification process has penetrated 'the leisure market' and has manufactured new and novel forms of activities to attract consumers.

Sociologists of leisure and sport have questioned the assumption that most people have the freedom and the means to construct their lifestyles. This assumption oversimplifies a complex process. Since the commodification of lifestyle requires that people have the ability to pay for products and services, there are financial barriers to constructing a lifestyle of their choice. Nevertheless, people often work and save to buy what they want. It seems obvious that not everyone can afford regular snow skiing holidays, a tennis court in the garden or a yacht. Nevertheless, within their financial circumstances, many people participate in, and contribute to, the commodification of lifestyle.

So, for most Britons, lifestyle is partly constructed through their own efforts and partly constructed for them through commitments to work, family, home and friends. An individual's 'freedom' to choose is constrained by these factors, finances and by a host of other life circumstances and social forces such as gender, race, disability and health. There is then a tension, a dynamic interplay, between freedom to choose and life circumstances, between work and play, self and others.

Young adults are a large target group for the manufacturers and advertisers of leisure and recreation products and services. This is because they are perceived to have fewer constraints operating on them in terms of relationships, responsibilities for children or other members of their family, and work and career. They are also likely to be quite healthy and to have a higher proportion of disposable income than other groups. Young adults can be viewed as a group who, more than other members of British society, are involved in constructing their lifestyles and their emerging self-identities through their participation in commodified leisure and recreational pursuits.

Within this context of the commodification of leisure and lifestyle, exercise and sport are two forms of physical activity that are of particular importance in the lives of young people. Both forms of physical activity have been subject to similar pressures and processes as leisure and lifestyle.

THE COMMODIFICATION OF EXERCISE

The notion of exercise has as long a lineage as physical recreation. It was not until the 1950s, following developments in the use of progressive resistance activity, that a contemporary notion of exercise began to emerge. Since the 1950s, exercise has acquired associations with physical fitness and health, and with body shape and wellbeing. Sport can be an exercise activity for some people, although more commonly exercise tends to be thought of in terms of activities such as walking, swimming, cycling, jogging, gym work and aerobics, where we believe there are explicit health outcomes. Of course, exercise can also be a leisure activity.

The specific ways in which the process of commodification has affected exercise are in some respects different from leisure and lifestyle. But at the same time you can see the influence of the emerging exercise industry in Britain since the mid-1970s. The existence of an 'industry' presupposes a number of things, including a service or product that people will buy, a group of paid workers who claim to have specialised skills and knowledge, and the reasonable prospect of profit-taking for the owners of the businesses.

In the early days of the exercise industry, many gyms were set up as small businesses and, like many other small businesses, struggled to survive. In some cases, the closure of a gym left people who had bought services in advance, such as a 12-month membership, without their money and without the service. There were also concerns that some gym owners and instructors lacked the necessary expertise to deliver the services they claimed to offer, such as fitness assessment and exercise prescription. There was no regulation of the field, and virtually anyone could set up an exercise business, regardless of qualifications. Accusations of charlatanism were not uncommon.

These early experiences of the exercise industry caused some damage to its public credibility. One of the ways in which the industry responded was to begin to regulate who was qualified to offer services such as exercise instruction. Since the 1980s, a number of organisations have offered fitness leader courses. As confidence in the industry has returned, degree-level courses have appeared in universities that equip professionals to make fitness assessments using scientific techniques and to offer advice and counselling on developing an exercise programme.

The existence of exercise gyms is not as recent as this story would suggest. From at least the middle of the 1800s, professional physical culturists ran commercial gymnasia where the public could pay to receive a massage or instruction in callisthenics, lifting weights, swimming and Indian clubs. Some exercise gyms or clubs catered solely for women and were popular among sections of the middle classes in the major cities.

However, the mid-1970s marked a new point in the history of commercial gymnasia. One important difference between the old and the new form of gym was that the latter were intended to appeal to a mass market rather than a small cross section of wealthy people. This intention was fuelled by the desire to maximise profits and affected the ways in which the gyms presented their services. Weight control or loss was, and remains, a predominant theme, reflecting sociocultural pressures relating to media representations of bodies and body image. Another feature of the new wave of commercial gyms was their emphasis on the use of technology such as computerised treadmills and other sophisticated exercise equipment. The technology also included scientific equipment for measuring and monitoring the important physiological and anthropometric effects of exercise on the body. One more recent difference is the claim that some of the services offered by workers in exercise gyms require extensive training in the exercise sciences.

The exercise industry is based on the idea that exercise is a commodity, a product that can be exchanged through a financial transaction. The existence of the industry presupposes the idea that people will pay for services that improve their appearance and health through exercise. As with any other commodity, people need to be made aware that it exists and persuaded that they need it. The existence of an exercise industry also presupposes the idea that most individuals left to themselves lack the knowledge or motivation, or both, to achieve the goal of looking and feeling better. In order to exist, the exercise industry needs to sell the message that the best and most effective way to get fit is to buy the services and expertise available.

Critics question some of these assumptions. They suggest that the level of knowledge required to exercise safely and effectively is not especially complex and that most people with a sound physical education can identify their own needs and, if they are in sound health, exercise to meet those needs. They also point out that it is in the business interests of the exercise industry to persuade individuals that they need the services the industry sells. Some of their advertising and marketing strategies may exacerbate the problems they claim to solve. A good example of this would be using images of **mesomorphic** (slim, muscular) male and female models in advertisements for a gym, where weight loss is emphasised. Critics argue that this technique is widespread in the exercise industry and may be contributing to body shape anxiety and unrealistic ideas about 'normal' body shapes among many women and girls and some men and boys. They also make the point that the cost of membership of a commercial gym is beyond the means of many people. If the

Mesomorphic bodies are muscular, with slim hips and waists and broad shoulders.

services these gyms offer are, according to their own claims, essential, why should many people who can't afford to buy a membership miss out on the health benefits of regular exercise instruction and advice?

Over to You

In a group, make a list of some of your local facilities for participation in physical activity. Note the images and messages they use to sell their services. Analyse these messages and identify whom the messages are targeted at. Chapter 6.1 outlines a method that you might find helpful in analysing advertisements.

The commodification of exercise is part of the broader process of the commodification and construction of lifestyle. For some people, exercise plays a major role in the process of 'styling' their lives. Exercise is one way in which people can work on their bodies. As one sociologist puts it, 'the body becomes a project'. Part of this project is to shape the body in the particular ways that an individual desires. This shaped and maintained body then comes to represent that individual's preferred view of him- or herself. Of course, many people who embark on this body project, using exercise as a major tool, do not achieve their aims.

THE COMMODIFICATION OF SPORT

Sport is a set of specialised practices that form a key part of the physical culture of British society. Social theorist Pierre Bourdieu has suggested that one of the central tasks of a social history of sport is to identify from what set of conditions and at what moment it became possible to speak of sport in its contemporary sense. He argued that modern sport emerged from the practices of the British public schools of the nineteenth century, a proposal that is strongly supported by much subsequent historical research. Understood historically, the term 'sport' refers to a complex set of practices that feature highly developed techniques and strategies, organised competition and specialised facilities.

Sports such as cricket, the various forms of football, and track and field athletics have been spectator sports for more than a century and have served as a form of entertainment for many people. Sport on television began in earnest in the 1950s. With the mass availability of television sets a decade later, it became a regular feature of everyday life. Before the 1950s, if an event had not been seen live, it could be replayed in cinema newsreels. However, the televising of sport as entertainment had little direct effect on the sports themselves, and most continued to exist in the forms in which they had emerged in the late nineteenth century. Minor modifications to rules and styles of play came from within the sports, and only in a few cases did considerations for spectators influence changes.

The introduction of one-day cricket in Australia provides just one example of a profound change in the nature of sport as entertainment that began to emerge in the late 1970s. Here was a sport modified from its original format and designed specifically for television. Players wore brightly coloured uniforms rather than traditional whites, and the technological development of powerful floodlights made it possible for play to continue into the night. One-day cricket was based on the idea that limited overs could be packaged in a more accessible form for a television audience than the five-day match. Broadcasts during peak viewing times meant that additional revenue could be generated through advertising, screened during the time it took to change overs. The net result of these changes turned cricket into a faster, more attacking and more entertaining sport.

We can see from this example of one-day cricket that **'media sport'** is, in several important respects, different from traditional forms of sport. One important difference is that key aspects of the rules and styles of playing the game are changed in order to enhance its entertainment value for a television audience. Another important difference is that television makes the televised event accessible to many thousands, even millions, more people than would normally be possible. This increased audience opens up the potential for huge revenue to be generated through selling advertising space during the broadcast. It also helps generate an entire secondary industry in sports goods and other memorabilia and paraphernalia, to the extent that the profits from selling Chicago Bulls or Manchester United merchandise, for example, are many times larger than the revenue generated by the basketball and football matches themselves.

You can see that media sport marks an important departure from traditional notions of sport as entertainment. This process does not affect all sports. But all sports that feature regularly on television now have begun to make changes to rules, uniforms and styles of play in order to retain their share of the sport entertainment market. Not all sports have been able to persuade the owners and operators of television companies that they have a public profile high enough to warrant the televising of the sport. It is no accident that the sports that have claimed the lion's share of televisual media exposure are the traditional male team sports. Sports played predominantly by women, such as netball, tend to receive much less media attention, a matter you can read about in chapter 6.3.

> Media sport is a modified or novel form of traditional sports or the invention of new sports to suit television broadcasting.

Over to You

With a partner, choose a sport that is not shown regularly on television. List some things you could do to the sport to increase its media and spectator appeal.

Media sport can be viewed as a part of the broader process of the commodification of sport. In fact, it is not only televised sport that has been commodified, although it is media sport that has been the prime example of this process at work. Commodification affects all levels of sport and all kinds of sport, in some cases indirectly, but never without some social and cultural significance. What does it mean to suggest that sport has been caught up in the process of commodification?

As you read earlier, commodification is a process through which items or objects become commodities. Typically, these items or objects did not begin life as commodities and only become commodities in the course of their existence. Usually, the commodification process changes the nature of the item or object. In what sense might sport be described as a commodity? The answer is that sport is commodified when its primary purpose, the main reason for its existence, is to produce wealth for owners.

A good example of the process of the commodification of sport is Super League, a version of the traditional game of rugby league. Rugby league did not begin life as a commodity. It developed as a separate game from rugby union after a split in the code

© Human Kinetics

Commodification affects all kinds of sport.

towards the end of the first decade of the twentieth century. From the start, rugby league was a professional sport and was strongly supported by the working classes in the North of England, whereas rugby union remained amateur and middle class in its affiliations.

Rugby league initially paid players on a part-time basis and quickly became a popular form of local entertainment. The use of league as entertainment and its professionalisation suggest that the game was in the early stages of being commodified during the first few decades of the twentieth century. However, it lacked the wide, mass exposure that television offers and the intensive marketing that characterises Super League as a commodified version of the game.

Super League was created specifically for television and was the outcome of a battle between Australian media barons Kerry Packer and Rupert Murdoch to control the television rights to the sport. In short, Super League would not have existed but for the combined influence of money, media and power. Particular sports become commodities when their existence depends on their profitability, when teams can be bought and sold, relocated from state to state and city to city, and success or failure depends on the ability of a team or club to buy talented players.

The commodification of sport affects all levels of sport to some extent. For example, sponsorship of competitions and teams is now commonplace, even in school and junior sport. Sports merchandising, particularly of equipment and uniforms worn by teams, is a multibillion pound business operating on a global scale. Talented young sports performers, particularly those in the most prominent sports, might have realistic expectations of earning large sums of money from their sports and through associated merchandising. The process may soon reach the stage where participation in some sports becomes too expensive without sponsorship.

Technology and Sport

You have already read about the ways in which technology, from floodlights through to the computerised exercise treadmill, has had an impact on sport and exercise. Because you are surrounded by so many technological innovations in sport, it is easy to form the impression that the entry of technology into sport is quite recent. However, this is not the case. The invention of the wheel not only made a valuable contribution to transportation, it also made possible sports such as chariot racing. Much later, around the end of the nineteenth century, this same technological innovation, with some additions such as the invention of the rubberised pneumatic tire, was responsible for the emergence of cycling as a sport.

The ability to time footraces has also been developing since the emergence of reliable clocks towards the end of the seventeenth century. The earliest clocks could time races to within half a minute, fine for the longer distances, perhaps, but not so good for the shorter races. Over a period of 200 years, clocks became precise and reliable enough to time a race to within a quarter of a second and, by the early decades of the twentieth century, to a tenth of a second. It was not until the 1980s that sprint races were timed to a hundredth of a second. Electronic timing rather than hand timing made such precision possible.

The technological development of clocks had a fundamental impact on how we think about the measurement and recording of human performance in sports such as running, cycling, swimming, downhill skiing and speed skating. As clocks have become more sophisticated, it has seemed appropriate to measure performance in increasingly minute fractions of time. People seemed prepared to accept the dead heat in sports such as track and field and swimming before the 1980s and the widespread use of the photo finish linked to electronic timing. Now every effort seems to be made in running events, in horse racing, swimming and other sports, to separate the winner from the 'also-rans'.

However, only occasionally have sociologists of sport questioned the appropriateness of this use of technology. These sociologists have questioned whether — even though a particular technology exists, such as electronic timing to a hundredth of a second — it is appropriate to use it in, say, track events. Does a hundredth of a second indicate a significant difference in performance over a short distance such as 100 metres? What about the marathon? If it is not possible to separate runners with the naked eye, is the minute difference between them, measurable by technology, important enough to require that they be separated into winner and also-rans? Some sociologists have also asked where this process might stop. If it becomes possible to measure performance in terms of a thousandth of a second, will we use this technological development next?

The use of increasingly sophisticated technology to time running and other races is just one case in which the appropriateness of the relationship between sport and technology has been questioned. Often underlying these questions is the idea that the use of technology somehow makes sport less natural and more artificial. The use of video playbacks to assist the decision making of umpires and referees in cricket and rugby league has been cited as one such case. The surfaces of hockey and gridiron football fields are often referred to explicitly as 'artificial turf'. The switch to Astroturf in field hockey has resulted in significant changes to the rules and techniques of the game. Technological developments that have impacted on the design and manufacture of sports equipment provide yet another field of controversy about the denaturalising impact of technology.

Sometimes overlooked by advocates for this position is the fact that all sports are social creations or constructions and so hardly qualify as 'natural' activities in the first place. The formalisation of the rules and methods of play of many major games and sports in the late nineteenth and early twentieth centuries was the decisive moment in moving these activities away from their folk origins and any kind of natural state. It is also the case, as you have already read, that technology has, since the invention of the wheel, had an intimate relationship with sport. Players and the manufacturers of sports equipment and facilities have constantly looked for superior materials and better designs. They have done so in the belief that the new design will improve some aspect of the game. Examples include changes to the head of the hockey stick to allow players to use the reverse stick dribble and to hit the ball harder, and the use of better materials that are more reliable, durable and effective, such as the change from wood to metal golf clubs.

Over to You

With a partner, assess the impact of technology on one of the physical activities you are studying. Provide a definition of technology and an assessment of the significance and appropriateness of this impact. Explain in writing how technology contributes to the commodification of sport.

Globalisation and Sport

The term **'globalisation'** refers to the ways in which technological developments have made it possible for people, manufactured goods, information and ideas to travel to what were once diverse and distant cultures. For instance, as airline travel and sophisticated telecommunications have become commonplace features of our everyday lives, time and space appear compressed. Today the world seems much smaller today than it used to be because it takes much less time to cover distances.

Globalisation refers to the ways in which technological developments disseminate information, people and products around the world.

Places become 'closer' than they once were, making it easier for ideas, customs and practices to travel.

As a consequence, what was once a local practice becomes globalised when it is taken up in other places. In the process of being taken up, this practice changes in some way the new place in which it has arrived. An example of the globalisation of dietary practices is the spread from the United States to other parts of the world of the McDonald's chain of fast-food restaurants. Fried potato chips and hamburgers have now become part of the dietary practices of countries in which this kind of food otherwise might never have been consumed.

The example of McDonald's provides some clues to the key features of globalisation. One feature is uniformity. Regardless of where in the world the McDonald's hamburger is being served, the customer can be sure that it will look and taste the same. Another feature is that practices that become global tend to emanate from only a small number of very powerful countries in the world. The dietary practices of people in the so-called developing countries tend not to become globalised. A third feature is that globalisation is strongly dependent on televisual communications and advertising. This means that globalisation is, in part, an outcome of the commodification of various aspects of culture, including sport.

Earlier in this chapter we discussed sport as a commodity and the influence of television and advertising on the commodification of sport. From this discussion we can see how the marriage of advertising and business with televisual communications can lead to the globalisation of practices in sport. The razzmatazz that formerly surrounded sports such as gridiron football and basketball in the United States is now evident in many other parts of the world and in other sports such as rugby league in Britain.

One of the important issues raised by the globalisation of sport is the changes exerted on local culture caused by the transfer of practices from one country to another. An example of cultural change connected with globalisation is the ways in which some young people in Britain have taken up the forms of dress and codes of behaviour associated with basketball in the United States, such as wearing back-to-front caps, baggy trousers and basketball boots as everyday forms of dress. Globalisation is most profound when it influences aspects of everyday life about which we typically remain unaware. Cultural transformation through globalisation takes place when people forget that the styles of dress and ways of behaving associated with basketball originated in the United States and so begin to believe that these practices are their own.

The process of time–space compression has greatly accelerated the globalisation of sport towards the end of the 20th century. Some sociologists argue that the United States has now overtaken Britain as the source of cultural imperialism and that it is practices in sport and everyday life originating in the United States that are now taken up in other places, including former British Commonwealth countries such as Australia. Whereas there is evidence to support this argument, it is worth bearing in mind that 100 years of accelerating globalisation has not necessarily erased local culture and practices. Good examples of the tenacity of local sports to survive are the various Gaelic sports in Ireland such as football and hurling, and Australian Rules football on the other side of the globe.

SUMMARY

The chapter began with a definition of physical culture. Physical culture relates to three major categories of organised, institutionalised physical activity: sport, exercise and leisure. We then discussed the emergence of notions such as recreation, leisure and lifestyle over time. Then we examined in detail the commodification of leisure, exercise and sport. We suggested that the process of commodification draws physical cultural activities into the cycle of buying and selling. As a reflective performer in physical education, you must be able to recognise and respond appropriately to this process because the commodification of physical culture has a direct influence on how we as individuals construct our lifestyles and our embodied identities.

Test Yourself Questions

1. Define the term physical culture.
2. Define sport, recreation, leisure and lifestyle.
3. Explain what is meant by commodification. Show how this concept can be applied to an analysis of sport, exercise or leisure by providing one example from any of these categories.
4. List three reasons why the sport, exercise and leisure industries target young people as potential clients.
5. Give four examples of the impact of technology on sport.

The Social Construction of Gender in Physical Education and Sport

Learning Outcomes

When you have studied this chapter, you should be able to

☑ define the words 'sex' and 'gender',

☑ explain the relationship between sport and gender,

☑ list the factors that discourage girls from participating in physical activity and sport,

☑ describe some strategies for making sport more 'girl friendly',

☑ identify problems for the social construction of gender in sport and physical education, and

☑ understand the role the media plays in terms of maintaining gender stereotypes in sport.

INTRODUCTION

You can read in chapter 3.3 that, from at least the 1940s, physical education as a school subject has been defined by considerations for 'the sex of the individual'. Chapter 3.3 showed that in the struggle over what version of physical education should be taught in schools, the male version became dominant and the female version was **marginalised.**

It should come as no surprise for you to learn that there is an extensive and wide-ranging literature on gender, sport and physical education and, in particular, on factors affecting the participation of girls and women. The existence of this literature suggests intense interest in, and concern for, girls' access to active and healthy lifestyles. Feminist researchers have shown that sport has traditionally been a 'male preserve'. From the middle of the nineteenth century, men created the rules and actions that constitute many of today's most popular sports.

In other words, men created sport for men, not for women. Sport has built into it many of the qualities associated with dominant notions of masculinity, such as strength, physical size and aggression. Netball, a sport created for women by women in the last decade of the nineteenth century, was a modification of basketball and was designed intentionally to emphasise middle class Victorian ideals of femininity and womanhood.

The associations between sport and masculinity have been troublesome for girls and women who wish to be physically active, resulting in the questioning of their femininity and sexuality. Historical research presents overwhelming evidence that the association of sport and masculinity is deeply rooted in Western societies such as Australia, Britain and North America. There are strong undercurrents of beliefs about the appropriateness of girls' and women's participation in sport across all sections of these societies.

There can be no question that attitudes have changed over time and that we now view girls' participation in sport more positively than ever before. Some people wish to argue that in this day and age gender is no longer a significant issue in physical education and sport. However, in this chapter you will read that the issue remains significant and that the process of socially constructing gender is complex and multidimensional. As a reflective performer in physical education and sport, you should be aware of how gender affects an individual's opportunities to be physically active.

DEFINING SEX AND GENDER

It is important in any discussion of gender and sport that we define the two terms basic to this discussion, sex and gender, and note the differences between them. For our purposes, **sex** refers to biological characteristics that distinguish between females and males, and **gender** refers to a socially constructed pattern of behaviour recognised as feminine or masculine. As it is socially constructed, gender is dynamic, responding to social change. Accordingly, gender differs from one society to another across social classes, ethnic and cultural groups and within the same society.

Sport, physical recreation and exercise involve work on the body. Moreover, the body is important to the construction of self-identity, of who we think we are, and of self-esteem or self-worth. It is gendered bodies that are socially constructed since we attribute different social values to female and male bodies. The stereotype of the homosexual who has a limp wrist and walks with a hand on his hip provides a good, if wildly inaccurate, example of the ways in which basic movements, posture and comportment are used to denote appropriately or inappropriately gendered behaviour.

When people are marginalised, their interests and welfare are not considered important to everyone.

Sex refers to the biological characteristics that distinguish females and males.

Gender denotes socially constructed patterns of behaviour which, when combined with sex, is recognised as feminine or masculine.

Within a naturalistic perspective on the body discussed in chapter 6.1, matters of gender, involving social values, are invariably reduced to matters of sex or biology. A social constructionist view of the body, in contrast, suggests that biology and social values interact to construct forms of femininity and masculinity. Neither can be reduced to the other. These distinctions between sex in terms of femaleness and maleness and gender in terms of femininity and masculinity are significant to any discussion of gender and sport. This is because arguments used to exclude females from particular sports or treat them differently from men are often forms of **sex discrimination** in the guise of biological arguments about sex differences.

The issue of gendering the body emerges as crucial to a discussion of the social construction of gender because it confronts directly the nature/culture dichotomy. As the examples of homosexuality, transvestism and cross-dressing reveal, biologically male or female bodies do not necessarily denote culturally masculine or feminine people. The body is not merely the measure or manifestation of a sexed self; it is a shaper of gendered identity and is shaped by dominant notions of femininity and masculinity. Sexuality, like the body, is socially constructed, but biology sets limits on the extent to which femininity and masculinity are possible for any individual. There is, in other words, a meshing of natural and cultural considerations around the question of the gendered body.

The gendering of the body is very much a cultural process that appropriates the biological body as its raw material. This is not a matter of assigning priority to either realm, but rather of stating the relative contributions of each to the process of gendering the body. The body's surfaces may be the script upon which femininity and masculinity are mapped and which others read. Physical appearance alone does not provide a complete account either of sexuality or self-identity. More accurately, it is the interaction of nature and culture that produces gendered bodies, rather than cultural inscription or biology by themselves. It is the subtle shades of physical size, the occupation of space, the embodiment of force that attributes varying degrees of femininity and masculinity to individuals.

> Sex discrimination is the act of treating someone differently on the basis of their femaleness or maleness.

Over to You

Create two columns on a piece of paper with the headers 'Masculine' and 'Feminine' at the top. With a partner, make a list under each header of the physical features that are commonly assumed to characterise masculinity and femininity. Now share your list with another pair, noting agreements and disagreements within the group and any reasons for these disagreements.

SPORT AND GENDER

It becomes obvious very quickly from even a superficial examination that many sports were originally developed either for males only or for females only. As mentioned earlier, netball, a sport that continues to be played mostly by women and girls, was developed as a modification of basketball. In fact, netball in Australia and New Zealand was for many years known as 'women's basketball' until women began to play the male version of basketball, thus forcing the name to be changed. Middle class women developed the rules and styles of play in netball at the end of the nineteenth century in Australia, Britain, New Zealand and North America. Their ideas about appropriate behaviour for 'young ladies' are clearly demonstrated in the rules, such as the absolute prohibition of physical contact.

Netball stands in stark contrast to a game such as rugby union where rough physical contact, including knocking other players over, is accommodated within and actually required by the rules of the game. Historians have noted that the explicit educational goals for rugby union were the development of 'character', where a boy who had been knocked down would get up and rejoin the fray, and 'manliness', which required that players show appropriate levels of controlled aggression and competitiveness. Whereas games such as netball and hockey emphasised physical dexterity over strength, speed and force, the rules of rugby and other football codes often advantaged the fast and strong over the skilful player.

So it is important to note that the team games that remain major sports in contemporary British society and that emerged in the late nineteenth century, were firmly and explicitly designed to emphasise the social characteristics of femininity and masculinity valued at that time. This means that, throughout its modern history, sport has been an important means of stressing differences between men and women and of maintaining those differences.

Nowadays, some women play rugby and some men play netball. Does this mean that we have made progress and eliminated gender as a factor in the conduct of sport?

The fact that some women now play 'male' sports and some men now play 'female' sports owes much to women's long struggle and perseverance in the face of extreme hostility from male organisers and administrators of sports. Even so, women cannot be full members of golf clubs in many parts of Britain. In addition, the best women performers in sports such as soccer, running, golf, swimming and tennis are not allowed to compete in the same competitions as men and therefore do not have access to the same levels of prize money. Nor do they receive the same media attention as men in sport or the benefits that accompany this, such as sponsorship. Sport does not exist outside society but instead actively contributes to the social construction of gender in other spheres of life. The inequalities and injustices in sport between females and males are also present in British society more generally.

Over to You

In a small group with equal numbers of females and males, list the arguments commonly used to exclude women and girls from some sports. Decide as a group whether you think these arguments are justified. Write a brief summary of your discussion, noting points of agreement and disagreement.

DIFFERENCES IN SPORT PERFORMANCE: BIOLOGY OR SOCIETY?

One of the arguments commonly used to justify the continuing use of sport as a means of constructing power relations on the basis of gender is that females and males are 'naturally' different, both biologically and emotionally. Men, so the argument goes, will always be bigger, stronger and more aggressive than women. Here you might recognise the naturalistic view of the body discussed in chapter 6.1.

In the case of elite level performers in sports such as rugby, there may be some evidence to support this claim. But this point isn't as strong as it seems when we recall that the rules of this sport were made in the first place with particular characteristics in mind that were attributed to 'manliness', such as strength, speed (figure 61) and aggression. Elite athletes aside, does the argument hold for other levels of ability that females are inevitably inferior performers to males?

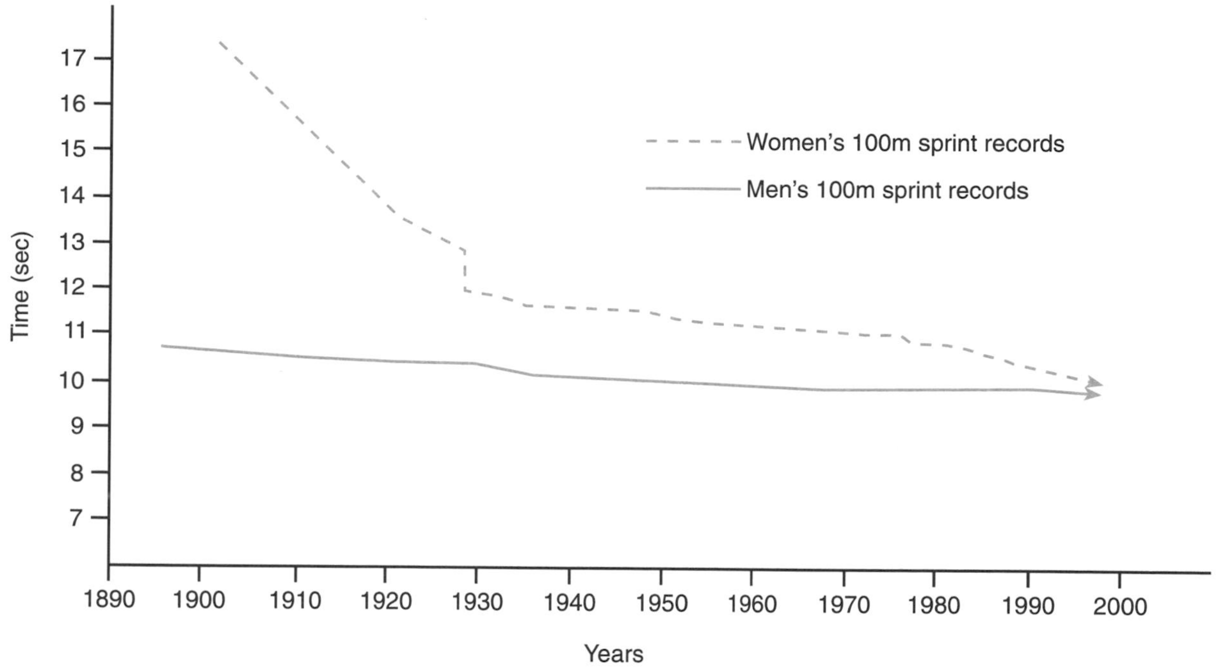

Figure 61 The gap narrows, but will it ever close.
Reprinted, by permission, from Kirk et al., 1999.

Over to You

As a class, discuss and then note which of the following sports segregate females and males on the basis of sex differences (due to biological factors) and which sports segregate on the basis of gender differences (due to social and cultural factors)? Think of all levels of sport participation, not only the elite level.

- Golf
- Rugby league
- Sailboarding
- Snooker
- Basketball
- Artistic gymnastics
- Tennis
- Soccer
- Synchronised swimming
- Netball
- Freestyle skiing

Summarise briefly the arguments for segregation in sports where the basis is biological differences and also where the basis is sociocultural differences.

MEDIA AND THE SOCIAL CONSTRUCTION OF GENDER

The media plays a key role in maintaining a view of women's participation in sport as being of inferior quality to sport involving men. Surveys of media coverage of sport, on television and in print, show that sports involving women receive only a fraction of the coverage of the major team sports involving men. In defence of their selective coverage, representatives of the media argue that ratings and audience approval drive the process and that their viewers and readers find women's performances in sport less entertaining than men's performances. The problem with this argument, as sport sociologists have noted, is the classic 'chicken and egg' dilemma: which came first, uneven media coverage or lack of popularity of some sports? As you will have observed in chapter 6.2, the media are not a neutral relay of sport to the television audience. The media actively market and promote sport and in so doing use sexist images to appeal to their target audiences.

© Sport, The Library

© Sport, The Library/Darrin Braybrook

Would Venus Williams' performance decline if she wore baggy shorts like Pete Sampras? Would television ratings decline?

When women's participation in sport does receive media coverage, often the emphasis is placed on the attractiveness of women's bodies and their revealing costumes or uniforms, with less attention paid to physical performance. A male journalist wrote a magazine article in the early 1990s questioning whether netball would need to get 'sexier' before the game could hope to attract sponsorship and media attention. His view of sexier netball involved the players wearing high-cut leotards. Few articles have appeared that have posed the same question for the football codes or cricket involving men.

For some time, sociologists have been investigating the social construction of gender through media representations of sport and exercise. A prominent line of research has investigated how mass media images reinforce stereotypical notions of femininity and masculinity, often in ways that are oppressive for most women and some men. Researchers have shown that female bodies are most likely to be portrayed as inactive, and women's performance subjected to sexist commentary. In a study of women's gymnastics, a researcher demonstrated that cultural norms demand that female gymnasts display feminine qualities of grace, flow, dramatic expression and rhythm, and physical attractiveness, consistent with notions of women as sexual objects, while their sport demands of them strength, power, speed, courage and aggression.

In another study that focused on men and television, the researcher explored the consequences of changing representations of sport in ways that enhance the speed, power and physical prowess of male bodies. The researcher suggested that the commodification and visual representation of the sporting body is 'associated with a limited and stereotype view of masculinity'.

In a study of photographs in a popular sports magazine for children, researchers noted that photographs constructed and legitimatised differences between females and males and presented these differences as natural. They noted that female athletes appeared in only a small percentage of photographs in this magazine and that, in the few categories where female athletes outnumbered males, they were typically shown in individual and aesthetic roles that contrasted notably with males' association with team sports and power activities. More recent developments in this line of research have analysed language to show how media representations of the 'new' sporting women have worked to limit the range of acceptable activities for women. Researchers have also examined the relationships between representations of black sportsmen and their alleged natural physical prowess, and how everyday representations of sport naturalise male power.

 ■ ■ ■ ■ ■ ■ *Over to You* ■ ■ ■ ■ ■ ■ ■ ■

Select a newspaper. Analyse the content on the sports pages in terms of

- number of articles on men;
- number of articles on women;
- length of articles on men;
- length of articles on women; and
- differences in style/content of report – for example, to what extent does the reporter concentrate on attractiveness/femininity of female performers and on strength and physical attributes of male performers?

What message about women's and men's sport does this give to people reading the newspaper? Write a paragraph summarising your conclusion.

THE PROBLEM OF TRADITIONAL PHYSICAL EDUCATION

Some sport administrators have blamed the unequal treatment of women in sport on the basis of gender, involving social values, as a major factor in adolescent girls' dropping out of sport in larger numbers relative to boys. They have argued in support of 'girl friendly' sport (figure 6.3.3). This advocacy has been influential in the development of a number of government-funded initiatives since the mid-1980s aimed at increasing the sport participation of girls.

You can read in chapter 3.6 about a new male version of physical education based on team sports and scientific measurement that became dominant in schools from the 1960s. Some researchers now view this 'traditional' form of physical education as a source of problems in relation to the social construction of gender. A large volume of research suggests that the way in which physical education has traditionally been organised and the attitudes and actions of teachers actually contribute to gender discrimination.

Sport administrators have begun arguing against gender-based programmes of activity.

A number of researchers have shown that deeply held beliefs about girls and their participation in physical education and sport have persisted and have proven hard to change. A study of girls' participation in physical education and sport in three schools found six major influences on girls' attitudes to physical education: the activity offered, the learning context and environment, class procedures, perceptions of competence, attitudes of peers, and teachers' attitudes and teaching styles. The researchers commented that 'few of our findings are new, but it is disappointing to find such gendered practice after more than 20 years of work towards more equitable educational provision for girls and boys' (Williams and Bedward, 1999).

A researcher noted that physical education was the only area of the curriculum where not only are boys and girls taught separately, but they are offered, in many cases, totally different programmes of physical activities. Another study surveyed physical education teachers to examine teachers' involvement in, and attitudes towards, the National Curriculum for Physical Education (NCPE), discussed in detail in part 4 of this book. The researcher found that the attitudes and actions of many physical education teachers continue to reflect gender stereotyping, with marked tendencies for male teachers to perceive dance as a 'female-appropriate' activity and female teachers to perceive outdoor physical education as a 'male-appropriate' activity.

Analysts of educational policy have suggested that the introduction of an NCPE in 1991 did little to alter the way in which physical education is taught in schools. The researchers suggested that the conservatism and one-dimensional, dogmatic activities of some teachers could be denying girls the educational experiences that they need and deserve. Supporting these findings, a study in the mid-1990s discovered that many everyday practices within physical education departments reinforce and reproduce gender inequalities and stereotypical ideas about femininity and masculinity.

■ Is Single-sex Groupings or Co-Ed Physical Education the Answer?

Researchers have paid particular attention to the possibilities for co-educational or single-sex classes overcoming or contributing to problems for girls in physical education. The results of studies in Australia, Britain and North America have suggested that there are advantages and disadvantages associated with each approach. Although girls and boys appear to prefer single-sex groupings within gender-appropriate sports, younger students prefer single-sex groupings generally; older students prefer co-educational classes. Teachers appeared to prefer single-sex groupings because co-educational classes are sometimes more difficult to teach due to teasing and harassment of girls by boys.

Over to You

As a class, list some things a school could do to make physical activity and sport more attractive to girls.

HOMOPHOBIA AND SPORT

Increasingly, feminist researchers are reaching the conclusion that **homophobia** lies behind the apparent reluctance on the part of some people to accept that gender is a significant factor in limiting girls' participation in physical education and sport. Writing in the United States, a researcher noted incidences of homophobia in sport in the form of silence, denial, apology, promotion of a heterosexual image, attacks on lesbians and preference for male coaches. In Britain, another study discovered examples of sexism and homophobia while studying initial teacher education in physical education. The researcher argued that many physical educators have yet to recognise and challenge the operation of sexism and homophobia in their own classrooms, and it is only through this process, the author claimed, that real progress in gender equity can be made.

> Homophobia refers to hatred of individuals on the basis of their homosexuality.

IS HEGEMONIC MASCULINITY A PROBLEM?

The overwhelming concern for girls within debates about sport and gender has tended to divert attention away from the part sport plays in constructing masculinity among boys and of contributing to the maintenance of dominant forms of masculinity that celebrate extreme behaviours such as aggression, competitiveness and physical violence. Feminist researchers now suggest that gender equity interventions in education on behalf of girls have left **hegemonic masculinity** intact; that much work is still needed in this area with both boys and girls.

R.W. Connell (1994) is an Australian sociologist who has identified the key characteristics of hegemonic masculinity as specific combinations of force and skill and the occupation of space. He suggested that sport is by definition centrally concerned with these characteristics. For many adult males, bodily prowess and physical size form the key ingredients of hegemonic masculinity, generalised beyond sport into work, sexual activity and fatherhood.

> Hegemonic masculinity is a form of masculinity that is widely and unquestioningly accepted by many people as the 'normal' or 'correct' way to be a man.

This version of masculinity is ideological and value-laden; the linking of its various elements appears to be natural and inevitable, but what is happening instead is a process of social construction, an arbitrary forging of associations that have no necessary relationship to each other. Hegemonic masculinity acts as a structuring discourse for boys' experiences of school physical education and for others' expectations of normal behaviour for boys in this setting. Significantly, health does not feature in this privileged definition of masculinity; and, indeed, boys' engagements in many of the physical activities informed by this discourse of hegemonic masculinity are health threatening, often endorsing physical violence and sometimes leading to serious injury.

Researchers argue that we need to question and reform hegemonic masculinity in order to tackle gender discrimination and equal opportunities. But it is not only girls and women that hegemonic masculinity disadvantages. Boys and men who do not wish to conform to such behaviours on the sports field and in other areas of their lives may be disadvantaged or discriminated against. Researchers suggest that men and women who feel such behaviour is inappropriate need to act together to bring about an acceptance of a broader range of femininities and masculinities that can find expression in and through sport.

Over to You

As a class, list some things a school could do to make physical activity and sport more attractive to all pupils, girls and boys. Compare this list to the one you developed earlier for girls only. Note any similarities and differences.

SUMMARY

This chapter began by noting the gendered history of physical education in British schools. Definitions of sex and gender were provided. The close association between sport and the social construction of gender was investigated. The chapter then examined and criticised the media's role in promoting stereotypical versions of femininity and masculinity through sport. Traditional forms of physical education were identified as a further contributing factor to the construction of dominant versions of femininity and masculinity. The chapter closed with a brief mention of the problem of homophobia in sport and asked whether hegemonic masculinity needed to become a target for gender equity interventions.

Test Yourself Questions ■ ■ ■ ■ ■ ■ ■ ■ ■ ■ ■

1. What are the differences between 'sex' and 'gender'?

2. How have arguments based on biological differences been used to discriminate against girls and women in sport? How have arguments based on sociocultural differences been used to discriminate against girls and women in sport?

3. List at least two reasons why girls might be put off taking part in sport at school.

4. Explain the role the media plays in maintaining gender stereotypes of women and men in sport.

5. Describe some of the ways in which physical education and sport could be made more attractive for girls.

6. Define hegemonic masculinity. Explain why the characteristics associated with hegemonic masculinity might discourage girls and boys from playing sport.

Comparative Perspectives on Physical Education and Sport

Learning Outcomes

When you have studied this chapter, you should be able to

- ☑ describe the systems for administering sport in a number of selected countries,
- ☑ identify some of the key factors influencing participation in sport and recreation in a number of selected countries,
- ☑ describe provision for physical education in a number of selected countries,
- ☑ compare and contrast the administration and organisation of sport and physical education in selected countries, and
- ☑ identify trends in physical education and sport common to a number of countries.

INTRODUCTION

The purpose of this chapter is to provide information on the organisation of sport and physical recreation, on the provision of physical education, and on trends and issues in sport and recreation in a number of selected countries. The countries included in this chapter represent a basis for comparison with Britain on a number of levels. Northern European countries such as Norway and Belgium and former Commonwealth countries such as Australia share many aspects of social organisation with Britain — in the case of Australia, a shared heritage until recently. The United States also shares some of those characteristics of other Western nations, but provides insights into different forms of organisation based on private, rather than public, ownership of sport. Spain has only more recently begun to adopt the forms of social organisation characteristic of these Western capitalist democracies. China's sheer size and its position as a communist country, as well as its unique traditional physical activities, offer a useful contrast to Western nations.

Through comparative study of other countries, you can develop a clearer understanding of sport and physical education in Britain. Because of the globalisation of sport culture, you will find many similarities between the countries included in this chapter. You will also discover how trends in some countries begin to influence trends in other countries. Media sport is one example of this process. Originating in the United States, media sport is now a growing force in other Western nations. The commercialisation of sport is another global factor, although what you will find is that sport is commercialised at different rates and in different ways in the countries included here. You will also find that despite the globalisation of sporting culture, local traditions and activities remain in place. Examples include the various Nordic sports traditional to Norway and other Scandinavian countries, sports such as cricket in former Commonwealth countries and gridiron in the United States.

An expert from each country has provided the most up-to-date information on the organisation and provision of sport, physical recreation and education in that country. The same task can be applied to each country to develop your knowledge and comprehension.

Over to You

In a small group, allocate each person responsibility for highlighting in dot point form the following information: (1) how sport is organised in *this* country, (2) provision for physical education, (3) some key issues and trends in participation in sport and physical recreation. Share this information with your group members.

AUSTRALIA

Education is the constitutional responsibility of the state governments in Australia. Even though national guidelines for all aspects of curriculum have been in place since 1994, time allocation and content of physical education vary from state to state. In primary schools serving children aged 5 to 12, most children receive one to three lessons of physical education per week. There are specialist teachers in some states, though it is most common for physical education to be taught by generalist teachers in primary schools. The daily physical education initiative promoted in the early 1980s continues to have an influence on primary school physical education, where a 15-minute aerobic exercise session several times per week remains common. Recently, there has been concern over low levels of sport skills among Australian primary school children, and some initiatives such as a sport education programme in the state of Victoria have attempted to address this concern by focusing on fundamental sport skills.

Specialist teachers in secondary schools teach physical education to young people aged 12 to 18, where most students receive between one and three lessons per week. The development of new syllabuses and curriculum guidelines in all states has promoted a conceptual approach to physical education and related topics such as health. However, many schools continue to offer a range of traditional sports (such as football, netball, cricket) as the main content of lessons, although physical education teachers often teach classes in personal development and health also. In the senior high school, most states offer an equivalent subject to A-level physical education. In the state of Queensland, senior physical education is one of the most popular subjects among senior high school students.

There have been strong school sports associations in all Australian states for over one hundred years. Competitions in a wide range of sports are available at local, district, state and inter-state levels. Large schools support a number of teams in a wide range of sports. However, most school teams select only the most talented performers.

The **Australian Institute of Sport (AIS)** was formed in the early 1980s and attracted considerable attention from other countries. The AIS is located in the Australian capital city of Canberra and provides residential training and sport science support facilities for elite young performers in a wide range of sports. In the 1990s, the AIS began to locate some of its sports in state capital cities in preference to Canberra. Around the same time, institutes began to be developed in each state. The state institutes cater for state instead of national-level performers and work in a loosely coordinated way with the AIS.

The AIS provides facilities and assistance to elite athletes.

Although the AIS and state institutes have attracted much attention, the main unit in Australian sport is the local club. Clubs exist in all sports and are affiliated with local governing bodies. Local organisations are in turn affiliated with state-level governing bodies. The exact arrangements for the administration of sports vary from sport to sport.

There have been regular surveys of Australians' participation in sport and recreational physical activities since the mid-1980s. Studies conducted over a 10-year period between 1984 and 1993 show that 60 to 70 per cent of the Australian population over the age of 14 participated in physical activities on a regular basis.

The most popular physical recreational activity for both females and males and across all age groups is walking. Recreational swimming, fishing, aerobics, jogging and golf were the most popular activities overall. There were some differences in the types of activity preferred by females and males. More women than men walked and did aerobics, whereas more men than women jogged, worked out in the gym and played team sports. About equal numbers of men and women swam regularly.

Walking is the most popular recreational physical activity.

A 1992 study by the federal Department of Arts, Sport, Environment and Territories (DASET) showed that the reasons men and women give for not exercising varied according to the sex of the individual. For women, the perception that they were 'too fat', mentioned by almost 90 per cent of respondents, is strong evidence of the social pressures women feel to 'look right' and confirms the issue discussed in chapter 6.1 that bodies are socially constructed.

Almost 80 per cent of women in this 1992 survey reported that caring for children was a major reason for their not exercising, whereas this was a factor for less than 30 per cent of men. This finding provides evidence of the structure of Australian families and the considerably larger role women play in caring for children compared with men. This is a highly significant factor in reducing the opportunities for women to be physically active.

Family demands limit women's participation more than men's.

These two factors alone suggest there is more to the issue of participation than people's will to be active or their knowledge about exercise and health, factors that are often cited by health promoters. Many of the other reasons for non-activity listed in the 1992 survey, such as 'don't enjoy' and 'not sporty', 'no time' and 'can't afford to ', suggest complex social structural and educational factors well beyond people's individual inclinations to choose not to be active.

Age influences the popularity of activities.

There were also notable differences in popularity of activities across age groups. A study conducted by another federal department with responsibility for sport between 1984 and 1988 showed that walking grew in popularity as people get older; golf and tennis remain about the same across all adolescent and adult age groups; and lawn bowls increases markedly as people get older. However, the survey showed that participation levels generally fall as people get older. Of course, we might have expected this finding because as people get older they become less physically able to be active and are more likely to suffer from illness. At the same time the ageing process is having this affect, people in their fifties begin to have more time to themselves with less responsibility for small children and by their mid-fifties may even have retired. It may be among the over-fifties age group that health promotion campaigns could be effective in persuading people of the benefits to their health and general wellbeing from regular exercise.

Another factor influencing participation that has far-reaching implications for a country such as Australia is its multicultural population. The Australian Bureau of Statistics (ABS) conducted a national survey in 1994. It reported that Australians born in Australia, New Zealand and other Oceania countries, Britain and Ireland are more likely to participate in recreational physical activity than Australians born in European countries (other than Britain) and Asian countries.

This finding suggests that the cultural norms and values people bring with them to Australia from their home countries have considerable impact on their participation in physical activity. For a Muslim girl, to take one example, participation in physical activity is shaped by factors that may not affect non-Muslims, such as the requirement that she keep her body covered in public, avoid activities considered to be masculine and participate in physical activity only with other females.

There is little evidence in the survey research to show a relationship between socioeconomic status and the likelihood of participation in physical activity. This is a surprising finding when you consider that access to some activities requires higher levels of wealth than others. A 1988 federal government study did report that there is a relationship between level of education and activity. It has been well established by sociologists that the socioeconomic background of an individual is an important determinant of the level of educational attainment. This may be an indirect indicator that wealth and social class have some influence on the type and level of physical activity participation.

Less is known about activity preferences and participation levels among younger Australians. Among school age children and adolescents, participation in physical activity seems to be dominated by their school sport and physical education programmes. The few surveys that have been conducted with this age group show that competitive team sports tend to be the dominant activity up to about 13 or 14 years of age and are most popular among boys. Adolescents over fifteen, particularly girls, begin to show preferences for individual, exercise-type activities.

The Australian Sports Commission is the government body responsible for funding and developing sport at all levels.

Participation in sport by young people under 15 is dominated by the traditional team games of football (rugby union, rugby league, soccer and Australian rules) and cricket for boys, and hockey and netball for girls. In the last decade, there has been a growth in opportunities for children as young as six to play organised sports in community settings in contrast to school settings. However, a recent study sponsored by the **Australian Sports Commission** showed that up to 80 per cent of the children who play club sport come from middle class families. This is because there exists a range of significant direct and indirect costs of participation, including fees, equipment and clothing, transportation to training and competition venues, and parents' time.

These findings suggest that schools remain the major provider of sport for many Australian children. At the same time, it is important to note that not all children have the same quality of experience in school sport and physical education and that there may be significant differences in the facilities, equipment and teaching expertise schools are able to offer.

The development of a National Junior Sport Policy in 1994 was a response to increasing perceptions from the mid-1980s of an apparent increase in the dropout rate from sport among adolescents. The ASC funded several studies in the late 1980s and early 1990s that suggested that dropout from sport was highest among adolescent girls, and this finding stimulated a campaign to encourage girls to stay in sport. Another study reported in 1991 that a majority of young people who were active participants in sport most disliked being forced by their parents or their coaches to take their participation too seriously. Many ranked fun as the major reason for participating in sport and cited a 'winning at all costs' attitude to be the factor most likely to cause them to give up the sport. This study suggested that sport is highly valued by these young sports participants, and most said they would spend more time playing sport if they could, as long as it remained fun.

The surveys show that there is a significant decline in levels of participation in sport from around the age of 15, with only a very small minority of Australians playing sport at any level beyond their mid-thirties. Even though there has in the last decade been an upsurge of interest in veterans or **masters sport,** the number of participants over 40 years of age currently remains very small. We can conclude from these findings that sport, with the exceptions of golf, tennis and lawn bowls, is played in significant numbers only by young people.

Masters sport is sport for adults, although the minimum age for entry varies across sports.

BELGIUM

Paul Wylleman, Paul De Knop and Marc Theeboom, Vrije Universiteit, Brussels, Belgium

Belgium, with a population of approximately 10 million inhabitants, is constitutionally divided into Flemish-, French- and German-speaking communities. Each community is responsible for, among other things, education (including physical education) and sport.

Primary (6- to 12-year-olds) and secondary (13- to 18-year-olds) education is autonomously organised by three different educational networks: namely, the board of education of each community, the board of education of the major cities and provinces, and schools run by the Catholic Board of Education. At secondary level, all schools offer, independently of the network, a six-year general and occupationally oriented curriculum. Extracurricular school sports activities are organised by an umbrella organisation comprising the Flemish Foundation for Schoolsports (Stichting Vlaamse Schoolsport; SVS) and the French-speaking community's Association of Francophone Federations of Schoolsports (Association de Fédérations Francophones du Sport Scolaire; AFFSS).

Each network also provides higher education at polytechnic and university level. Whereas polytechnics generally organise three-year study programmes, universities provide four- to five-year study programmes and doctoral programmes. Higher education is open to all pupils with a secondary-level degree (entrance exams are only required for civil engineers, medical doctors and dentists). Physical education is organised at polytechnic level in a three-year programme and provides, among other things, physical education teachers for primary education. Universities offer a four-year physical education programme, generally allowing students to specialise in physical education teaching (for secondary education), in training and coaching, in sports management, or in fitness and health education. Inter-university or inter-

BUSF is equivalent to the British Universities Sports Association (BUnited States).

collegiate sports are organised by an umbrella organisation comprising the Flemish Student Sports Federation (Vlaamse Universitaire Sportfederatie; VUSF) and the French-speaking community's equivalent (Association Sportive de l'Enseignement Universitaire et Supérieure; ASEUS). Both associations are members of the Belgian University Sports Federation (Belgische Universitaire Sportfederatie; BUSF).

Secondary-level education has always been a setting in which young people participate in physical activities (e.g., physical education classes, extracurricular sports activities). Whereas pupils have a minimum of two hours physical education per week, some sport-oriented study programmes (e.g., sport sciences) enable schools to schedule in up to four extra hours of physical education per week. Extracurricular sports activities include inter-scholastic recreational and competitive sports programmes. During the 1998/1999 school year, for example, 116,000 pupils (58 per cent in primary, 42 per cent in secondary-level education; from 740 different schools) participated on average 4.7 times in extracurricular school sports activities in the Flemish community. During the school week, secondary schools also organised classes combining athletic and educational (e.g., use of computer, learning a foreign language) activities.

The dropout rate of 16- and 17-year-olds from organised sports and the lack of compulsory physical education in the study programmes lead to a drop of participation in physical activities by students in polytechnics and universities. For example, in the 1998/1999 academic year, only 4 per cent, or 7,300 students (from 32 different polytechnics and universities), participated in activities organised by the Flemish Student Sports Federation (VUSF). On average, one student in two participates once or more per year in intra-mural (e.g., inter-faculty) competitions and Sport for All events (e.g. swim-marathon), or rents sports infrastructure and equipment for individual or team use (e.g., squash, tennis, basketball).

In the Flemish community, specific initiatives have been developed in favour of young talented athletes. At secondary level, a joint initiative between the respective Flemish Ministries of Sports and Education led to the development of nine 'topsport schools' throughout the Flemish community. These topsport schools enable some 350 young talented athletes and players (in alpine ski, badminton, basketball, golf, Olympic gymnastics, horse riding, judo, Olympic handball, sailing, soccer, table tennis, tennis, and track and field) to combine their educational and athletic careers during secondary-level education. These 'pupil-athletes' have in their (general or occupationally oriented) curriculum a 12-hour weekly training programme delivered by the technical directors of their respective sports federation. At university level, the Vrije Universiteit Brussel (VUB) has since 1987 given its elite 'student-athletes' studying in one of its eight faculties, specific academic flexibility as well as sports facilities and sport science support. Other Belgian universities have since followed this initiative.

Sport in Belgium is organised at various levels: national, community, governmental and non-governmental. A constitutional revision gave the three communities in Belgium responsibility for, among other things, sport. However, the national government still retains a number of prerogatives closely related to sport, such as public safety at sports venues and events, responsibility for air sports and tourist routes, and control over building criteria for sports facilities.

Each of the three Belgian communities has its own separate Ministry of Sport and sports administration. The Ministry of Sport is the policy-making body, whereas the sports administrations have an executive function. The Bestuur voor Lichamelijke Opvoeding, Sport en Openluchtleven (BLOSO) is the sports administration for the Flemish community; the Direction d'Administration de l'Education Physique, des Sports et de la Vie en Plein Air (ADEPS) for the French community; and the Deutsche Gemeinschaftsanwalt für Sport for the German-speaking community. These sports administrations are, in general, responsible for sports technical services (e.g., sports promotion, sports camps, in-service training and coach education programmes), as well as administration (e.g., distribution of subsidies) and management (e.g., sports centres). They also relate to the sports governing bodies (e.g., sports federations) at community level, as well as to the community sports services at local level.

At non-governmental level, organised sports associations (e.g., sports clubs) are grouped into national (e.g., soccer, basketball, motorcross) or community sports federations (e.g., swimming, judo, tennis). All community-based sports federations are members of the Flemish Sports Federation (Vlaamse Sportfederatie; VSF), and most sports federations (nationally as well as community-based) are also members of the Belgian Olympic and Interfederal Committee (BOIC). Organised sports and sports-related activities are also organised by, among others, private sports organizations (commercial and non-profit) and non-sports organisations, such as the Flemish Department of the Red Cross (Vlaamse afdeling Rode Kruis) or the King Baudouin Foundation (Koning Boudewijnstichting; KBS).

Since the mid-1960s, Belgium has been at the forefront of organising 'Sport for All' campaigns focusing not only on mass participation but also on the promotion of sport for specific target groups, such as women. During the latter part of the 1980s, the emphasis shifted towards the promotion of youth sports. Belgians' active sports participation has generally involved between 40 and 60 per cent youth participation (depending on the year and community), with walking, swimming and cycling being the most popular sports. Participation in organised sports is generally located in sports clubs, with soccer, tennis and basketball clubs having the greatest number of participants. For example, in 1996, Flanders counted 15,066 sports clubs members of Flemish sports federations subsidised by the Flemish community sports administration BLOSO and 4,290 sports clubs members of nationally structured sports federations. This sets a ratio of 3.8 sports clubs per 1,000 inhabitants. In sports clubs there is generally a 2:3 ratio of members aged under 18 and those above, with youngsters becoming members at the age of 5 to 6 years.

A number of initiatives were developed for, and by, organised sport in Belgium, aimed at increasing the rate, the structural and legal organisation, and the quality of sport participation.

A first set of initiatives was aimed at using the integrative function of sports activities to promote the integration of specific populations in Belgian society. During the last decade, sport, as one of the most popular leisure activities for youngsters, was used as a means of social integration for underprivileged urban youth in Belgium. Sport became a valuable instrument for teachers and welfare workers in their work with socially deprived youth. For more than a decade, the King Baudouin Foundation has provided for a 'youth sports' programme in Flanders, in which it tries to raise awareness of the problems and possibilities concerning the relationship between underprivileged youth and sports. Other projects have also been set up in cooperation with schools, sports clubs, youth welfare and local authorities. The French-speaking community has also launched similar initiatives.

A second set of initiatives followed, aimed at providing an organisational structure for specific populations, such as youngsters. Aimed at children and youth at local level, the concept of the 'sports academy' was developed which provides, through a cooperation between local sports clubs and community sports services, 6- to 12-year-olds with an after-school omni-sports programme in different sports. Specific legal initiatives, which determined the way in which professional and semi-professional athletes could participate in sports, also confronted the world of organised sports. The 'Bosman ruling' is perhaps the best known of these initiatives and refers to the Belgian soccer player who won his plea in the European court for the free transfer of players between soccer clubs. This decree established the rights of the individual player above those of the club.

A final set of initiatives was aimed at improving the quality of the management of, and coaching in, sports clubs. An integral quality instrument for sports ('IKSport') was employed: a quality control system implemented for some 2,500

Flemish sports clubs to provide them with specific recommendations to improve their performance. This system of quality control might be extended to other sports settings, such as sports services at local community level.

THE PEOPLE'S REPUBLIC OF CHINA

Robin Jones, Loughborough University, England

The People's Republic of China comprises 22 provinces, five autonomous regions and four municipalities, with a growing economy and a population of more than 1,200 million. China has become increasingly important as a potential market for the products of Western industrialised nations and also a labour pool for manufacturing. This has given the Chinese government a degree of recognition among its Western counterparts that has helped to accelerate its emergence from a relatively secluded past.

Founded in 1949, after almost 30 years of conflict between the Chinese communists and the nationalists and surviving the years of occupation by the Japanese during the Second World War, the People's Republic is now the world's major communist power. Fifty years after the founding of the People's Republic, China is becoming stronger economically, it is open to the West, living standards are rising and the five-day working week has been established. The government of President Zhiang Zemin has retained the determination of the previous government to reform the country according to market forces but 'with socialist characteristics'. In short, this meant the acceptance of the principles of supply and demand, but with government control over the pace and direction of reform.

Over the centuries, China has developed various forms of health-related or therapeutic exercises that have unique and distinctive characteristics. Commonly seen in the Hong Kong–produced action movies, the kung fu fighting routines are part of a much broader range of exercises, including t'ai chi ch'uan and qi gong, that are still extensively practised throughout the country, especially by older people. However, influence from the West in the nineteenth and early twentieth century also introduced sports that today form part of the Olympic and international programme, with the result that there is a blend of old and new, Eastern and Western in the country.

Compulsory schooling in China lasts for nine years. It begins with six years of primary school (from age six), followed by three years of junior middle school. After junior middle school, about 35 per cent of students are selected to go on to three more years of senior middle school to become eligible for the state entrance examination for universities. Throughout the period of primary and middle school education, physical education is compulsory. Government regulations aim to ensure that there is daily physical activity for all students, either by the timetabled physical education lessons, the extracurricular sports clubs at the school or the morning exercises at the start of the school day.

Students at university, regardless of the subject they are studying, also have to undertake two hours a week of physical activity, at least for the initial two years of higher education. There is some variation in this pattern in different parts of China. The activities offered usually depend on the facilities available and typically include games such as basketball, soccer, volleyball, tennis and badminton. The university sports department staffs and organises these activities. There is a military link also. The army drills students in basic military training for up to a month at the start of their university programme.

The Chinese authorities consider success in high-level sports competition to be worthy of recognition alongside academic work. Accordingly, by referring to approved tables of sport performances (in successive age groups from primary school up to university), a student's sporting performance is credited with a number of points, which is then added to their academic points score at key stages of their

Physical activity in China is increasingly a mix of traditional exercises and modern sports.

education. For example, in the state university entrance exam, a student who has also achieved a high level of performance in an approved sports competition may be credited with up to 200 points for his or her sport. When added to his or her entrance test score, this would contribute significantly to the 500 or more points typically required for entry to a good university.

Lower-level sports performances also receive recognition from around 30 points upwards. One consequence of this system of reward for sports performance is that the status of physical education in schools is enhanced. This is an important consideration when parents are balancing the merits of a purely academic education against the commitment of their child to sport, especially those parents whose children show high sporting potential.

A key feature of the Chinese sports system is the opportunity for talented young sports people to be selected for transfer out of their normal school into a special sports school. Here, for five half-days every week they have normal lessons. For the remainder of the time, they train for their particular sport under specialised coaches, monitored by sport scientists. The transfer into these special sports schools is highly selective and follows a series of intermediate stages that young sports people may be exposed to before fully committing their future to sport, including special classes in their normal schools, spare-time training with specialist coaches, and evening and vacation classes. The net result is that, for those with the potential, the state provides a system of support and progression in sport. The sports schools operate throughout the provinces of China, forming the basis of the provincial sports teams that compete at various levels up to the national championships.

The last decade in China has seen the arrival of a considerable number of reforms that have directly and indirectly affected sport and physical education in schools and the sports system in general. Government regulations published in 1995 give more attention to health and fitness. The curriculum of the senior middle school has been liberalised. Sport, particularly soccer, basketball, volleyball and tennis, has moved towards a professional model with the reduction of state financial support. There has also been a consequent growth in commercialisation and sponsorship.

The introduction of the five-day working week in 1996 gave individuals more time in which to follow their own leisure interests but also increased the need to provide opportunities to satisfy the demand. However, the size of China dictates that changes will not occur overnight. Signs of change in leisure activities can be seen in the major cities, such as facilities for tenpin bowling, golf driving ranges, new restaurants, fast-food bars, shopping malls, computer stores, roads crowded with taxis and private cars, mobile phones and pagers in every quarter, and busy street markets. Sports fans flock to the local stadium to watch the rising number of professional sports or watch them on the television.

In 1998, the Chinese government announced further, major restructuring of the various offices and departments of the state, including the state Sports Commission. For sport, the key part of the restructuring involved the closure of the Sports Commission as a state ministry and its replacement by a Sports Bureau that, in effect, represented a lowering of status. Fifty per cent fewer personnel were to be employed in the Sports Commission offices at state and provincial level, and, over a three-year period, the government was to reduce or phase out funding. Increasingly, physical education and sport in China are feeling the winds of change. For students in school, opportunities for the gifted performer remain strong, and, with the development of professional sport, the chance of future stardom in pro-club sport will affect what is on offer to young students. As for citizens, they will have to adapt to a pay-as-you-play-or-watch culture. And sports organisations will have to find sources of revenue to pay for their continued survival.

China narrowly failed in its bid to host the 2000 Olympic Games, but is still keen to host the Olympics and has won the bid for the 2008 Games. By then, it should be evident whether the reforms of the 1990s have taken firm root.

Sport success is valued alongside academic success.

Talented young people are selected to attend special sports schools.

GERMANY

Wolf-Dietrich Brettschneider, Universität Paderborn, Germany

Youth sport in Germany is primarily the responsibility of sports clubs. These clubs are autonomous and operate free from government control. Physical education is part of the school curriculum and is controlled by governmental bodies. Despite profound structural and functional differences, there is a strong relationship between the two institutions of club-based youth sport and school physical education. This is reflected in many programmes that seek to offer sport experiences to young people.

The umbrella organisation for youth sport is the German Sport Federation (Deutscher Sportbund; DSB). The DSB delivers general guidelines for promoting youth sport. This body and its various sports associations and federations are responsible for establishing competitive systems and for organising nationwide sports events. However, the full responsibility for attracting girls and boys to organised sport and keeping them in this system is in the hands of the local sports clubs. The clubs are free to choose which sports they offer and how they organise and present them.

Participation rates in sports clubs are high. One-third of the overall population are members of sports clubs. In 1999, 27 million people out of 80 million were members of 86,000 sports clubs. In the 7- to 14-year-old group, every second girl was a member of a sports club. Among boys the rate was even higher at 64 per cent. Participation decreases during adolescence. As representative youth studies show, among the 15- to 18-year-olds, about half of the male and a third of the female adolescents are active members of sports clubs.

School physical education aims to improve physical fitness and develop the motor skills that enable young people to take part in play, games and sports. It also aims to promote the adoption of a physically active lifestyle through adulthood. Physical education is assigned the task of contributing to the social, cognitive and effective development of young people through physical activity.

Physical education is compulsory from grade 1 (age 6) to grade 13 (age 19). In elementary schools (grades 1–4), three hours per week are allocated; in high schools the time allocated to physical education differs according to the status of the subject in the school curriculum. Generally, three hours per week are allocated from grades 5–13. If physical education is selected as part of the **'Abitur'** (a kind of A level), six hours are allocated. Theoretical issues such as principles of training, physical activity and deviant behaviour, sport and mass media are an integral part of physical education in this special course.

At present physical education is under pressure. The weekly physical education hours are being cut from three to two in some states. The remaining hour of physical education in the curriculum is no longer guaranteed. Evidently the arguments currently put forward to prove the indispensability of physical education have not convinced policy makers and education bureaucrats to retain the time allocation traditionally enjoyed by physical education.

At present, about 25 elite sports schools exist in Germany where about 10,000 talented young people live, learn and train. The schools aim at supporting elite sports performers in the process of coping with the stress resulting from the demands of school and training. These schools are part of the educational system and controlled by the government. It is clear that education and development are at the top of the priority ladder, and training comes second. Admission criteria to the sports schools are excellence in sport and high academic performance. The school functions as a coordinator between classes and training.

Abitur is similar to A levels.

Talented young people are selected to attend elite sports schools.

The German educational system for physical education teachers differs from other countries in many respects. One of the major features is that two different kinds of courses are offered. University-based programmes offer courses for primary and secondary specialist teachers. The primary teacher course is six semesters or three years long, and the teacher is prepared for teaching three subjects, one of which can be physical education. The course for high school teachers takes an additional two semesters and prepares the teacher to teach physical education and one other subject.

One other pathway into physical education teaching exists. After graduating from university the student can complete an additional two years of teacher training in the teacher training centre and in schools. This programme is practically oriented.

NORWAY

Fiona Dowling-Næss, The Norwegian University of Sport and Physical Education, Norway

Sport in Norway has a long, strong tradition of being steered by central policy. The state has provided economic support for the last 140 years. Originally it was financed by *ad hoc* grants, but, in the post-war years, national football pools have provided the funding. The rationale for such state interest has been based on the idea that sport is a worthwhile cultural activity in its own right. It is also believed that participation in sport provides an invaluable opportunity for individuals to experience a sense of community at local, national and international levels. Finally, sport can make an important contribution to a person's health. Since the 1970s, the Ministry of Cultural Affairs has adopted a 'sport for all' policy that aims to provide for everybody, irrespective of age, ability, gender, ethnic background or geographical location, the right to take part in organised sport.

Today there are 1.8 million members of sports clubs. Although the same individual may be a member of several sports clubs, the authorities estimate that nearly a third of the Norwegian population participate in organised sport. Indeed, sport is Norway's largest voluntary activity. This volunteering activity is based upon principles of choice, democracy, loyalty and equality. The Norwegian Confederation of Sports (NCS) and the Norwegian Olympic Committee (NOC) state that they promote the values of community, health, honesty and the joy of sport.

Within the NCS there are 56 member associations representing over 100 different sports. Each association has a team of representatives at national, county and local level. Every four years the 'Sports Parliament' (Idrettstinget) is convened to discuss current issues and to pass laws and regulations. The agenda is set by the Norwegian state Sports Council, a council consisting of 11 members appointed jointly by the government and sports associations. Representatives from all the sports clubs also contribute to setting the agenda. Various associations — at the national, county and local level — implement policies and new practices.

Current issues in Norwegian sport have centred on maintaining participation levels, particularly among young people, in the face of growing competition from commercial training studios. There has also been an emphasis on integrating disabled athletes in mainstream clubs. Authorities have been fighting drug misuse in sport, with the Ministry of Cultural Affairs recently awarding two million kroner for research to combat this growing problem.

Elite sport is also an important feature of Norwegian sport, and it, too, has received much economic support from the state because it is seen to play a vital role in developing a Norwegian cultural identity. Athletes receive grants and have access to a national training centre with a broad range of support services. Increasing commercialisation of certain sports, however, poses a great challenge for the future, if the NCS's principles are to be respected.

Returning to participation patterns, it must be stated that a gender bias exists in participation levels. Despite a number of campaigns targeting women and a general social policy of gender equity in society at large, there are not equal numbers of women and men or girls and boys in organised sport. Sport in Norway is to a large degree dominated by men, and issues of gender equity remain pertinent in the 21st century.

Physical education is a compulsory subject at all levels of the Norwegian school system. It originated as a subject exclusive to boys with the aim of nurturing fit young men capable of bearing arms in the defence of the nation. It has since been justified by a variety of reasons such as its health benefits, its contribution to pupil discipline, and as a 'break' in an otherwise highly academic day. It ranks as one of the most popular school subjects among pupils, but popularity has not been a sufficient argument for politicians to retain many hours of curriculum time. Currently, pupils in primary and middle schools (students between 6 and 16 years of age) are taught physical education three times a week, whereas pupils in the upper schools receive only two lessons weekly of about 45 minutes' duration.

National curricula have existed in Norway for more than 150 years and have determined the content of physical education lessons. The 1990s witnessed major school reforms with new curricula in all subjects, which aim to guarantee that pupils receive very specific learning experiences.

A health focus is fairly central to physical education. There is also an attempt to retain traditional Nordic activities such as outdoor activities and folk dance because team games such as football, basketball, volleyball and handball assume an increasingly larger role in lessons. It remains to be seen whether physical education teachers are able to deliver such an ambitious curriculum within the scarce resources made available, and, in practice, physical education remains a very practical, activity-based subject.

Physical education lessons have been taught in mixed-sex groups since the mid-1970s when an equal opportunity policy was introduced in all subject curricula. It is particularly disturbing, therefore, that recent research findings reveal that girls receive on average consistently lower grades than boys, and lesson content is dominated by what we might call traditional 'masculine' activities (e.g., football). Grades in physical education are important for entry into further education or the job market, so many girls are being disadvantaged.

SPAIN

José Devís-Devís, Universitat de València, Spain

Current forms of physical education and sport in Spain are the products of the social, political and economic conditions and transformations that have occurred since the 1960s. A number of broad trends in Spanish society have had a significant impact on the development of sport and physical education. These include the following trends:

- Social and economic liberalisation during the 1960s and early 1970s while Spain was still under the dictatorship of General Franco and the introduction of capitalist economy structures and ways of life similar to other European countries that have been considerably developed since then

- The adoption of a democratic political system in the late 1970s with the wide participation and support of the Spanish population and a decentralised model of government that the Spanish Constitution defines as the 'state of Autonomies'

(Margin notes)

Fewer women than men participate in physical activity.

National Curriculum includes traditional Nordic activities and team games.

• The evolution of social policy in the 1980s based on European welfare state principles and the development of this policy along neoliberal lines after Spain joined the EEC in 1986

Consistent with these broader social, economic and political trends, two main features of the Spanish sport system are decentralisation and the belief that access to sport is a right for all citizens. The decentralisation and democratisation of sport private institutions such as clubs, federations, and the Olympic Committee initially required the development of new laws and regulations concerning how sport could be administered. In the late 1980s, more democratic participation was promoted within private institutions, and public institutions gained more say over sport administration. Local institutions played a particularly significant role by promoting wider access to sport for the general population. A local policy of building sports facilities and offering sports services supported by public funds contributed to this aim. For some researchers, this 'sport for all' trend was the real democratising factor of sport in Spain, although others have suggested this trend was more apparent than real.

The nomination of Barcelona as the host city for the Olympic Games was crucial for the development of Spanish sport. It had a great impact on different levels of the sports system including administration, investments, consumption, research and higher visibility in everyday life. It required real and effective collaboration among local and state institutions to run such an international event, as well as the investment of public money in sport, which doubled during the five years following the announcement of Barcelona's successful bid. Sport became an important economic sector that represented 1.2 per cent of gross national product, with a growing job market. Sport also received special research funding because it was included for the first time and with preferential attention in the National Quadrennial Plan of Research and Development. Furthermore, sport became more visible in everyday life through media programmes due to liberalisation of television. Sport was promoted as an integral part of people's lifestyle through various means, including a television show that conducted large-scale surveys of sport participation.

After the Barcelona Olympic Games in 1992, there was a public budget cut in sport as a consequence of an economic recession. Public investment in sports facilities was reduced and rationalisation was demanded through effective and efficient management of public sport. Since then, new approaches to public services management, including mixed forms of public–private funding and compulsory competitive tendering, have emerged to reduce costs.

Traditionally, funding for sport was sustained by money generated from the football pools, but, after the announcement of the Barcelona Olympic Games, the government mainly sustained the funding. Two different policies emerged, one concerned with Olympic sport and the other with professional sport. Olympic sport received public funds directly from government budgets to support various sports federations as well as the Spanish Olympic Committee, to support athletes through grants and to create 'high performance centres', initially in Barcelona and later in other Spanish locations.

In addition, the Association of Olympic Sports (*Asociación de Deportes Olímpicos*, ADO) was established, a special organisation that aimed to generate private money for sport through enterprise sponsorship. Professional sports policy was revised in order to give economic independence to sports clubs, and this allowed mainly football clubs to become stock companies.

Both approaches to sport funding are still functioning after the Barcelona Olympic Games, although there has been a substantial decrease in government funding and an increase in private funding. Some local government support for professional and performance (as opposed to recreational) sport has continued because of the symbolic benefits of image and politics, although this funding is directed to

Hosting Olympic Games impacted on sport development and organisation.

promoting significant events and sponsorship rather than as it was in the 1980s to the building of sports facilities.

Following the first study on patterns of sport participation developed by the research organisation Icsa-Gallup and published in 1975, a remarkable series of five-year studies on sport participation was developed by Spanish sociologist García-Ferrando. His large-scale descriptive surveys have revealed a gradual increase in participation in physical activities of the Spanish population aged 15 to 65 during the 1980s and 1990s. These surveys have also shown the positive association of level of participation with income and education, and the negative relation with age. Despite a significant increase in the participation of women, they remain less active as a group than men. Even larger gender differences appear in relation to elite sport participation.

Sport has diversified in the 1990s due to this increase in recreational participants, new types of games and increasing numbers of multisport participants. About two-thirds of the general population participate in recreational sport, and one-third are involved in performance sport.

Emerging studies on general health practices, with limited emphasis on physical activity, and those especially centred on physical activity of youth and adult populations report different levels of participation depending on the criteria and type of measurement used (e.g., frequency of practice, heart rate or estimation of energy expenditure). A recent study based on an estimation of total physical activity energy expenditure showed that over half of school-age adolescents in Spain are active or moderately active, with more boys in the active category than girls.

There was a period of reform of the education system in Spain after the demise of the Franco government. In the 1980s, conditions appeared to be right for physical education to gain some parity with other school subjects. Although physical education has gained greater recognition as a school subject in the 1990s, changing some traditional practices based on competitive sport has been slow and difficult. Some teachers have been reluctant to accept new ideas.

However, educational reform has stimulated research in physical education. Studies have focused on health, attitudes and values, body expression, alternative approaches to teaching games and sports, outdoor activities and gender issues. More research is needed on how new ideas in physical education are implemented in practice.

THE UNITED STATES OF AMERICA

Peter Hastie, Auburn University, Alabama, United States

Physical education, like all areas of education in the United States, is the responsibility of each state. As a result, depending upon the policies and interests of state governments, the laws relating to physical education vary. Among these variations are things such as

- the amount of curriculum time for physical education;
- the qualifications of the teachers who teach the subject; and
- the content of physical education programmes.

Perhaps the biggest variation lies in the area of time allocation to physical education. However, one consistent factor is that no states have increased the time requirement for physical education for at least 25 years. Only the state of Illinois has required daily physical education for all grades, from grade 1 (aged 6) to grade 12 (aged 18). More common are states where the children receive two or three 30-minute lessons during their primary school years and complete a one-semester requirement during high school. In some states where the physical education requirement is judged in 'minutes per week', some schools allow the time children are in recess (i.e., 'play time') to count towards that total activity time.

Although physical education mandates do come from individual states, there are national associations that comment on, and raise debate about, the subject. For example, the National Association for Sport and Physical Education (NASPE) has identified four key characteristics of the 'physically educated person'. A physically educated person can demonstrate physical skills, is physically fit, participates regularly in exercise and knows how to plan and develop a programme to be active for a lifetime.

Other national influences on the practice of physical education include the recommendation from the Centers for Disease Control (CDC) that suggests 50 per cent of all time in physical education should be spent in moderate to vigorous physical activity. This statement has resulted in many schools spending more time in fitness and allocating less time to skill development. This development has caused much debate in education and other communities. In addition, in high school physical education, many states with the one-semester-only requirement are moving to a fitness education programme focus. In these courses, students learn to evaluate their own fitness, solve their own fitness problems, and learn to make decisions about how to stay active in adulthood.

To become a physical education teacher a four-year degree is required. However, the actual training required within this degree varies from state to state. For example, some states certify teachers for years 1 through 12, and others certify teachers for either the early school years (up to grade 6) or the later years (grades 7 to 12). States also vary in terms of the number of teaching specialities required (e.g., in states where you get only secondary certification, the teacher would normally need a second teaching area) and the amount of field/in-school experiences required during training.

The status of physical education at the university level varies. For physical education teacher education there is usually an activity requirement, but it varies from university to university. Among the general student population some universities have a physical education requirement for graduation and others do not. Some universities (e.g., Auburn University) issue 'certification in wellness and activity'. This is a certificate plus a transcript record that the student has been involved in healthy activity defined as three physical education classes and a wellness course.

Whereas physical education does not have a particularly high status in American schools, sport certainly does. Coaches of school teams receive a stipend to coach their teams. Players must achieve a certain standard in their schoolwork in order to be allowed to compete. However, school sport in the United States is very exclusionary. There are often at most two teams for each sport, called the varsity and junior varsity teams. This means that only the most talented players get the opportunity to participate in inter-school sport. Although many young people of primary and middle school age participate in local recreation leagues usually administered by that city's local government recreation department, club sport as it is understood in Commonwealth and European countries is virtually unheard of in the United States.

In the United States, only about a half of young people (aged 12–21) regularly participate in vigorous physical activity and a quarter report no vigorous activity. About 14 per cent of young people also report no light-to-moderate activity, with the rate of inactivity being higher in females and higher in black females compared with white females. Participation rates in all types of physical activity decline as age or grade in school increases. In addition, the percentage of high school students who were enrolled in physical education and who reported being physically active for at least 20 minutes in physical education classes declined from approximately 81 per cent to 70 per cent during the first half of the 1990s. From this data it would appear

School sport has a high status in the United States.

Gender and ethnicity influence participation in physical activities.

that some adolescents are particularly at risk of developing sedentary lifestyles. For the overall youth population (aged 12–18), girls are less active than boys, and older students are less active than younger. There are also differences in activity and inactivity patterns by ethnicity, with teenagers in minority groups engaging in less physical activity and more inactivity than their non-Hispanic white counterparts (U.S. Surgeon General Report, 1996).

One unique feature of American sport is the strong tie between the universities and sports competition. Sport is a multimillion dollar business in universities, with extensive television revenues, mega-stadia (some college football arenas seat more than 100,000 and fill to capacity every game) and, often, extensive sponsorship. Some athletes receive scholarships to attend specific universities and play for their teams, with this financial aid paying for the student's tuition, books, room and board. In the attempt to become competitive, many universities recruit athletes from overseas, particularly in sports such as tennis that are less popular in the schools.

One of the incentives of a college sports scholarship is not only the chance for a free education, but the opportunity to develop and showcase one's skills to professional sports teams. Professional sport in the United States is organised around leagues, with all teams being privately owned. These owners employ a commissioner who runs the daily operations of the league and makes all major decisions about the functioning of seasons. Whereas the owners and the commissioner have great power, so do the players, as professional sport is highly unionised. Players have team representatives as well as full-time union leaders, and many seasons have been disrupted by player strikes, mostly related to salary issues. In one extreme case, the 1994 Baseball World Series was cancelled because of a work stoppage by players.

Whereas many players have lucrative careers in professional sport, with the highest paid baseball player in 2000 earning more than 15 million dollars for the season, a career in sports coaching is also attractive to many Americans. Most professional coaches were at one time professional players, but, significantly, most of these coaches are Caucasians. There is a significant mismatch between the racial composition of professional sports players, particularly in basketball, baseball and football, and those of coaches. There remains a strong call for the appointment of more coaches from minority ethnic groups, not only in professional sport, but also collegiate sport.

As most coaches in the professional leagues are former players, few have any training in coaching. Whereas Britain, Australia and New Zealand all have government-sponsored coaching education schemes, there is no such equivalent in the United States. One publishing company has set up the American Coaching Effectiveness Program (now called the **American Sport Education Program**), but this is a private enterprise. Furthermore, although Commonwealth countries often require some form of certification for a coach to gain a specific coaching position with a regional or national team, there is no equivalent requirement in the United States. Coaching success is almost demanded by team administrators and supporters. It has been jokingly noted that a professional coach in the United States is in one of two situations: 's/he has just been sacked, or s/he is just about to be sacked'.

The American Sport Education Program aims to improve sport experiences for youth by providing workshops and resources for coaches, administrators and parents.

Perhaps the greatest influence on sport in America is television. The Superbowl is the most-watched single television event in the world. Matches are scheduled to appear in prime time. With such exposure, an underlying debate about sport in America is the extent to which athletes should be role models. Another debate concerns the place of women's sport. The Women's National Basketball Association was developed by the men's equivalent to promote the women's game, but, in the main, women's sport is less represented on television, in sponsorship and in general media coverage.

SUMMARY

This chapter provides you with information on the organisation of sport and physical recreation, on the provision of physical education, and on trends and issues in sport and recreation in a number of selected countries. The countries selected each have in common some approaches to the administration of sport and physical recreation and the provision of physical education. These similarities may be due to shared cultural heritage and to globalisation. There are also some significant differences that are related to local forces and traditions. Even though some differences exist, it is clear that sport and physical education are a major part of the culture of countries around the world.

Test Yourself Questions

1. Select a country and list the main features of how sport is organised and administered there.

2. Select a country and identify three major trends affecting participation in sport and recreation.

3. Select a country and describe who is responsible for providing physical education and the main activities offered.

4. Select two or more countries and compare and contrast three key features of the organisation of sport and physical education. Explain briefly any differences and similarities in terms of globalisation and local forces.

5. Select two or more countries and identify and explain common trends in physical education and sport.

References and Other Sources of Information

Chapter 1.1

Almond, L., (Ed.). (1997). *Physical Education in Schools* (2nd edition). London: Kogan Page.

Qualifications Curriculum Authority. (1999). *Terminology in Physical Education*. London: QCA.

Chapter 1.2

Evans, J. (1993, Ed.). *Equality, Education and Physical Education*. London: Falmer Press.

For information on participation trends in sport and recent initiatives responding to these, see chapters 5.1, 5.2 and 5.3, and refer to the websites of the following:

Sport England: **www.sportengland.org**

Sports Council for Northern Ireland: **www.sportni.org**

Sportscotland: **www.sportscotland.org.uk**

Chapter 1.3

Abernethy, A.B., L.T. MacKinnon, V. Kippers, R.J. Neal and S.J. Hanrahan. (1996). *The Biophysical Foundations of Human Movement*. Melbourne: Macmillan.

Kirk, D., J. Nauright, S. Hanrahan, D. Macdonald, and I. Jobling. (1996). *The Sociocultural Foundations of Human Movement*. Melbourne: Macmillan.

Mosston, M. and S. Ashworth. (1994). *Teaching physical education* (4th edition). New York: Macmillan.

Chapter 1.4

Cox, R. (1998). *Sport Psychology: Concepts and Applications*. Boston, MA: WCB McGraw-Hill.

Weinberg, R. & D. Gould. (1999). *Foundations of Sport and Exercise Psychology* (2nd edition). Champaign, IL: Human Kinetics.

Chapter 2.1

McGinnis, P. (1999). *Biomechanics of Sport and Exercise*. Champaign, IL: Human Kinetics.

Watkins, J. (1999). *Structure and Function of the Musculoskeletal System*. Champaign, IL: Human Kinetics.

Whiting, W. C. and R. F. Zernicke. (1998). *Biomechanics of Musculoskeletal Injury*. Champaign, IL: Human Kinetics.

Chapter 2.2

Abernethy, B., V. Kippers, L. T. Mackinnon, R. J. Neal and S. Hanrahan. (1996). *The Biophysical Foundations of Human Movement*. Melbourne: Macmillan

Wilmore, J. H. and D. L. Costill. (1994). *Physiology of Sport and Exercise*. Champaign, IL: Human Kinetics.

Chapter 2.3

Abernethy, B., V. Kippers, L. T. Mackinnon, R. J. Neal and S. Hanrahan. (1996). *The Biophysical Foundations of Human Movement*. Melbourne: Macmillan

Enoka, R M. (1988). *Neuromechanical Basis of Kinesiology*. Champaign, IL: Human Kinetics.

Wilmore, J. H. and D. L. Costill. (1994). *Physiology of Sport and Exercise*. Champaign, IL: Human Kinetics.

Chapter 2.4

Abernethy, B., V. Kippers, L. T. Mackinnon, R. J. Neal and S. Hanrahan. (1996). *The Biophysical Foundations of Human Movement*. Melbourne: Macmillan

Enoka, R M. (1988). *Neuromechanical Basis of Kinesiology*. Champaign, IL: Human Kinetics.

Wilmore, J. H. and D. L. Costill. (1994). *Physiology of Sport and Exercise*. Champaign, IL: Human Kinetics.

Chapter 2.5

Abernethy, B., V. Kippers, L. T. Mackinnon, R. J. Neal and S. Hanrahan. (1996). *The Biophysical Foundations of Human Movement*. Melbourne: Macmillan

Carr, G. (1997). *Mechanics of Sport*. Champaign, IL: Human Kinetics.

Enoka, R.M. (1988). *Neuromechanical Basis of Kinesiology*. Champaign, IL: Human Kinetics.

McGinnis, P. (1999). *Biomechanics of Sport and Exercise*. Champaign, IL: Human Kinetics.

Chapter 2.6

Abernethy, B., V. Kippers, L. T. Mackinnon, R. J. Neal and S. Hanrahan. (1996) *The Biophysical Foundations of Human Movement*. Melbourne: Macmillan

Carr, G. (1997). *Mechanics of Sport*. Champaign, IL: Human Kinetics.

Enoka, R.M. (1988). *Neuromechanical Basis of Kinesiology*. Champaign, IL: Human Kinetics.

McGinnis, P. (1999). *Biomechanics of Sport and Exercise*. Champaign, IL: Human Kinetics.

Chapter 3.1

Board of Education. (1909). *Syllabus of Physical Exercises for Schools*. London: HMSO.

Board of Education. (1933). *Syllabus of Physical Training for Schools*. London: HMSO.

Jolly, W. (1876). *Physical Education and Hygiene in Schools*. London: John Kempster and Co Ltd.

Macintosh, P.C. (1968). *Physical Education in England Since 1800*. (2nd edition). London: Bell.

Newman, G. (1933). Prefatory Memorandum in Board of Education, *Syllabus of Physical Training for Schools*. London: HMSO.

Smith, W.D. (1974). *Stretching Their Bodies: The History of Physical Education*. London: David & Charles.

Chapter 3.2

Hargreaves, John. (1986). *Sport, Power and Culture*. Cambridge: Polity Press.

Hargreaves, J.A. (1994). *Sporting Females: Critical Issues in the History and Sociology of Womens' Sport*. London: Routledge.

Mangan, J.A. (1983) Grammar Schools and the Games Ethic in Victorian and Edwardian Eras. *Albion*, 15 (4), pp. 313-335.

Mangan, J.A. (1986). *The Games Ethic and Imperialism: Aspects of the Diffusion of an Ideal*. Harmondsworth: Viking.

McCrone, K.E. (1988). *Playing the Game: Sport and the Physical Emancipation of English Women, 1870-1914*. London: Routledge.

McIntosh, P.C. (1952). *PE in England Since 1800*. (1st edition). London: Bell.

Munrow, A.D. (1958). Physical Education in the Universities. Proceedings of the Second British Empire and Commonwealth Games Conference, Barry, Glamorgan.

Smith, W.D. (1974). *Stretching Their Bodies: The History of Physical Education*. London: David & Charles.

Chapter 3.3

Fletcher, S. (1984). *Women First: The Female Tradition in English Physical Education, 1880-1980*. London: Althone.

Brown, H.C. (1958). The Training of the Man Teacher of Physical Education. *Physical Education*, 50, pp. 91-94.

Hargreaves, J.A. (1994). *Sporting Females: Critical Issues in the History and Sociology of Womens' Sport*. London: Routledge.

Mangan, J.A., and R.J. Parks (Eds.). (1987). *From 'Fair Sex' to Feminism: Sport and the Socialisation of Women in the Industrial and Post-Industrial Eras*. London: Frank Cass.

McCrone, K.E. (1988). *Playing the Game: Sport and the Physical Emancipation of English Women, 1870-1914*. London: Routledge.

McIntosh, P.C. (1957). From Treadmill to Springboard. *The Leaflet*, 58 (5), p. 23.

Munrow, A.D. (1963). *Pure and Applied Gymnastics*. (second edition). London: Arnold.

Randall, M. (1961). *Basic Movement: A New Approach to Gymnastics*. London: Bell.

Wardle, M. (1947). Free Formation and Individual Work. *Journal of Physical Education*, 39.

Chapter 3.4

Henry, F.M. (1965) Physical Education as an Academic Discipline. *The Leaflet* 66 (1), pp. 6-7.

McDonald, A. (1957). Some Reflections Upon the 'Physical' in Physical Education. *Physical Education*, 50, p. 33.

McIntosh, P.C. (1957) From Treadmill to Springboard. *The Leaflet*, 58 (5), p. 23.

Morgan, R.E., and G.T. Adamson. (1957). *Circuit Training*. London: Bell.

Schrecker, K.A. (1954). Physical Fitness. *Journal of Physical Education*, 46, pp. 45-52,55.

Wand-Tetley, H.T. (1946). Purposeful Physical Training in the Army. *Journal of Physical Education*, 38, pp. 140-143.

Chapter 3.5

Anthony, D. (1980). *A Strategy for British Sport*. London: Hurst.

Hargreaves, J. (1986). *Sport, Power and Culture*. Cambridge: Polity Press.

McIntosh, P.C. (1963). *Sport in Society*. London: Bell

McIntosh, P.C. (1968). *PE in England Since 1800* (second edition). London: Bell.

Presswood, R.E. (1954) in *The Leaflet*, 55 (8), p. 5.

Wolfenden Report.(1960). *Sport and the Community*. London: CCPR.

Chapter 3.6

Jacobs, V. (1961). The Planning and Organization of Physical Education in a New Comprehensive School. *The Leaflet*, 62 (6), pp. 45-48.

Whitehead, N. and L. Hendry (1976). *Teaching Physical Education in England - Description and Analysis*. London: Lepus.

Chapter 4.1

Almond, L. (1997). *Physical Education in Schools*. (2nd edition). London: Kogan Page.

Evans, J. (1986). *Physical Education, Sport and Schooling. Studies in the Sociology of Physical Education.* London: The Falmer Press.

Evans, J. (1990). Defining a Subject: The Rise and Rise of the New PE? *British Journal of Sociology of Education,* 11 (2), pp. 155–169.

Evans, J. (1993). *Equality, Education and Physical Education.* London: The Falmer Press.

Green, K., and S. Scraton .(1998). Gender, Co-education and Secondary Physical Education: A Brief Review. In K.Green & K.Hardman (Eds.) *Physical Education. A Reader.* Aachan, Germany: Meyer & Meyer.

Harris, J. (1997). A Health Focus in Physical Education. In L.Almond (Ed.) *Physical Education in Schools.* (2nd edition). London: Kogan Page.

Kirk, D., and R. Tinning (Eds). (1990). *Physical Education, Curriculum and Culture: Critical Issues in the Contemporary Crisis.* London: Falmer Press.

Penney, D., and J. Evans. (1999. *Politics, Policy and Practice in Physical Education.* London: E. & F.N. Spon, an imprint of Routledge.

Penney, D., and M. Waring. (2000). The Absent Agenda. Pedagogy and Physical Education. *Journal of Sport Pedagogy,* 6, 1, pp. 4-37.

Scraton, S. (1993). Equality, Co-education and Physical Education in Secondary Schooling. In J. Evans. (1993). *Equality, Education and Physical Education.* London: The Falmer Press.

Thorpe, R. (1992). The Psychological Factors Underpinning the 'Teaching for Understanding Games' Movement. In T. Williams, L. Almond & A. Sparkes, (Eds.) *Sport and Physical Activity: Moving Towards Excellence.* London, E. & F.N. Spon.

Thorpe, R., and D. Bunker. (1986). Landmarks on Our Way to 'Teaching for Understanding'. In R. Thorpe, D. Bunker & L. Almond, (Eds.) *Rethinking Games Teaching.* Department of PE and Sports Science, University of Loughborough.

Chapter 4.2

Almond, L. (1997). *Physical Education in Schools*. (2nd edition.). London: Kogan Page.

Armstrong, N. (1996), (Ed.). *New Directions in Physical Education. Change and Innovation.* London: Cassell.

Curriculum Council for Wales. (1992). *Non-statutory Guidance for Physical Education in the National Curriculum.* CCW: Cardiff.

Department of Education and Science. (1989). *National Curriculum - From Policy to Practice* London: DES.

Department of Education and Science/Welsh Office. (1991). *Physical Education for Ages 5-16. Proposals of the Secretary of State for Education and the Secretary of State for Wales.* London: DES.

Department of Education and Science/Welsh Office. (1992). *Physical Education in the National Curriculum.* London: DES.

Department for Education (DFE)/WO. (1995). *Physical Education in the National Curriculum.* London: DFE.

Department of National Heritage (DNH). (1995). *Sport - Raising the Game.* London: DNH.

Fox, K. (1992). Education for Exercise and the National Curriculum Proposals: A Step Forwards or Backwards? *British Journal of Physical Education,* 23 ,1, pp. 8-11.

Penney, D., and J. Evans. (1999). *Politics, Policy and Practice in Physical Education.* London: E. & F.N Spon, an imprint of Routledge.

Williams, A. (2000). (Ed.). *Primary School Physical Education. Research into Practice.* London: RoutledgeFalmer.

The Youth Sport Web site: **www.youthsport.net** details the Youth Sport Trust programmes and developments.

Chapter 4.3

Almond, L. (Ed.). (1997). *Physical Education in Schools*. (2nd edition). London: Kogan Page.

Armstrong, N. (Ed.). (1996). *New Directions in Physical Education. Change and Innovation*. London: Cassell.

Blunkett, D. (1999). Letter of Introduction in QCA. (1999). *TheReview of the National Curriculum in England. The Secretary of State's proposals*. London: QCA.

Davies, G.A. (1999). Blunkett's Fatal Blow? Minister's Edict Would Further Destroy Team Ethic. The *Daily Telegraph* 5/6/99, p .8.

Department for Education and Employment (DfEE)/Qualifications and Curriculum Authority (QCA). (1999). *Physical Education. The National Curriculum for England*. London: QCA.

Green, K., and K. Hardman. (Eds.). (1998). *Physical Education. A Reader*. Aachan, Germany: Meyer & Meyer.

National Assembly for Wales/Awdurdo Cymwysterau Cwricwlym Ac Asesu Cymru (ACCAC). (2000). *Physical Education in the National Curriculum in Wales*. Cardiff: ACCAC.

Qualifications and Curriculum Authority (QCA). (1998). *Maintaining Breadth and Balance at Key Stages 1 and 2*. London: QCA.

Williams, A. (Ed.). (2000). *Primary School Physical Education. Research into Practice*. London: RoutledgeFalmer.

Chapter 5.1

Biskup, C., and G. Pfister. (1999). I Would Like to be Like Her/Him: Are athletes Role Models for Boys and Girls? *European Physical Education Review*, 5, 3, pp. 199-218.

DCMS. (2000). *A Sporting Future for All*. London: DCMS.

DCMS. (2001). The Role of DCMS Web page. Retrieved July 13, 2001 from the World Wide Web: **http://www.culture.gov.uk/role/index.html**

Health Education Authority. (1998). *Young and Active?* Policy Framework for Young People and Health-enhancing Physical Activity. London: HEA.

Health Education Authority. (1999). *Physical Activity and Inequalities*. A Briefing Paper. London: HEA.

Houlihan, B. (1997). *Sport, Policy and Politics: A Comparative Analysis*. London: Routledge.

Sports Council for Wales. (1999). *A Strategy for Welsh Sport. Young People First*. Cardiff: SCW.

Chapter 5.2

Biskup, C., and G. Pfister. (1999). I Would Like to be Like Her/Him: Are athletes Role Models for Boys and Girls? *European Physical Education Review*, 5, 3, pp. 199-218.

DCMS. (2000). *A Sporting Future for All*. London: DCMS.

Health Education Authority. (1998). *Young and Active?* Policy Framework for Young People and Health-enhancing Physical Activity. London: HEA.

Health Education Authority. (1999). *Physical Activity and Inequalities*. A Briefing Paper. London: HEA.

Sports Council for Wales. (1999). *Young People First: A Strategy for Welsh Sport*. Cardiff: SCW.

Sport England. (2001). World Class Web page. Retrieved July 13, 2001 from the World Wide Web: **http://www.sportengland.org/whatwedo/world_class/class.htm**

Chapter 5.3

The British Sports Trust. (2000). Leading into the New Millennium. *The Leader*, Spring, 2000.

DCMS. (2000). *A Sporting Future for All*. London: DCMS.

For information on participation trends in sport and recent initiatives responding to these, refer to the websites of the following:

The British Sports Trust: **www.thebritishsportstrust.org.uk**

Charnwood Borough Council: **www.charnwoodbc.gov.uk**

Department of Culture, Media and Sport (DCMS): **www.culture.gov.uk**

Leicestershire County Council, 2000: **www.leics.gov.uk**

National Council for School Sport: **www.schoolsport.freeserve.co.uk**

Sport England, 2000: **www.sportengland.org**

Sportsmatch: **www.sportsmatch.co.uk**

Chapter 6.1

Connell, R.W. (1990). An Iron Man: the Body and Some Contradictions of Hegemonic
Masculinity, in: Messner, M. and D Sabo (Eds.) *Sport, Men and the Gender Order*. Champaign,
IL: Human Kinetics.

Fitzclarence, L.(1990). The Body as Commodity, in: Rowe, D. and G. Lawrence.
(Eds.). *Sport and Leisure: Trends in Australian Popular Culture*. Sydney: Harcourt Brace
Jovanovich.

Shilling, C. (1993.) *The Body and Social Theory*. London: Sage.

Theberge, N.. (1991). Reflections on the Body in the Sociology of Sport. *Quest*, 43 (2), pp.
123-135.

Turner, B. (1984). *The Body and Society*. Oxford: Blackwell.

Chapter 6.2

Goldlust, J. (1987). *Playing for Keeps: Sport, the Media and Society*. Melbourne: Longman
Cheshire.

Chapter 6.3

Birrell, S., and C.L. Cole. (1994). *Women, Sport and Culture*. Champaign, IL: Human Kinetics.

Connell, R.W. (1994). *Masculinities*. Sydney: Allen & Unwin.

Clark, G., and B. Humberstone. (1997). *Researching Women and Sport*. London: Macmillan
Press Ltd.

Hall, M.A. (1996). *Feminism and Sporting Bodies: Essays on Theory and Practice*. Champaign,
IL: Human Kinetics.

Messner, M., and D. Sabo (Eds.). (1990). *Sport, Men, and the Gender Order*. Champaign, IL:
Human Kinetics.

Williams, A., and J. Bedward. (1999). *Games for the Girls: The Impact of Recent Policy in the
Provision of Physical Education and Sporting Opportunities for Female Adolescents*.
Summary Report of a Study Funded by the Nuffield Foundation.

Vertinsky, Patricia. (1992). Reclaiming Space, Reclaiming the Body: the Quest for Gender-
Sensitive Physical Education. *Quest*, 44 (3), pp. 196-218.

▨ Chapter 6.4

Cantera-Garde, M.A., and J. Devís-Devís. (in press). Physical Activity Levels of Secondary School Spanish Adolescents. *European Journal of Physical Education* \bb\.

De Knop, P., P. Wylleman, M. Theeboom, K. De Martelaer, J. Van Hoecke and L. Van Heddegem. (1999). The Role of Contextual Factors in Youth's Participation in Organised Sport. *European Physical Education Review, 5 (1)*, pp. 91-106.

Kirk, D., J. Nauright, S. Hanrahan, D. Macdonald and I. Jobling. (1996). *The Sociocultural Foundations of Human Movement.* Melbourne: Macmillan.

Puig, N. (1996). Sport Policy in Spain. In L. Chalip, A. Johnson and L. Stachura (Eds.) *National Sport Policies: An international Handbook*, pp. 346-369. Westport: Greenwood Press.

Riordan J. and R. Jones (Eds). (1999). *Sport and Physical Education in China.* London: E & FN Spon, an imprint of Routledge.

Brownell S. (1995). *Training the Body for China: Sports in the Moral Order of the People's Republic.* Chicago: University of Chicago Press.

Test Yourself Answers

Chapter 1.1

1. The six categories of activities are games, gymnastics, athletics, dance, outdoor and adventurous activities, and swimming and water safety.

2. Four examples are sociology of sport and leisure, biomechanics, exercise and sport physiology and the pedagogy of physical activity.

3. The four key learning processes in physical education are acquiring, applying, evaluating and appreciating knowledge and skills.

4. The four educational principles are integrating knowledge, making knowledge personal, equity and inclusion, and synopsis. Integrating knowledge refers to linking knowledge in a 'practical' activity such as rugby with the subject matter of a 'theoretical' activity such as biomechanics. Making knowledge personal refers to the ways of presenting new information in a meaningful way to you as an individual. Equity involves valuing and celebrating rather than merely accommodating difference, and inclusion refers to making meaningful and appropriate provision for all people. Synopsis involves drawing on knowledge from a range of subdisciplines to better understand an issue, such as examining the use of drugs in sport from ethical, social, psychological and biological perspectives.

5. Reflective performers in physical education are people who think and do at the same time because they learn effectively from their experiences of physical activities.

6. The social construction of physical education refers to the organisation of knowledge according to the preferences, interests and cultures of individuals and groups of people. For example, particular sports and forms of physical education such as rugby union and rowing were first developed in elite independent schools and continue to reflect some of the values of people in that section of society at the particular period in time when they were developing.

Chapter 1.2

1. Offering the same activities to both girls and boys is one such move. However, experiences in lessons and opportunities to develop skills, knowledge and understanding are not the same for all children involved.

2. (i) From an equality perspective, difference is viewed as 'deficiency'. Some people are regarded as 'lacking' in comparison to others and this is seen as a problem to be addressed; and (ii) from an equity perspective, difference is viewed as a resource to be valued and celebrated as a richness of society.

3. (i) Differences that need to be considered include different abilities and interests in physical activity and sport, different cultural values, religious beliefs and practices relating to participation and performance in physical activity and sport, and differences in socioeconomic circumstances that may inhibit or enhance opportunities to participate. (ii) Changes may need to be made to the *range of activities* offered in order to embrace diverse interests and difference cultural values; and to the *form of provision*, so that there are opportunities for people to participate in ways that reflect their interests (such as to have fun and be with friends, or to improve their performance and reach

elite levels) and to move between different sports if they wish. In addition, changes may need to be made to *organisation and planning* procedures in order to include young people in the planning process.

4. The framework involves the following five levels. There is a dynamic relationship between each level so that, for example, actions at the individual level are shaped by those at the interpersonal level but, at the same time, actions at the individual level act to shape those at the interpersonal level. The *cultural level* refers to the shared assumptions, beliefs and values that are embedded so that they are regarded as 'the norm' within particular societies. The *structural level* relates to the distribution of resources within sport and within society. The *institutional level* is concerned with routine practices, rules and procedures within organisations. The *interpersonal level* addresses our interactions with others. The *individual level* relates to our own attitudes and beliefs.

Chapter 1.3

1. (i) It relies on directive or command styles of teaching. (ii) It assumes that learning is a passive process. (iii) It assumes that learning skills is mainly concerned with perfecting movement execution. (iv) It caters for the whole class rather than the individual.

2. Traditional approaches to learning often fail to consider cognitive and creative aspects of performance of games, sports and other activities. They also tend not to cater for individual differences and needs as command styles of instruction are best suited to whole group or class teaching. A third weakness is that traditional approaches focus on the acquisition of technique and so fail to provide adequate explanations of how people learn.

3. The information-processing approach likens learning in humans to the workings of a computer. A human being is considered as a system that receives input through the senses like a computer receives input from a keyboard or other device. The central nervous system is thought to work like the central processing unit of a computer, using a combination of hardware and software. The central nervous system sends messages to the muscles in the form of neural commands, just as a computer sends output to a printer or another computer.

4. The three main phases are perceiving, deciding and acting. During the *perceiving* phase, a player is trying to work out what is happening and what information is relevant. For example, a basketball player who has just received the ball must interpret the position of team-mates and opponents, their own position on court, distance from goal, the stage of the game, the score, levels of fatigue, etc. During the *deciding* phase, a player decides the best course of action. For example, the player needs to decide whether to pass, dribble or shoot, and decide on the kind of pass, dribble or shot. During the *acting* phase neural impulses stimulate the muscles to execute selected movements with appropriate timing, coordination and force.

5. The three components are: learning is an active process, learning is developmental, and learning is multidimensional. In the case of learning as an active process, players in a basketball game must actively search their surroundings to determine their own position in relation to the basket, other players and the ball, and make appropriate interpretations of environmental cues.

6. Experienced players in contrast to novices (i) adapt more readily to new circumstances; (ii) make faster, appropriate and more accurate decisions; (iii) anticipate what is likely to happen next in a game; and (iv) may be more technically proficient.

7. The teacher or coach as a facilitator (i) creates opportunities for players to learn the relationship between their own abilities, the task at hand and the environmental conditions in which it is to be performed; (ii) caters for a range of ability; (iii) provides different kind of feedback; and (iv) uses a range of instructional strategies.

Chapter 1.4

1. *Motivation* is the effort and persistence we put into the activities we choose to do. *Arousal* refers to the level of psychological and physiological activation ranging from deep sleep to high excitement. *Cognitive anxiety* refers to feelings of nervousness and worry associated with changes in arousal. *Somatic anxiety* refers to physiological responses such as increased heart rate and sweaty palms associated with increased arousal. *Self-confidence* is the realistic belief that you have the ability to achieve your goals. *Self-talk* is the things that we say to ourselves. *Social cohesion* refers to how much team members like each other and enjoy each other's company. *Task cohesion* refers to the degree to which team members work together to achieve a specific goal. *Task orientation* is a focus on learning new skills and comparing performance with personal standards. *Ego orientation* is a focus on beating others and comparing performance against other people.

2. This is going to be different for each student but you should mention something about your level of motivation, arousal, confidence and concentration levels. For example, my mental climate when I perform best is one where I am highly motivated (motivation), see the competition as a challenge (arousal, motivation), am excited with a few butterflies (arousal), feel positive about meeting the challenge (confidence) and am really focused on what I have to do (concentration).

   Strategies: Again this could be different for each student but might include things such as (i) goal setting to get your motivation right and make sure that you are focusing on the task, not the outcome (helps with arousal and concentration); (ii) relaxation/breathing techniques, stretching, if you need to calm down (arousal down); (iii) loud music, jumping on the spot, if you need to wake up (arousal up); (iv) using positive thoughts to replace negative thoughts (for confidence and cognitive anxiety; (v) having a pre-game or pre-shot routine (helps concentration and arousal management); (vi) having cue words to focus your concentration; and (vii) employing positive imagery (confidence, arousal, motivation).

3. If you attribute success or failure to stable causes, you will expect to succeed or fail again in the future. Therefore, if you have succeeded, you expect to succeed again and participate in the future. If you have failed, you expect to fail again, and future participation is less likely.

   If you attribute success to internal factors (things within your control, e.g., ability or effort) you experience greater pride and satisfaction than if you attributed success to external factors (things that are out of your control, e.g., task difficulty or luck; therefore you are more likely to participate again in the future.

   If you attribute failure to internal factors you experience greater shame than if you attribute failure to external factors, therefore you are less likely to participate in the future.

4. Task orientation is motivationally adaptive because it provides greater personal control – you are focusing on what you can do and how well you do it and not on how well someone else does (which you can't control).

5. Goal setting may help because (i) it sets out smaller steps (goals) on the way to the ultimate goal, so that you can see where you have come from and what improvements you are making; (ii) it helps identify strengths and weaknesses which can be worked on to make sure you get to your ultimate goal in the best state of preparation; and (iii) it gives you a sense of purpose and direction – you know what you are working on and why.

   Steps in effective goal setting include (i) set specific goals, (ii) set challenging goals, (iii) set long-term and short-term goals, (iv) set performance goals, (v) identify strategies that will help you achieve your goal, (vi) write down your goals, and (vii) evaluate your goals regularly.

6. The catastrophe model is the best explanation. It suggests that, when cognitive anxiety is low, increases in somatic arousal will follow the inverted-\ssU\ (i.e., there will be gradual decreases in performance beyond optimal levels of somatic arousal). But, if cognitive anxiety is high, the model suggests that once somatic arousal passes optimal there will be a sudden and dramatic decline in performance. Robert, on the days he is not bothered by feeling 'physically really tight' (somatic arousal), has low cognitive anxiety, so the tightness doesn't affect performance. On the days he worries about the tightness (increased cognitive anxiety), the tightness (increased somatic arousal) affects performance.

7. Arousal and concentration are linked. If arousal is high, concentration may not be on the right things (you are too busy worrying), or it may be too narrow; hence you might miss vital cues and therefore your performance decreases. If arousal is optimal, then you are free to concentrate on appropriate things and performance is optimal. If your arousal is low, your mind tends to wander onto irrelevant details, and therefore concentration is lower and performance decreases.

8. Lowering somatic arousal: You would use physical techniques such as stretching, deep breathing, physical relaxation techniques. You would use physical techniques because this is the type of arousal you are trying to change.

   Lowering cognitive anxiety: You would employ cognitive techniques such as thought stoppage, positive imagery, and cue words, which concentrate the mind on positive things and therefore reduce the capacity for worrying (cognitive anxiety).

9. Tennis – the familiarity of a consistent mental and physical preparation routine means that you are more likely to be appropriately focused when you actually serve (i.e., it makes it more likely that you are in the present and being positive). It can also help you your my arousal levels to appropriate levels and, because of the relationship between arousal and concentration, this can also help your concentration.

   An example of a tennis pre-serve routine might include (i) check stance; (ii) decide on serve; (iii) imagine the serve going in; (iv) bounce the ball twice and take a deep breath in and out; (v) visualise the target; (vi) think of the cue word 'target'; and (vii) serve.

10. It would be appropriate to use positive thoughts. Be aware of the negative things you say to yourself. Come up with positive statements to counter these negative thoughts. These positive thoughts should be task-oriented (i.e., focus on what to do), be in the present, and encouraging. When having negative thoughts in the future, use the positive statements to replace them (i.e., repeat them to yourself). Make sure you say them like you mean them. Focus on challenging but achievable task goals (rather than outcome goals). Because you are focusing on things you can control, you are likely to feel more confident.

11. If a sport requires a high degree of mutual interaction (e.g., basketball, where passing, and offensive and defensive patterns are required), then task cohesion is more important than in sports where little of no interaction is required between team members during the event (e.g., archery, team

triathlon). That is, the degree of interaction determines the importance of task cohesion; the greater the interaction, the more important is task cohesion.

12. Arrange for some easy games early on to ensure early team success; have a team T-shirt or uniform that identifies members; have a team goal; or, focus on performance, not outcome, as a measure of success.

Chapter 2.1

1. Three mechanical functions of bone are (i) support and allowing movement (e.g., long bones of arms and legs); (ii) protection (e.g., skull, pelvis, ribs); and (iii) increasing the moment arm, and hence the turning effect of muscles (e.g., the patella).

2. *Anisotropic* refers to the fact that the strength of bone depends on the direction of the applied load. Bone is better able to withstand loads that coincide with the long axis (such as the loads during locomotion). *Viscoelastic* refers to the fact that the strength of bone depends on the rate at which load is applied. Bones are stiffer and stronger when loads are applied at higher load rates (for example, in impact-loading situations such as running and jumping).

3. How this process occurs is not completely understood, but something like the following occurs. Bones are continually experiencing a turnover of cells. Bone is continually being resorbed, and new bone deposited. The loading experienced by bone in daily living causes microdamage, and this microdamage is repaired as part of the normal processes. Additional bone is deposited where microdamage occurs, leading to increased density and strength. The reverse also occurs. Where less microdamage occurs, resorption occurs more rapidly that deposition, and a net loss of bone density (and hence loss of strength) occurs.

4. A stress fracture occurs when the cumulative loading experienced by bone is excessive (high forces and prolonged exposure) and the rate of microdamage is too fast to be repaired. Such stress fractures are very common in the lower limbs of athletes training for endurance-running events. They are even more likely if hormonal dysfunction impairs the mechanisms of bone deposition. A classic example is the stress fracture to the tibia of a female endurance runner exposed to long periods of repetitive high-intensity impact loading while simultaneously experiencing hormonal disruption due to insufficient energy intake. Stress fractures can also occur in non-weight-bearing situations. For example, rowers commonly suffer stress fractures of the ribs. Here the forces exerted arise from prolonged exposure to repeated high-intensity muscular contractions.

5. Articular cartilage and menisci provide cushioning between bones and, in conjunction with synovial fluid, lower the friction in the joint to very low levels.

6.

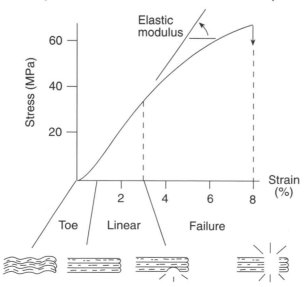

7. Intervertebral discs are composed of an outer layer (annulus fibrosus) which consists of many layers of collagen fibres in many different orientations, providing resistance to tension in all directions. The centre of the intervertebral disc is a gel-like nucleus (pulposus). The intervertebral disc acts to transfer forces and allow movement of the vertebral column. The intervertebral disc has poor vascular supply and, if damage to the fibres of the annulus occurs, it cannot be repaired rapidly. If damage to the fibres of the annulus continues, and full-width ruptures develop, the gel-like nucleus begins to seep out through the rupture and impinge on the spinal nerve roots which lie immediately posteriolaterally to the intervertebral disc, causing chronic back pain.

8. The microstructure of muscle consists of overlapping actin and myosin filaments. The cross-bridges between the actin and myosin attach and detach cyclically, pulling the fibres longitudinally and creating tension.

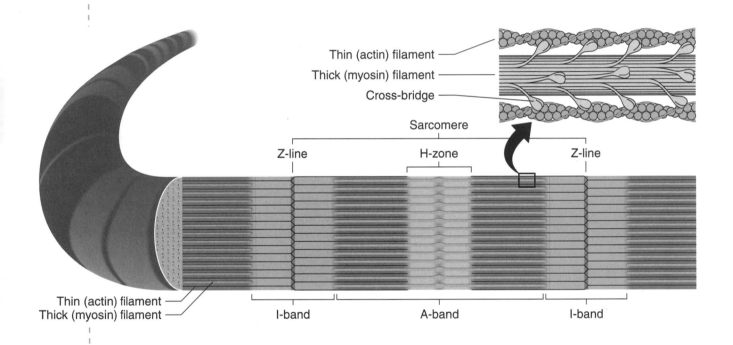

The tension-generating capability of each fibre at any time depends on the overlap between actin and myosin, which is a function of the length of the muscle. An optimal muscle length exists at which an optimal overlap exists and tension-generating potential is maximised. If the muscle is shorter than this length, the increased overlap reduces the cross-bridge attachment sites available and consequently the tension-generating potential. Similarly, if the muscle is longer, the reduced overlap also reduces the attachment sites available.

Within the whole muscle there are also passive connective tissues in both series and parallel with the contractile fibres, and these passive tissues act like non-linear elastic bands. If stretched beyond their resting length, they contribute additional tension. When muscle is shortened, its tension-generating capabilities are impaired. At long lengths, passive tissues contribute tension, but less active tension is possible.

In addition to length, the tension-generating potential of muscle is also influenced by the velocity of muscle length changes. During concentric contractions (muscle shortening while producing tension) the ability of a muscle to generate tension is reduced as the velocity of shortening increases. Greater forces are possible during eccentric contraction.

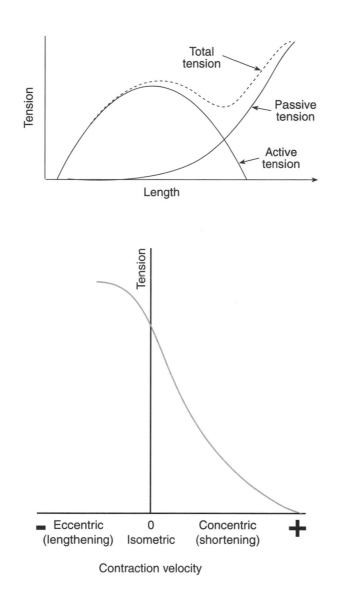

Chapter 2.2

1. Energy for muscle contraction comes from turning the molecule adenosine triphosphate, or ATP for short, into adenosine diphosphate (ADP). An enzyme (ATPase) splits one of the three phosphate molecules from ATP. This action releases chemical energy that the muscle fibre turns into mechanical energy. Only a very small amount of ATP is stored within the muscle cells and, for movement to continue, other parts of the muscle cell then turn the ADP back into ATP using energy obtained from other sources.

2. The fastest way of turning ADP back into ATP involves creatine phosphate. Although this system acts very quickly, it doesn't last long and provides enough energy only for about 10 to 15 seconds of maximum effort before the stores of creatine phosphate run out. Athletes aim to increase the stores of creatine phosphate by taking creatine supplements. Activities involving repeated bouts of short, high- intensity efforts may benefit from additional creatine stores.

3. Anaerobic glycolysis involves breaking down glycogen or glucose without using oxygen. A by-product of this process is pyruvic acid. If sufficient oxygen is not available to the cells, the pyruvic acid is converted into lactic acid. If lactic acid accumulates, the anaerobic glycolysis process is slowed, resulting in fatigue. Anaerobic glycolysis provides energy for up to three minutes of

maximal effort before the build-up of lactic acid prevents further energy production by this system.

The aerobic, or oxidative, system can take the pyruvic acid produced by glycolysis and turn it into more energy instead of turning it into lactic acid. The aerobic energy system also produces electrons and hydrogen ions, which are eventually turned into water and excreted through sweat, and carbon dioxide, which is transported by the blood to the lungs where it is exhaled. In addition to using glucose or glycogen derived from carbohydrates, this system can also be fuelled by fatty acids which come from fat stores in the body or amino acids which come from protein stores. The aerobic system is the slowest way of providing energy, but if enough oxygen can be delivered by the heart and lungs, energy can continue to be supplied for as long as the on-board supplies of glucose and glycogen derived from carbohydrates, fat and protein last. The aerobic system supplies most of the energy required in activities lasting longer than about three minutes.

4. 'Hitting the wall' occurs when an endurance athlete has used up all the stored glycogen, and must rely on fat for the energy for further muscle activation. Glycogen provides energy faster than fat, and results in more energy per litre of oxygen consumed. When glycogen stores are depleted, the athlete will either have to reduce the intensity of exercise or increase oxygen consumption by increasing the volume of air breathed and blood pumped around the body.

5. Athletes who train intensely for several hours each day should consume a high-carbohydrate diet (i.e., 60 per cent or more of total energy intake). A normal diet typically supplies sufficient protein; up to 15 per cent of the energy consumption is appropriate. High-protein diets or supplements are unnecessary. Adequate supplies of vitamins and minerals are essential for the body to function, and these are normally supplied by a balanced diet. Supplementation to levels above normal will not lead to improvements in performance.

Chapter 2.3

1. The lactic acid threshold is the exercise intensity above which the aerobic system cannot utilise all the pyruvic acid produced by anaerobic glycolysis. In untrained people, the threshold is equivalent to an oxygen consumption about 60 per cent of their $\dot{V}O_2$max; for endurance-trained athletes it might be 80 per cent. Fatigue results rapidly if the intensity of exercise is increased above this level.

2. This oxygen is used, in part, to create the energy needed to replace the stores of creatine phosphate and glycogen used up during exercising. Extra oxygen is also needed because the heart is pumping extra blood to return body temperature to normal, and respiration remains elevated to clear the build-up of carbon dioxide from the blood.

3. The initial gains in strength that occur in response to training are a consequence of changes in the functioning of the nervous system. In part, this is related to increased skill and coordination of muscle contraction, but there are also increases in the ability to activate muscle fibres. After the initial gains in strength due to neural changes, any further gains are a consequence of increases in the size, or number, of muscles fibres. Which fibres increase in size depends on the specific nature of the training performed. Type II fibres will increase in response to strength and sprint training. Type IIB fibres, although having the greatest potential for hypertrophy, will only increase in size if near-maximal forces are involved in training.

4. Type I fibres contract slowly and use energy from the aerobic process. Consequently, they are very useful for physical activities requiring low forces

over long periods of time. The large type II fibres that contract quickly are useful for physical activities requiring large forces. However, because they obtain energy via anaerobic glycolysis, they produce lactic acid. Type I fibres are smaller than type II, and are used to produce force before the larger type II fibres. Only when more force is needed are the larger type II fibres used as well.

5. The size and strength of the heart increases with endurance training, leading to an increase in the stroke volume. Maximum heart rate does not change with training but, because of the increase in stroke volume, the cardiac output of endurance-trained athletes at maximal heart rates is much larger, perhaps up to double that of untrained people. There is also an increase in the number of capillaries within muscle. This allows more oxygen to be delivered to the muscle cells and, in part, accounts for the increase in the ability of muscle to extract oxygen from the blood that the cardiorespiratory system delivers.

6. On average, differences exist between females and males. $\dot{V}O_2$max, for example, is higher, on average, in males than in females, although the magnitude of the difference is small until after puberty. When trained female and male endurance athletes are compared the differences in aerobic capacity are small (< 10 per cent).

   In general, the differences between females and males in physiological capacity are small in children, and the differences are probably caused by differences in activity levels due to social rather than biological factors. After puberty, larger average differences are seen between females and males, especially in terms of muscle mass and, consequently, strength and power. Females and males respond similarly to training, and strength differences are reduced when similarly trained females and males are compared. How much of the average strength differences is a consequence of social factors affecting activity levels, and how much is a consequence of physiological differences, is unknown.

Chapter 2.4

1. The four principles of training are specificity, progressive overload, reversibility and individuality. The implication of specificity is that to gain maximum benefit in terms of improved capacity for performance of any particular physical activity, training should involve movements that are, as far as possible, identical to the movements involved in the actual activity and be similar in frequency, duration and intensity to that of the physical activity. The implication of progressive overload is that for continued improvements in physiological capacity to occur, the programme of training must include progressive increases in the demands placed on the body. The implication of reversibility is that the demands must be maintained if adaptations are to be maintained. The implication of individuality is that the timing and extent of increases in exercise demands must be flexible and be adapted to the individual.

2. The principle of specificity dictates that a high jumper's training programme would focus on very short-duration, explosive muscle contractions with ample rest. The programme for a hockey player would involve high-intensity bouts of anaerobic activity repeated for up to 70 minutes.

3. Plyometrics might be used by athletes attempting to develop very high-velocity and short-duration muscle contractions such as jumping.

4. Reducing the volume of training before a competition allows healing of tissue damage caused by intense training and provides time for the body's energy stores to be fully replenished.

5. Improved physiological capacity for physical activity has many benefits for health, including preventing or reducing the risks of obesity, osteoporosis, heart disease and diabetes.

Chapter 2.5

1. Speed is a scalar quantity having a magnitude only; velocity is a vector, having both a magnitude and a direction.

2. Average velocity is the change in displacement during a time period divided by the duration of the time period.

3. The movement of a golf club during a swing is conveniently described in terms of angular displacement, velocity and acceleration.

4. An arrow shot towards a target will travel in a curved path. In the absence of air resistance, this path has the shape of a parabola. The initial velocity of the arrow may be resolved into horizontal and vertical components. In the absence of air resistance, the horizontal component of velocity remains constant while the arrow is in flight; the vertical velocity changes as a consequence of the constant acceleration due to gravity. The result is a curved path.

5. The centre of mass, or centre of gravity, of an object is the point at which the force due to gravity appears to act. The location of the centre of mass of an object depends on the arrangement of mass within the body. If an object is a regular shape and its mass is evenly distributed then the centre of mass will be at the centre of the object. Objects with irregular shape or arrangement of mass can have a centre of mass quite distant from the centre of the object, and sometimes even outside the object. Examples include a boomerang and a high jumper executing a Fosbury flop.

6. A volleyball blocker can raise their legs by bending at the knees after takeoff, and then lower their legs as they reach the peak of the jump. Lowering the legs has the consequence of lowering the centre of mass of the body relative to the upper body and arms. The player's trunk remains higher for longer than it would have if the legs had not been lowered.

Chapter 2.6

1. *Newton's Law of Inertia:* The velocity of a body remains constant unless a force acts on it. *Newton's Law of Action-Reaction:* Every action by a force is accompanied by an equal action in an opposite direction. *Newton's Law of Acceleration:* The change in velocity caused by a force acting on a body is proportional to the force and inversely proportional to the mass of the body.

2. The turning effect of a force (the moment or torque) is the product of the magnitude of the force and the moment arm, where the moment arm is the perpendicular distance from the line of action of the force to the axis of rotation.

3. A body is in equilibrium when the vector sum of forces and torques acting on the body is zero. If the linear and angular velocity of a body are constant, the body is in equilibrium.

4. The moment of inertia of a diver's body about a somersault axis is greater in a layout position. The moment of inertia is a measure of the body's resistance to turning about a particular axis of rotation. This resistance is increased by locating mass farther from the axis of rotation. In the layout position, the mass of the body is located further from the somersault axis of rotation than in a tucked position.

5. If a force is constant, then the linear impulse is equal to the force multiplied by the time for which it is applied to an object (Impulse = Force × Time). The

linear momentum of an object is equal to the object's mass multiplied by its linear velocity (Momentum = Mass × Velocity). When a force is applied to an object for a defined time period, the impulse is equal to the change in momentum that results. To propel a ball at high velocity we can apply a very high force for a very short period of time, such as hitting a ball with a bat, or we can apply relatively small forces for a longer period of time, such as pitching a softball or baseball.

6. Divers and gymnasts in flight can alter their moment of inertia, and thus their angular velocity, by altering their posture. For example, for a diver to rotate fast enough to complete a double somersault before hitting the water, she tucks, bringing the mass of the limbs closer to the axis of rotation, reducing her moment of inertia. Her angular velocity increases to maintain constant angular momentum, and she is able to complete the required number of revolutions in the time available. The diver does not want to be rotating quickly when she enters the water, and so she straightens her body again before entry. This increases the moment of inertia again, resulting in a reduction of her angular velocity.

7. The mechanical work done is zero. Mechanical work is the product of the force applied and the displacement through which an object moves. If upwards is the positive direction, positive mechanical work is done to raise the load against gravity, and an equal amount of negative mechanical work is done to lower the load.

8. A standing long jump can be divided into a crouch phase, an extension phase, a flight phase and a landing phase. During the crouch phase, the centre of gravity of the body is lowered (using chemical energy from food stores), and a small amount of gravitational potential energy is briefly stored as elastic potential energy in tendons and muscles. During the jumping phase, this elastic potential energy and further chemical energy is converted into gravitational potential energy (as the centre of mass of the body is raised) and kinetic energy (as the body moves). During the upward portion of the flight phase, the gravitational potential energy increases and the kinetic decreases, and the reverse occurs during the downward part of the flight phase. During the landing the kinetic energy is converted into heat.

9. When a spinning ball moves through the air, on one side of the ball the spin opposes the direction of motion, increasing the fluid pressure on that side. The consequence is a lift force acting towards the side of lower pressure. The consequence of spin is to alter the trajectory of the ball. In the cases of a golfer whose club is not perfectly perpendicular to the direction of travel at the moment of impact, the consequence is for the ball to deviate laterally from the intended path.

Chapter 3.1

1. The Ling system was a way to regulate children's bodies in space and time and so make them obedient citizens and useful workers.

2. The four problems were the deterioration of physique, hereditary factors such as physical disability ('organic defects'); diseases of the eyes, nose, throat, chest and spine; and ignorance of good hygiene. He thought these could be overcome by providing grants to schools if they taught physical education and hygiene. He also recommended that physical education should be compulsory for teachers in training.

3. Members of the Royal Commission were impressed by teachers' resistance to military drill and accepted their views that the wrong kind of exercise, or

exercise for poorly fed children, could be harmful to them. They also believed ordinary physical exercise could remedy some minor physical problems such as poor posture.

4. An argument for physical training to promote health was that it helped remedy minor physical problems, thereby enabling children better use of their bodies for work. An argument against physical training to promote health was that it cured disease. This was shown to be false.

5. There was little change because the rationale for physical education contained in the 1933 Syllabus was based on the arguments for physical education developed in the late 1900s.

6. The Syllabus presented a broader version of physical education in theory than previous syllabuses, although this may not have been realised in practice due to constraints of facilities and lack of teachers. It also contained a new chapter on the organisation of games and sports.

7. The working classes were believed to be in need of therapy for physical disabilities. It was believed that they needed to be taught about hygiene.

Chapter 3.2

1. The belief that games build character, games develop loyalty, games teach young people to accept defeat graciously, and that games provide rules for how to live.

2. The games ethic was applied with less enthusiasm for competition and vigorous physical activity.

3. It was believed that games developed the qualities of gentlemen, schools aspiring to be socially elite adopted them. In order to play team games such as football, schools needed to own and maintain playing fields, which were very expensive. Playing fields were an obvious symbol of social superiority. Schools that wished to in the social elite used games and playing fields to demonstrate their status.

4. Raising of the school leaving age prompted schools to look for physical activities that could supplement Swedish gymnastics and that would be of more interest to older children. It was thought that games could diminish conflict between social class groups. It was also believed that games could help develop national identity.

Chapter 3.3

1. Olympic gymnastics was based on German gymnastics. Because Britain had been at war with Germany between 1939 and 1946, British people did not readily accept anything associated with Germany.

2. Swedish gymnastics aimed to develop precise performance of exercise with the whole class doing the same thing at the command of a teacher. Educational gymnastics encouraged individual creativity and non-uniformity. Olympic gymnastics was a competitive sport involving work on the floor and several pieces of apparatus.

3. Swedish gymnastics was believed to be too formal, promoting unnatural movements and conformity and obedience. The mass participation required by Swedish gymnastics was too similar to activities used by the German youth movements (such as the Hitler Youth), and there was hostility to this at the end of the Second World War. Swedish gymnastics was thought to be out of touch with developments in society more generally, particularly the increased availability of games and sports to working class people.

4. Critics of educational gymnastics claimed it was too individualistic. Children were allowed to do what they wanted, and so the quality of movement was poor. Educational gymnastics failed to teach children specific skills. It also ignored the role of competition in physical education.

5. The women believed it was possible to develop a general base for more specific skills. The men believed skill learning was specific in all cases.

6. The pupil's emotional, spiritual and intellectual development was considered to be as important as her physical development.

7. Motor learning approaches to skill acquisition promoted the idea of whole/ part/ whole learning, where a skill is dissembled and reassembled to allow learners to concentrate on small aspects of the skill and then incorporate these parts of the skill into the whole skill. The female educational gymnasts took a holistic approach that included cognitive, spiritual and emotional learning alongside physical learning.

8. The change of emphasis placed games and sports at the centre of physical education, replacing gymnastics. Degree programmes also developed and the study of physical education became possible, particularly through biophysical science. These shifts reflected a male approach to physical education.

Chapter 3.4

1. Brigadier Wand-Tetley suggested that the skills and fitness developed through the war would allow ex-soldiers to play games and that this would provide a recreational break from work.

2. De Lorme suggested that injury would be reduced and efficiency of movement increased.

3. Morgan and Adamson claimed that the hard core of fitness was strength and endurance, meaning that with these two capacities other activities would be more easily developed.

4. Circuit training involved developing strength and endurance, which may have been considered unfeminine at this time. Morgan and Adamson stated that boys begin to take an interest in their physical development early in adolescence. They also stated that boys begin to take an interest at this age in activities that require strength and endurance.

5. Fitness activities were restricted mainly to boys' physical education. Even for boys, activities such as circuit training occupied only a small percentage of curriculum time, unlike games.

Chapter 3.5

1. The NPFA was formed by middle and upper class philanthropists to provide fields and other facilities where working class people could play games. They believed that games playing had a civilising effect on the working classes.

2. The NPFA's role was to provide funds to build sports facilities.

3. The shift in focus was away from recreative physical training using activities such as Swedish gymnastics to games and sports. The major concern after the war was to produce community sports leaders.

4. Higher levels of organisation and formality surrounding participation in sport.

5. They thought that their behaviour could be supervised and regulated by adults.

6. Between 1941 and 1947, working class adolescents had to be registered in a youth organisation. It was believed that working class youth were more likely

to become involved in criminal activity than their grammar school peers. It could be argued that this was partly because the grammar school youth had gained the benefits to their characters of playing games, whereas at this time working class young people had not.

Chapter 3.6

1. Two forms of physical education were offered, with the form depending on the social class of the pupil. Working class children experienced a drilling and exercising form of physical education (Swedish gymnastics and marching). Middle and upper class children played games.

2. The major factors were the increasing state intervention in sport and recreation provision; the belief among the middle and upper classes that sport was a unifying force that could overcome social class conflict and develop national identity; and a concern for public order and the control of working class youth.

3. There is evidence to suggest that the values of the games ethic, such as character development, loyalty and deferred gratification, did not fit with working class lifestyle. There is also some evidence that these values may not have been taught effectively as games were often taught by nonspecialist teachers who may not have applied these educational principles in their coaching.

Chapter 4.1

1. Within mixed-sex groups, the curriculum experience for girls might be quite different than for boys. Research has shown the ways in which girls may be marginalised in some mixed- sex group settings and that there may be limited interaction between girls and boys.

2. TGFU seeks to integrate the development of specific skills with experience of 'game play', and develop skills and strategic understanding in parallel with one another. This contrasts with the sequential pattern of traditional approaches, in which there is often a focus on learning specific skills first and, after this, moving into game play situations. TGFU directs greater attention to pupils developing an understanding of strategic and tactical aspects of games and highlights the way in which this understanding may enhance performance across several sports. Finally, TGFU encourages the use of 'modified games' to facilitate the progressive development of both skills and game play.

3. There were some critics who thought that some initiatives, in emphasising cooperation between pupils, were failing to teach pupils key attitudes and values 'for life'. Specific concerns related to the attitudes and values that are traditionally associated with experience of competitive team games. In directing attention to the need for teaching to address strategic aspects of game play, TGFU was regarded as a threat to skill development in particular sports. Critics were concerned that new activities or new ways of teaching lacked 'educational rigour'.

4. Differences: HRF has largely focused upon development of fitness for participation and performance in sport. In contrast, HRE has focused more on the ways in which physical activity and participation in sports can contribute to general health and wellbeing. To some extent, HRF and HRE have promoted different activities, so that HRF has, for example, often featured fitness testing, circuit or weight training, and cross-country running; HRE has often included activities such as aerobics, multi-gym and weight training.

   Similarities: Both HRF and HRE have tended to focus upon the physical aspect of health, and pay limited attention to mental health and the links between physical activity, sport and mental health. An example of this link is the way in which participation in sport may enhance or may damage self-esteem. Secondly, both HRF and HRE have tended to adopt an uncritical approach to health and to the relationship between participation in physical activity, sport and health. Relatively little attention has been paid to the ways in which participation or the pursuit of excellence in sport might threaten or damage one's health. In addition, there has been little recognition that what we regard as a health lifestyle, or a healthy body, is socially constructed. In different times and in different cultural settings, the patterns of behaviour or body shapes that we regard as healthy would not be seen as such.

Finally we can reflect that in many physical education programmes, both HRF and HRE have been given a rather 'marginal' position, with far more time and attention devoted to units of work and lessons in which the focus is upon the development of skills, knowledge and understanding that is specific to particular activities or sports.

5. Examination courses in physical education have been developed at CSE, then GCSE level, and at A and A/S levels. Titles of courses have varied and include 'sports studies' and 'games' and 'dance' as well as 'physical education'. Vocational courses have been developed relating to the sport and leisure industries and are increasingly linked to the National Vocational Qualifications framework. The national governing body award and the CCPR leadership award courses are examples of vocational courses that you may experience within physical education.

These developments have helped to raise the status and profile of physical education, within and beyond schools. They have generated increased interest in, and understanding of, the subject among staff and parents. In addition, the developments have meant that some departments have gained additional resources (equipment or funding) that have been used to improve the quality of provision of all physical education.

Chapter 4.2

1. The attainment target identifies the knowledge, skills and understanding that pupils of different abilities and maturities are expected to develop. They therefore establish learning objectives. Originally three attainment targets were proposed for the NCPE, focusing on planning, performing and evaluating.

The issues influencing the decision to establish a single attainment target were twofold. There were ideological issues involved, relating to the government's view of physical education (focusing on it being a 'practical subject'). There were also pragmatic issues involved, with the government wanting to keep requirements to a minimum.

2. 'Programmes of study' refer to the matters, skills and processes that must be taught to pupils in order for them to meet the objectives set out in the attainment target for the subject. The six 'areas of activity' that provided the framework for the POS were games activities, gymnastic activities, athletic activities, dance activities, outdoor and adventurous activities, and swimming activities and water safety. Initially it was proposed that, in each of Key Stages 1, 2 and 3, children should experience all six of the identified areas of activity and, in Key Stage 4, at least three areas, including games, and either gymnastics or dance.

In 1992, it was decided that the curriculum in Key Stage 1 must include the five areas of games, dance, gymnastics, athletic activities and outdoor and adventurous activities plus, if desired, swimming. At Key Stage 2 all six areas had to be addressed, with the exception of swimming if the programme of study for swimming had already been completed in Key Stage 1. At Key Stage 3, swimming was removed as an area of activity in its own right and instead identified as an activity that could be pursued in the context of the remaining areas. At Key Stage 3, it was then stipulated that games must be included in *each year* of the key stage and at least three other areas should be experienced during the key stage. In Key Stage 4 pupils who were not following GCSE physical education were required to follow two activities from either the same or different areas.

In September 1995, requirements changed again. At Key Stage 1, schools were required to include games, gymnastics and dance in each year of the key stage. If they wanted, they could also include swimming in Key Stage 1. At Key Stage 2, only games, gymnastic activities and dance had to be included in each year of the key stage. The other areas of activity had to be covered at some point in the key stage (again, with the exception of swimming if the programme of study for swimming had been covered at Key Stage 1). At Key Stage 3, games was now the only area of activity that schools had to include in each year of the key stage. At some time in the key stage they would also have to address three other areas of activity, with one of these being gymnastics or dance. In Key Stage 4, the requirements were changed so that at least one of the two activities included in the curriculum had to be a game.

3. The position of health and health-related exercise was somewhat unclear in the NCPE. There was no distinct programme of study for HRE, but health-related issues were mentioned in the NCPE. In some respects, the position of health and HRE in the NCPE were 'marginal' to other interests and priorities. However, there was, in practice, the scope within the requirements for teachers to make health and HRE a focus of attention.

4. The National Curriculum in Wales included Welsh as a core subject in Welsh-speaking schools, and a foundation subject in non-Welsh-speaking schools.

   In addition Curriculum Cymreig was a focus for the development of the requirements for all National Curriculum subjects. In physical education, for example, Welsh culture and history could now be expressed in dance.

5. The requirements for the NCPE allowed schools a lot of scope to decide upon the particular activities to be included within the physical education curriculum and the way in which they could be taught. It also did not stipulate the amount of time for physical education in the curriculum. This meant that many factors could influence what the National Curriculum looked like 'in practice'. Differences in facilities, in physical education teachers' expertise and interests, in school sporting traditions, and in the time allocated to physical education could be among the factors influencing the content and focus of the NCPE in any one school. Schools could meet the required minimum requirements for the NCPE in many different ways. Some schools might choose to go beyond the minimum provision, but others would not. Children's experiences of the NCPE could therefore be very different in different schools.

6. Local management of schools could effect the funding for physical education and decisions relating to staffing and in-service training for teachers. There was a danger that in some schools, other subjects would be considered a priority for funding and staffing and that the quality or range of provision in physical education might suffer as a result. Open enrolment linked funding for schools to their recruitment of pupils. This could result in the provision of physical education and school sport, and achievements in these, being regarded as something that could attract pupils (or their parents) to choose a school. With this in mind, attention could become focused upon the achievements of a few pupils in school sport.

7. In the second half of the 1990s a number of developments have led to an increasingly close association between physical education and sport development. Most notably, the government policy document *Sport – Raising the Game* set out plans for many initiatives directed towards physical education and sport in schools, including the introduction of awards relating to provision of physical education and sport. Since 1994, the Youth Sport Trust has emerged as a key provider of resources and training to support the development of physical education and sport in schools, (particularly in primary schools). The YST programmes that have been developed to support a 'sporting pathway' for children are well established in many schools.

Chapter 4.3

1. (i) Acquiring and developing skills; (ii) selecting and applying skills, tactics and compositional ideas; (iii) evaluating and improving performance; (iv) knowledge and understanding of fitness and health

2. In 1995, it had been established that Key Stage 4 should include a minimum of two activities and that at least one of these must be a game. The new requirements were for two areas of activity to be addressed in the key stage. The change was controversial as it meant that games would no longer be a compulsory area of activity for all children.

3. (i) Setting suitable learning challenges; (ii) responding to pupils' diverse learning needs; (iii) overcoming barriers to learning and assessment for individuals and groups of pupils.

4. (i) The NCPE in Wales included specific programmes of study for health-related exercise. At each key stage, the curriculum therefore had to address the programmes of study for health related exercise and for the specified areas of activity. (ii) At Key Stage 4, the NCPE in Wales adopted a new system of categorising activities. The following four areas of experience were introduced: sport (competitive focus), dance (artistic and aesthetic focus), adventure activities, and exercise activities (non-competitive forms of exercise). At Key Stage 4, schools were required to include health-related exercise and two practical activities selected from one or more of these areas of experience.

Chapter 5.1

1. The Department for Culture, Media and Sport. Key agencies funded by the DCMS are the sports councils: UK Sport, Sport England, **sport**scotland, The Sports Council for Wales, and the Sports Council for Northern Ireland.

2. (i) National governing bodies of sport; (ii) local authorities, and (iii) national and regional organisations concerned with sport, recreation, education and the environment.

3. (i) Increasing participation in sport – in terms of numbers of people involved and frequency of activity; (ii) raising standards of performance and excellence in sport; (iii) improving provision of sports facilities; and (iv) providing information and advice about sport and recreation.

4. (i) Widening opportunities – creating a country where sport is more widely available to all; (ii) developing potential – creating a country where sporting talent is recognised and nurtured; (iii) achieving excellence – creating a country that posts and sustains world-class performances in sport.

5. (i) Coaching and team management programmes; (ii) the setting-up of working parties to address specific issues; (iii) the establishing of pre-Games preparation and warm-weather training camps; (iv) the accreditation of training centres; (v) support via doctors, physiotherapists, psychologists and

physiologists within the British Olympic Medical Centre; and (vi) financial assistance to elite athletes to assist with the expense of elite training.

6. The NCF has developed coach education courses to enhance the quality of sport coaching in Britain and has established a regional network for coordinating coach education provision. The NCF courses are integrated into the sport-specific coach education conducted by national governing bodies. The NCF has also established a national register of sports coaches and runs an information service for coaches. The NCF thus supports and complements the work of the individual governing bodies.

7. (i) To optimise physical fitness, current health and wellbeing, and growth and development; (ii) to develop active lifestyles that can be maintained throughout adult life; and (iii) to reduce the risk of coronary heart diseases in adulthood.

8. (i) The inactive, (ii) girls aged 12–18, (iii) young people of low socioeconomic status, and (iv) older adolescents (16–18 years).

Chapter 5.2

1. (i) *Sport – Raising the Game,* (ii) *England the Sporting Nation,* and (iii) *Young People First.*

2. (i) Time devoted to physical education and sport in the core curriculum; (ii) breadth and balance within the core curriculum programme; (iii) opportunities for students to develop their interests outside the core curriculum; (iv) planned development routes for talented performers; (v) links with sports organisations and other schools; (vi) community activities; (vii) leadership development and opportunities; and (viii) opportunities for further training and updating qualifications.

3. (i) More People, (ii) More Places, and (iii) More Medals.

4. (i) Young people and sport, (ii) active participation throughout life, (iii) performance development, and (iv) achieving excellence.

5. (i) Active Schools, (ii) Active Sports, and (iii) Active Communities.

6. *Performance Funding* aims to assist performers with the potential to win medals in significant international competitions and events within the next six years. *Potential Funding* aims to assist the development of talented performers with the potential to win medals in significant international competitions and events within the next ten years. *Start Funding* aims to identify and nurture those performers with the necessary characteristics to achieve future World Class success within the next ten years. The funding schemes link respectively with the following programmes: World Class Performance, World Class Potential, and World Class Start

7. (i) Dragon Sport, (ii) Club Cymru, (iii) Elite Cymru.

Chapter 5.3

1. Although the local authority would retain ownership of the facility, management of facilities would be subject to a process of competitive tendering, with contract periods running for four to five years. Attention was clearly directed towards facilities operating in a financially efficient (and ideally profit-making) way, and provision being shaped by financial interests.

2. Best Value.

3. (i) Club coaches may become involved in provision of sport in schools; (ii) teachers may also be involved in clubs for local junior sport; (iii) junior clubs may use school facilities as their base; and (iv) information about local clubs can be displayed in schools.

4. Professional clubs in several sports now have junior development sections. They provide coached sessions and tournaments for children and may become involved in development work with local schools.

5. Youth clubs and organisations such as the Scouts and Guides, and church groups and other voluntary organisations such as the Red Cross also provide sporting opportunities.

Chapter 6.1

1. A naturalistic view sees the body as biological and so likely to act on drives and instincts. A constructionist view sees the body as both biological and cultural. This means that values are attached to the shape, size and appearance of a body. It also means bodies are part of the process of communication because we use bodies to make sense.

2. The varieties of shape, size and overall appearance of the female body have remained roughly the same over time. However, how we view beauty and femininity has changed. Tennis players' bodies provide one example from sport. It is now more acceptable for female tennis players to have a masculine physique with broad shoulders and narrow waist and hips.

3. Body image is a combination of our personal view of ourselves and the values other people link to particular looks, shapes and sizes. Body image is a major contributing factor to self-esteem. Researchers have linked poor body image and low self-esteem.

4. The body is commodified when it is drawn into the processes of buying and selling. One of the less desirable effects of commodification is when the body becomes an object to be maintained and worked on. Another less desirable effect is when bodies are used to sell products, and so the values attached to them are reorganised to convey new ideas – for example, that a slender body is evidence of fitness and health.

5. Bodies are regulated scientifically through a whole range of processes involving technology and science. One form of scientific regulation of the body is working with computerised equipment such as the treadmill machines common in most gyms. Drugs to enhance sport performance is another form of such regulation..

6. Advertising emphasises selected associations between bodies and values. The representations of bodies included are said to be inside the frame; and those excluded are outside the frame. In order to be effective at selling products, advertisements are targeted at specific groups of people and encourage those people to identify with the product and the values surrounding it. An example may be the association of a product such as a car with a particular look and lifestyle. The repetition of advertising over time constructs and reconstructs those links associating particular body shapes, sizes and appearance with particular qualities.

Chapter 6.2

1. Physical culture refers to production of social values and meanings in and through the highly organised and institutionalised practices of sport, exercise and leisure.

2. Sport refers to organised and codified physical activities that are centred on competition. Recreation refers to our ability to recreate or regenerate through activities that are alternatives to work, whether this be the domestic work of running the home or wage labour. Leisure is a broader notion than recreation and has generally referred to all of the time available to an individual when

they are not engaged in work. The notion of lifestyle assumes that people have some degree of freedom from the responsibilities to work, family and other commitments, plus the time, self-discipline and the money to shape their lives in particular ways.

3. Commodification is the process of turning something or someone into a commodity, to be bought or sold for profit. For example, the commodification of lifestyle takes place when we are 'sold' the idea that particular ways of life can be constructed through the commodities and services we buy and, along with this, a corresponding self-identity. One-day cricket is an example of the commodification of sport, where a traditional game is changed to suit the medium of television and promote a secondary industry such as merchandising.

4. (i) Young people have quite high disposable incomes; (ii) they have few constraints operating on them in terms of dependants and careers; (iii) they are likely to be healthy compared with other groups in society; (iv) they are in the process of developing their self-identities as adults.

5. (i) More precise measurements of performance, (ii) new forms of equipment; (iii) new surfaces; (iv) increased use of video playbacks to make decisions in professional sports.

▇ Chapter 6.3

1. Sex refers to the biology of femaleness and maleness; gender refers to the combination of biological and social factors, such as femininity (ways of being feminine) and masculinity (ways of being masculine). Gender is influenced by biology and society because dominant forms of femininity and masculinity can vary within and between cultures.

2. Biological arguments usually refer to women and girls being weaker, less aggressive and having a lower pain threshold compared with men and boys. Sociocultural arguments usually refer to women and girls being less feminine when they play sports traditionally played by men such as rugby. Such arguments sometimes also question women's and girls' sexuality.

3. (i) They are required to wear skimpy or revealing clothing such as leotards or short skirts; (ii) they are required to take communal showers; (iii) they suffer 'put-downs' and harassment from boys and male teachers.

4. Women receive less media attention than men and lower pay and prize money. When media does attend to women, skimpy clothing, appearance and sexual appeal are frequently the focus, and sport performance is portrayed as being of secondary importance.

5. (i) Girls could be allowed to wear clothing that is comfortable for them; (ii) changing rooms could be pleasant to be in and showers have curtains; (iii) girls could be encouraged and rewarded for their effort; (iv) activities could be modified to suit levels of interest and ability, and provide opportunities to experience success.

6. The occupation of space, the use of physical force, and physical size and process are the characteristics of hegemonic masculinity. is hegemonic When this form of masculinity is accepted unquestioningly by many people as the only way to be masculine, it is said to be hegemonic. Sport often requires these characteristics for successful performance. However, many girls and boys cannot, or will not, display these characteristics, and so may be destined to be unsuccessful in sport unless it is modified to suit their forms of femininity and masculinity.

■ Chapter 6.4

1. **Australia:** (i) School sport associations organise competitions at local, district, state, and inter-state levels; however, these tend to be for only the most talented performers; (ii) the Australian Institute of Sport provides residential training and sport science support for elite performers; (iii) the principal organising unit in Australian sport are the local clubs. These are affiliated to local governing bodies, which are affiliated to state-level governing bodies, which are affiliated to national governing bodies.

   Belgium: (i) There are three communities (Flemish, French and German) who have responsibility for sport constitutionally. Each has its own ministry of sport and sports administration. The ministry of sport is the policy maker; the sports administration has an executive function providing technical services, management and administration (e.g., of subsidies); (ii) the Flemish Ministry of Sport and Ministry of Education have nine 'topsport schools' in the Flemish community to assist the development of elite youngsters; (iii) at universities, elite student athletes get assistance; (iv) extracurricular school sports are organised in the Flemish community by the Flemish Foundation of Schoolsports and in the French-speaking community by the Association of Francophone Federations of Schoolsports

   China: There are special sports schools for talented young people (students do a half-day of classes and the rest is in specialist training). These schools are highly selective but, for those accepted, the state provides support and progression in sport. Increasingly, this is a pay-as-you-go approach for non-elite participants.

   (i) Youth sport is the responsibility of sports clubs (autonomous bodies). Physical education is in the school curriculum and controlled by the government but there is a strong relationship between the two; (ii) the German Sport Federation is responsible for establishing competitive systems and organising nationwide events, but the responsibility for recruiting and retention of young people in organised sport is in the hands of the local sports clubs; (iii) in addition, there are approximately 25 elite sport schools to develop talented young people. These are under government control.

   Norway: (i) Sport is supported by the state on the basis that sport is a worthwhile cultural activity. It is believed that sport provides a chance for individuals to experience a sense of community at local, national and international levels; (ii) there are many sports clubs; (iii) the Norwegian Confederation of Sports is made up of 56 associations, which represent 100 sports with representatives at national, county and local level; (iv) there is a four-yearly 'sports parliament', which discusses current issues, develops policy, laws and regulations; (v) elite sport is largely state funded through grants and access to facilities.

   Spain: Sport is decentralised and access to sport is a right for all citizens. Funding traditionally came from football pools but, when Spain was awarded the Barcelona Olympics (1992, government funding increased. Two policies emerged – one for Olympic sport and one for professional sport. Olympic sport gets funding direct from government to support athletes and to create High Performance Centres. Professional sport policy was revised to give greater economic independence to sport clubs (e.g., many football clubs became stock companies). Since the Barcelona games, there has been a decrease in government funding and an increase in private funding.

   The United States: (i) Sport in schools has a very high status (contrast this with the relatively low status of physical education). Players must achieve a certain standard in their schoolwork in order to be allowed to compete. It is very exclusionary, with only the most talented getting the opportunity to participate; (ii) primary and middle school children can participate in local recreation leagues normally administered by the local government recreation department; (iii) there is a strong tie between universities and sports competition (multimillion-dollar industry). Some athletes receive scholarships that pay tuition, books, room and board. Some even recruit athletes from overseas; (iv) professional sports are organised around leagues with individual teams being privately owned. Power in professional sport rests with the owners, the commissioners (who run the daily operations of the leagues) and the players (pro sport is highly unionised).

2. **Australia:** (i) There are social pressures on women to 'look right'; (ii) childcare has a negative impact on participation, but more so for women; (iii) reasons for not participating include lack of enjoyment, lack of time and lack of money; (iv) the multicultural population means that some activities are more, or less, acceptable in different cultures; (v) social structural and educational factors effect activity participation as well as personal inclinations.

   Belgium: (i) Increasing age results in lower participation. The dropout rate from organised sport at around 16-17 years of age, plus a lack of compulsory physical education in polytechnics and universities, means a decreased participation among older students; (ii) there are initiatives aimed at using sport to promote integration of specific populations in Belgian society (e.g., underprivileged urban youth); (iii) the sports academy concept provides for cooperation between local sports clubs and community sports services (6-12 year olds) resulting in an omni-sports programme for young people; (iv) there are 'sport for all' campaigns; (v) there are initiatives to improve the quality of management and coaching in sports clubs.

   China: (i) There is a high regard for success in sport, and sport performances can help towards points required for university entrance; therefore the status of physical education is enhanced and there is greater participation; (ii) in 1996, a five-day working week was introduced, resulting in more leisure time, and facilities are increasing to meet this demand; (iii) a government restructuring of sport in 1998 means that only the elite will not have to adapt to a pay-as-you-go culture.

   Germany: (i) Participation rates are high, although there is a drop-off during adolescence; (ii) participation rates are higher among boys compared with girls.

   Norway: (i) Since the 1970s there has been a 'sport for all' policy; (ii) there is a gender bias — more boys and men participate than girls and women.

   Spain: (i) There is a positive association between level of participation and income and education (i.e., those who earn more and are better educated participate more); (ii) there is a negative relation between level of participation and increasing age (i.e., older people participate less); (iii) women and girls participate less than men and boys.

3. **Australia:** (i) State governments are responsible for education. Time allocation and content of physical education varies from state to state; (ii) the main activities for primary school are aerobic activity and sport skills; for secondary schools, traditional sports, personal development and health.

   Belgium: (i) Constitutionally, Belgium is divided into Flemish-, French- and German-speaking communities, with each being responsible for physical education within their community; (ii) there is a minimum of two hours per week in secondary school, although in some sport-oriented programmes this can be increased by up to four hours; (iii) some classes are combined across subjects (e.g., athletics plus a foreign language).

China: (i) Physical education is compulsory daily during primary and middle school; (ii) government regulations aim to ensure that all students do daily physical activity through timetabled physical education lessons, extracurricular sports clubs or morning exercise; (iii) university students also have to do two hours a week of physical activity for at least the first two years. The activities depend on facilities but include games (e.g., basketball, soccer, volleyball, tennis, badminton) and basic military drill.

Germany: (i) Physical education is compulsory between the ages of 6 and 19; (ii) in elementary schools (for children aged six to nine), there is a provision for three hours a week of physical education; in high schools, it is generally three hours per week. If physical education is being taken as part of the A-level equivalent, then six hours are allocated; (iii) the times allocated for physical education are under pressure; (iv) the German system aims to improve physical fitness and develop the motor skills that enable young people to take part in play, games and sports; to promote the adoption of a physically active lifestyle through adulthood; and to contribute to the social, cognitive and affective development of young people through physical activity.

Norway: (i) Physical education is compulsory at all levels of the Norwegian school system; (ii) physical education in primary and middle schools is for three classes a week; (iii) for upper schools there are two classes a week (typically 45 minutes a time); (iv) the national curriculum includes a central health focus, traditional Nordic activities and team games; (v) grades in physical education effect entry to further education or the job market.

The United States: (i) Physical education is the responsibility of each state, meaning that the laws relating to physical education vary; (ii) the biggest variation is probably in time allocation; only one state requires daily physical education for all grades. More common is for children to receive two or three 30-minute lessons a week during primary schools and complete a one-semester requirement during high school. Some states allow recess time to count towards the total activity time; (iii) content is based around fitness and skill development.

4. Use the answers from questions 1 and 3 to identify key features. Possible explanations will depend on the countries selected but could include things like the following: (i) In most countries the majority of elite sport is government-funded; (ii) increased commercialisation is threatening core values of some organisations (e.g., the Norwegian Confederation of Sports); (iii) there is pressure on physical education within the school curriculum and, in many situations, the time allocation is under threat (e.g., Germany, the United States).

China: (i) New government policies that reform the country according to market forces and reduced state funding means that professional sport is on the increase and this may effect the sports and activities that are on offer to the rest of the population; (ii) success in international sport (e.g., Olympics) is seen as very important, therefore influencing activities available (e.g., there is increased availability and funding for Olympic sports); (iii) increased contact with Western countries has led to the popularisation of some Western-style sports.

Spain: (i) The introduction of a capitalist-like economy, the adoption of a democratic political system, a decentralised model of government and the evolution of a social policy based on European welfare state principles, have all significantly influenced the way sport is organised; (ii) Barcelona's hosting of the 1992 Olympics has influenced sports (e.g., meant more money available and increased collaboration between local and state institutions).

The United States: (i) Sport in the United States is a multimillion-dollar business and as such exerts great influence; (ii) owners of sports teams have great power; (iii) athletes also have great power (witness the player strikes); (iv) television exerts a strong influence — it affects scheduling, sponsorship (if not on TV, sponsorship is more difficult); the exposure of athletes raises questions about to what degree they should be role models.

5. Use answers from questions 1–3.

Index

About the Authors

David Kirk, PhD, is a Professor of Physical Education and Youth Sport in the department of physical education, sport science and recreation management at Loughborough University, where he earned his doctorate in philosophy in 1987. He also holds an honorary chair in human movement studies at the University of Queensland and is adjunct professor of physical education at the University of Limerick. Dr. Kirk has 18 years of experience as a physical education teacher, researcher, and teacher educator. He has authored or coauthored numerous books, including three previous textbooks: *Senior Physical Education: An Integrated Approach, Sociocultural Foundations of Human Movement,* and *Learning to Teach Physical Education.* Dr. Kirk is a member of the Physical Education Association of the United Kingdom and a consultant to the Qualifications Curriculum Authority (QCA) for the accreditation of A-level physical education courses. He enjoys exercising, watching sports, and gardening. He and his wife, Susan, and their three children live in Loughborough.

Dawn Penney, PhD, is a senior research fellow and a lecturer in contemporary issues in the department of physical education, sport science and recreation management at Loughborough University. A visiting lecturer at many other institutions, Dr. Penney has published numerous articles and coauthored two previous books, *Politics, Policy and Practice in Physical Education* and *Senior Physical Education: An Integrated Approach.* She received her doctorate in education from the University of Southampton in 1994, and in 1996 and 1997 she served as evaluator of the Queensland Senior School Physical Education syllabus during its pilot development phase. Dr. Penney is a member of the Physical Education Association of the United Kingdom and of the British Association of Advisers and Lecturers in Physical Education. A resident of Loughborough, she enjoys swimming, cycling, and running.

Robin Burgess-Limerick, PhD, is a senior lecturer in biomechanics in the school of human movement studies at The University of Queensland, Australia, where he earned his doctorate in biomechanics in 1994. Dr. Burgess-Limerick has conducted research on diverse topics including field hockey, locomotion and manual lifting and has published many research articles in biomechanics, motor behaviour and ergonomics journals. He is a member of the International Society of Biomechanics and the Ergonomics Society of Australia. In his spare time Dr. Burgess-Limerick enjoys playing field hockey. He resides in Queensland.

Trish Gorely, PhD, has worked as a sport and exercise psychologist with athletes of various ages and abilities, including young people in schools, and has conducted research to establish how best to help people reach their goals. A former lecturer on sport and exercise psychology at the University of Queensland, she currently lectures on the topic of young people and sport in the department of physical education, sport science and recreation management at Loughborough University. Dr. Gorely earned her doctorate in sport and exercise psychology in 1996 from the University of Western Australia. She belongs to the Association for the Advancement of Applied Sport Psychology. In her leisure time Dr. Gorely enjoys trekking, tennis and golf. She and her husband, Matthew Seed, and daughter Rachel live in Loughborough.

Colette Maynard, BEd (Hons), is a teacher adviser for physical education at the Finstall Centre in Worcestershire, where she supports and advises teachers in the Worcestershire Local Education Authority. Ms. Maynard taught A-level physical education in two secondary schools for several years. She is a member of the British Association of Advisers and Lecturers in Physical Education. She enjoys cross country running, road racing, skiing, and windsurfing. She resides in Worcester.